AF657593

Pilgrimage

Sacred Landscapes and Self-Organized Complexity

PILGRIMAGE

— Sacred Landscapes and Self-Organized Complexity —

edited by

John McKim Malville
Baidyanath Saraswati

with a foreword by

R.K. Bhattacharya

Indira Gandhi National Centre for the Arts
New Delhi

D.K. Printworld (P) Ltd.
New Delhi

Cataloging in Publication Data — DK
[Courtesy: D.K. Agencies (P) Ltd. <docinfo@dkagencies.com>]

International Seminar: Pilgrimage and Complexity (1999 : New Delhi, India)
Pilgrimage : sacred landscapes and self-organized complexity / edited by John McKim Malville, Baidyanath Saraswati ; with a foreword by R.K. Bhattacharya.
p. cm.
Proceedings of the International Seminar: Pilgrimage and Complexity, held at New Delhi in January 1999.
Includes bibliographical references.
Includes index.
ISBN 13: 9788124604540 ISBN 10: 8124604541

1. Pilgrims and pilgrimages — Congresses. 2. Hindu pilgrims and pilgrimages — India — Congresses. 3. Sacred space — Congresses. 4. Sacred space — India — Congresses. 5. Self-organizing systems — Congresses. 6. Integrity — Religious aspects — Congresses. I. Malville, J. McKim (John McKim), 1934- II. Saraswati, Baidyanath, 1932- III. Indira Gandhi National Centre for the Arts. IV. Title.

DDC 203.50954 22

ISBN 13 : 978-81-246-0454-0
ISBN 10 : 81-246-0454-1

First Published in India in 2009
© Indira Gandhi National Centre for the Arts, New Delhi.

All rights reserved. No part of this publication may be reproduced or transmitted in any form or by any means, electronic or mechanical, including photocopying, recording, or any information storage or retrieval system, without prior written permission of both the copyright owner, indicated above, and the publisher.

The views expressed in this volume are those of Participants, and are not necessarily those of Editors and Publishers.

First published in India by:
Indira Gandhi National Centre for the Arts
Central Vista Mess, Janapath, New Delhi - 110 001

and

D.K. Printworld (P) Ltd.
Regd. office : '*Sri Kunj*', F-52, Bali Nagar
Ramesh Nagar Metro Stn., New Delhi - 110 015
Phones : (011) 2545 3975; 2546 6019; *Fax* : (011) 2546 5926
E-mail: dkprintworld@vsnl.net *Web*: www.dkprintworld.com

Printed in India by: D.K. Printworld (P) Ltd., New Delhi - 110 015

We dedicate this volume to our friend and mentor
Dr. Kapila Vatsyayan,
the founding Member Secretary and Academic Director
of the Indira Gandhi National Centre for the Arts.

Her all-encompassing vision of art has created
an extraordinary home for artists of all kinds
as well as anthropologists and astronomers.

Foreword

The present volume *Pilgrimage: Sacred Landscapes and Self-Organized Complexity* jointly edited by John McKim Malville and Baidyanath Saraswati is a collection of the proceedings of the international seminar "Pilgrimage and Complexity" held in the Indira Gandhi National Centre for the Arts, New Delhi in January 1999. The contributors are from diverse disciplines and their papers cover a wide range of ideas in this connection. Pilgrimage is a worldwide phenomenon. There is a lot of philosophical, theological and textual content in the context of pilgrimage and an attempt has been made to include all these aspects in this volume.

The obligations and duties on the one hand and the penance and renunciation on the other are intimately related to pilgrimage, as the idea is of earning merit. People also expect miracles to be logically possible in such places. Places of pilgrimage are often identified by the mythical associations of their being abodes of gods, goddesses, prophets and religious preceptors or containing their body parts. The former is a mythical idea while the latter is believed to be supported by 'material' remains. This brings about an emotional connection in people regarding these places and gives them strength to encounter the vicissitudes of life. A few of the papers in this volume have explored the modern context of pilgrimage and vice-versa, i.e., pilgrimage in modern life. The transformation that is most noticeable lies in the provision of amenities like roads, transport, accommodation as well as encouraging tourism to develop in the places of pilgrimage which nowadays cater to not only those seeking a spiritual experience but also those who desire to travel. The divide between the sacred and the secular is gradually narrowing and getting more blurred as people are happy to mix both for a more complete experience.

Pilgrimage centres are hubs of economic activities and sometimes we find temple complexes functioning like an industry due to the variety and amount of services required. Often these centres become places where alternative medicine practitioners can practise their trade. These centres are also places supporting a wide variety of networking between visitors, service providers and business enterprises. There is almost a niche-based market economy that develops in these centres. Apart from the economic activities and spiritual experiences, places of pilgrimage perform the social function of providing shelter for the poor. In the context of India, old age homes and shelters find an appropriate ambience in these places, especially in those in which pilgrimage is not seasonal or linked with some festivals and occasions.

The broadening effects of travel are experienced in pilgrimage; it is a socially approved way of release from the humdrum of daily life, of heightening one's awareness through travel, of learning about different ways of life and of stimulation of one's aesthetic sensibilities. It may be the scenic beauty of the place, the wonder of architecture and carvings, the tranquillity of the environs or its contrary like in some places, or even the feeling of brotherhood with other pilgrims — in short, enriching oneself.

Many of these aspects have been discussed in the papers in this volume which provide quite a vicarious experience to the reader who is free to make a pilgrimage to any place in this wide world. The papers are interesting and the book in its entirety traces the many forms of tradition and their transformation.

R.K. Bhattacharya

Contents

Introduction

The Cosmos of Pilgrimage

John McKim Malville
Baidyanath Saraswati

THE 19 papers in this volume were presented at a five-day conference held at the Indira Gandhi National Centre for the Arts in January 1999. We are drawn to *cosmos* as a metaphor for pilgrimage for a number of reasons. The Greek word, *kosmos,* implies a universe as a harmonious system that has evolved out of chaos, which we feel is a fine metaphor for pilgrimage. In addition, many pilgrimages celebrate and re-enact the origins of the cosmos. Cosmic cycles of time play a major role in the scheduling of pilgrimages and in festival calendars.

Pilgrimage involves movement of people, either as individuals or as members of a group, in search of the sacred. Spontaneous behaviour, miraculous events, and/or ecstatic visions of individual pilgrims have often resulted in complexity in ritual, meaning and movement. As pilgrimage traditions mature, ecclesiastical or political authority may increasingly control them, supressing spontaneity and innovation. But before that mature stage is reached, pilgrimage is an example of the complexity that arises from the combination of human individuality and group coherence. Pilgrims create an integrated whole that is greater than the sum of its parts.

In our planning for the conference, we proposed the following themes:

Complexity in space: By their movement, pilgrims create personal and universal maps of ritual spaces, which may involve vast amounts of territory. Cosmic geometries connect the macrocosm of the heavens with the microcosm of the pilgrimage landscape. These geometries may be cardinal or they may be influenced by local topography. Once a pilgrimage destination has been reached, circumambulation of the centre is a common experience. A spiralling path into the centre may symbolize the merging of the individual with the absolute.

Complexity in time: The development of the accurate pilgrimage calendar was a major achievement of human culture. The expansion of a pilgrimage from local to regional scale awaited the invention of precise methods for measuring and structuring time. Not only were precise observations of the cycles of the sun and the moon necessary to develop an accurate calendar, but also calendrical knowledge had to be communicated across the pilgrimage "catchment" area. Few other events of humankind involve such precise *voluntary* behaviour of ordinary people.

Complexity in symbol and meaning: An important aspect of pilgrimage centres is the presence of multiple interpenetrating levels of meaning and symbolism. The symbolic power of pilgrimage landscape may not only transform the individual, but also may transport the pilgrim into alternate realms that transcend time and space.

Ritual complexity: Pilgrimage involves highly complex ritual traditions that embrace continuity and change, predictability and surprise, order and chaos. Does complex ritual behaviour arise spontaneously from the pilgrims or does an authority impose it?

Social complexity: Pilgrimage is a major force of social integration. The pilgrimage mega-community of shared ideals often achieves high degrees of complexity and stability. Societal stratification may grow out of a pilgrimage system, if leaders acquire ritual suzerainty.

Self-organizing systems: What is the origin of the rich multilevel complexity of pilgrimage systems? Most pilgrimages are not ordained by kings or hierarchical power, but emerge as the collective behaviour of free individuals, each in search of a spiritual ideal. Similar examples of complex self-organization are found in forest and ocean ecosystems. An essential quality of pilgrimage systems specifically and of self-organizing systems in general is their openness. The difference between open and closed systems is especially illuminating when one compares the longevity of pilgrimage centres with the brief florescence of the closed imperial city. In closed political systems, processes are put in place that suppress innovation and accident.

Visual astronomy: In addition to providing the cosmological setting for pilgrimage, astronomy plays roles in organizing time through the calendar and in visual rituals such as viewing astronomical objects, e.g., the sun at dawn. Organized by the pilgrimage calendar, vast numbers of people move across the landscape in resonance with the motions of astronomical bodies. Pilgrimage is one of the primary examples on our planet of a dynamic parallelism of macrocosm and the human microcosm.

Saraswati's essay, which deals with a sacred theory of pilgrimage, abounds with cosmic themes and with issues related to the theory of complexity. One of the very profound emotions that humans can experience when gazing at the night sky is that of an infinite universe, filled with mystery, surprise and unfathomable meaning. Hinduism resonates with that vision of infinity when it refers to *Brahman* (in Saraswati's words), "the ever-expanding Universe identified with both fullness and emptiness, and is beyond all kinds of dialectical opposition between formed and unformed, time and timelessness, mortal and immortal."

The self-organization of the universe has proceeded through time. In the Hindu cosmos the flow of time is described in term of *yugas*, *mahayugas*, and immense Brahma-years. These periods of time are as vast as anything we know of in astrophysics, in which our present universe started approximately 15 billion years ago. These cycles of time may be embedded in even greater expanses of time, which are shared with multiple universes that appear out of and dissolve back into a boundless ocean of superspace and supertime.

Pilgrimage intertwines theory and landscape; both are necessary. Saraswati uses Kashi as a concrete example of the theory. The inner complexity of the (infinite) cosmic Kashi is made simpler and comprehensible in the (finite) earthly Kashi. Self-similarity and scale invariance could not be clearer: exact size is irrelevant. The shrine of Madhyameshvara, the Lord of the centre, is the centre of both the infinite and finite Kashi. The pilgrims move along the 3 concentric circles: the inner sanctum formed by 3 sectors represents the microcosm; pilgrimage in the radius of 5 *kosa* signifies the mesocosm, and the larger circle in the radius of 84 *kosa* stands for the macrocosm of *Brahman* where all the 33 crore of Gods and Goddesses reside. Pilgrimage follows a cycle of time, which contains elements that are similar to the large cosmic cycles of birth and death.

The paths of clockwise circumambulation may not form a perfect circle or triangle or quadrangle, but the pilgrims' movement amplifies all the possible forms of cosmic geometries resulting in a complete picture of the Universe. Because of the principle of self-similarity, pilgrims visiting Kashi get the feeling that they moved into the boundless cosmic space in all its directions, all its constellations, planets, stars, and Gods through the 6 seasons, driven in the solar car. The earthly Kashi is a paradigmatic model that includes within itself the patterns of all other places of pilgrimage. All the sacred spaces, all the Gods and Goddesses, all the sacred rivers and mountains, and all the planets and stars are manifest in Kashi. The clockwise circumambulation of Kashi-kshetra may be conceived as an imitation of the great solar system.

The movement of the pilgrims around a fixed centre, e.g., temple, *stupa*, tree, or deity, is like the movement of the Sun, Moon, and planets and hence is archetypical. What follows is the great principle of Life. Everything is moving. Even Dhruva (pole-star) is only relatively fixed, as, in fact, it also moves in the heavens. Numerical symbolism provides an abstract and profound link between the pilgrim and the invisible forces of God. The use of numerical concepts helps one to visualize the unity of places and peoples, objects and ideas, visibles and invisibles.

Malville introduces the idea of self-organization by contrasting the two types of stable systems that can be found in the physical universe: the death state of perfect equilibrium and the infinitely fertile condition of self-organization. The latter provides useful models for many complex features of the natural world, which are characterized by fractal geometries, cooperative behaviour, self-similarity of structures and power law distributions. He proposes that pilgrimage systems may be viewed as natural and self-organizing structures wherein complexity develops through the spontaneous and coherent behaviour of free people. Examples of such systems in the natural world range from earthquakes, schools of fish, forest fires and rain forests. Openness to the outside environment and coherent behaviour are necessary conditions for self-organization and the growth of complexity.

Forces that disrupt equilibrium may drive cultural systems and individuals into a state of metastability or self-organized criticality lying between frozen inactivity of equilibrium and disordered hyperactivity. As systems depart more from equilibrium the amplification of small fluctuations by non-linear processes may result in stress-releasing avalanche-like movement of people to pilgrimage centres. The resulting cultural systems may be highly non-adaptive as judged by prior paradigms. Self-organization lacks an overall goal or teleology because the future is an unfinished project. At each stage, along the trajectory of cosmic time, emergence of new purpose provides new meaning.

Because of a common conceptual framework that threads the system, a self-organizing system is characterized by self-similarity and scale invariance: similar patterns are repeated with different sizes or time scales without changing their essential meaning. The body, temple and universe are perceived as self-similar and fundamentally identical in many traditions. The pilgrim may follow a pathway that represents the universe from centre to periphery or that mimics the evolution of the universe from birth to death. In field studies at Mt. Kailasa and Varanasi Malville is able to show that circumambulation pathways have the characteristics of self-organization.

Bhardwaj combines the Hindu pilgrimage traditions of linear *tirthā yatra* and circular *pradakshina-parikrama* as interlinked concepts. He notes that the geographers, Vidal and Sore, identify circulation of people as a transformative process that can upset traditional cultural equilibria and encourages the growth of new lifestyles and paradigms. The stirring of the cosmic ocean by the *devas* and *asuras* is a fine example of such circulation which destabilizes but also creates something absolutely new and life affirming, *amrita*. Churning disrupted the calm of the Sea of Milk; swirls in the ocean have smaller and smaller self-similar eddies. There is another metaphor of circulation and holism in the form of the serpent as he encircles the mountain and is pulled back and forth by the *devas* and *asuras*, whose differences are momentarily dissolved.

Circulation of blood in the human body is a means of connecting the local to the whole and achieving coherence of the system. Another well-known example is that of Gaia, through which the whole biosphere has been unified and transformed into something entirely new through the circulation of oxygen and carbon dioxide.

Bhardwaj observes that circulation not only diffused traditional ideas but also changed traditions. As a somewhat ironic consequence, tradition and change are converted from opposing entities to complementary components of a self-organizing system.

There is a "push-pull" quality to a pilgrimage centre. The centre has to have its power of place, but in order to be influenced and personally transformed by the pilgrimage process, there has to be a personal sentimental attachment to the place. "Aimless wandering" does not lead to pilgrimage; nor does trekking through an alien, albeit dramatic landscape such as adventure tourism.

The individual and his/her goals change through the process. The pilgrimage landscape is not like the wheel with its still-point in the fixed geometric centre and the repetitive revolutions of the rim, the image of perfection in the Greek world of movement without change. Pilgrimage is, instead, like a growing, changing living system.

As in the living system, circulation purifies and energizes both the moving agent and the system; both pilgrim and landscape are mutually transformed. The procession re-awakens, rejuvenates, re-energizes the land and city, as an internal cycle is necessary to maintain and energize a stable system. The circulation of people is often in resonance with the great cycles of the cosmos. That circulation brings the human microcosm and the macrocosm into synchronism.

Part of the springtime celebration involves returning to and union with the place of origin. A continuous cycle pilgrimage is consistent with the essential circulatory pattern of the world, which has no beginning and end. There is non-verbal communication between landscape, pattern of the movement, and individual pilgrim. One of the consequences of the processional circulation is social and symbolic integration of the individual into the system to achieve unity and holism.

These open systems in which there are great flows of people and ideas are subject to change. By contrast the equilibrium system has negative feedback loops, which suppress change. The non-equilibrium system has non-linear processes, which amplify small changes. The strange attractor has a complementary quality, as an endless journey and a goal. There is a centre toward which energy flows: it can only be approached but never fully reached. This is a classic existentialist dilemma of seeking the centre as if it were reachable, but knowing all along that it can never be reached.

Gutschow continues the discussion of circulation and *pradakshina* in his in-depth study of pilgrimages at Bhaktapur, Muktinath and Varanasi. He notes that circumambulations identify "inner" and "outer" spaces. In quoting Panikkar, "there is no outer without inner space," which referred to human being, Gutschow acknowledges the condition of self-similarity, in which the size of the territory is irrelevant. Beyond the "inside" exists an "outer" space, which, on a different level, might be the "inside" of another entity with a different size. And so it goes, upward or downward, meaning and form are repeated.

The case of Varanasi reveals such circumambulatory routes, which enclose each other in order to incorporate an ever-increasing space. The case of Muktinath provides a different model. There, the six villages of the valley are circumambulated individually, while only on rare occasions are all six villages circumambulated in order to reconfirm a political entity. In the case of Bhaktapur all representations of "place" are worshipped on the occasion of New Year along a circular route that encloses the city.

A self-organized system must reject and eject those anti-entropic processes that lead to disintegration and loss of complexity. Bhaktapur is protected from those demonic forces by eight shrines to *Ashtamatrika*, which form a complex *mandala* that surrounds the sacred realm. Spring equinox is a "cosmo-drama," celebrating renewal of the world on *Mesha Samkranti*. The celebration involves killing the serpent, which is associated with the darkness and water of the period between fall and spring equinoxes when the sun is below the cosmic ocean. The erected pole symbolizes the *axis mundi*, which pillars apart the world while uniting and stabilizing the world.

The procession re-awakens, rejuvenates, re-energizes the world. The circulation of people is in resonance and parallelism with the great cycles of the cosmos. The continuous cycle of the procession is consistent with the essential circulatory flow of energy that stabilizes the system, which has no beginning and end. There is non-verbal communication between the landscape, the pattern of the movement of people through the landscape, and individual pilgrim. One of the consequences of the processional circulation is social and symbolic integration of the individual into the system and every part thereof to achieve unity and holism.

Ritual circumambulation of the cultivated area of Muktinath is a festival of renewal that confirms and energizes the protective deities. The protecting Grandfather and Grandmother are located at the north and south poles of the land, which are themselves self-similar to the north-south axis of the cosmos. On the procession there are halting places at four cardinal roads, which are blocked by piles of stones to protect the interior from the threat of chaos and dissolution from the outside.

The outside is necessary as a place into which disorder and low grade energy can be exported. Without the outside, the interior world would dissolve into the meaninglessness of pure equilibrium. Thus, we can invert Panikkar's dictum: there can be no inside without an outside.

The *Caurasikrosi-yatra* of Varanasi is a perfect circle with Madhyameshvara at its centre. It is an "ideal" figure, which is not walked today, and perhaps in reality when it was walked, it was not "perfect." The *Panchakrosi-yatra* is an approximate oval but quite irregular, more natural, and apparently self-organized, as suggested by Malville's measurements.

In contrast to the Muktinath and Bhaktapur circumambulations, the *Panchakrosi-yatra* has

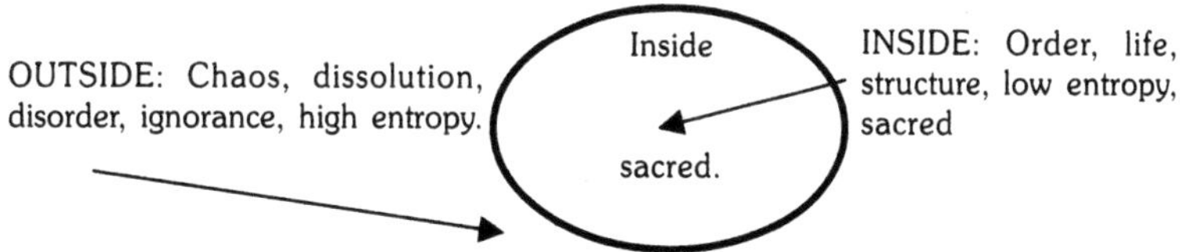

a formal start and end, and the *yatra* may take place, at any time. Starting at the Jnanavapi well, which symbolizes the axis of the universe, the pilgrim re-enacts cosmogony, mimicking the evolution of the universe from beginning to end. The space of Kashi-kshetra is continuously "redefined and confirmed by the feet of pilgrims," an example of self-maintaining internal cycles of energy.

Kashi contains numerous examples of self-similarity and scale independence. In theory, it contains all outer space within its inner space. Structures are repeated in miniature scale within Kashi such as the twelve *Jyotirlingas* and the four *Dhamas* that mark the four quarters of the subcontinent. The 108 shrines of the *Panchakrosi-yatra* are also contained in miniaturized form in the Panchakrosi Mandir. That temple, with its 272 niches, symbolizes, in its self-similarity, the entire sacred territory of Kashi and a circumambulation of the temple is, in essence, a circumambulation of the entire territory and of the entire cosmos. Finally self-similarity is expressed in the body of the pilgrim who can locate Kashi within his/her body and "perform the entire *Panchakrosi-yatra* within himself."

Singh provides further analysis of the *Panchakrosi-yatra*. Along the route existing 108 holy shrines and spots archetypally connote the integrity of cyclic time, 12 constellations of the zodiac and 9 planets. Another meaning of the number108 involves the 27-day sidereal cycle of the moon and the 4 directions of space. This circular route is a unique example of "mesocosm" where the celestial realm (macrocosm) meets with the devotee's consciousness. The alignments of shrines on the route with corresponding shrines on the other pilgrimage routes inside the circuit area create another pattern of complexity. This spatial complexity is paralleled by the human complexity, involving the interconnections of pilgrims' faith, specific rituals at various shrines and the actual experiences of pilgrimage.

Singh, Malville and Marshall consider the processes that have resulted in Gaya's central role as a pilgrimage centre for performance of *shraddha* ceremonies. Gaya is an ancient pilgrimage centre: most its shrines have been known since the time of the *Vayu Purana c.* CE 500, and some are mentioned in the *Vishnu Sutra c.* CE 100. Gaya is named for the holy demon, Gayasura, who, after being killed by Vishnu, was transformed into the series of rocky hills, that make up the landscape of the Gaya-kshetra. After his death, many people have flocked to Gaya to perform *shraddha* sacrifices on his body for their ancestors. Gods and goddesses had promised to live on Gayasura's body after he died, and temples to Rama-Shila, Preta-Shila, Ram Gaya Pahar and Brahmayoni surmount the hilltops. All are part of the pilgrimage circuit, with grand staircases, leading up to most of them. The most popular temple today is Vishnupad, a place along the Phalgu River, marked by a footprint of Vishnu incised into a block of basalt, which symbolizes one of the three steps of Vishnu as the sun. It also marks Vishnu's subduing the demon of chaos, Gayasura, by placing his foot on Gayasura's chest. Singh, Malville and Marshall made a GPS survey of the major shrines of the area and find that the small hill above Vishnupad may have been a station for observing the rising and setting sun at the solstices. They suggest that Gaya may have been initially a place for sun worship and advance several models to describe its transformation to a pilgrimage centre dominated by *shraddha* ceremonies.

Kropf investigates the *Navagraha-yatra*, located in the Kumbhakonam area of Tamil Nadu, consisting of nine temples, each associated with one of the nine *grahas* or planetary deities. The nine *grahasthalas*, that she discusses, are:

(1) Tirunallaru (Tirunallaru): Saturn — Shani
(2) Vaithisvaran Koil (Vaittisvaran Koyil): Mars (Tamil: Cevvay)
(3) Perumpallam (Perum Pallam): Ketu
(4) Thiruvenkadu (Tiruvenkatu): Mercury — Budha
(5) Kanchanur (Kancanur): Venus — Shukra (Tamil: Velli)
(6) Suryanar Koil (Curiyanar Koyil): Sun — Surya
(7) Thingalur (Tinkalur): Moon — Chandra
(8) Thirunageshvaram (Tirunakeccuram Koyil): Rahu
(9) Alangudi (Alankuti): Jupiter — Guru

Kropf suggests that the travel agents provide effective travel itineraries for the *yatra* and she gives an example of the advertisement, appearing on a *Navagraha-yatra* homepage:

> The Tamil Nadu Tourism Development Corporation announced on June 26, 1997 in Chennai, a "Navagraha worship package Tour," covering nine temples in the State dedicated to the Navagraha deities. Pilgrims, wishing to visit the temples, can leave from Chennai on Friday night and return on Monday morning.

While every temple presents an elaborate list of worships, provided by the priests at the temple, most of the pilgrims seem drawn due to astrological compulsions, which are primarily to remove negative influences of some of these planets. The prominent shrine for Shani at Tirunallaru and that for Rahu at Tirunagesvaram are important pilgrim destinations because of the negativity and evil consequences the planets bring about in the life of man. By contrast, the shrines of the more positive planets, Guru and Shukra, do not have such elaborate ritual programmes.

She notes that the *Navagrahas* do not belong to a category of divine phenomena, be they deities, saints or naturally given sacred sites that should generate pilgrimage visits. Because the *Navagraha* shrines represent an instrumental means to an astrological end, the basic mood of the pilgrims is one of anxiety and fear rather than spiritual growth or insight.

The borders between pilgrimage and tourism are blurred in the *Navagraha-yatra*. The pilgrimage tour, as it is promoted on the Internet, has a fashionable touch. The concept of the *yatra* doesn't seem to convince the priestly authorities of the temples involved; there is no intensified exchange or even cooperation among the corresponding temple trusts as it could be expected of an integral and welcomed pilgrimage concept, embracing all the nine temples.

Even though the cycle of the nine temples with the *grahas* has some of the characteristics of a pilgrimage centre, the promoters of the tours seem less interested in meeting the needs of pilgrims than increasing the popularity and fame of the sites. Neither myths nor textual references suggest interconnections to all of the *graha*-shrines, which leads Kropf to conclude that, in the absence of a tradition, tour directors have designed the *yatra*. The priests do not see themselves as the promoters of the pilgrimage tour but are quite willing to provide the appropriate services for pilgrims to earn boons from the gods.

Amita Sinha compares landscapes described in Valmiki's *Ramayana* with existing ones associated with Rama and examines the pilgrimage landscapes of Ayodhya, Chitrakut and Kishkindha, in detail. Without archaeological data to establish the authenticity of the epic tale, the sites of the drama have acquired their identities through the activity of pilgrims. Today, the landscapes of Chitrakut and Kishkindha retain much of their original wildness and beauty, and the natural world is a significant part of the pilgrimage experience at these sites, as, in fact, one should expect at a *tirtha*. In the case of the *Ramayana* tradition, theory has preceded landscape. The transformation of natural landscapes in accordance with textual tradition took place over two thousand years. As pilgrimage destinations, their physical characteristics and role in sustaining belief are worth examining, since they throw light on cultural construct of nature. Recent research by Malville and Singh shows how pilgrimage landscapes of Chitrakut and Kishkindha can be read as cosmic geometries, which connect different levels of the cosmos as well as different psychological levels of the pilgrims, i.e., inner experience with outer physical reality. Pilgrimage landscapes evoke cosmic time as well as shrines are visited in a certain order. The movement of the pilgrims collapses the passage of time into hours or days, reinforcing the idea of the eternal, bringing mythic time and space into the consciousness of the believer. Certain landscape features, described in the epic, such as ecologically diverse niches of river valleys, changing course of river, hills aligned with cardinal directions and marking solstices and planetary movement, formed the ideal context for *Ramayana* legend to grow, as they attracted holy men, pundits and their patrons. We see here an example of positive feedback as the region grew in significance due to the mutual, self-reinforcing influences.

Behrendt examines some of the broad parameters that governed early Buddhist pilgrimage.

He considers the categories of local and distant pilgrimage. Monks typically undertook long distance pilgrimages to visit the sacred geography, associated with Shakyamuni's life, and these pilgrimages are well documented in inscriptions, early religious texts and the ancient accounts of pilgrims. Parallel to this system is the larger local pilgrimage tradition of the lay population that has left only a few traces. We know that sites associated with the life of Shakyamuni, such as Bodh-Gaya or Sarnath, were the main focus for foreign monastic pilgrims, coming from places like China, Sri Lanka, Burma and Thailand. Thus we can understand these sites, to some extent, in terms of foreign concerns and "multi-national" patronage. Economy was also an element in these pilgrimage sites, as pilgrims and monks were often engaged in trading enterprises.

The well-documented monastic long-distance pilgrimage tradition provides valuable insight into the world of local practices. Centres like Bodh-Gaya or Sanchi would have acquired their financial base in the localized lay pilgrimage traditions. Behrendt considers the key sites associated with the sacred geography of the Buddha's life both as part of an international pilgrimage itinerary and as hubs of regional lay traditions, linked to the Gangetic urban centres. These places developed "miraculous landscapes" due to positive feedback as more and more visitors had extraordinary experiences, associated with relics and other aspects of Buddha's life.

Stoddard examines the knowledge of spatial geography by pilgrims in the Kathmandu Valley of Nepal. According to holy texts and religious scholars, the religious geography of the Kathmandu Valley coincides with an enveloping *mandala* of temples and sacred topography. This geometrical configuration is reinforced annually when pilgrims undertake a 40-km circuit while worshipping sequentially at a set of four Narayana temples within a single day. The symmetries of these temples in the Kathmandu Valley indicate that actual cosmological geometries are important. However, according to the responses of sampled persons residing in the Kathmandu Valley, very few persons actually envision an encompassing *mandala* as the basis for temple locations or have a very good idea of the local sacred geography. As is true in the case of many pilgrimages, such as the *yatras* of Varanasi, a theoretical spatial pattern is overlaid upon the actual topography.

Mack discusses the role of economy as an essential element in complex systems of pilgrimage, in which the exchange of goods and information plays a fundamental role in integrating the overall structure. Pilgrims must be fed and housed at the pilgrimage centre, and may return home with ritual objects or souvenirs. The economic establishment is then perpetuated by the return of pilgrims, each year. Spatial arrangement of medieval temple centres indicates that the economic aspects of pilgrimage are inextricable from the ritual and cosmological aspects. Archaeological studies of the temple district of Vitthalapuram at Vijayangara show the physical layout and distribution of activities that combined ritual geometries as well as markets providing services to pilgrims. Temple districts were thus primary loci for both the ideological and economic transactions that are engendered by pilgrimage, creating a complex dyanamic underlying the organization of the larger royal centre.

Shimazaki describes the popular pilgrimage to the 88 temples on Shikoku Island, Japan, associated with Kobo Daishi (AD 774-835), the founder of the Shingon sect of Buddhism. There is a large scale representative circular pilgrimage covering some 960 miles. The changing nature of how pilgrimages to the 88 sacred places are made and how rituals are conducted at each sacred site reflects Japanese cultural preference. Behind the dynamic process is the self-organizing "mechanism" to resolve conflict through compromise and to adapt to the changing goals and needs of pilgrims. While modern modes of transportation have increased the speed with which the pilgrimage can be completed, the traditional walking pilgrimage is still considered to yield the greatest religious merit. Conflict between the attainment of religious merit and the time available for such pursuits parallels the larger set of incongruities in Japanese society, associated with the increased pace of life in secularized societies and the yearning for the security of some sacred absolute. The resolution of the conflict between religious merit and convenience has been sought in a variety of areas, including the way in which the pilgrimage can be made (order of temples visited, segmentation of the total pilgrimage system, establishment of miniature pilgrimages, acceptance of modern modes of transportation) and how the rituals are performed at each sacred site. The resolutions of these conflicts reveal the underlying strength of the ongoing popularity of this Buddhist pilgrimage and the complex nature of this particular self-organizing system as it has evolved over the last three centuries.

Noschis compares traditional pilgrimage with movements of migratory birds, in which there are collective, repetitive and unquestioned urges to travel long distances with considerable effort. Among Christians, some Catholic groups experience pilgrimage in this way also today, with annual journeys to holy places like Lourdes, Fatima, Compostela, etc. Among other Christians, such as European Protestants, where the relationship to the spiritual dimension is predominantly individualistic, pilgrimage has lost its collective appeal after being stopped by the Reformation in early sixteenth century. Yet the effort of travelling (and particularly walking) long distances towards a spiritually significant place while surrounded by the beauty and challenges of nature, has recently gained attractiveness for numerous non-practising people also of Protestant and, generally, Christian origin. Noschis discusses this relatively new interest in spiritually-oriented trekking, drawing upon Trondheim pilgrimage as an example. In 1997, on the occasion of the 1000 years celebrations of Trondheim, efforts were made to reawaken the ancient pilgrim's route from the South to the North of Norway. Pilgrim wanderings to St. Olav's shrine in Nidaros began shortly after St. Olav's death in 1030 and lasted up to the Reformation in 1537. Today, with more touristic than religious ambitions, the project of reopening the pilgrim route has again become a reality.

Barrie views sacred architecture as a cultural artefact that traditionally has symbolized religious beliefs and facilitated the enactment of shared rituals. Drawing upon Eliade, Campbell and Jung, among others, Barrie explores common myths of spiritual quests and their relationship to the form and symbolic narratives in sacred architecture. In particular, he discusses the journey of the hero and the recurring theme of the spiritual quest as manifest in sacred architecture. Barrie suggests that the entry, path and sanctuary in churches often symbolized the spiritual path and its goal. The 660 foot labyrinth of Charters, for example, is reportedly designed as a miniaturization of the pilgrimage journey to Jerusalem. The Basilica of La Madeleine in Vézelay is the paper's case study and is examined in depth. The ecclesiastical and political power of the Basilica symbolized the treacherous labyrinthine path that the religious pilgrirns had to negotiate. Their movement along that path was a recapitulation of the age-old spiritual journey to places of spiritual authority and sacrality and, most significant of all, it was meant to be a mimesis of Christ's journey to apotheosis.

Zuidema identifies Pachacamac, on the coast of Peru, and the island of Titicaca as the major poles of attraction for pilgrimages in pre-Inca, Inca and modern times. An axis of the Inca Empire extended from Titicaca to Cuzco, and a system of straight ritual movements paralleled that axis. These movements were essential to Inca astronomy and they helped to lay out the Inca calendar over the landscape of Cuzco's valley. The socio-political complexity of the Empire included the interweaving of different social classes, an elaborate ritual calendar, which tied time together, and the ritual movement across the landscape, which tied space together. The two poles of religious attraction in the Inca Empire may have functioned in a manner similar to the strange attractor in chaos theory. A single fixed-point attractor does not energize systems but pulls everything into itself for a final fixed stillness, while two poles maintain aliveness and dynamic tension.

The sudden collapse of Inca state may be attributed to a number of causes but, from the viewpoint of self-organizing systems, it may have been a closed system and thus vulnerable to dissolution. Openness, which is dangerous to any authoritative political system, was suppressed by the Inca. The Spanish pushed the system to the edge of chaos. In a manner similar to biological mutations, a disruption of equilibrium can destroy as well as transform. In such a metastable, non-equilibrium state, normal stabilizing negative feedback loops may not function to quench disturbances. Non-linear processes, such as provided by Pizarro's greedy thugs, may amplify small disturbances, and push the system into a new realm. These events are also known as bifurcation points. At the point there is complete indeterminacy, at which non-linearity causes huge amplification of small changes.

Ritual movement expressed the self-similarity of heaven and earth. Processions by priests daily during the month of June solstice, imitated the daily course of sun through the sky. The race on the fourth night after the first full moon after December solstice was an event that resonated with a number of cycles. The race-ritual was performed to end the rainy season. Runners followed the ashes of the previous year's sacrifices as they flowed down the river. Resonance must be precise to be effective and these events moved with precision on solar-lunar dates. The pilgrimage and race complemented each other; six months apart were mirror images of each other in terms of following the river and then moving through the mountains. All three shared a common "solstitial axis" along which they traveled.

The race and pilgrimage were associated with seasonal variations of rain, flow of water in rivers and in the use of irrigation canals. The runners had to move fast to mimic the rapid flow of water in the rivers. The opening of the canals synthesized ideology, ritual and practical needs of agriculture.

Zuidema notes that two modern festivals of Peru provide interesting contrasts: Corpus Christi and Coyllur Riti. Corpus is an official feast, organized by the Church and Municipality of Cuzco and attracts many tourist-pilgrims. While it is certainly not an example of self-organization, there are many Peruvians who inject their own "uninvited" festivities into the occasion. Coyllur Riti grew spontaneously out of popular fervor and maintains many local customs. It attracts thousands of pilgrims mostly indigenous, from all over Southern Peru and the festival has many characteristics of a self-organized system. Nevertheless, Coyllur Riti is influenced by the Church but to a much a lesser degree than Corpus. Thus, each festival has features of self-organization and authoritative control; each lies somewhere between pure spontaneity and perfect order.

Torres considers the sanctuaries that the concheros or dancers of tradition visit every year as a pilgrimage. The concheros are groups of people organized in brotherhoods whose ritual activities include public daily performances in honour of the saints and private nocturnal dances which are wakes in honour of the souls of the departed spirits. .

One of the most important activities of the concheros is to dance ritually in the five sanctuaries which are arranged in the form of a cross. The church of Santiago Tlatelolco is located at the centre of the cross and four sanctuaries or winds radiate from this local: to the north, Our Lady of Guadalupe; to the west, Our Lady of Remedies; to the south, the Christ of Chalma; and to the east, the Christ of Sacromonte.

Why did the concheros of the city of Mexico choose these particular sites as their main obligations? Torres believes that this is because these are linked to a very old sacred geography of the people of the Valley of Mexico. These sites mark the limits of their most sacred realm with Tlatelolco as the *axis mundi*, with Santiago, saint of conquest — god of war — sun god, surrounded by saint-gods who represent the time of the year and their sacred space which may extend without limits to the four quadrants of the universe. The persistence of myth and pilgrimage tradition in sacred Mexico is extraordinary. The old cosmo-vision of the

Mesoamerican Indians continues to permeate the modern pilgrimage landscape.

Meyer explores the usefulness of the idea of pilgrimage to interpret the meaning of the ceremonial core of Washington. Religious terms have been used to describe the U.S. capital since it was first planned. Thomas Jefferson called the capitol a "temple of Liberty" and made use of analogies with ancient Rome: the House of Congress, modelled on the Pantheon, was considered comparable to the temple of Jupiter on the Capitoline Hill. Both overlooked a Tiber river. Both cities were built as the centre and made for the world.

Meyer emphasizes the importance of centring, in space and time, a capital city whose major building is perceived as a microcosm of the universe. He examines three major axes which constitute the ceremonial core of Washington: the great axis from Capitol to the Lincoln Memorial, the shorter axis from the White House to the Jefferson Memorial, and Pennsylvania Avenue which links the two power centres to White House and Capitol (and Supreme Court). Two of these axes have become the loci of important rituals. Some of the rituals, like the quadrennial inauguration, are organized by political elites.

Prorok's paper on the creation of new sacred places cuts to the core of the issue of self-organization of complexity pilgrimage systems. In order to create new pilgrimage traditions, new shrines, and/or new sacred places, there probably are three necessary conditions, i.e., the system must be open, it must be unbalanced and in a state of non-equilibrium and there must be an internal coherence and connection between its elements. Because it is out of balance, the system contains non-linear processes such the results of very tiny fluctuations and impulses may be multiplied many times over. This condition certainly applies to transplanted cultures. The system must be open to the flow of new ideas, new energy and people from a variety of backgrounds. It cannot have powerful negative feedback loops already in place, which suppress new ideas or any potential disruptions of socio-political stability. There must be a certain amount of imbalance, non-equilibrium and metastability in order to encourage and amplify newness. In other words, the cultural landscape must have those qualities of luminosity that have been identified by Turner. Finally the individual must be in a space in which he/she feels connected, at home. Naipaul's comments are insightful and appropriate about how difficult it is to create new sacred spaces in alien landscapes, with which the individuals have no sentimental, historic or mythological attachment. Noschis also discusses how nature may inspire epiphanies and hierophanies and the creation of new shrines but that the trekkers to Trondheim must see themselves following the footprints of the saints. It takes more than simply walking through "someone else" landscape, no matter how dramatic it may be.

Indigenous sacred sites may or may not influence the visitor. Some are offended. In the case of the new world, a common approach was to destroy evidence of the devil, as in the destruction of Templo Mayor to build the Cathedral in Mexico City and the Coricancha of

Cuzco over which a church was built. The Spaniards did everything they could to scrape clean any vestige of sacrality in the landscapes of both Peru and Mexico. The Virgin of Guadeloupe, as discussed by Torres, is fascinating because the original vision was probably the mother of Aztec gods and not Mary. The vision occurred in a stressful time, which is a fertile time for the creation of new shrines because there is non-equilibrium and imbalance.

The development and evolution of pilgrimages and sacred sites may follow the following sequence:

1. Individual ecstatic visions. unusual strange unworldly experiences; these are the experiences of "ordinary" people, certainly not of priests or politicians; there are bleeding and weeping images, which may embarrass the authorities. As Eliade notes, the sacred is not created but discovered.

1a. People discover part of themselves and their past at special sites. Native Americans do that in Chaco Canyon and countless other places in the Southwestern United States. The Vietnam memorial, which has turned out to be more powerful and symbolically deeper than its builders could probably have imagined.

1b. Ritual movement is conceived as protective and rejuvenating for home or country, such as the marches on Washington D.C discussed by Meyer and the circumambulation of Bhaktapur and Muktinath.

2. Newly created sacred sites become formalized in organized socio-political systems with economic overtones.

3. The site becomes even more controlled by tradition and texts, increasingly closed to outside influences and change.

4. The pilgrimage may finally be taken over by religious and/or political authority, loses its spontaneity and becomes frozen in time. But even in these situations, in which large numbers of people may gather, there is a tremendous amount of "primal" energy in which innovations and visions may be evoked.

Pilgrimage is an inseparable synthesis of theory, meaning and landscape. The first paper by Saraswati emphasized the theory of pilgrimage and this last paper emphasizes the transforming power of landscape. **Dhillon** notes that the extraordinary acceptance of Harrer and Aufschneiter as fellow pilgrims by the Tibetans is an acknowledgement of the fundamental openness of the Tibetan pilgrimage tradition. For a variety of reasons, the Tibetan landscape and the Tibetan people transformed Harrer and Aufshnaiter and their hosts in Lhasa recognized them as fellow pilgrims. For the two Germans, goals of victory over people and over mountains, so much in vogue in Nazi Germany of 1939, were converted into victories over oneself. Harrer's recollection of his life in Tibet involves images of "gigantic mountains" and the power of the Tibetan landscape. The powerful and beautiful landscape and physical hardship combined to create a luminosity, such as suggested by Turner, in which the normal world is turned upside down and the pilgrim opened to change.

Dhillon suggests that the crucial element of the journey of the pilgrim, perhaps, even a necessary and sufficient condition for personal transformation, is the dissolution of distinction between subject and object. Until that recognition occurs, the traveller remains a tourist, largely untouched by the landscape. In a search for a centre the pilgrim moves through a sacred ecosystem, only to find that it is so intricately interconnected that there is no centre. Madhyamikan emptiness emerges naturally from the complex landscape. The pilgrimage journey is the discovery that the journey need not have been taken, for the goal disappears in the process of approaching it, and can never be fully grasped. As the poet (T.S. Eliot) says "We shall not cease from exploration and the end of all our exploring will be to arrive where we started and know the place for the first time."

PART I

THEORY AND CASE STUDIES

1

Sacred Theory of Pilgrimage

Baidyanath Saraswati

THE Hindu institution of pilgrimage stands on four legs: the Cosmic principle, the Life principle, the Organizing principle and the Transforming principle. Sacred is the proper context of pilgrimage. I shall briefly reflect on each of these.

Cosmic Principle

The theory of pilgrimage has sprung up from the conception of *Brahman*, the ever-expanding Universe. Metaphysically, *Brahman* is identified with both fullness and emptiness and is beyond all kinds of dialectical opposition between formed and unformed, time and timelessness, mortal and immortal. Biologically, *Brahman* is a living organism that "breathes without breath."

Within the expanding Universe of *Brahman* there are many universes formed by a divine entity called *deva*, God. As an aspect of *Brahman*, God is transcendent, as an architect of the Universe, He is immanent. The *Brahman* is without name, without form and without function. The God is with name, with form, and with function. As an innermost aspect of *Brahman*, the God operates within the self-existing Universe of *Brahman*, and hence has no absolute freedom. However within his own sphere, God exercises his intrinsic powers and hence is named Brahma, the creator, Vishnu, the preserver and Mahesha, the destroyer. One God assumes many forms and therefore many, many Gods. Gods are so much a part of the creation that with the extinction of their universes they also dissolve in the same manner that other beings die.

The God takes three kinds of incarnation: that which has full power, that which has a power only for the time being and that which is only partial incarnation. Complete incarnations are ten in number. Of these, the first three are the animal forms (Fish, Turtle, Boar), the fourth is a composite form (Lion-Man), the fifth is a dwarf and the next five are fully developed humans.

Animals are the earliest form of creatures. They are also the most variable species living in the varied ecological conditions. As God has assumed the powers of *Brahman*, so have the animals derived the qualities and powers of God. Animals seem to have set standards for man in his productive powers, in swiftness, energy and strength, in mien and courage, in docility and inoffensiveness, in intelligence and faith, and so on. Ontological changes in the moral order of time follow the degree of respect for animals. Man is also a virtual animal, *pashu* the roped one. So are the Gods. They are also "roped" by the cycle of birth and death. Every human has two births: one from a human mother, another from a female animal, depending on the asterism at birth.

God, animal and man are not seen in terms of phylogeny. There is no path of linear evolution, no selection, no survival of the fittest. No species develops out of other species. The First Threes (God, Animal and Man) form a divine triangle on the surface of the Universe. The Hindu cosmological principle links all of them in a remarkable manner. Thus the theorem:

Brahman Zero God One
God One Animal Two
Animal Two Man Three

Life Principle

The Cosmic principle coincides with the Life principle. The conception of the "breathing *Brahman*" allows the assumption that life throughout the Universe exists by itself. That which is self-existent is also self-organized. In the Universe of *Brahman*, the *coincidentia oppositorium*, life and death coexist.

The smallest unit of time is *yuga*, celestial time. Four *yugas* make up a *mahayuga*. One day of Brahma constitutes a thousand fourfold *yuga*, and during the life of a Brahma, fourteen Indras fall down from heaven and die. This is the Brahma-age. The age of two Brahmas constitutes one Vishnu. At the end of the age Vishnu perishes. The age of the Mahesh is double the age of Vishnu; Mahesh also perishes at the end of his age. When everything perishes there comes the deluge. After that, for 120 Brahma-years the Universe remains a desolate void. In that eternal silence Vishnu sleeps on a banyan leaf on the surface of water. That is the beginning of the next great age.

There are two kinds of creation: natural and unnatural. The Brahma creates in his first morning not only persons having a long life, as that of himself, but also creations which have history only up to the end of that day, such as *lokas* or worlds. The worlds of Brahma signify the cosmic division of space. There are three *lokas*: the earth, the middle region and the heaven. There are seven higher regions and seven lower regions.

There are seven planets in the higher regions. Planets are persons, identified by sex and *caste*. Mercury and Saturn are neuters. The Moon and Venus are females. The Sun, Mars and Jupiter are males. Jupiter and Venus are brahmana, the learned priestly caste. The Sun is a kshatriya, the royal caste. The Moon and Mercury belong to vaishya, the commercial caste. Saturn is associated with shudra, the serving caste. Each planet has a distinctive persona.

The central point to be recognized is that the life-forms in the sky resemble the forms of life on earth in their basic characteristics. As divine persons, the planets are closely linked with humans. The underlying unity of all lives has been the essential realization of the seers of all cultures.

Organizing Principle

Quite evidently, the revealed knowledge of the Universe is complex. Being formless and suprapersonal, *Brahman* escapes the ordinary human thought, but it gets crystallized in the sacred geometry (*fig.* 1.1). There appears a circle with 360° in circumference. The centre is a dimensionless point symbolizing the expanding *Brahman*. The dotted circle is the point expanded. Within the circle, the cosmos appears as a *svastika* with four angles of 90° each, forming a square which signifies the four dimensions of space, the four-faced Brahma. The quadrangle within the circle represents the four divisions of celestial time. The three lines come together to form a cosmic triangle representing the First Threes: the three forms of life (God, animal, man), the three worlds (earth, middle region, heaven), the three Gods (creator, preserver, destroyer), the three microcosmic-macrocosmic properties (light, energy, inertness), the three principles of life (assimilation and elimination, growth, procreation), the three aspects of time (past, present, future) and the three *vidyas* (*Yajurveda*, *Rigveda*, *Samaveda*) and other similar triads. These primary forms of the Universe are fundamental to the Hindu conception of pilgrimage.

The Universe is self-organized, and the principle of life has also its own momentum. Both form the basis of all types of organization. All realms are hierarchical or else chaotic. This idea is invariably applied in the Hindu organization of space. Places of pilgrimage (*tirtha*, *kshetra*) are associated with the *hierohistory* of the Universe. Among the natural places of pilgrimage, all rivers flowing into the sea and all great mountains and forests are holy. Some of them are especially holy. There are seven seas, seven mountains and seven forests of great merit. Thermal springs are *agni-tirtha*. There are several holy places associated with animals and birds. *Tirthas* are associated with the incarnations of God. Gods,

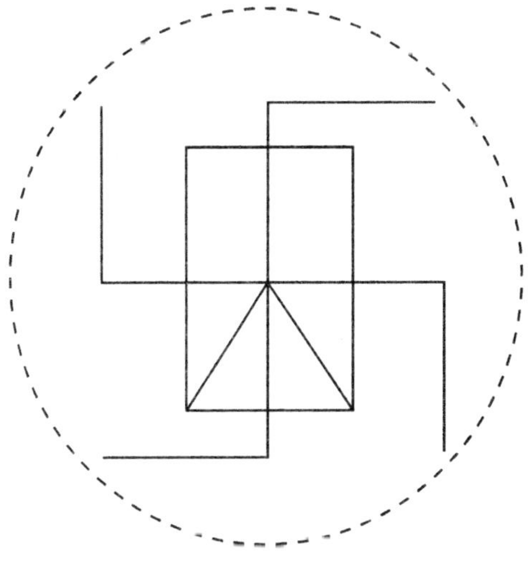

fig. 1.1: Universe of Brahman.

demons, sages and the noble kings have created a number of *tirthas*. In the *tirthas* the past is continuous with the present. The mysterious presence of the spirit of a *tirtha* is shown in the anthropomorphic (*fig.* 1.2) and Zoomorphic (*fig.* 1.3a, 1.3b) forms. All rivers, excluding the Brahmaputra (the son of Brahma), are females. The sacred hills and oceans are males. The Ganga is the mother of all creatures. The Narmada is the Daughter of the *pitris*, ancestors. Being female, all the rivers undergo a menstrual period of impurity for three days. These characteristics reveal a truth stranger than myth: *places of pilgrimage are complex living organisms.*

The grand design of a place of pilgrimage is hidden in the geometrical scheme. For instance, Kashi-kshetra (*fig.* 1.4) is represented by a holy circuit, a conch and the image of Shiva, signifying the Universe. Here the circle symbolizes the cosmic space, the quadrangle symbolizes the cosmic time, the conch symbolizes the life principle and the anthropomorphic image symbolizes the universal Self (*kshetrajna*).

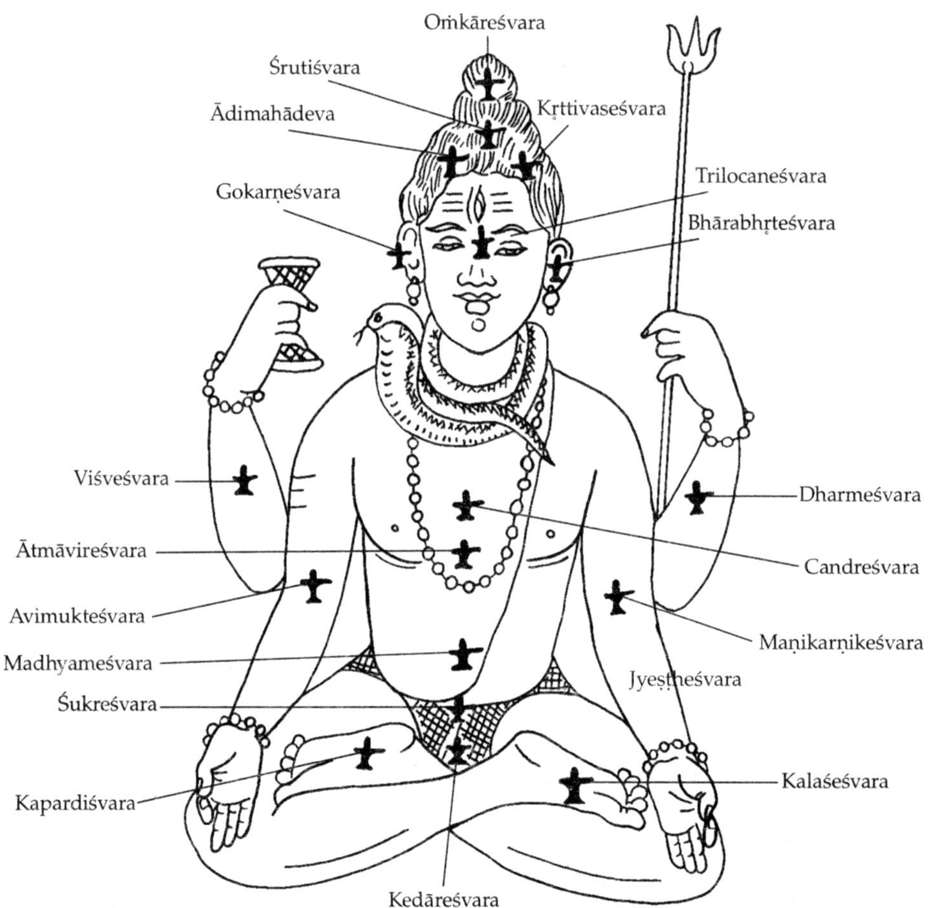

fig. 1.2: Body of Shiva as the sacred Kashi.

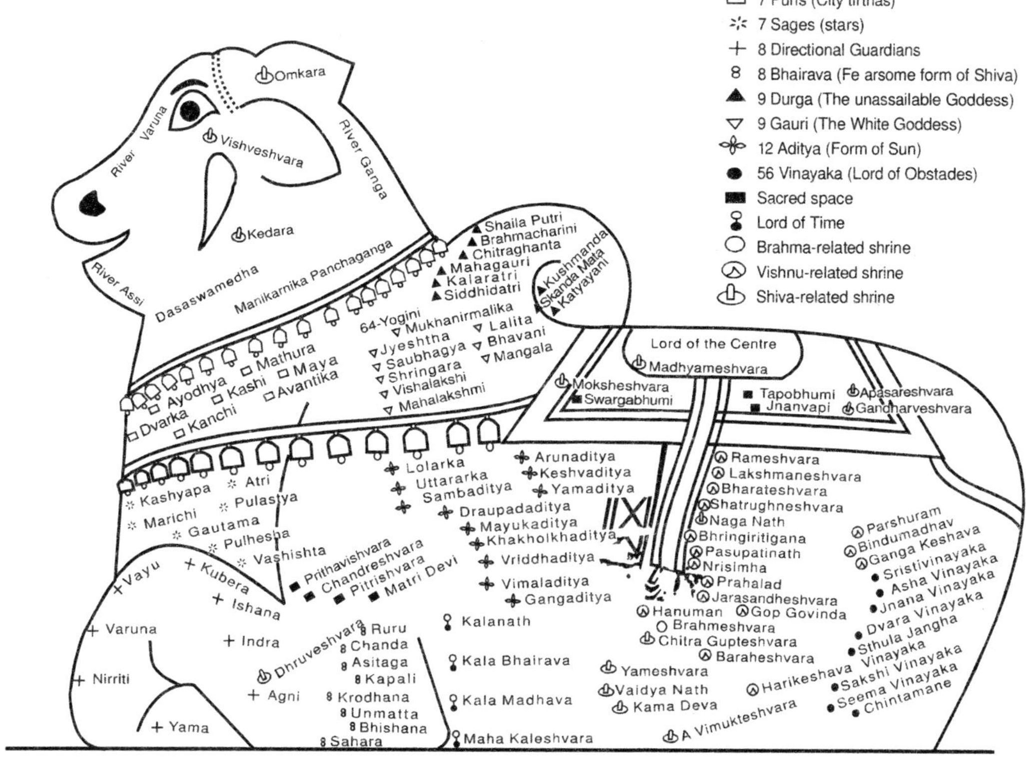

fig. 1.3a: Body of Nandi (Shiva's bull) as the sacred Kashi.

At another level, Kashi, the luminous space, is conceptualized in the mathematical arrays. Kashi-kshetra is situated on Shiva's trident at the centre of space and time. Its cosmological structure, marked by a holy circuit in the radius of five *kosas*, represents five fundamental configurations: five sheaths or envelopes (the food sheath, the vital sheath, the psychic sheath, the knowledge sheath, the blissful sheath), and five materials (earth, water, fire, air, sky). Kashi's three segments signify the totality of the Universe: three worlds, three microcosmic-macrocosmic properties, three Gods, three principles of life, three stages in the life, three aspects of time, three *vidyas*, three fire, etc. All of them coexist and cooperate. Kashi is a place where earthly dissolution is overcome and all beings rest here forever. This Kashi is an infinite void, *Brahman*. The finite Kashi is *mahashmashan*, a great ceremonial ground.

The inner complexity of the infinite cosmic Kashi is made simpler and comprehensible at the finite earthly Kashi. The shrine of Madhyameshvara, the Lord of the centre, is the centre of both the infinite and the finite Kashi. The pilgrims move along the three concentric circles: the inner sanctum formed by three sectors represents the microcosm; pilgrimage in the radius of five *kosa* signifies the mesocosm, and the larger circle in the radius of 84 *kosa* stands for the macrocosm of *Brahman* where all the 33 crore of Gods and Goddesses reside (*fig.* 1.5). In this scheme of pilgrimage one moves toward the full realization of the innermost spiritual experience. Pilgrimage follows the cycle of time. All important shrines hold annual functions. A pilgrim

fig. 1.3b: Puri as Shankha-kshetra (in the shape of a conch).

fig. 1.4: Cosmic Kashi-kshetra.

makes this an occasion for worship. The year is divided into the summer solstice and the winter solstice. In both parts of the year the pilgrims perform the *parikrama* of the Kashi-kshetra. Pilgrimage through six seasons means a visit to all the seven salvation-bestowing *tirthas* enshrined in Kashi. There is a scheme of pilgrimage for all the 12 months of the year, fortnightly pilgrimage, pilgrimage on specific lunar days, all the seven days between Monday and Sunday dedicated to the seven planets, on certain moments of auspicious time, moments of crisis, on occasions connected with astronomical conjunctions, and as and

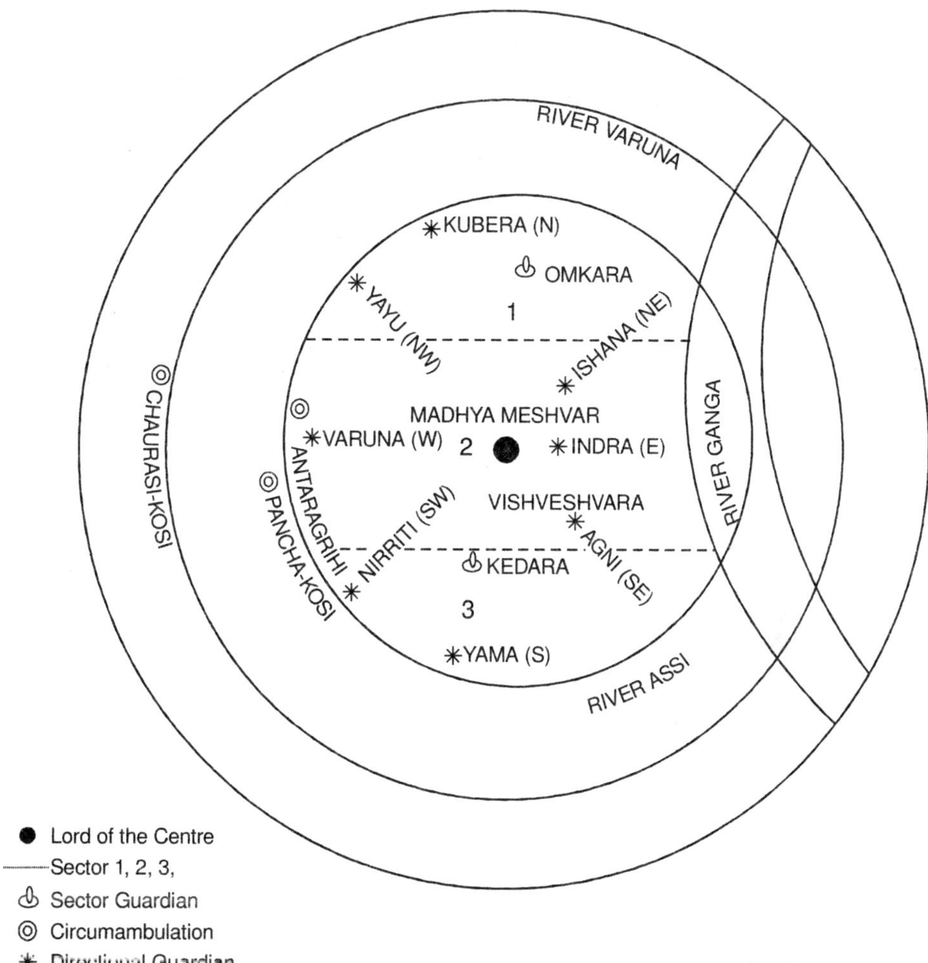

fig. 1.5: Earthly Kashi-kshetra.

when one feels the urge and the necessity for pilgrimage.

Let us admit that the scriptural description of Kashi-kshetra may or may not correspond with the empirical reality. Geographically, the shrine of Madhyameshvara does not seem to be the centre of the metropolis Kashi. Cosmologically, we are well aware that this is true as much as for Kashi-kshetra as for any place in the Universe. Similarly, the holy paths of clockwise circum-ambulation may not form a perfect circle or triangle or quadrangle but the pilgrims' movement amplifies all the possible forms of cosmic geometries that give a complete picture of the Universe. The scheme of pilgrimage takes them beyond the barriers of language and form, provides a window that illuminates their mind and carries with it a blissful momentum. A pilgrim visiting Kashi gets the feeling that he has moved into the boundless cosmic space in all its directions, all its constellations, planets, stars and Gods through the six seasons, driven in the solar car. Residing in Kashi for nine months is akin to living in the mother's womb. Taking refuge or ending one's life in Kashi means securing salvation and immortality: the ultimate goal of pilgrimage.

The earthly Kashi is a paradigmatic model that makes the reality of position and pattern in all other places of Hindu pilgrimage. Without doubt, it is a place of Shiva; but clearly it does not derive its importance from Shiva alone. All the sacred spaces, all the Gods and Goddesses, all the sacred rivers and mountains and all the planets and stars are manifest here in their revealed aspects. The presiding deity is Visheshvara, the Lord of the Universe, one of the thousand (infinite) forms of Shiva, representing *Brahman* itself. Shiva as Nataraja is the same as Surya, the Sun. Kashi the luminous space is especially significant for enshrining all the 12 forms of Surya. The clockwise circumambulation of Kashi-kshetra may be conceived as an imitation of the great solar system. Much of this description implies that the institution of pilgrimage moves the wheel of life and culture.

Transforming Principle

All places of pilgrimage are sacred-effective places. Entry into a sacred space is an extraordinary event in man's life. It transforms him completely and brings him closer to the original self, the supreme Sacred. For instance, a pilgrim to the Ayappa shrine, at the Sabari Malai hills in Kerala, undergoes a remarkable transformation. The mysteries of this pilgrimage are unspeakable but expressible through ritual acts of the pilgrim. A pilgrim dies temporarily as a secular man and attains the godhood during the time of pilgrimage. One becomes Ayappa as soon as his secular personality is switched off. He is addressed as Ayappa, and not by his personal name. Having observed a 30-day vow, the aspirant pilgrim is required to make a fire-walking ritual to prove that he has followed the rules of pilgrimage faithfully. Having proven worthy of pilgrimaging, he breaks a coconut at the doorstep of his house, just before starting the sacred journey. On the way he bathes in the river Pumpa and climbs 18 steps from the foot of the Sabari Malai hills to the Ayappa shrine. On his ascent he breaks a coconut on the relevant step corresponding to the number of his sacred journey to the Ayappa shrine. All preparatory rituals such as fire-walking, bathing in the river and breaking the coconut symbolize the death of the secular man. Now the pilgrim is exalted in rank as an Ayappa who sees the divine bird Garuda and also the self-effulgent light *makaravilaku* across the Sabari Malai hills. This, only a true Ayappa pilgrim can see and no one else. Upon completion of the pilgrimage, the pilgrim returns to his worldly realities and, once again, becomes a secular man. This is done again in a ritual way. On his return journey he breaks another coconut on the relevant step in the descending order, bathes in the Pumpa River once again and, back home, breaks the last coconut. Thereafter he no longer remains Ayappa, no one calls him Ayappa. The ritual of breaking the coconut and bathing in the river now symbolizes his return to the normal state, his re-descent to the temporal world. He regains his secular identity and his name. This extraordinary pilgrimage, involving ritual death and rebirth of the secular-man and his transformation, as God is indescribable.

This experience of the supreme sacred energy transforming the person is personal.

Transformation from *within* the sacred tradition causes a condition which might be called "homeomorphy." This type of transformation brings continuous acceleration of faith in the sacred realities. During the medieval age, when the temples of Kashi were being destroyed and its shrines were desecrated, a great pundit Narayana Bhatt declared that God Shiva resides in every pebble of Kashi, and the power of the Supreme flows in the life of the people. The cosmic design of Kashi was thereafter restored by regular circumambulation, the wakefulness of the faithful. There are also instances of transformation of another kind which does not seem reconcilable within a specific context. For instance, the Buddhist and the Hindu pilgrims sharing a common sacred site (Gaya, Varanasi, Badrinath) have a revolutionary implication. Historically it is true that one faith stimulates another which may appear dissimilar. Hajo, on the river Brahmaputra, is a pilgrimage centre where Hindus, Buddhists and Muslims assemble. For the Assamese-Muslims, this place has a quarter of the sanctity of Mecca, hence Hajo is called Pau-Mecca. Such instances of the shard religious traditions, involving transformation, may be termed, "heterochromous homeo-morphs," transformation into multicolour in each religious tradition producing similar response: seven colours in each ray of the sun.

Transformation from *without* the sacred tradition causes a situation in which a highly aberrant form evolves. We may call it "heteromorphy," whereby a place of pilgrimage degenerates in its functional structures. In many parts of India today the sacred places are turning into political and commercial cities. The Nation State, committed to secularism and modernity, has taken over the rights and duties of the hereditary sacred specialists who were once the traditional guardians of the shrines and rituals. Perhaps nothing makes a greater mockery of State claiming development of the sacred traditions through cultural tourism.

Theoretical Conclusions

Seven Sutras

- Pilgrimage has a *parahistory*. From the Hindu point of view, it is more than visiting a sacred place on earth. As a spiritual exercise of the human mind, it captures the mysteries of the expanding Universe of *Brahman*. Here religion and science are inseparable. Call it the Sacred Science.
- Pilgrimage may be defined as a cosmic drama of which God, animal and man are the actors and the earth the theatre. Places of pilgrimage are the manifested cosmoses. Pilgrimage on the earth is sky-bound. As a heavenly movement it is visible, but the power that makes a pilgrim move is elusive. The movement of the pilgrims around a fixed centre (the presiding deity) is something like the movement of the Sum, Moon and other planets and constellations, and hence archetypical. What follows is the great

principle of Life. Everything is moving. Even Dhruva (pole-star) is only relatively fixed but factually itself moves in the heavens.

- From cosmic intelligence to all forms of human knowledge. From complex to simple is the transcendent law. The inner complexity of the meaning of pilgrimage gives way to the outer simplicity of performances. The reality of complexity obeys a definite cultural Law. The equivalence between knowledge and power is central to this theory.
- Intellect looks inward. Faith looks forward, to receive all. Scriptures are the authority of the morning of faith. Here truths are stated in simple words. The symbols echo the message straight away. Man's thinking and experiencing flow from his self-image. Anthropomorphization is, therefore, a kind of necessity for comprehending mystery.
- Numerical symbolism provides an abstract and profound link between the pilgrim and the invisible forces of God. The use of the numerical concept helps recognize the conceivable unity of places and peoples, objects and ideas, visibles and invisibles.
- Pilgrimage is a personal venture. The merit accrues at the level of individual self. Essential to this claim is that interaction between man and God is direct, and no mediator (priest) is required. At the highest level of realization there is no need to visit a place of pilgrimage. Pilgrimage has to be realized within one's own body.
- Pilgrimage has the capacity to transform matter into spirit, human into divine in a space-time continuum. Two types of transformation are taking place in today's world of Pilgrimage : (1) Homeomorphy, which is a gradual progressive change within the sacred tradition, retaining the essential identity. Simulation in the shared religious traditions may be termed heterochromous homeomorphy. (2) Heteromorphy, which is a change without thoughtful consideration of tradition. It upsets the internal organization in the deepest way.

References

Agrawala, Vasudeva S., 1968, *Matsya Purana: A Study*, Varanasi: All India Kashiraj Trust.

Saraswati, Baidyanath, 1984, *The Spectrum of the Sacred: Essays in the Religious Tradition of India*, New Delhi: Concept Publishing Company.

———, 1985, "Kashi Pilgrimage : The End of an Endless Journey," in Makhan Jha (ed.), *Dimensions of Pilgrimage: An Anthropological Approach*, New Delhi, Inter-India Publications.

———, 1991, "Ritual Space: Tribal-Nontribal Context" in Kapila Vatsyayan (ed.), *Concept of Space: Ancient and Modern*, New Delhi, Indira Gandhi National Centre for the Arts.

———, 1992, "Ksetra", in Bettina Baumer (ed.), *Kalatattvakosa* (*Concepts of Space and Time*), vol. II, New Delhi, Indira Gandhi National Centre for the Arts.

Vatsyayan, Kapila, 1983, *The Square and the Circle of the Indian Arts*, Delhi, Roli Books International.

2

Complexity and Self-organization in Pilgrimage Systems

John McKim Malville

The Non-equilibrium Universe

WHEN two different liquids are placed in the same vessel they will diffuse into a homogeneous mixture, thereby achieving an equilibrium state with the greatest disorder and maximum entropy. Such behaviour is the prediction of the Second Law of Thermodynamics.

At some future time, far into the future, hundreds of billions of years in the future, all configurations of matter and energy in our universe will be similarly homogenized and will approach the condition of thermodynamic equilibrium. Stars will cool and become dark, as temperature differences between them and their surroundings will vanish. Black holes and neutron stars may dissipate their concentrated mass and fade into the homogeneous background. In its most perfect form, thermodynamic equilibrium involves a detailed balancing of all processes, such that each process is precisely balanced by its inverse. In such a balance no information, structure or complexity can persist. The state of thermodynamic equilibrium is frozen into timelessness, remembering no history, containing no information and incapable of sustained change. Perfect equilibrium is perfect death.

Today portions of our universe depart significantly from equilibrium, and these are the regions where we find life, complexity and beauty. It is fair to say that we humans are the fragile children of non-equilibrium. A glance at the night sky reveals the non-equilibrium of our universe. The sky of stars and galaxies is an inhomogeneous soup. Hot, bright, dense stars are surrounded by cold, dark, vacuous space. Planet Earth has a hot star on one side and cold space on the other. Expansion of the universe prevents stagnation by keeping space cold. Expansion has allowed the formation of complex low entropy structures like us and our fellow inhabitants of the earth's biosphere.

We truly live between fire and ice. We also live between the extremes of complete chaos and perfect order, for in that intermediate state structures can have their greatest complexity and contain maximum information (*fig.* 2.1). There is no information contained in either pure disorder or perfect order. In his book *At Home in the Universe* the theoretical biologist, Stuart Kauffman (1995), argues that evolution occurs at the "edge of chaos." At that edge, intermediate between chaos and order, biological systems have their greatest flexibility, greatest opportunity for creative impulses, and most effective responses to environmental threats.

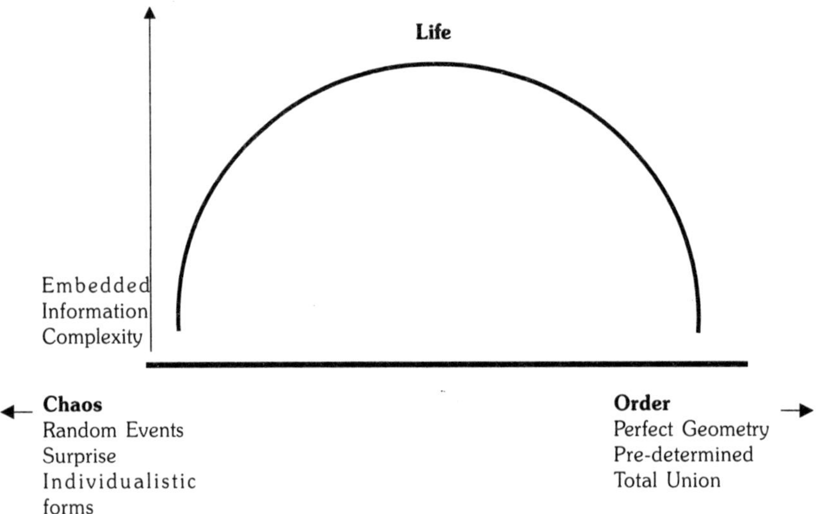

fig. 2.1 Variation of information contained within a system between states of pure chaos and perfect order. Note that the greatest complexity lies between these two extreme states.

Biological evolution is but one example of the general class of non-equilibrium systems that self-organize. As it has moved along its trajectory of time during the last 15 billion years since the big bang, the universe is the largest example of self-organization. Pilgrimage is another form of spontaneous complexification, as individual creativity and group coherence join to produce human systems that are greater than the individual parts (Malville 2001).

Dissipative Structures

The physical chemist Ilya Prigogine (1980) was one of the first to demonstrate the thermodynamic and chemical benefits of non-equilibrium by showing that certain configurations of low entropy and great complexity can be stabilized if they are open to the inward and outward flow of energy and matter. Prigogine and his colleagues (Prigogine 1980; Nicolis and Prigogine 1989; Jantsch 1980) called these stable systems *dissipative structures* and argued that they may spontaneously develop great complexity and become reservoirs of considerable information.

The pathway to the formation of stable dissipative structures involves a condition of metastability in which processes amplify small fluctuations so that they can have influences far beyond themselves. As a result, the system can suddenly transform into something radically different, similar to rapid phase transitions from a supersaturated liquid to ice. In the metastable state just prior to transformation, the future system may be entirely unknowable. Order and complexity in the dissipative structure are created from disorder precisely because the system is out of equilibrium. We humans should feel comfortable by the ideas of self-organized complexity and dissipative systems for we are the ultimate improbable structures in our cosmic neighbourhood.

In order to achieve a decrease in entropy, the system needs to be open and transmit, radiate, and/or excrete "low quality" energy into its surroundings. A chicken egg is able to develop internal complexity by dissipating heat to the outside. Preventing dissipation by surrounding the egg with an insulating layer would kill its contents. Likewise, if we were to enclose the inner part of the solar system by an insulating shell and thereby prevent dissipation of "low quality" energy into interstellar space, we would eventually destroy life on our planet. The de-coupling of an internal combustion engine from its radiator will similarly kill the engine.

Self-organized Criticality

An alternate approach to self-organizing systems that emphasizes discreet events rather than a continuous flow of matter and energy is that of *self-organized criticality* (SOC). The theory of SOC was first developed by Bak (Bak, Tang and Wiesenfeld 1988; Bak and Chen 1991; Bak and Sneppen 1993; Bak 1994) modelling avalanches of sand piles that achieve critical slopes. When sand grains are first added to a low pile, they function as entirely separate and isolated objects, having little if any effect upon neighbouring grains. Once the pile has achieved a critical slope (34° for dry sand) individual grains may acquire large ranges of influence and, acting in cooperation with other grains, initiate avalanches. The sand pile acquires thereby a cooperative and coherent mode of behaviour and achieves SOC. The system is open, requiring a constant throughput of energy and matter: sand must be constantly added and must be eliminated at the edges. Building a wall around the base of the pile would destroy the coherent behaviour of the system. Because it is an improbable low entropy structure, any randomizing process such as a strong gust of wind or an earthquake would also eliminate its coherency. By contrast, the equilibrium condition of maximum entropy would be one in which sand is scattered randomly across the floor.

Once criticality has been achieved in a sand pile (or a rice pile), avalanches occur with a power law distribution in sizes. It turns out that avalanches of real piles of rice grains when measured in the laboratory actually show fractal geometries and power law distributions better than real piles of sand (Frette *et al.* 1995). Occurring at all scales of time and space, these avalanches have no special size or frequency and are therefore called scale independent.

A power law distribution (Appendix I) of the sizes of avalanches is a "litmus" test for SOC. The initial nature of the grains of sand (or rice) or the rate at which the grains are added does not influence the distribution of avalanche sizes. A highly significant feature of SOC is that its details are not determined by the exact nature of the individual elements or initial conditions: it happens, in spite of specific details. SOC is a robust, holistic and universal process, which is found in countless situations in the natural world such as earthquakes, forest fires, solar flares and biological extinction events. In contrast to the sudden transformation of the chemical systems studied by Prigogine, the sand pile model slowly approaches the state of criticality.

Flares on the sun are impressive examples of metastability and avalanches in a self-organized system (Lu 1993). In the early phase of its 11-year sunspot cycle, the global magnetic field becomes increasingly twisted due to differences in the rates of rotation between the equator and the poles. As the magnetic field is twisted further from its equilibrium condition, metastable regions appear in the form of sunspots, each containing twisted magnetic fields that are just at the edge of instability. Very slight perturbations of those magnetic fields can cause sudden releases of stress and avalanches of flares of all sizes. As the number of sunspots grows, the frequency of appearance of flares of all sizes follows the *same* power law distribution, a dramatic indication that self-organized criticality has been achieved across the surface of the sun. The release of magnetic energy becomes a coherent global phenomenon. The correlation length of dynamic changes of the magnetic field has vastly expanded from a tiny bundle to the entire surface of the sun.

Resonance

Dynamical systems can undergo major transformations due to resonance, whereby small fluctuations may slowly accumulate if they have the same frequencies as the natural frequencies of the system. The world is filled with examples of resonant behaviour that can produce system-wide changes, such as the destruction of the Tacoma Narrows Bridge, near Seattle, due to the resonant amplification of small gusts of wind. Elsewhere in the solar system gaps in the asteroid belt and in the rings of Saturn are established by resonance. Some features of human behaviour and most pilgrimage systems are influenced by resonant phenomena involving the heavens, such as solar days, the 29.5 day cycle of the moon or the 365.25 day cycle of the sun. The joining of three resonant cycles may be observed in Varanasi at a great festival on the morning of the first full moon after *makara-samkranti* (precessed winter solstice). Resonance between the lunar cycle and human social rhythms may have influenced the length of the human menstrual cycle and other features of early human culture (Knight 1998).

The 11.86-year cycle of Jupiter resonates with the dates of the Kumbha Mela (Dubey 1987). The 18.6-year standstill cycle of the moon establishes periods of high and low ocean tides at middle and high latitudes and consequently has great influence on coastal fishing cultures. Attention to the standstill cycle is evident in the archaeological record of the ancestral Pueblos of the American Southwest (Malville and Putman 1993).

An important example of resonance occurs in noisy systems such that a background of random fluctuations can enhance the influence of a particular periodic event in the process known as *stochastic resonance* (Wiesenfeld and Jaramillo 1998; Gluckman *et al.* 1998). For each situation there is an optimum level of noise that will have an influence but will not overpower the signal. This phenomenon of stochastic resonance can enhance the ability of sharks to detect weak electrical signals produced by prey fish in the noisy ocean (Adair, Astumain and Weaver 1998). One of the first natural systems in which evidence for stochastic resonance was detected is the changing climate of the earth, particularly that of the ice ages. The period of advance and retreat of ice is close to 100,000 years, which synchronizes with a very weak periodic variation of solar energy due to the changing shape of the earth's orbit, first pointed out by Milankovitch in the 1920s. In the presence of random fluctuations of the earth's atmosphere, the small periodic signal from the sun may have been amplified to produce the large climate fluctuations of the ice ages.

Large periodic aggregations of people at the Kumbha Mela or other great pilgrimage events are further examples of large consequences of small periodic signals that are amplified in our noisy world. In the natural world with a rich spectrum of background noise, such as a rural Indian village, relatively weak influences due to the cycles of the sun and moon may be amplified by stochastic resonance to result in periodic pilgrimage or other social aggregations. By contrast, people living in noise free "sterile" modern environments or alternately in ones that are dominated by noise may not become aware of periodic signals emerging from their terrestrial and celestial surroundings.

Self-organization in the Biosphere and in Pilgrimage

All three types of self-organization (rapid transformations of metastable states; slow build-up to criticality; resonance) are present in the biosphere of the earth. We acquire high quality energy from the sun (T= 5800 K) and export lower quality energy (T = 300 K) into interstellar space. In his Gaia hypothesis, Lovelock (1979) has proposed that the total biosphere functions as a single organism that is integrated by the movement of atmospheric oxygen and carbon dioxide. Lovelock's ideas have provoked lively controversy but the self-organization of the biosphere is beyond dispute.

Our biosphere is a highly non-equilibrium system with concentrations of O_2 and CO_2 that greatly depart from equilibrium. Life could not exist on the earth were it an equilibrium system. The non-equilibrium levels of oxygen and carbon dioxide are maintained by a complex network of feedback loops, some of which first appeared in the atmosphere and oceans of our planet some 2-3 billion years ago with the appearance of life. Like blood flowing through the human body, atmospheric oxygen and carbon dioxide flow through the biosphere and provide the medium by which separate living systems interact with each other.

One consequence of the Gaia hypothesis is that the biosphere functions as unified system in which all parts are interdependent. A consequence of that unity and interdependence is that a loss of a part affects the whole. When a comet or asteroid strikes one part of the earth, such as the K-T event 65 million years ago or the great Permian extinction event some 230 million years ago, the whole of the biosphere is imperiled.

Similar to the biosphere, pilgrimage systems often have the appearance of self-organized complexity. When people spontaneously interact with each other they can develop a pattern in space and time that is self-organized and scale invariant. The movement of people and ideas through a pilgrimage landscape stabilizes the system and is analogous to the movement of oxygen and carbon dioxide through the biosphere or blood through the body. The mega-system of pilgrimage throughout the vastness of Hindu India has the appearance of a natural system similar to the biosphere in which it is embedded.

Self-similarity

Self-organizing systems are characterized by the phenomenon of self-similarity, wherein similar geometric patterns may be repeated again and again at different sizes. Self-similarity is expressive of a fundamental unity of the system. Meaning and process are continuous across all levels of scale. With no fundamental scale or characteristic size, self-similar structures are unchanged after increasing or shrinking their size.

The parallelism of macrocosm and microcosm is a deep and ancient human intuition, which led to the first naming of night time constellations and the building of cities that were intended to be miniature versions of the cosmos. Wheatley (1971: 414) is speaking precisely of self-similarity, as it was manifest in the traditional city, when he refers to parallel planes of reality. Architecture that mimicked celestial realms converted cities, temples and homes into self-similar structures. That parallelism included time as well as space and produced . . .:

> an intimate parallelism between the regular and mathematically expressible regimes of the heavens and the biologically determined rhythms of life on earth as manifested in the succession of the seasons, the annual cycles of plant regeneration, and within the compass of an individual life, birth, growth, procreation and death.

The pathway walked by the pilgrim may represent the layout of the universe from centre to periphery, and it also may represent the evolution of the universe from beginning to end.

The cosmic cycles of sun and moon, which entrain the pilgrim, are similar to the cycles of birth, maturation and death of terrestrial life. Since they can be enlarged or decreased without changing their essence, the space-time geometries of pilgrimage, whether held in the mind of a pilgrim, drawn on the page of a manuscript, or embedded in a pilgrimage landscape retain their universal meaning and their power.

The cardinal *dhamas*, the four "abodes" of the gods of the Indian subcontinent parallel the cardinality of the Hindu temple. Varanasi-Kashi is a paradigmatic example of self-similarity. It contains those four *dhamas* within itself as well as most, if not all, of the other pilgrimage destinations that span the sub-continent (Eck 1983; Singh 1993; Saraswati 1985). Kashi is one of the Seven Cities, *Saptapuri*, and it achieves another form of self-similarity by including the other six cities within itself. The Panchakrosi route encloses the universe, but it is also believed to be contained within the body of the individual pilgrim.

The cosmic mountain that the pilgrim circumambulates may be both the axis of the universe and the spire of a temple; a change in scale does not change the significance or efficacy of the movement. The *garbhagriha* of the Hindu temple is both the dark and watery womb of life and the point of creation from which the universe expanded outward from chaos. Circulation about the temple may be revolution about the cosmic axis, the motion of the sun in the sky, and a spiral backward into the beginning of time. The labyrinthine patterns in the floors of certain Gothic cathedrals through which penitents would crawl were meant as miniaturized pilgrimage journeys to the centre. The 660 ft circumambulation path at Chartres cathedral symbolically recreates the pilgrimage to Jerusalem (Barrie 1996).

Self-similarity is the key to the story of Shiva and Parvati asking their two sons to demonstrate their love by racing each other around the universe (see also Bhardwaj, Chapter 3). Ganesha circumambulates his parents, who are also the entire universe, while his brother begins the immensely long journey along its perimeter. Both pathways are equally valuable and meaningful for the pilgrim, each providing different benefit.

Fractals

Fractals are composed of self-similar structures and have overall geometries with fractional dimensions (Schroeder 1991). The well-known fractal named after Mandelbrot is a striking example of the endless inclusion of patterns within patterns. No matter how much its tiniest element is magnified it still contains the essence of the entire structure.

In its repetition of triangles of different sizes, the fractal known as the Sierpinsky triangle demonstrates self-similarity and scale invariance. The same distributions of larger and smaller triangles are seen everywhere, regardless of the magnification of the image. It has a fractional dimension of 1.585.

fig. 2.2 Sierpinsky Triangle

Fractals are the free spirits of the world of mathematics and geometry and range in the natural world from clouds, cauliflowers, leaves, braided streambeds and coastlines (Porter and Gleick 1990; McGuire 1991). It should come as no surprise that pilgrimage landscapes have fractal geometries when the natural movement of people generates their geometric patterns.

Meyer (1994) suggests that "psychic maps" and cosmograms are created by most cultures and are "absorbed and held unconsciously by members" of those cultures. Mentally-held cosmograms may be elements of the pilgrimage experience for some pilgrims as they walk along fractal pathways. The complex geometry of the Hindu *yantra* is an example of such a mental map, which holds great power and significance for the Hindu pilgrim and which may play a role in organizing the ideal landscape through which pilgrims move. In its expression of unity across all scales of the universe, the well-known *Shri Yantra* is fractal both in geometry and in fundamental meaning.

Power Law Distributions

Self-similarity of the large and small is also expressed in mathematical power law distributions in which different sizes and lengths are united. In fractals, for example, there are many more small structures than large ones. Their respective numbers are represented by a power law distribution, such that the number of objects or events (N) is proportional to size(s) raised to a negative power (α), $N = s^{-\alpha}$. For example, if one counts the number of triangles of various sizes found in the Sierpinsky triangle and plots those numbers on log-log paper, the line has a slope of 1.585.

A power law distribution is a fundamental feature of self-organization. The natural world is full of such power law distributions between the large and the small: earthquakes, words of the English language, interplanetary debris and coastlines of continents. Further discussion of power laws can be found in Appendix I.

Origins of Pilgrimage

The catchment basin of a pilgrimage centre contains villages, which themselves may be self-organized complex systems, as has been noted by Saraswati (1995). In a manner like slowly increasing the slope of a rice pile or the build-up of magnetic stress on the sun, a village may be brought to a critical state, which Saraswati identifies as bio-spiritual stress. The village is another example of a complex Gaia-like ecosystem that is stabilized by a myriad of interconnecting feedback loops. Release of stress in a metastable village may inspire local festivals as well as periodic departures of residents on pilgrimages. Certain festivals and pilgrimage journeys thus might be understood stress-releasing events that are triggered by the solar-lunar calendar.

The critical event leading to the onset of a particular pilgrimage tradition may have been a charismatic leader, a powerful individualistic vision, a miraculous cure, a novel idea, or simply a wealthy patron. A pilgrimage tradition may start with surprising suddenness when the cultural system departs sufficiently from equilibrium such that a very slight fluctuation or bio-spiritual impulse can produce a transforming avalanche of spontaneous change. The circulation of pilgrims from village to pilgrim centre creates an open system that in some cases transcends regional diversity and social stratification and opens up possible pathways for innovation and individual social mobility (Bhardwaj 1973). Like the stirring of the cosmic ocean to create *amrita*, pilgrimage stirs the cultural landscape, produces new life-giving options and prevents the stagnation of equilibrium.

Preston (1992) alludes to the "spiritual magnetism" that draws people into a pilgrimage centre, but it is important to note that such attraction is not toward a simple point in space and time. There is no single, persistent end-point to be pursued. The goal changes as the pilgrim changes. The journey may be endless and ever different (Saraswati 1985), in which participants are drawn forward by "strange" attractors (Cambel 1993). The "strange" attractor is an important concept in the physics of complex systems and refers to the process wherein matter is pulled toward self-transformation by unpredictable, changing, and ambiguous forces.

There clearly are powerful attractors at work to cause pilgrims to journey far and undergo (sometimes) extreme physical hardships in search of an ideal. In its ambiguity and unpredictability the metaphorical attractor of pilgrimage shares features with the strange attractor of mathematical chaos theory. In his description of complex physical systems Cambel (1993: 4) comes remarkably close to a description of pilgrimage: "Complex systems are dynamic and not in equilibrium; they are like a journey, not a destination and they may pursue a moving target." Because of various junctions and bifurcations along the pathway in space-time of a pilgrimage landscape, future developments are typically unpredictable.

Complex Landscapes

Interactions between humans and the heavens, between the microcosm and macrocosm, have initiated and maintained many pilgrimage traditions. Such appears to have been the case in the Nubian Desert of southern Egypt, when repetitive visits by nomadic cattle herders during the summer monsoons between 10,000 and 7,000 years before the present established a ceremonial complex at the western shore of Nabta Playa. Perhaps the world's first recorded pilgrimage tradition developed at Nabta Playa involving periodic cattle worship set amongst megalithic structures aligned to the sun and stars (Malville *et al.* 1998). The onset of the summer monsoons, which made the desert habitable for a few months, established the rhythm of nomadic pilgrimage.

A similar resonance between humans, the terrestrial landscape, and the cycles of the heavens may have played a role in the development of the Chaco regional system among the ancestral Pueblos of the American Southwest. The region may have been pushed into self-organized criticality by environmental forces and population growth. The result was a rapid onset of periodic movement of people into Chaco and construction of great houses, great kivas, roads and other possible accoutrements of pilgrimage (Malville and Malville 2001). Near the middle of the eleventh century there appears to have sudden transformation of the culture as its correlation length, L_c, i.e., the distance over which myth, ritual and architecture is correlated, increased by a factor of more than 100 from the kilometer radius of a village to the hundreds of kilometers of the Chaco culture system.

The first cities of the world, which appeared during the third millennium BCE, were self-organizing, non-equilibrium systems, which often underwent rapid self-transformation. The first major examples of urban order appeared suddenly in the Indus valley following 2600 BCE, giving the appearance of "a paroxysm of change" (Possehl 1990; Parpola 1994). A variety of stimuli may have triggered the vast modifications of socio-cultural behaviour that led to the Mature Harappan culture: the onset of maritime trade, a powerful new ideology, and a writing system. The Harappan culture area covered an area of more than 1,250,000 km^2 and consisted of approximately 1000 settlements, many with orthogonal systems of streets, ritual baths, standardized construction bricks standardized, and sophisticated sanitation and water systems. Parapola (1994) has suggested that the sudden transformation of the Harappan landscape was paralleled by the development of a complex astronomy, which may be manifest in part by the Harappan script containing the remarkable self-similarity of stars and fish, each swimming in their respective oceans.

The *tirthas* of India provide further examples of self-amplifying interactions between people and their landscapes. *Tirthas* are "crossing-over" places with many levels of meaning. Some were initially places to pause in the process of fording a river, such as the Ganga at Varanasi, at which place a symbolic resonance was evident because the Ganga flows northward out of the realm of death toward the place of birth. Repetition of simple acts and the confluence of countless mytho-historical events have led to the vast significance of pilgrimage to Varanasi, also known as Kashi. In that location multiple realms can be crossed and many of the features of self-organizing systems can be experienced such as self-similarity, resonance and fractal geometries (Saraswati 1985; Singh 1993; Malville and Singh 1995).

Concluding Remarks

In the beginning stages, pilgrimage may be a vigorously open self-organizing system, which creates new meaning, myths and rituals. In its more mature state opportunities for spontaneity and innovation may be reduced, although not entirely eliminated. Openness always invites spontaneity, surprises, and unconventional behaviour, often disproved by authority. A summary of the characteristics of self-organizing systems is presented in Appendix II.

When a human system has become self-organized and reached the critical state, it may sustain ideational avalanches such as new concepts, theories, and perspectives. Within the "catchment basin" of a pilgrimage system, these avalanches involve people as well as ideas. In the case of Hindu India, the scale of interaction extends across the entire country, involving the coherent behaviour of hundreds of millions of people who are not organized by any central authority, but who, by their movement, provide social continuity and cohesion for the entire land (McNamara 1995).

Often pilgrimage acquires cosmogonic and cosmological meaning as pilgrims re-enact the origin of the myths of the cosmos, mimic great events of the past, and move in parallel with the cycles of the heavens.

There is immense depth to the pilgrimage landscape and its associated mythology, generated by many levels of meaning, many sources of energy, and multiple centres of attraction. The entry of the mathematics, physics, and chemistry of self-organization into the discussion does not diminish in any way the deep mystery and grandeur of the pilgrimage experience. There is breath taking mystery and spaciousness to the fractal of Mandelbrot, for example, which in its scale-invariance continues inward to the heart of the tiniest piece of matter and outward to its expanding boundaries of the universe. In the actuality of dawn on the Ganga, there is mystery to the rising of the sun greeted every morning by thousands of pilgrims.

The greatest wonder of all is that these complex pilgrimage structures were created by free individuals walking in concert over the land, each in search of meaning and in pursuit of an ideal.

Appendix I

FRACTALS AND POWER LAWS

Self-organization is characterized by a power law distribution of the sizes of its elements such the number of elements of a size r is given by

$$N = Ar^{-D}$$

where the power, D, may be defined as the fractal dimension.

Scale-invariance or self-similarity is demonstrated by changing the scale of measurement from r to kr, where k is a scaling factor, as if one were to magnify or de-magnify an image. The image in its essence remains. The power law behaviour remains unchanged and retains the same dimension:

$N = Ar^{-D}$ becomes $Ak^{-D}r^{-D}$
or simply
$N = Br^{-D}$

We may test for scale invariance and self-similarity by means of log-log plots of distributions of sizes of structures.

Square or rectangular geometries with a dimension precisely equal to 2 are found in planned pre-conceived ritual landscapes such a royal city designed as the geometrically perfect "cosmic" cities of China or a Hindu temple built according to precise mathematical rules. With only a single dimension, these structures do not show power law distributions.

Scale invariance and self-similarity are fundamental characteristics of fractals. First introduced by Mandelbrot, fractals were so named because of their fractional dimensions, such as 1.6 for the sea anemone or 2.35 for clouds. Freedom from imposed dimensions of 1, 2 or 3 make fractals common features of the natural world. The real fractals found in nature are not geometrically precise or mathematically deterministic. Like the actual snowflake with its damaged edges and broken symmetries, fractals of nature possess a statistical self-similarity in that patterns at different levels of scale are similar but never exactly duplicated.

In order to test for self-similarity and scale invariance in pilgrimage systems, we have investigated the structure of shrines along the pilgrimage circuit of Mt. Kailasa in Tibet, by measuring the positions of the 54 major shines of its kora using the Global Positioning System.

A glance at the map of the shrines reveals that they are neither perfectly ordered nor randomly spaced. The four major gompas of the circuit (Nyreni, Diraphuk, Zutul Phuk, and Darchan) are ordered along approximate cardinal directions. But the individual shrines have not been placed in an obvious pattern. Randomness would appear as an error function or

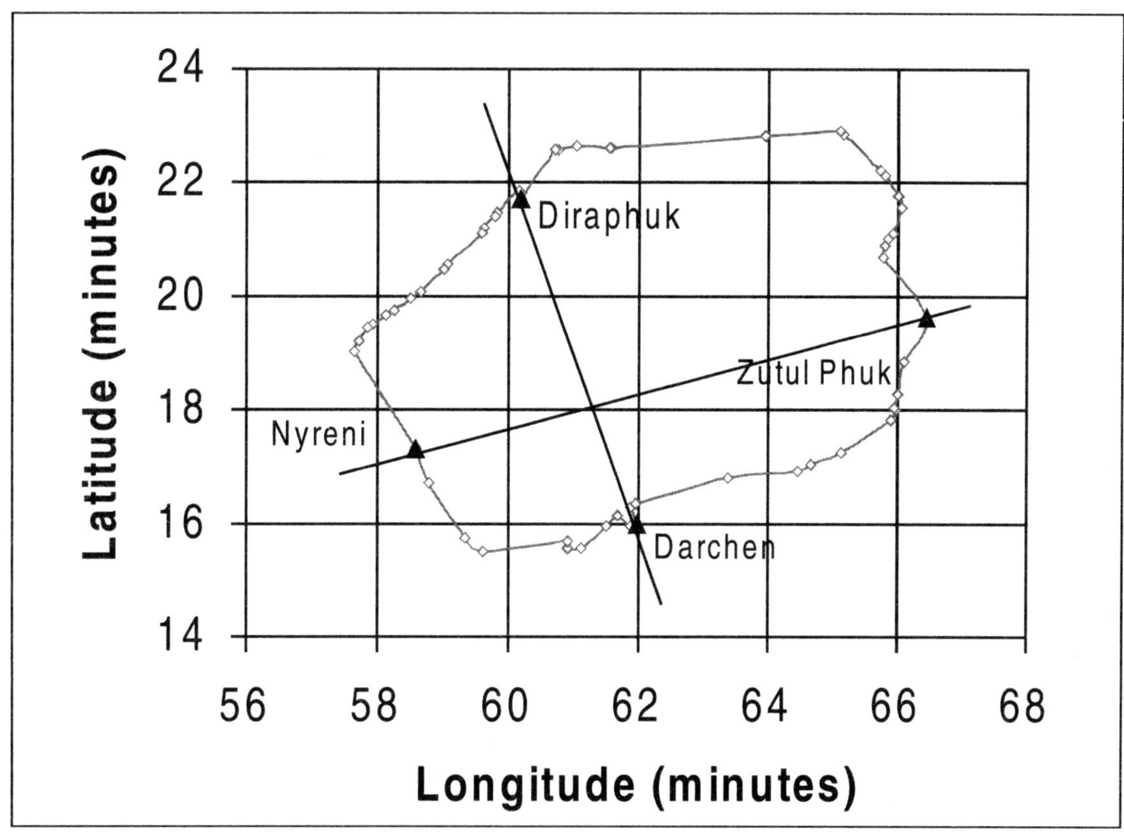

Map. 2.1 Shrines and Gompas of the Kailash Kora

Poisson distribution, which we do not find. On the contrary, there is a power law in the spacing of adjacent shrines, i.e., a straight line on a log-log graph. The frequency distribution of separation distances varies with a power of –1.5.

We extended our measurements to the 108 shrines of the *Panchakrosi-yatra* and found a similar distribution with a power of –1.4. Further measurements of all the shrines along the four inner *yatras* of Varanasi, a total of 324 shrines, gave a distribution with a power of –1.5

Note that these distributions do not involve perfect straight lines, but they are "on-the-average," i.e., statistically, power law distributions, such as a snow flake with its broken symmetries. The recurrence of a power law distribution in these two different pilgrimage systems is remarkable. The fact that both have similar powers (dimensions) close to –1.5 is even more noteworthy and suggests that we may be in touch with a fundamental aspect of human behaviour, i.e., the self-organization that emerges from human freedom and spontaneity during pilgrimage.

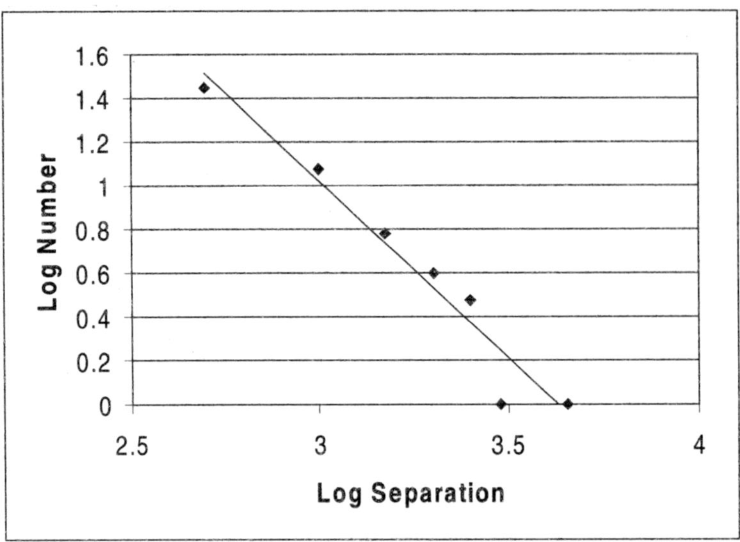

fig. 2.3 Shrines of Kailas Kora

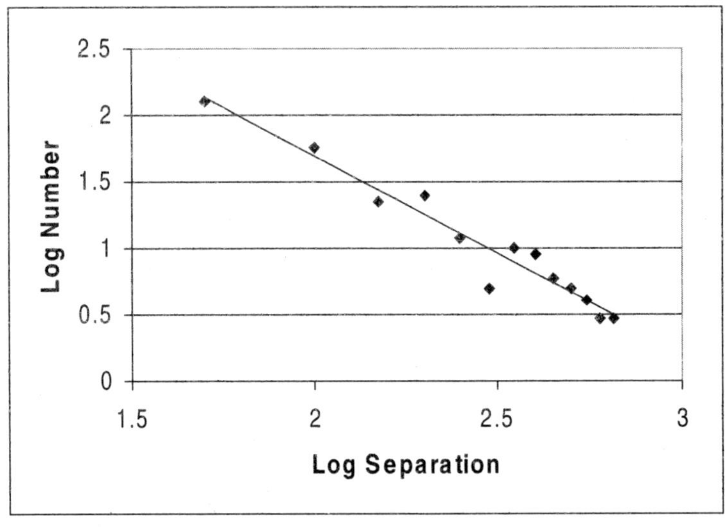

fig. 2.4 Shrines of Kashi Yatras

In the table below are compared the dimension of various self-organized, fractal structures.

Pattern	*Dimension (Cambel 1993)*
Koch snowflake	1.262
Sierpinsky triangle	1.585
Atmospheric clouds	2.35
Woods Plants	1.28-1.79
Sea anemone	1.6
Coast lines	1.05-1.25
Turbulent flames	2.33
Pilgrimage circuits	*1.5*

Appendix II

CHARACTERISTICS OF SELF-ORGANIZING SYSTEMS

1. Openness

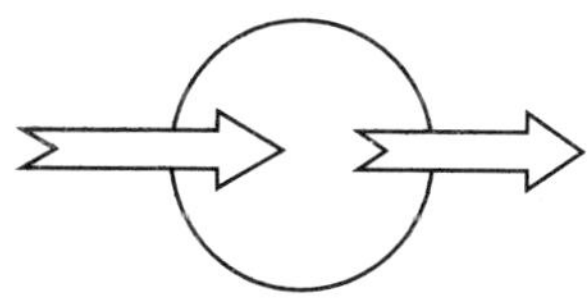

Matter, energy, and ideas must flow through the system, which must be able to "eject" lower quality energy in order for complexity to grow. The earth radiates infrared energy into space in order to keep our biosphere alive. Pilgrimage systems need the open flow of ideas inward and outward.

2. Non-equilibrium

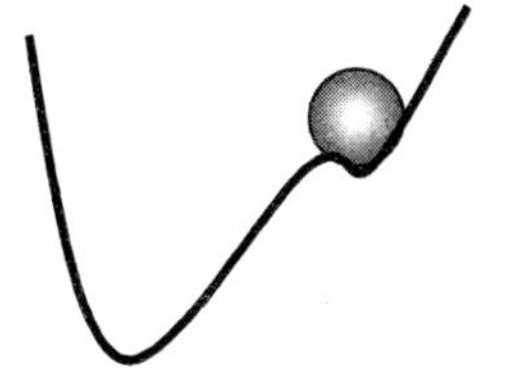

Equilibrium is a state of death. Detailed balancing of opposing forces prevents change and innovation. Only systems that depart from equilibrium can achieve significant complexity.

3. Coherent Behaviour

Isolated, non-communicating elements cannot achieve self-organization. Non-linear processes amplify interactions between individuals.

4. Resonance

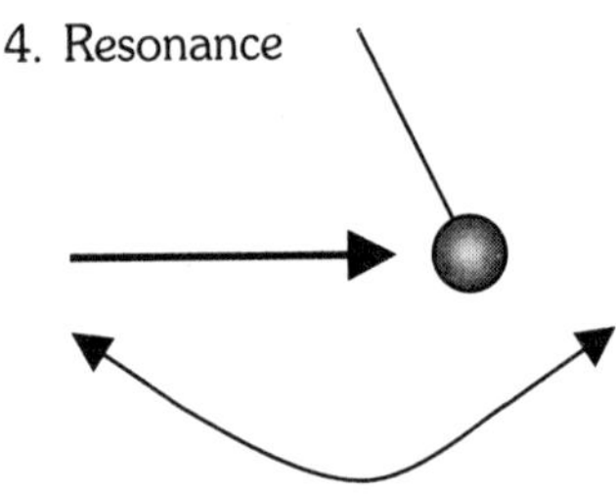

Cycles within a system can be coupled when they possess similar characteristic frequencies. When frequencies agree, power flows into the system and sudden transformations can occur. Resonance is a powerful means of achieving holistic behaviour. Many pilgrimages involve the mythology of resonance between the macrocosm and microcosm.

5. Strange Attractors

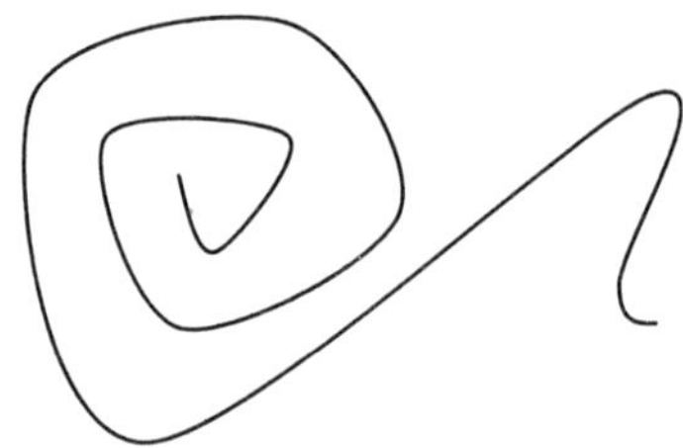

The system is dynamic and changing, drawn toward increasing complexity and transformation by "strange," constantly changing, and unpredictable forces.

The "strange attractor" is a metaphor for the experience of pursuing an unreachable and ever-changing goal.

6. Metastability

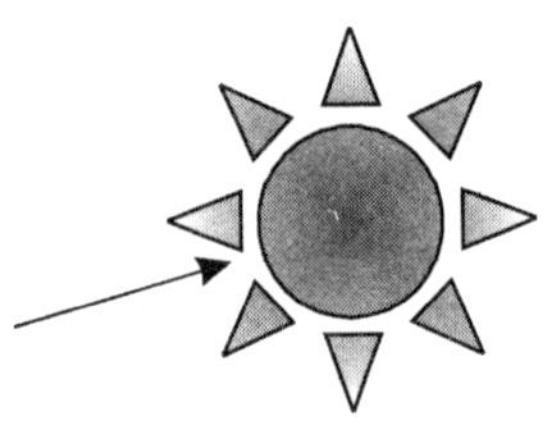

When driven away from equilibrium the system may approach a threshold, similar to super-saturated saline solutions, at which small fluctuations may cause major and sudden transformations. In such a meta-stable condition, very slight human inputs and unpredictable ecstatic visions may be greatly magnified.

7. Self-reference

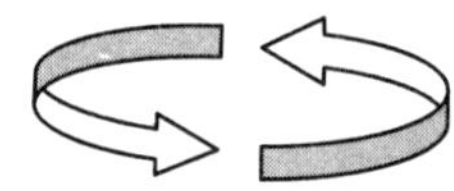

The system develops without dependence upon external authority, stabilizes itself through internal feedback loops and creates its own meaning (teleonomy). Autocatalytic loops constantly re-energize the system.

8. Symmetry Breaking

Perfect geometries and exact symmetries have no uniqueness and no information content. Broken symmetries are necessary for surprise, variety and complexity.

9. Indeterminancy

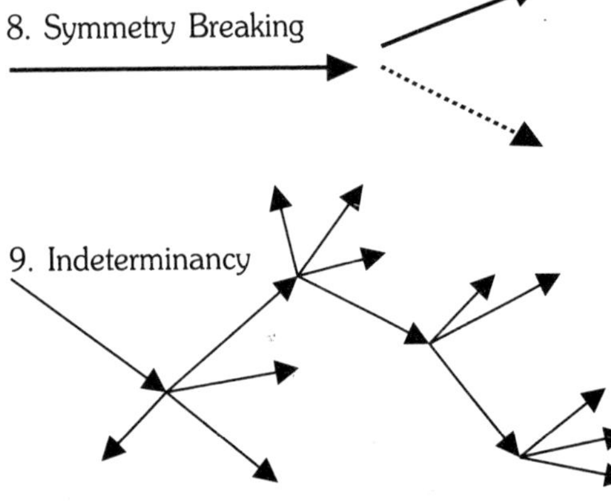

Because new states are created by the amplification of small fluctuations, the outcomes of change are unpredictable. Self-organizing systems lack a goal or teleology.

Acknowledgements

The studies of pilgrimage circuits in Varanasi were carried out in conjunction with Rana P.B. Singh.

References

Adair, R.K., R.D. Astumain and J.C. Weater, 1998, "Detection of weak electric fields by sharks, rays and skates," *Chaos: An Interdisciplinary Journal of Nonlinear Science,* 83: 576-87.

Bak, P., 1994, "Self-organized criticality: A holistic view of nature," in *Complexity: Metaphor, Models and Reality,* ed. D. Pines and D. Meltzer, Reading, MA: Addison-Wesley.

———, 1996, *How Nature Works: The Science of Self-Organized Criticality*, New York: Copernicus, Springer Verlag.

Bak, P. and K. Chen, 1991, "Self-organized criticality," *Scientific American*, 246: 46-53.

Bak, P. and K. Sneppen, 1993, "Punctuated Equilibrium and criticality in a simple model of evolution," *Physical Review Letters*, 71, 4083-86.

Bak, P., C. Tang and K. Wiesenfeld, 1988, "Self-organized criticality," *A Physical Review*, 38, 364-74.

Barrie, T., 1996, *Spiritual Path, Sacred Space: Myth, Ritual and Meaning in Architecture,* Boston: Shambhala.

Bhardwaj, S.M., 1973, *Hindu Places of Pilgrimage in India: A Study in Cultural Geography*, Berkeley: University of California Press.

Cambel, A. B., 1993, *Applied Chaos Theory: A Paradigm for Complexity*, Boston: Academic Press.

Coleman, S. and J. Elsner, 1995, *Pilgrimage: Past and Present in the World Religions*, Cambridge: Harvard University Press.

Dubey, D.P., 1987, "Kumbha Mela: Origin and historicity of India's greatest pilgrimage fair," *The National Geographical Journal of India*, 33: 469-92.

Eck, D., 1983, *Banaras, City of Light*, London: Routledge & Kegan Paul.

Frette, V., *et al.*, 1992, "Avalanche dynamics in a pile of rice," *Nature*, 379, 49.

Gluckman, B.J., P. So, T. I. Netoff, M.L. Spano and S.J. Schiff, 1998, "Stochastic resonance in mammalian neuronal networks," *Chaos: An Interdisciplinary Journal of Nonlinear Science*, 8, 588-98.

Jantsch, E., 1980, *The Self-organizing Universe: Scientific and Human Implications of the Emerging Paradigm of Evolution*, Oxford: Pergamon Press.

Kauffman, Stuart, 1995, *At Home in the universe: The Search for the Laws of Self-Organization and Complexity*, New York: Oxford University Press.

Knight, C., 1989, "The lunar analogue and the origins of culture," *Cosmos* 3: 72-106; also, *Menstruation and the Origins of Culture*, Ph.D. thesis, University College, London (1987).

Lu, E.T., R.J. Hamilton, J. M. McTiernan and K. R. Bromund, 1993, "Solar flares and avalanches in driven dissipative systems," *Astrophysical Journal*, 412: 841-52.

Lovelock, J., 1979, *Gaia, A New Look at Life on Earth*, Oxford: Oxford University Press.

Malville, J.M., 2001, "The Paradigm of Self-Organization: From Village to Pilgrimage," in *The Nature of Man and Culture: Alternative Paradigms in Anthropology*, ed. by Baidyanath Saraswati, New Delhi: Indira Gandhi National Centre for the Arts and Aryan Books International.

Malville, J. M. and N. Malville, 2001, "Pilgrimage and periodic festivals as processes of social integration in Chaco Canyon," *Kiva*, 66: 327-44.

Malville, J.M. and C. Putnam, 1993, *Prehistoric Astronomy in the Southwest*, Second Edition, Boulder: Johnson Books.

Malville, J.M. and Rana P. B. Singh, 1995, "Visual astronomy in the mythology and ritual of India: The sun temples of Varanasi," *Vistas in Astronomy*, 39: 431-49.

Malville, J.M., F. Wendorf, A.A. Mazar, and. R. Schild, 1998, "Megaliths and Neolithic astronomy in southern Egypt," *Nature* 392: 488-91.

McGuire, M., 1991, *An Eye for Fractals*, Redwood City: Addison-Wesley.

McNamara, J.D., 1995, "Hindu pilgrimage as a force of Indian spatial cohesion and temporal continuity," in *Pilgrimage Studies: Sacred Places, Sacred Traditions*, ed. D.P. Dubey, pp. 31-44, Allahabad: The Society of Pilgrimage Studies.

Meyer, Jeffrey B., 1994, "The Buddhist Cosmogram in the Twentieth-Century Taiwan," *Cosmos,* 10: 171-82.

Nicolis, G. and I. Prigogine, 1989, *Exploring Complexity*, New York: W. H. Freeman.

Parpola, A., 1994, *Deciphering the Indus Script*, Cambridge: Cambridge University Press.

Porter, E. and J. Gleick, 1990, *Nature's Chaos*, New York: Viking.

Possehl, G.L., 1990, "Revolution in the urban revolution: the emergence of Indus urbanization," *Annual Reviews of Anthropology*, 19: 216-82, Paolo Alto: Annual Reviews.

Preston, J.J., 1992, "Spiritual magnetism: an organizing principle for the study of pilgrimage," in *Sacred Journeys: The Anthropology of Pilgrimage,* ed. A. Morinis, Wesport: Greenwood Press.

Prigogine, I., 1980, *From Being to Becoming*, New York: W.H. Freeman.

Saraswati, B.N., 1985, "Kashi pilgrimage: the end of an endless journey," in *Dimensions of Pilgrimage: An Anthropological Appraisal,* ed M. Jha, pp. 91-104, New Delhi.

———, 1995, "Lifestyles in traditional cultures: a conceptual framework," in *Computerizing Cultures*, ed. K. Vatsyayan and B.N. Saraswati, New Delhi: Indira Gandhi National Centre for the Arts.

Singh, Rana P.B., 1991, *Pancakroshi Yatra, Varanasi: Sacred Journey, Ecology of Place, and Faithscape*, Varanasi: Tara Book Agency.

———, 1993, "The sacred geometry of India's holy city, Varanasi: Kashi as cosmogram," in *The Spirit and Power of Place,* ed. Rana. P.B. Singh, pp.189-216, Varanasi: National Geographical Society of India.

Schroeder, M., 1991, *Fractals, Chaos, Power Laws: Minutes from an Infinite Paradise*, New York: W. H. Freemen and Co.

Turner, V., 1979, *Process, Performance, and Pilgrimage: A Study in Comparative Symbology,* New Delhi: Concept Publishing Company.

Wheatley, P., 1991, *The Pivot of the Four Quarters*, Chicago: Aldine.

Wiesenfeld, K. and F. Jaramillo, 1998, "Minireview of stochastic resonance," *Chaos: An Interdisciplinary Journal of Nonlinear Science,* 8: 539-48.

3

Circulation and Circumambulation

Surinder M. Bhardwaj

Introduction

IN the Hindu pilgrimage tradition, *tirtha yatra* and *parikrama* are inter-linked concepts. *Tirtha yatra* refers to undertaking a pilgrimage to sacred places whereas *parikrama* (or *pradakshina*) means circling the sacred object. In geographic literature pilgrimage circulation has been used to describe pilgrimage flows, but circumambulation has been given little attention, probably because it has been identified as a purely ritual activity in the general process of pilgrimage. Circumambulation has a deeper meaning in the religious space, however, as it connects the pilgrimage to the larger cosmos. This paper strives to connect these two activity utilizing the model of self-organized complex systems.

While this exploration is both preliminary and tentative, the application of the theory of self-organization appears to be potentially valuable at least as a heuristic device to advance pilgrimage studies by reinterpreting the processes and patterns of pilgrimage. This approach also appears to have value in the convergence of interdisciplinary and intercultural perspectives and the evolution of holistic viewpoints.

Circulation in the Context of Geography

The concept of circulation has its roots in French human geography in the early twentieth century. Paul Vidal de la Blache (1922: 347-443), professor of geography at the Sorbonne, is credited with the early use of this concept. For Vidal, circulation seemed to have been a double-edged sword. It was seen as a destructive force transforming traditional regional equilibria and stable *genres de vie*, but also a creative process promoting the diffusion of ideas, the emergence of a real comparative advantage and the radiation of socio-cultural influences from nodal centres (Buttimer 1971: 190). The concept has been interpreted by Buttimer to mean the network of physical and social communication. Later Max Sorre (1962: 410) echoes Vidal's views when he observed: "Circulation not only develops, transforms and specializes already existing genres de vie but it also encourages the formation of new ones." Circulation has come to describe transportation and communication in all its manifestations. Thus, it refers to movement or flow in general: flow of goods, services, ideas, information and people. Analogous to the circulation of blood in the human body, geographic circulation connects localized ways of life to the outside world and vice versa. Circulation brings in outside influences as well as exports local ones. Circulation emphasizes continuous flows and movement and assumes the system to dynamical, with energy input from external sources, analogous to the behaviour of biological systems.

Vidal's characterization of circulation as a destructive process that upsets cultural equilibria is a perceptive description of the consequences of the openness of a system and the resulting destabilization. A departure from equilibrium is a necessary requirement for self-organization of both physical and cultural systems, complex systems (Malville 2001). Working together openness and non-equilibrium actualize processes leading toward new modes of organization and creative impulses within a society. Sorre's understanding of circulation foresees the possibilities of new lifestyles and even new paradigms to emerge from the process of circulation of people and ideas. Self-organization is also predicated upon the development of communication between the elements of the system and its consequence-coherence. In the cultural sense, circulation transmits shared belief but, paradoxically, it also changes tradition. In a circulation system, tradition and change do not necessarily behave as opposing entities but rather they become a dynamic dyad, the complementary poles of an actively evolving cultural system.

CIRCULATION IN THE GEOGRAPHY OF PILGRIMAGE

The circulation of pilgrimage generally means a round trip to a holy place or a circuit of holy places. Both round trip and circuit pilgrimages are common in India and in other cultures especially Japan (Tanaka 1977). David Sopher (1968: 392) first applied the concept of circulation explicitly to the study of pilgrimage in his work *Pilgrimage Circulation in Gujarat*, and considered pilgrimages to holy places as circulatory flows. Sopher (1968: 392) has argued that although Hinduism lacked the formal organization of religion in the West, even so "common forms and a sense of community have been maintained by means of largely informal, autonomous circulatory flows." Other geographers have used this or similar ideas, and in my examination of the pilgrimage phenomenon (Bhardwaj 1973), circulation has been a central concept.

Sopher, nevertheless, assigned a rather passive role to pilgrimage in reinforcing and maintaining regional or national identity (Sopher 1968: 425). I am certain that he did not mean passive in the sense of ineffective, for pilgrimage can be a powerful metaphor in matters of nationalism. One has only to recognize the political commotions caused by L.K. Advani's *ratha yatra* toward the Babari Mosque to understand the awesome power of pilgrimage.

IS PILGRIMAGE CIRCULATION AN EXAMPLE OF SELF-ORGANIZING SYSTEM?

I have argued that the principles of self-organization seem to be embedded in the geographic term *circulation.* Pilgrimage circulation is not a random activity nor does it have a random spatial imprint. A massive circulation system has evolved over the millennia as an integral part of Hindu belief. Pilgrimages are strongly vectored toward specific places ranging from local to national and even supranational. In terms of the concept of self-organizing systems, pilgrimage circulations are internal self-referencing processes that maintain and stabilize a non-equilibrium system without the need of external forces or authorities. It is amazing that in spite of a lack of central religious authority in Hinduism, millions of pilgrims from different parts of India spontaneously participate in pilgrimage circulation from local through pan-Hindu levels. Especially remarkable are the massive Kumbha Melas which maintain a twelve year periodicity. Such cyclical movement of people appears to rejuvenate, reawaken, purify and auto-catalyze the pan-Indian pilgrimage system in a manner very similar to that of other stable non-equilibrium systems.

Pilgrim circulation requires the existences of centres that possess attractive powers, which Preston (1992: 33) calls "spiritual magnetism." Qualities of such attractive centres such as power, awe, mystery and magnetism are meaningful only in relation to the persons who perceive them as such and who have the sentiment that motivates them to undertake journeys to such places. Sacred places are human constructs in terms of the meaning they embody and convey to the pilgrims. Operating within the framework of non-equilibrium system theory, Prigogine and Stengers (1984: 293) observe this construction of meaning in relation to our understanding of "reality": "Whatever we call reality, it is revealed to us only through the active construction in which we participate."

Preston (1992) has employed the term "spiritual magnetism" to emphasize the pull of place, which has always been critical to pilgrimage. Geographers tend to consider such "magnetism" more generally as the "power of the place," a terminology which has almost become a cliché in geography. If spiritual magnetism is what attracts a pilgrim to the place, it can be equally argued that the power of personal sentiment is what impels the pilgrim inward. Pilgrimage appears to be a result of both such magnetism of the place and the sentiment of the individual. One without the other is difficult to imagine as they appear to be complementary and co-dependent in the development of pilgrimage circulation.

I have suggested elsewhere that sentiment is what distinguishes pilgrimage from a touristic journey (Bhardwaj 1990). Unless the visitor feels a sentimental attachment to the place of veneration, a journey to it will not constitute a pilgrimage. For example, a visit to the Vatican by a Hindu may not be a pilgrimage even though the place is considered sacred by Christians. On the other hand, we can consider a journey to nationalistic shrines (for example, Jallianwala Bagh, Mahatma Gandhi's *samadhi* or the Vietnam Memorial) a pilgrimage because they are repositories of powerful collective sentiment. They have almost a spiritual magnetism and many visitors possess deep sentiment for what those places signify. Therefore, magnetism of the place or deity and the sentiment of the pilgrim (religious or secular) are both inseparably part of the pilgrimage phenomenon. They are interdependent and complementary (Allen 1994: 594-95) and this interweaving of pilgrim and place lies at the root of the self-organization of the pilgrimage over long periods of time.

Pilgrimage circulation may be seen as self-organizing in terms of two other concepts of chaos-complexity theory: *strange attractors* and *basins of attraction* (Cambel 1993). The attractor of a self-organizing system can be a point, a path or a series of states, all of which may be changing with time. Likewise, pilgrimage is not limited to a fixed, unchanging point-specific destination but includes the sacredness of the journey and as the individual pilgrim may be changed by the journey, so too may the meaning of the pilgrimage destination changes with time. The journey may also be along a path of special meaning for the pilgrim, such as the re-tracing of Buddha's or Christ's footsteps.

In chaos theory, the basin of attraction contains pathways in space-time that converge on to the attractor. A pilgrimage field contains the places of origin of pilgrims and the centre of attractions; the field is dynamic as it includes language, religion and other cultural distributions that define it. Pilgrimage activity, though fairly well defined, is never exactly replicative. While pilgrim flows constantly tie the pilgrim field to the sacred centre, the pilgrimage circulation system is not analogous to a wheel, which is a static structure, ever turning but ever the same. Instead, pilgrimage circulation is like a living system, such as a cell with its nucleus and constant movement of molecules or a human body with its circulation of blood. The circulation of pilgrims is often understood to be in parallelism with the great cycles of the cosmos, returning to the source of which one is an integral part.

Growth and change are coded in the pilgrimage process. Just as the circulation of blood feeds, nourishes, purifies and develops the body, in a similar way pilgrimage nourishes and purifies the pilgrim. Pilgrims hope to return with a renewed and purified body and soul. Just as blood circulation assumes simultaneously, growth and change in the human body, pilgrimage circulation also assumes there will be social and political changes in its basins of attraction. Complex flows and multiple nodes are constituents of pilgrimage. Whereas in the human body there is only one centre of purification (symbolized as the human heart), the Hindu social system has developed a much greater complexity, with a large number of purification centres, from parochial to the pan-cultural centres.

It seems to me that the concept of "basin of attraction" has particularly interesting possibilities for studies of pilgrimage in changing social, economic and political landscapes. The size of the basin of attraction is very sensitive to even minor changes. Since the processes in self-organized systems are non-linear, very small changes can have enormous consequences. This idea should be particularly applicable for examining the impact of religious fundamentalism and political polarization of different communities, such as happened in the Punjab during the twentieth century. Thus, it is well known that before the political polarization of Hindus and Sikhs, many Sikhs used to patronize goddess shrines but the numbers of pilgrims has now significantly declined. Likewise the number of Hindu pilgrims to the preeminent Sikh holy place, the Golden Temple at Amritsar, have been reduced to a trickle. Thus although political considerations should be minimal in the mind of a devout pilgrim, the change in the political landscape on the basin of attraction can have major cumulative effects on the overall geometry of the pilgrimage circulation system. By the same token, modest changes in the nature of the basin can cause huge increases of numbers of visitors to new pilgrimage centres that have become "inexplicably" very popular.

PILGRIMAGE CIRCULATION AND HIERARCHY

Super-ordination and sub-ordination are essential elements of a formal hierarchical system. In Hinduism, however, there is no single authority dictating which holy place shall be at the apex. Instead, a complex but informal hierarchy of holy places has taken shape over time, growing up from numerous individual sacred shrines, which emerged independently, and forming partially overlapping circulation systems.

Unlike Islam in which the primacy of Mecca is absolute, the Hindu pilgrimage system accepts several places of great importance, but none as the primary place. Moreover, there are many religious traditions and sects each with its own hierarchy of sacred centres. The primacy of Varanasi, though generally accepted as the most important pilgrimage destination within the literary tradition, does not have the same force for the Hindu as does Mecca for the Muslim or Jerusalem for the Jews. In that sense, we do see a tendency toward self-organization of a partially hierarchical circulation system operating at different levels. Considering the long involved history of the diverse people of India, this is hardly surprising. Such informal hierarchical circulation, evident through our pilgrim surveys in India (Bhardwaj 1973) can be re-interpreted as a general tendency as a system moves from chaotic disorganization to self-organization.

Our examination of Hindu building activity in diaspora in the United States indicated the emergence of an informal hierarchy of Indian sacred centres somewhat resembling those in India (Bhardwaj and Rao 1988, 1998). Of all the Hindu temples in the United States the S.V. Temple in Pittsburg is by far the primary one. This is not because of its size, for there are other temples with greater square footage or ones with higher *gopurams*. Its primacy is evident from the size of its basin of attraction. Because it was among the earliest consecrated Hindu temples in North America, its importance is partly due to the presence of a network of affluent and dedicated donors. The temple, as is true with other Hindu temples elsewhere in North America, was truly self-emergent. It was not imposed upon American Hindus by any Hindu authority. The idea of the temple was culturally coded in Hindu beliefs and would have been expressed as a temple eventually when the Hindu population reached a certain threshold. Now there are Hindu temples in virtually all major cities of North America. Although the S.V. Temple is not situated in the largest city of the U.S., it has emerged as the one with the largest basin of attraction. Other Hindu temples of diverse Indian regional traditions have their own more localized pilgrim fields, but they seem to nestle in the S.V. Temple's basin of attraction.

The emergence of Hindu temples in America in the last twenty-five years with the attendant development of an informal hierarchy seems to be an interesting example of self-organization in the developing system of affluent Hindu society in North America. Self-organization was similarly present in nineteenth-century Trinidad, where abjectly poor indentured labourers imported from India sweated in the sugar-cane fields. There too an impressive landscape of temples and religious culture emerged spontaneously (Prorok 1982). Similar processes have been at work in Canada, Britain and Malaysia. When the equilibrium and balance of a system is disrupted there is a burst of innovation. New cultural patterns are created without the imposition of any external authority. In the case of pilgrimage landscapes, these patterns are nourished, purified and, maintained by the circulation of pilgrims. It does appear that the principle of self-organization is useful, at least at the heuristic level, for an examination of the growth and development of complex religious landscapes.

Circumambulation

There is a popular story in Hinduism about the childhood rivalry of two deities, Ganesha and Karttikeya, both considered to be the sons of Parvati and Shiva. The vehicle of elephant-headed Ganesha is a tiny mouse. Karttikeya, on the other hand, is a handsome and eager boy whose mount is the swift and beautiful peacock. When a dispute arose about the speed of both the children, on approval of their parents, a competition was conducted and both of them were asked to go around the universe and reach a particular point, quickest, to decide who is greater of the two. Following this, Karttikeya promptly mounts his peacock and proceeds to encircle the universe, leaving Genesha, looking slightly ridiculous riding his tiny mouse. While Karttikeya flies at breakneck speed, confident of victory, the wise but ponderous Genesha aghast cleverly circumambulated his father and mother, who for him symbolized the entire universe. Ganesha was declared as the winner of the race because of the principle of self-similarity, which is a property of self-organized systems. Similar patterns and meanings are repeated at all scales of size. From this principle emerges one of the great rituals and architectural themes of the world's religions: the similarity and parallelism of the microcosm and macrocosm.

THE VARIED MEANING OF CIRCUMAMBULATION

Circumambulation (*parikrama* or *pradakshina*) is imbued with meaning for the devotee. In the *Encyclopedia of Religion* Dianna Eck lists a number of meanings of circumambulation, including honouring, centring bonding, setting apart and reaffirmation of the claim of sacred territory (Eck 1987: 509-11). Additionally, I believe circumambulation symbolizes the fluidity of meaning and tension of opposites that is characteristic of Hindu thought: completeness yet continuity, fulfilment and quest, contentment and pursuit, comprehension and mystery. The pole star, for example, is the epitome of desired — for firmness in Hindu cosmology (Eliade 1987, 4:110). Yet the Hindu cosmos pulsates, dissolving and re-emerging.

Stoddard (1994: 18) identifies four key elements of pilgrimage: destination, movement, magnitude and motivation. Preston (1992) adds "spiritual magnetism." The most important component, of course, is the motivated pilgrim. Circumambulation involves all the above-mentioned elements but the movement is around not toward the sacred centre. It is the movement encompassing an object of veneration: a temple, a holy site, a sacred mountain, a lake, river city and even includes circling around oneself. A circumambulating pilgrim recognizes the controlling power of the centre and tries to remain in its orbit. It should be noted that Hindus and Buddhists circumambulate their sacred clockwise, following the sun, while Muslims circle the Ka'aba in the anti-clockwise direction.

Over thirty years ago, while trying to reconstruct the pilgrimage topography described in the *Mahabharata*, I was struck by the directionality and inherent meaning in the "Grand Pilgrimage of India" (Bhardwaj 1973: 44). No single authority, sacred or secular, structured this grand pilgrimage of India, for it has been self-structured and sanctified over many centuries. The pilgrimage started significantly in Pushkar, Rajasthan, the sacred place of Brahma, the progenitor, and roughly following the sun's direction, the *yatra* encompassed virtually the entire Indian sub-continent (*fig.* 3.1). In effect, this grand pilgrimage was not only a long *yatra* but it was also a circumambulation of the Hindu cosmic axis. As the sun circles the sacred Mt. Meru of the Hindu cosmos, so did the pilgrim follow the path of the sun. The centrality of the sun in Hinduism has ancient roots, going back at least to the Rigvedic times (Malville 1985, 1989; Singh and Malville 1995). Viewed in the terms of Eliade (1959: 39), by encompassing the entirety of the sacred landscape the grand pilgrimage of India reaffirmed the land as consecrated territory.

Pilgrimage and Hindu Cosmology

Pilgrimage is not just traversing distance or earning merit by enduring hardship on a difficult path. Perhaps it has a deeper cosmological (as well as personal) meaning. While purifying themselves in the process of pilgrimage, the pilgrims consecrate the very paths by their own footprints. Herein do we then see the fusion of distinction between the sacred and the sanctified, the cause and effect, the divine and the human.

In his study of Indian cosmogonic mapping, Schwartzberg (1992: 332-82) presents several images of the Hindu cosmological schemata. Hindu cosmology from the Vedic times onward became increasingly elaborate, especially due to the influence of the Puranas but also became ethicised due to Hindu belief in transmigration of the soul (Schwartzberg 1992: 234). In such a humanized Puranic universe, pilgrimage was perceived as an activity that purified the

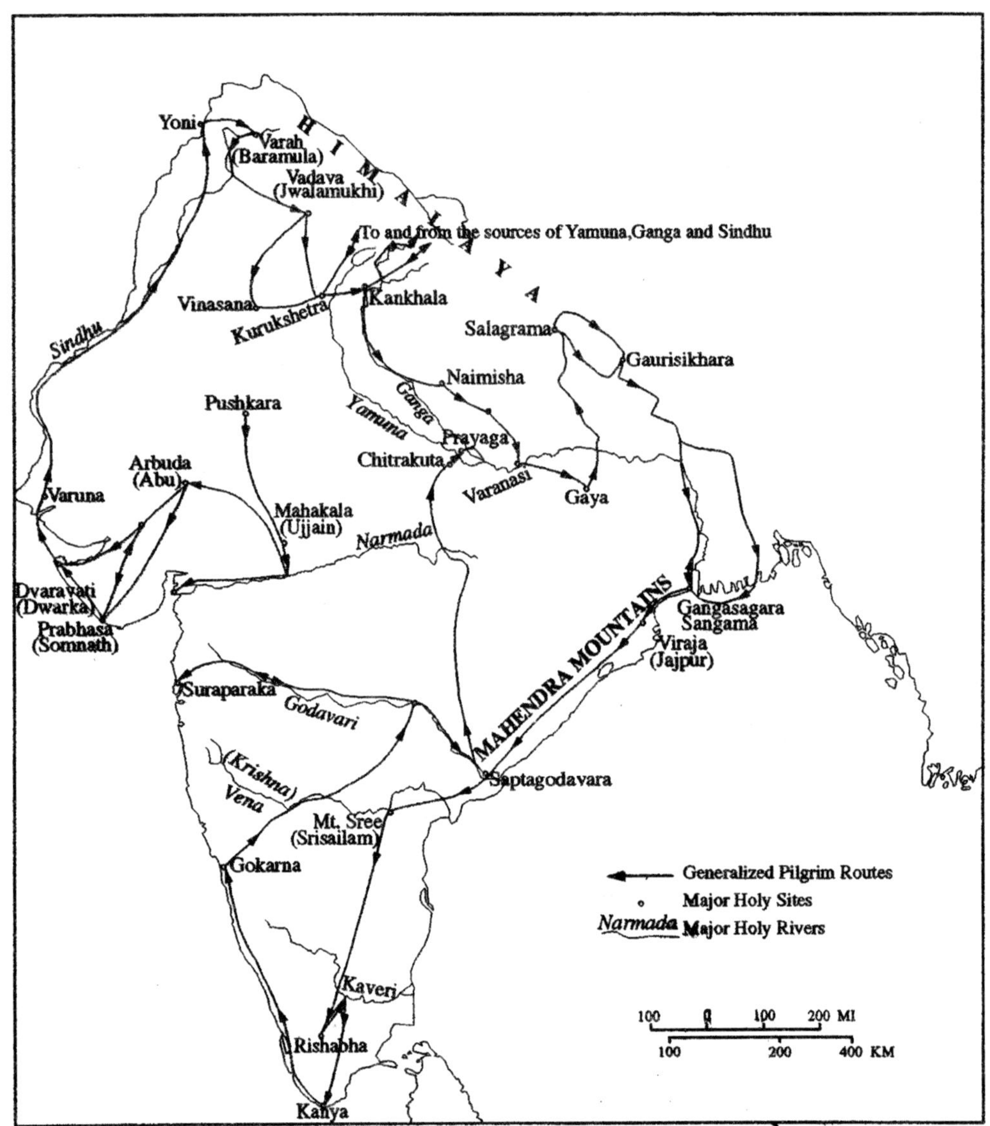

fig. 3.1: Circumambulation of India, according to the Mahabharata. Based upon Bhardwaj 1973, p. 44.

householder-pilgrims. *Tirtha-yatra*, therefore, became popular. New forms of *tirtha-yatra* emerged, such as visitations of *chara-dhamas* in the four cardinal direction in India, Puri in the east, Sringeri in the south, Dwarka in the west and Badrinath in the north. Mt. Meru, pointing toward the pole star, constitutes the cosmic axis, around which the sun and the moon are in a state of perpetual circumambulation.

Just as the universe, which has been thrust out of equilibrium by expansion, is pregnant with future galaxies, social chaos may be posited as an intensifier of pilgrimage (Turner and Turner 1978). Extensive research about the formation of shrines in western Europe by Mary Lee and Sydney Nolan (Nolan and Nolan 1989) appears to confirm the Turners' views. Shrine formation was accelerated during times of stress as, for example, around the highly unsettled conditions of the Thirty Year's War (Nolan and Nolan 1989: 85-89). More recently, David Smith (1995: 37) argues that the best opportunities for charismatic leaders to appear are during times of structural uncertainty, in effect during time of the disruption of equilibrium. Similarly, Michael Shermer (1995: 65) suggests that during conditions of extreme instability even persons with a threshold level of leadership ability can make enormous impact. Relating historical periods of uncertainty to the emergence of new pilgrimage sites in South Asia remains a fascinating potential research project.

Concluding Remarks

The concept of self-organization of complex systems of a powerful idea, Ilya Prigogine (Prigogine 1971: 2), quoting Bergson, writes: "The deeper we go into the nature of time, the more we understand that duration means invention, creations of forms, continuous elaboration of what is entirely new." This viewpoint helps us to pursue the possibility that organization from chaos is an ever emergent condition. In Hindu thought both entropy and order are reconcilable as part of the cosmic condition. In the dark ocean of chaos, organization and dissolution not only exist but are co-dependent. The Hindu universe is depicted as *brahmanda*, the primeval egg, symbolizing potential and self-emergence. Organization appears within this cosmic egg at various levels (*fig*. 3.2).

The concept of self-organization of complex systems can help in understanding how pilgrimage has created a landscape of its own, with having been imposed by outside forces. This landscape with its embedded geometry, which is always in the process of becoming, arises from the flow of people along lines of circulation between nodes of origin and destination and from central nodes and axes that are encircled. Hierarchies representing basins of attractions of multiple dimensions establish further depth to that landscape. These linear, axial and circular geometries have emerged, and continue to do so without any human organizing authority. As Per Bak (1996: 31) states: "Self-organized critical systems evolve to the complex critical state without interference from any outside agent."

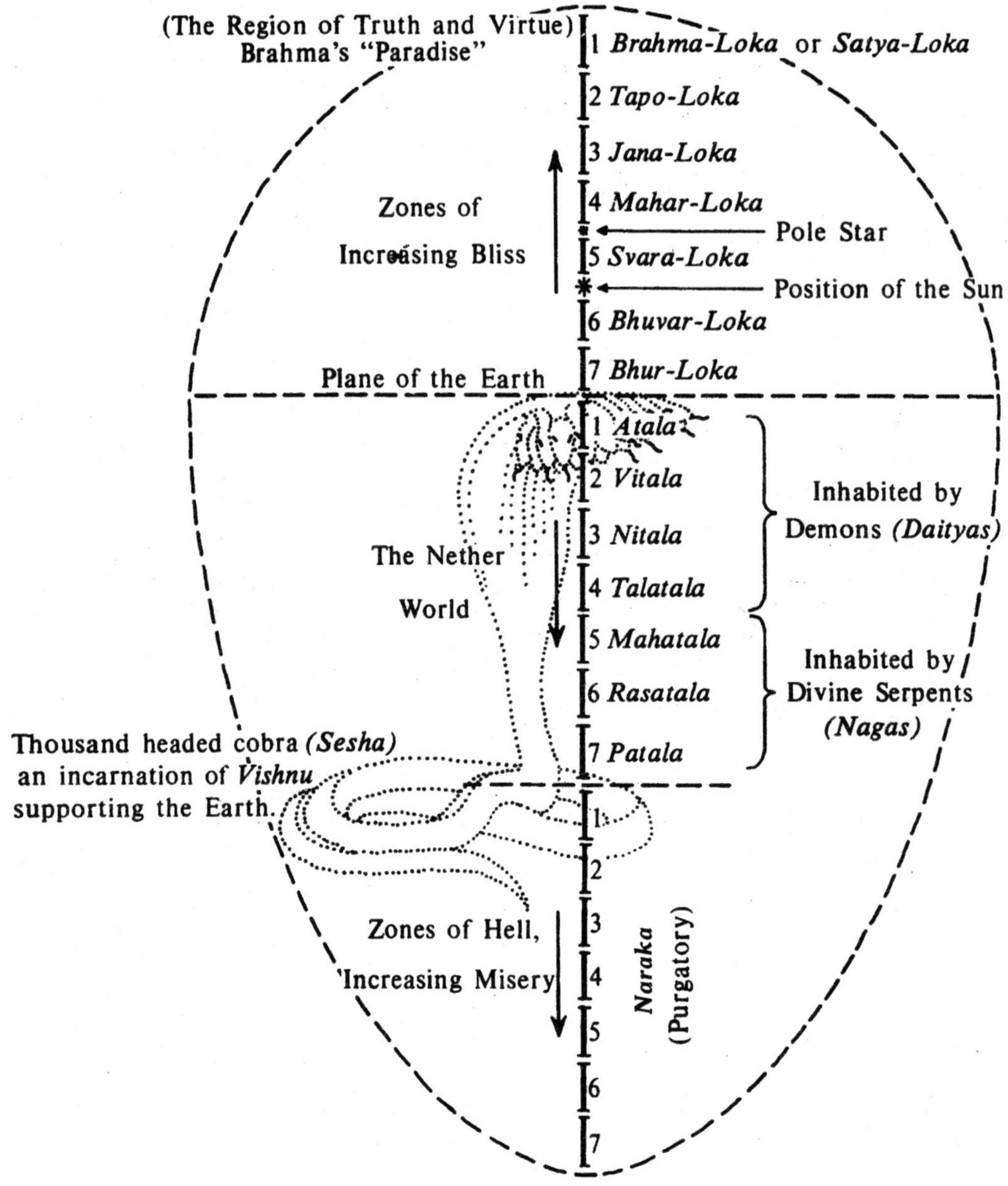

fig. 3.2: Generalized Diagram of the Hindu Universe.

While very intriguing in its many parallels to the pilgrimage process, the theory of complex self-organization skirts the issue of consciousness. Or, is it possible that consciousness is embedded in the cosmic complexity that is always self-emerging?

Acknowledgments

An earlier version of this paper was first presented at the 26th Annual Conference on South Asia (October 16-19, 1997) at the University of Wisconsin, Madison. A revised paper was presented at the conference on Pilgrimage and Complexity. The current form of the paper has benefited from the comments of Kim Malville, for which I am thankful.

References

Allen, Peter M., 1994, "Coherence, Chaos and Evolution in the Social Context," *Futures* 26: 583-87.

Bak, Per, 1996, *How Nature Works: The Science of Self-Organized Criticality*, New York: Springer-Verlag.

Bhardwaj, Surinder M., 1973, *Hindu Places of Pilgrimage in India: A Study in Cultural Geography*, Berkeley: University of California Press.

———, 1990, "Sentimental Journeys: Thoughts on the nature of Pilgrimage," Paper presented at the Association of American Geographers, Toronto.

Bhardwaj, Surinder M., and Madhusudana N. Rao., 1999, "Emerging Hindu Pilgrimage in the United States: A Case Study," *Geographica Religionum* 4: 159-88.

———, 1998, "The Temple as a Symbol of Hindu Identity in America," *Cultural Geography*, 17: 125-43.

Buttmer, Anne (sister Mary Annette, O.P.), 1971, *Society and Milieu in the French Geographic Tradition*, Chicago: Rand McNally.

Cambel, A.B., 1993,. *Applied Chaos Theory: A Paradigm for Complexity,* Boston: Academic Press.

Campbell, Joseph, 1949, *The Hero with a Thousand Faces*, New York: Bollingen Foundation.

Coleman, Simon and John Elsner, 1995, *Pilgrimage: Past and Present in the World Religions*, Cambridge: Harvard University Press.

Eck, Diana, 1982, *Banaras: City of Light*, New York: Alfred A. Knopf.

Eliade, Mircea, 1959, *The Sacred and the Profane*, New York: Harper.

———, 1987, *Encyclopedia of Religion*, New York: Macmillan.

Gleick, James, 1987, *Chaos: Making a New Science*, New York: Viking.

Lukermann, Fred E., 1965, *The cal des probabilites* and the *Ecole francaise de geographie*, Canadian Geograher 9: 128-37.

Malville, J. McKim, 1981, *The Fermenting Universe: Myths of Eternal Change*, New York: Seabury Press.

———, 1985, "Sun Worship in Contemporary India," *Man in India: A Quarterly Journal of Anthropology*, 65, 207-33.

———, 1988, "Solar Astronomy and Temple Traditions," *Journal of the Indian Anthropological Society*, 23,17-25.

———, 1989, "The Rise and Fall of the Sun Temple of Konarak: The Icon Versus the Morning Sun," in *World Archaeoastronomy*, ed. A.L. Aveni, Cambridge: Cambridge University Press, pp. 377-88 .

———, 2001, "The Paradigm of Self-Organization: From Village to Pilgrimage," in *The Nature of Man and Culture: Alternate Paradigms in Anthropology*, ed. by Baidyanath Saraswati, Indira Gandhi National Centre for the Arts and Aryan Books International, New Delhi.

Nolan, Mary L., and Sydney Nolan, 1989, *Christian Pilgrimage in Modern Western Europe*, Chapel Hill: University of North Caroline Press.

O'Flaherty, Wendy D., 1982, *Hindu Myths: A Sourcebook Translated from the Sanskrit*, New York: Penguin.

Pannikar, Raimundo, 1977, *The Vedic Experience: Mantramanjari*, Berkeley: University of California Press.

Preston, James, 1992, "Spiritual Magnetism: An Organizing Principle for the Study of Pilgrimage," in *Sacred Journeys: The Anthropology of Pilgrimage*, Alan Morinis, ed., Westport: Greenwood Press, pp. 31-64.

Prigogine, Illya, 1997, *The End of Certainty: Time, Chaos, and the New Laws of Nature*, New York: Simon and Shuster.

———, 1989, "The Philosophy of Instability," *Futures* 21: 396-400.

Prigogine, Illya and Isabelle Stengers, 1984, *Order Out of Chaos: Man's New Dialogue with Nature*, Toronto: Bantam.

Prorok, Carolyn, 1988, *Hindu Temples in Trinidad: A Cultural Geography of Religious Landscape and Ethnic Identity*, Ph. D. dissertation, Louisiana State University.

Schwartzberg, Joseph E., 1992, "Cosmographical Mapping," in *Cartography in Traditional Islamic and South Asian Societies*, Chicago: University of Chicago Press, pp. 333-87.

Shermer, Michael, 1995, "Exorcizing Laplace's Demon: Chaos and Antichaos, History and Metahistory," *History and Theory*, 59-83.

Singh, Rana P. B. and J. McKim Malville, 1995, "Cosmic Order and Cityscape of Varanasi (Kashi): Sun Images and Cultural Astronomy," *National Geographical Journal of India*, 41: 69-88.

Smith, David R., 1995, "The Inapplicability Principle: What Chaos Means for Social Science," *Behavioral Science* 40: 22-40.

Sopher, David E., 1968, "Pilgrimage Circulation in Gujarat," *Geographical Review*, 58: 392-425.

Sorre, Max, 1962, "The Concept of genre de vie," in *Readings in Cultural Geography*, ed. P. Wagner and M. Mikesell, Chicago: University of Chicago, pp. 399-415.

Stoddard, Robert H. and Alan Morinis (ed.), 1997, *Sacred Places, Sacred Spaces: The Geography of Pilgrimages*, Baton Rouge: Louisiana State University.

Tanaka, H., 1977, "Geographic Epression of Buddhist Pilgrim Places on Shikoku Island, Japan," *Canadian Geographer*, 21: 111-32.

Thompson, D'Arcy Wentworth, 1966, *On Growth and Form*, ed. J.T. Bonner, Cambridge: The University Press.

Turner, Victor and Edith Turner, 1978, *Image and Pilgrimage in Christian Culture*, New York: Columbia University Press.

Vidal de la Blache, P., 1926, *Principles of Human Geography* (ed. by Emmanuel De Marftonne), New York: Henry Holt.

Zausner, Tobi, 196, "The Creative Chaos: Speculations on the Connection Between Non-linear Dynamics and the Creative Process," in *Nonlinear Dynamics in Human Behavior*, ed. W. Sulis and A. Combs, Singapore: World Scientific.

4

Pilgrimage and Space

Case studies from Bhaktapur, Muktinath and Varanasi

Niels Gutschow

Introduction

THE following case studies present circumambulatory processions or pilgrimages which document a dichotomy between an inner and outer world. When eight years ago the philosopher Panikkar (1991) on a similar conference at the Indira Gandhi National Centre for the Arts on *Concepts of Space* made the statement that,"there is no outer without inner space," he referred to human beings. According to Panikkar, inner space is subjective, it belongs to an inner structure of the knower, the human being, while "outer space is supposed to be over there." In the context of the ritual journeys presented here, the "inner space" belongs to the "knower." In many cases it is a defined territory that represents his extended self — his habitat that on so many levels is imbued with sacredness. But sometimes the sacredness of such a territory radiates beyond its protective enclosure. Pilgrims come from the outer realm to identify with the inside and proceed to a centre. In such a case the closed world which is inside, represents the womb that incorporates the ultimate place of bliss.

The *American Heritage Dictionary* defines a pilgrimage as "a journey to a sacred place or shrine" but also says that a pilgrim is, "one who embarks on a quest for some end conceived as sacred." The first definition stresses a linear movement involving a finite destination. The second definition is open to include a variety of action and incorporates even the locus of the pilgrimage in an even more inner structure, either the body or the mind of the "knower" Panikkar was mentioning.

In this extended sense, any participant of a procession is a pilgrim — be it a person from the inner or the outer world of space. The aim is to share the quality of a defined "inner space" which is more than a protective enclosure. Kashi/Varanasi may serve as the model. There, the inside incorporates the outside. Pilgrims come from within and without; any of the many ritual journeys emerge from the centre — the Jnanavapi or well of knowledge near the temple of Vishvanath, the Lord of the Universe — and terminates there.

This paper concentrates on the complex notion of circumambulations, based on field studies that have been carried out over the past twenty years in Tibetan villages of the northern Himalaya, the Kathmandu Valley, and Varanasi. Answers are presented to the question how the mandalic inner space is set apart from an outer space that in itself is defined on various levels. The outside very often turns out to be the inside of a neighbouring entity. It is the mind of a community or a class of pilgrims that sets the standards.

Case Studies

BHAKTAPUR (NEPAL)

Bhaktapur is one of the three cities of the Kathmandu Valley, which by the end of the first millennium AD had developed an urban character. At times, these cities served as centres of small, independent and, since the fifteenth century, competing kingdoms with little hinterland. A specific townscape with public squares, temples and shrines in abundance, and with complex urban rituals developed in the sixteenth and seventeenth centuries. The spatial pattern of the towns mirrors the hierarchic principle of the accepted social order: In all cities the royal palace with its important temples dedicated to the royal cult marks the *ideal* centre, the pivot of an order that reflects the cosmos.

Bhaktapur must have developed from a cluster of small rural settlements along the low ridge that runs parallel to the river Hanumante. What legend calls the "foundation" of the town in the twelfth century, might have been a unification of these villages by means of a ritual involving a ceremonial circumambulation, a consecration of shrines dedicated to Mother Goddesses and the establishment of a palace as a seat of kingship. The main road with the two main squares forms the winding axis of a linear type of city: Running below the ridge, it generally keeps to a height of 1,330 metres. At intervals, the street widens to form a number of squares that occasionally turn into stages for the performance of urban rituals. The palace and its spacious palace square are not located in the geographic centre of the city but on the northern periphery, on a prominent spot of the ridge.

The territory of the city is experienced as a sacred realm, fenced off against the demonic surrounding countryside whose evil spirits must be repelled. Although there is no wall to delineate the protected and sacred realm, the edge is sharply demarcated through death rituals as processions carrying a corpse may never cross that imaginary line. Eight shrines dedicated to the *Ashtamatrika* (Eight Mother Goddesses) constitute the most powerful ritual fortification of the urban space. The eight shrines form the basis of a complex *mandala* that incorporates both worlds, the inside and outside. For the present context, it is of importance that these Mother-Goddesses, as well as 26 other powerful place-gods, receive blood-sacrifices — both in a process of propitiation as well as in honour of a rewarding experience. These gods and goddesses invariably enjoy a twofold representation, of which the non-iconic one is always present and accessible, while the iconic version is kept on the first floor level of a "god-house" (*dyahche*), from where it "comes down" only once a year on the occasion of the New Year ritual. The non-iconic representations (of rock or stone) are housed in an open chamber, accessible throughout the year; while the iconic representations are shut away, inaccessible to public worship.

Since time immemorial, the occasion of the vernal equinox has been considered appropriate and auspicious for celebrating the beginning of the New Year as a festival of renewal which is enacted as a cosmo-drama. The festival commemorates the foundation of Bhaktapur: It centres around a myth in which a foreign prince had to kill demon serpents in order to take into possession a dormant territory. The killed serpents are hung from a large pole to demonstrate victory. On a different level, the pole, that is to be erected on New Year's Eve, reflects the creation of the universe. The annual reenactment of the event stabilizes the cosmos and renews the quality of place, the urban territory.

Among the many events of the New Year festival which last for 9 days, of decisive importance is a concluding procession on the fourth day of *Baishakha*, which generally falls on April 18. The iconic representations of 34 gods and goddesses — all of them Matrikas, Ganeshas, Bhairavas — who have already been mentioned, leave their room "inside" the god-houses on New Year's eve in order to return or seek union with their place of origin "outside" the respective non-iconic representations. It seems as if the existing twofold order of the world is dissolved at the moment of crisis in order to be created again. As soon as the World Tree is erected the iconic representations are "reborn" and return to their "house." On the fourth day of the New Year the gods and goddesses appear again to be placed in open arcades where they are worshipped along a continuous route that leads through and around the city.

Almost everybody in Bhaktapur joins this *dyah svaga bijyaigu* procession at any point. There is no formal beginning or end. The counting of the 34 gods and goddesses on the map starts with Bhairava, the powerful guardian and master of the town, but in reality people join the procession at the point nearest to their house. In the morning, groups of women make their rounds with baskets, full of offerings, especially 34 eggs, one for each god or goddess. In the afternoon, groups of males take over with their drums and trumpets. More than 20,000 people will have completed the circuit by the end of the day.

The route largely follows the general processional route which was probably defined in the seventeenth century, acknowledging and incorporating newly built quarters of a growing urban place. On various occassions, gods or goddesses in iconic, or even living form, follow this route to prove, in a way, their existence and to bless the urban territory. On the occassion of the New Year's procession, the route deviates six times in order to incorporate the visit to a god

Map. 4.1. Bhaktapur: The urban fabric — clusters of courtyard houses form densely populated quarters (map based on a survey in 1978).

that has been added in recent years (some 8 out of the 34 gods and goddesses have been added in the course of the twentieth century). Obviously, every quarter of the town seeks to present its own god as part of the city's essential immaterial infrastructure. The festival concludes with the return of all gods and goddesses to their respective "god-house." After a period of unrest, crisis, and partial dissolution, the order is reinstalled and confirmed.

The route of the procession does not define a territorial unit along the edge. It is just a path that interconnects 34 places and, thereby, establishes a circuit within an urban territory that takes advantage of other tools to realize a ritual fortification along the periphery. The punctuated circuit rather represents the essence of the territory at the moment of crisis and recreation. The reborn gods and goddesses bear witness of continuity of time and space. The people of Bhaktapur become pilgrims on a journey that leads them once a year to the entirety of those powerful guardians that are propitiated with blood to fulfil their obligation. Only on this day is their split existence revealed, and only on this day the people turn beyond the guardian of their own neighbourhood to worship all of them. A twofold goal is achieved: the guardians ensure

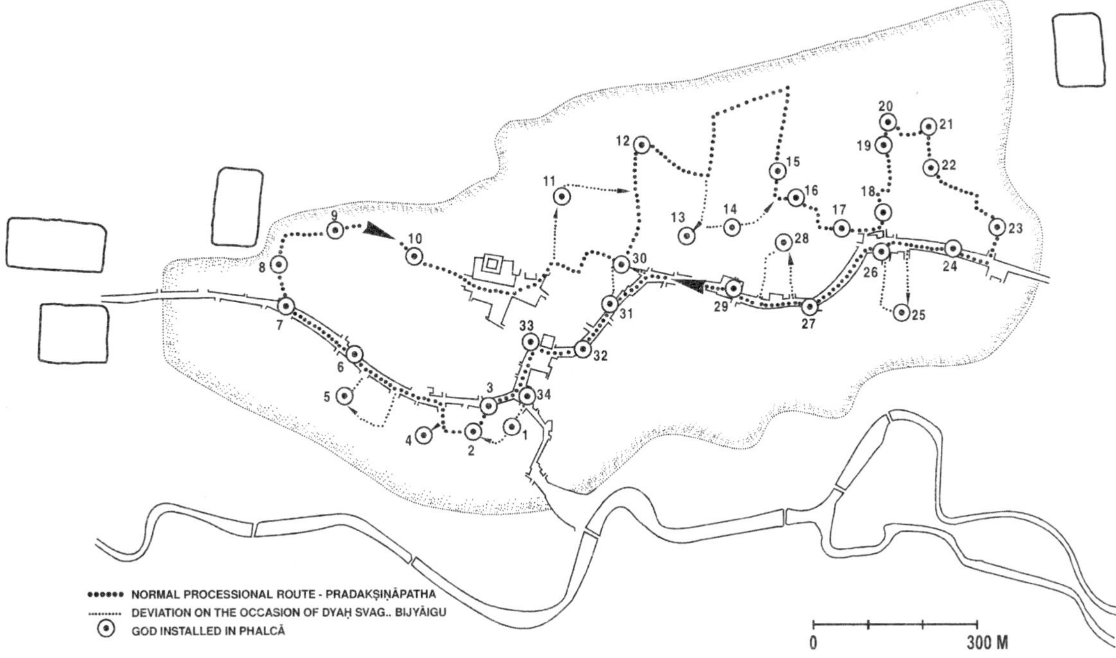

Map. 4.2. Bhaktapur: The processional route (marked with large dots) leads through and around an inner territory, tying important power places together. On the occasion of Bisket-jatra — the weeklong New Year festival — the route slightly deviates (indicated by small dots) in order to pass by all those 34 gods and goddesses who invite blood sacrifice.

the stability of their respective realms while the circuit addresses the territory in its entirety. It becomes a protected realm that supports life. The procession or pilgrimage, is reenacted to validate that protection and support for another 12 months.

MUSTANG — MUKTINATH

In order to illustrate the location of the following case studies, the circumambulation of Kag (one of the five villages on both banks of the Kali-Gandaki river) and the circumambulation of the Six Villages (*yul kha druk*) of the Muktinath Valley, it seems appropriate to present the wider geographical and topographical frame of the sacred landscape of the Himalaya. Three mountains — Tise in the West, Lapchi in the South and Tsari in the East — punctuate an imaginary line or edge that sets the high plateau of Tibet apart from the plains that are drained by Ganga. The three mountains are imagined to represent the uppermost three *cakras* of the human body. The ridge of the Himalayas thus is equal to the spinal column of the body. Other mountains along that ridge are inseperably tied to the notion of space on the micro-level. The

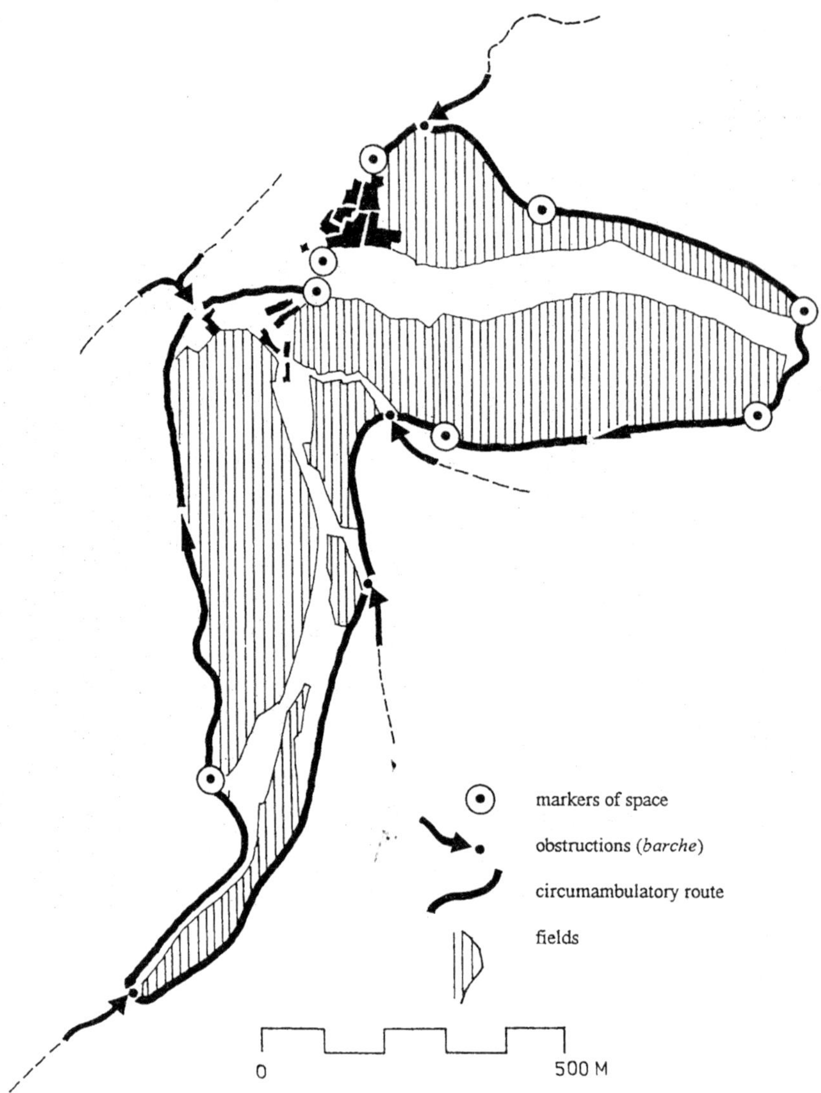

Map. 4.3. Kag: Ritual circumambulation of the fields. The processional path is punctuated by sixteen halting places. While three of these mark the northern and southern boundary of the village as well as its centre, eight are defined by markers such as rocks or boulders. At five places physical obstructions are produced against evil forces that have the potential to enter the protected space along the main access roads.

Blue Mountain (or Nilgiri, 26,492 ft.) and the Dhaulagiri (26,795 ft.), both form a gateway, through which a river leaves the arid valleys along a gorge. The rains rarely cross those high mountains, thus enforcing not only a change in climate but a decisive cultural change. Beyond the ridge agriculture is based on irrigation, villages have — until a generation ago — been built as multi-storied clusters. In such an environment the circumambulation of the cultivated area establishes a definitive edge against the desert.

KAG: THE CIRCUMAMBULATION OF THE CULTIVATED AREA OF KAG

Map. 4.4. The sacred landscape of Mustang and Muktinath: The Six Villages of Muktinath Valley and the Five Villages of Lower Mustang are located on both sides of the Kali-Gandaki river which merges into the Seven Gandakis and finally joins the Ganges. Two mountains — Dhaulagiri and Nilgiri — form a physical and spiritual gate that marks the boundary between the world of the plains and the high plateau with settlements based on irrigation. Three mountains (Tise, Lapchi and Tsari) mark this edge on a macro level. These three mountains are imagined as the three cakras of an anthropomorphic figure.

In the fourth month of the Tibetan calendar, which corresponds to May, the young people of the Chöde — the monasterial institution of the village — and practically all the young people of the village participate in a ritual circumambulation of the entire cultivated area. The procession is thus called "the walking around the cultivated area" (Tib. *klungs-skor*). Because the participants carry sacred books on their heads, it is also called "the scripture circuit" (Tib. *chos-skor*). While the young people set out for the procession, the old ones proceed to the Chöde to prepare consecrated food, which will be distributed to the participants.

On the occasion of the ritual, the constable of the village makes an early round to place piles of stones called *thowo*, at all halting points. Later, he, three women and two old monks accompany the procession up to the third halting point. From there they return. They will meet the procession again near the reservoir at the eighth halting point.

The procession starts at the northern entrance of the village (1) (see map), the gate that formerly enclosed the extended cluster of rammed earth houses at the end of the eighteenth century. Facing north, an image of the protective grandfather, the *meme,* is moulded in clay against the wall in half-relief. As part of the ritual of renewal that confirms and actualizes the protectiveness of the exemplary couple of "Grandfather" (at the northern gate) and "Grandmother" (near the south-western entrance), the figure is renewed annually. The path leads north along an extended wall of *mani*-stones (inscribed with the auspicious formula *om mani padme hum*) and stops first at a multistoried and stepped square structure, a Chörten (2) that serves as a receptacle for a person's remains. The halting point marks the edge of the present settlement just beyond the former archery ground that has been built up over the past two generations. Some 50 metre north the procession stops again at another chörten called Jin Chödro (3) which is placed in the middle of the road to protect the village against unnamed demons who threaten the village from the northern direction. A similarly protective chörten is seen on the crest of the hill north of Kag, powerfully protecting the path leading to Lo and farther on to Tibet. At Jin Chödro the path makes a sharp turn to lead along a wall that encircles the fields called Shön.

Below a meditation retreat (a cave in the cliffs) the procession stops (4) to pay respect to that sacred place. The easternmost tip of the cultivated area, named Tharkog, is marked by a stone boulder (5), which does not represent a particular divinity. Such a marker is not necessarily a religious site. Such markers may be classified as "sub-sacred," as my colleague Charles Ramble (1995) has written, and as such they collectively contribute to the definition of the territory. Only in a set do these markers assure the safety and prosperity of the cultivated area. They somehow emerge from a dormant state on the occasion of the procession, having received a stroke of red or white colour in order to be recognized. A narrow trail now leads down, crosses the river that originates from the glaciers of the Annapurna and is fed by the sacred springs of Muktinath, and climbs the cliff on the opposite side. There it crosses the upper leat,

Shango Yüra, the channel which irrigates Kag's southern fields. There, a rock (6) marks the easternmost tip of the cultivated area that is called Tangasa. Similar to the boulder mentioned above, this rock serves as a marker. Since 1974 the rock has been located in an orchard encircled by a wall, which on the occasion of the ritual circuit is broken down to allow the procession to proceed along the prescribed route. The sacred scripts are placed upon the rock, refreshments are brought from the village, and the participants enjoy songs and dance. After an hour's break the procession is resumed and leaves the orchard through the gate, continuing along the edge of the cultivated area towards the reservoir (7). This important source of water is probably honoured by the halt. After another 50 metres the procession stops near a rock, which is not merely a marker but is identifiable as the seat of a "wandering demon" named Tsen Khyampo (8). At that point the route turns south and stops where the path coming from Lubra crosses Shango Yüra, the leat that serves most of Kag's fields with water. A temporary pile of stones (9) is erected there, visualizing an obstruction (Tib. *barche*) that bars those demons who try to enter the village. Along the southern tip of the territory, the cultivated area is reduced to a narrow strip of fields called Kahlung. Another pile of stones (10) obstructs the main path that reaches the village along the Kali-Gandaki — in fact, the main road from the plains up toward Tibet. The route turns and leads along that main road for a short stretch before it turns down to the lowest terraced area called Nama. At the southern tip of that terrace another pile of stones (11), which were installed for this occasion, marks another halting point.

The procession leads now along the edge of the fields of Shung until it reaches the bridge (12) across the Kali-Gandaki, where for evil spirits trying to enter the village from the west, the entrance is blocked. From that bridge the route leads along the river Dzong Chu towards a second bridge. A double halt (13,14) on both sides of the bridge probably ensures the integrity and safety of this important passage within Kag's territory. It links the ancient core of the village to the fields south of the Dzong Chu. A few steps north lead to the representation of the protective "Grandmother" (Tib. *iwi* (15)), who guards the southern periphery of the village core — only a generation ago houses have been built beyond, or south of this place. The procession finally reaches Deya (16), the village square west of the castle. In the old days the annual Shontse dances used to be held here. In the early seventeenth century the first houses of Kag were built opposite the castle thus giving shape to the square.

The procession clearly defines the territory of Kag on various levels. First, the clustered settlement is defined by the placement of the mythic couple, the "Grandfather" at the northern gate, where it commences; and the "Grandmother" at the southern periphery, in a short distance from the edge of the original core of the village. The entire cultivated area is strictly circumambulated along the edges. Halting places at the extreme ends of the fields like Tharkog (5), Tangasa (6) and Khalung (10) convincingly demonstrate the purpose of the ritual in defining the area. While the halt near the path leading to Muktinath is dedicated to Tsen Khyampo's rock (8), the four remaining roads which arrive at Kag's territorial limits from the "Four Directions" are blocked by obstructions in the form of "conspicuous" piles of stones which have to be considered as part of an invisible fence that wards off evil influences to which every confined settlement is exposed. The "interior" has to be guarded and thus ritually set apart from a potentially evil and threatening "exterior." Evil influence is expected to follow the regular roads. The "obstruction" literally "cuts" the path, making the settlement inaccessible for any kind of demons. In a way these obstructions obtain the quality of the seats of the Three Protectors or Rigsum Gonpo which can be observed in the neighbouring villages of lower Mustang. There, four chörtens — small Buddhist votive structures — also gain a touch of renewal annually but remain as a physical obstructions throughout the year. In Khyinga, the village east of Kag, these Three Protectors even punctuate the processional route in the Four Directions. If the four obstructed entrances into the territory of Kag are seen as means to define the inner realm of a *mandala*, the final destination of the procession, the village square, could be seen as its centre.

It is open to speculation whether the number of the halting places mirrors the qualities of a cosmic order on more than one level. Sixteen places that punctuate the circuit suggest that it reflects four times four — thus reinforcing the spatial symbolism of the ritual.

The description of the procession stresses the point that no particular category of gods is revered and no particular category of demons is fought off. Certain divinities, sacred structures and sub-sacred markers of a non-descript kind are found along the circuit. Small landmarks in the shape of piles of stones are even created for the occasion to visualize the halting places.

The circumambulation of Kag's cultivated area carves space out of a continuum that has markers on yet a different level. The cultivated area represents the microcosmos which ensures the well-being of the people, it supports their life. Whether or not the number of halting points punctuating the route bears symbolic meaning: they provide an order, to the effect that the defined area becomes a stable entity in a potentially unstable world. It would probably be too much to call the inner realm "sacred," however it has a special quality, which is reinforced by the annual journey along its edges. The participants who exclusively belong to the inner world, can be called pilgrims although they are not heading for a sacred place beyond that inner world. They themselves act as the mount of the sacred scripts which bless the territory. A good harvest is the return of that meritorious action.

THE SCRIPTURE CIRCUIT OF MUKTINATH VALLEY

As the cultivated area of Kag is circumambulated, so are the cultivated areas of the six villages, the "Dzar-Dzong yul kha druk" comprising Khyinga, Putra, Dzong, Chongkhor, Purang and Dzar. Located in the wide valley of Muktinath, these six villages form a remarkably homogeneous entity at a height of 3300 to 3800 metre. The neighbouring entity of five villages, *Chügyü yul kha nga*, that includes Kag on the eastern bank of the Kali-Gandaki as well as Tiri, Pagling, Phelag and Dangardzong on the western side is less homogeneous, leaving every sub-entity in isolation. The territory of the six individual villages as defined by a circumambulation differs in extent. In Kyhinga, the route strictly follows the edge of the cultivated area or the main leat that is brought in a channel from Dzar, while in Dzar large tracts of uncultivated areas are included. In a way, clusters of fields are bound together by a route that largely crosses above the water reservoirs that are fed by the glacier streams of Khalung Mountain. Between Dzar and Purang a dividing line runs straight across the fields. It becomes apparent only on the occasion of the procession. Between Dzar and Khyinga, however, a marker in the shape of a whitish rock establishes the edge of Dzar, while the territory of Khyinga starts only a few hundred yards away. In between lie stretches of uncultivated land that only a decade ago had been utilized for orchards and willow saplings.

On a different level of scale, all Six Villages figure as a single entity that is circumambulated. Invariably this circumambulation is called Chökhor, the *scripture circuit*, as the 108 volumes of the *Kangyur* are carried around to bless the wider territory. The ritual is not carried out annually but only on rare occasions. The reading of the texts is sponsored by an abbot, a monk or somebody who seeks a son. Until recently, the *Kangyur* was only available in the monastery of Dzar. It had to be borrowed and read, either in halves or in full. Each sequence was followed by a circuit before the books were returned. Recently, copies of the *Kangyur* printed in India have been brought to Dzong and Chongkhor and before they have formally been installed in the respective monastery they have been carried along the prescribed circuit around the Six Villages.

The circuit also incorporates Chumik Gyatso, the sacred springs of Muktinath, that famous pilgrimage destination, which attracts pilgrims from the entire subcontinent. The inclusion of the springs, the water of which irrigate the fields of Purang and a much venerated flame that blesses the devout, add to the inherent quality of the circuit.

A NARRATIVE CIRCUMAMBULATION OF THE VALLEY OF MUKTINATH

The territory of the Six Villages is also circumambulated in the course of an invocation by the Nyingmapa priests of Chongkhor. The convocation recites 26 to 28 place names that dot the territory described above. It is a ritual journey that does not lead along the edges like the procession, but represents a continuous movement through and at the same time around the territory. The convocation starts with the visit of Jowo Shartsenpa, that powerful Lord of the Place who has his seat high up in the cliffs. A second seat of Jowo Shartsenpa is located along the processional circuit (3), before the ritual journey enters the cultivated area of Chongkhor, the village, where the convocation takes place. Five places within the village are named (at 4 and 5) before the journey again transcends the territory defined by the real circuit. From there

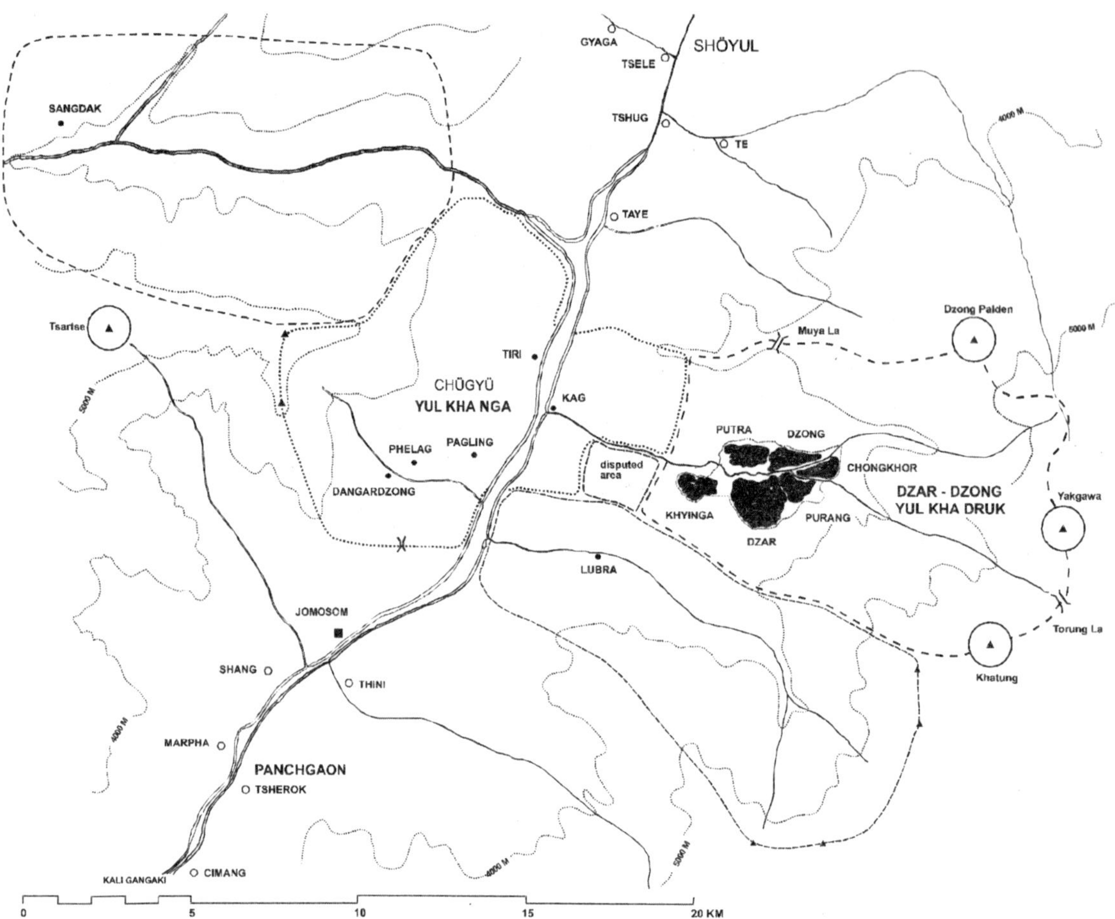

Map. 4.5. Dzar-Dzong (Yul Kha Druk): While the cultivated area of the individual villages (marked in black: Khyinga, Dzar, Purang, Chongkhor, Dzong, Putra) are circumambulated annually, the territory of the six villages are circumambulated collectively on certain occasions when the 108 books of the Kanjur is read in the context of a complex ritual. The circuit also incorporates Chumik Gyatso, the sacred springs of Muktinath. Beyond the route the natural space of Muktinath Valley is clearly defined by three imposing mountains, while the western border with the neighbouring entity of Chügyü Yul Kha Nga is disputed.

the journey moves to the sacred springs, Chumik Gyatso to Putra, Dzar, Khyinga, again to Putra and Dzong. An abandoned monastery (22) along the leat that serves Dzong with water is visited before it ends at the seat of Dagmo Trashi, another powerful Lord of Place in the cliffs.

Varanasi

Kashi, Avimukta or Varanasi, are names for spatial entities that incorporate different sections of the city and centered around different places. Names, that as Diana Eck, (1983a) has observed, "express the various powers and attributes of the city and reveal the dimensions of its sacred authority." Varanasi and Kashi seem to have been synonymous since the first century AD, but Varanasi is also the name for the capital of the kingdom Kashi. Later, Varanasi referred to the urban settlement that stretches along the Ganges (from Varana to Asi = Varanasi), while Kashi represented the sacred realm, the *kshetra* encircled by the *Panchakrosi-yatra*, the circuit, that some five hundred years ago became the outermost pilgrimage encircling a sacred "field" ideally defined by a radius of *panchakrosa* or 17.6 km, with the temple and *lingam* of Madhyameshvara as its centre.

When the *Panchakrosi-yatra* evolved during the twelfth century, it turned out to incorporate only one-fourth of a larger entity that once formed a perfect circle around Madhyameshvara. Its circuit covered 84 *krosa* or 269 km, thus the name *Caurasikrosi-yatra*. It is unknown why this extended circuit was given up. Today only a stretch of the *Panchakrosi-yatra* in the west — between Bhimacandi and Rameshvara — follows the ancient route. Otherwise, the Varana serves as a rough border in the north while the Asi stream marks the southern edge. While the Madhyameshvara *linga* only served as the geographical centre of the ancient Kashi, the *linga* of Avimukteshvara was the central object of worship and still remains to be so in the context of the *Avimukta-yatra*. But when the *Panchakrosi-yatra* evolved, the Lord of the Universe, Vishveshvara, became the central focus.

The present temple of Vishveshvara is in most rituals considered to be the *real* centre, although the original site has been destroyed in 1669 by a Mogul emperor, Aurangzeb. Subsidiary Vishveshvaras are either called Adivishveshvara or are simply considered to have survived the Mogul raid having been hidden by devout citizens of Varanasi or Mirzapur. A king of Nepal, Siddhi Narasimha Malla, even built a large temple in front of his palace in Patan nine years after the raid to offer refuge to Vishveshvara. With that temple he added a third one to those which have already been built in 1627 and 1647, one of which even incorporated 108 named reliefs of *lingas* of Kashi, suggesting the quest to participate in the bliss-bestowing qualities of Kashi.

Much has been written already about the *yatras* of Kashi by Rana P.B. Singh (especially 1987, 1993), Diana Eck (1983) and myself (1993, 1994). The present contribution focuses on the structure of the four circuits encompassing each other and the way the destination is reached. In contrast to the other case studies presented here, the circuits have a definite and meaningful destination. While in Bhaktapur the circumambulation is a continuous one in which individuals join and leave at any place and in Kag or the Six Villages of Muktinath the circuits originate from the village to which they return, the circuits of Varanasi are tied to an individual vow *sankalpa* in the presence of a priest. It resolves only with *darshana* of the *linga*

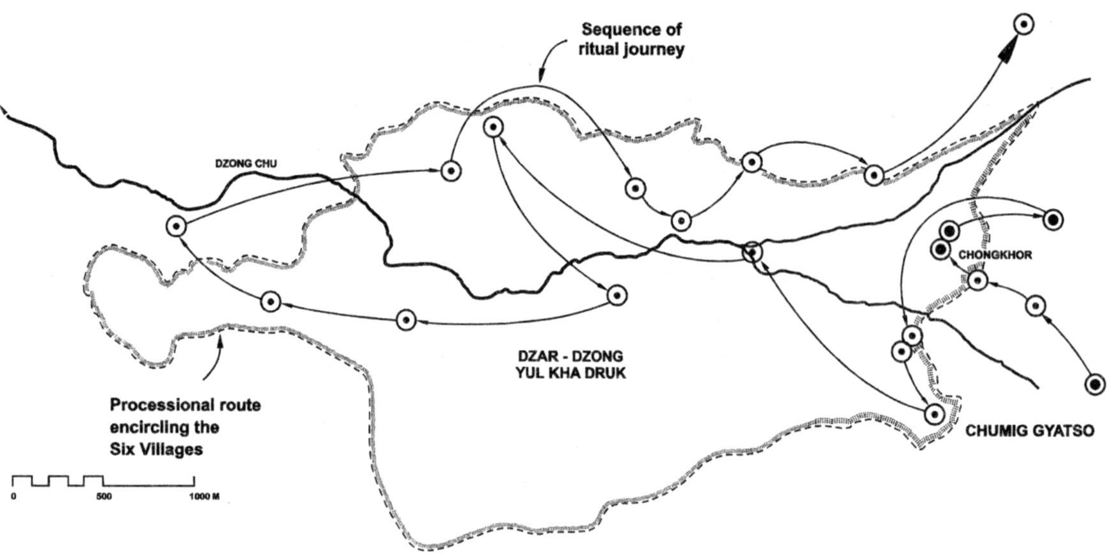

Map. 4.6. Dzar-Dzong: Ritual journey through the territory of the Six Villages of the Muktinath Valley.

that constitutes the destination. The circuit or pilgrimage thus has a formal beginning and a formal end, constituting a ritual frame that does not allow for any individual variations. The process itself is more complex, devoid of a rigid time frame. There are certain auspicious times that invite the different circuits but any other time is also possible.

The *Panchakrosi-yatra* (see map) commences — after the vow at Jnanavapi and a purifying bath at Manikarnika Ghat — at *Manikarnikeshvara* (see illustration), a *lingam*, which are flights of steps below the present level of Varanasi. The pilgrim not only returns to an ancient stratum of Kashi's history but also seems to vanish into an earthen womb. He or she emerges from there and passes along 104 sacred places before returning to Manikarnika Ghat. After the true circuit is completed, the pilgrim turns to the destination represented by Vishveshvara. Finally the neighbouring temples of Vishnu and Annapurna are visited and the ritual journey completed with a circuit around the inner realm, paying respect to the guardians of the Lord of the Universe, the Panchavinayaka.

The route of the *Panchakrosi-yatra* according to the *Kashi Rahasya* script is punctuated by 108 stops, a number which reflects various aspects of cosmic order. Moreover, along the route 8 of the 64 Vinayakas of Kashi are found, thus adding to the ordering of space by referring to the cardinal and intermediate directions. The dedication of the 108 places refer not only to the Great Tradition of Hinduism but incorporates also protectors (*gana*) associated with local tradition. Almost every second place has a *linga* as an object of worship. Others are devoted to Devi, Durga or Gauri and a few to Bhairava and Vishnu. Also worshipped are two sacred fields (*bhumi*), six water tanks and wells (*kunda, kupa, sarovara*), confluences of rivers and

fig. 4.1. Bhaktapur: On the final day of the New Year festival almost the entire population takes the chance to worship the 34 gods and goddesses. Women join the processional route in the morning, forming long queues (April 16, 1991).

fig 4.2. Kag: Ritual circumambulation of the fields. The processional path is punctuated by sixteen halting places. While three of these mark the northern and southern boundaries of the village as well as its centre, eight are defined by markers such as rocks or boulders. At five places physical obstructions are produced against evil forces that have the potential to enter the protected space along the main access roads.

*fig.*4.3. Kag: View across the fields and village towards north (February 19, 1998)

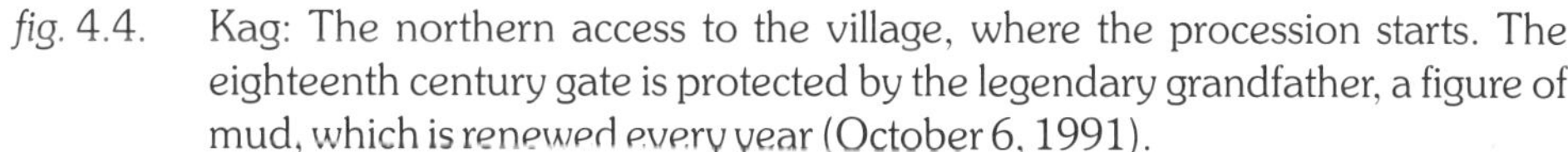

fig. 4.4. Kag: The northern access to the village, where the procession starts. The eighteenth century gate is protected by the legendary grandfather, a figure of mud, which is renewed every year (October 6, 1991).

fig. 4.5. Dzar-Dzong: View across Dzar towards West (October 12, 1991).

fig. 4.6. Kashi: Pilgrims from Mirzapur encircling the sacred realm along the route defined by the Panchakrosi-yatra, (near Rameshvara, April 22, 1991).

fig. 4.7. Varanasi: Linga of Manikarnikeshvara, placed seven metre below the courtyard of a matha, high above the Ganges. Panchakrosi-yatra and Avimukta-yatra commence with the worhsip of this linga (April 20, 1991).

fig. 4.8. Varanasi: Linga comprising 22 miniature lingas at Kapildhara, representing three series of fourteen lingas that mark the urban space which in turn are found scattered all over the subcontinent (December 2, 1990).

fig. 4.9. Varanasi: Panchagangaghat along the Ganges (April 24, 1991).

fig. 4.10. Varanasi: Detail of the wall of Panchakrosi Mandira with 20 niches representing figuratively tirthas which are visited in the context of various yatras — for example in the upper row from left to right Vishveshvara, Gabhastishvara (no. 98 of the 108 tirthas of Pancakroshi-yatra), Vaidyeshvara and Rinamocanakunda (November 7, 1991).

ghats. The sequence of the 108 places do not convey any specific order. They probably represent places, which were already there when the *Panchakrosi-yatra* was established. The route probably took advantage of an existing infrastructure and shaped it into a meaningful sequence and order.

More clearly than in other places, Kashi-kshetra — the sacred field of Kashi — is defined by the circuit as a space that differs profoundly from the profane continuum surrounding it. Kashi-kshetra or Kashi mandala — the circle of Kashi — is believed to be suspended in the sky, resting on the three prongs of the trident (*trishula*) of Shiva. The special quality of that space is said to be like the sun behind the clouds: you can't see it although it is there. Parry (1993: 108) quotes an informant, said that "the soil *is* gold, the city *is* suspended in space and Shiva *does* wander in it daily." In fact, the space even bears anthropomorphic traits: Shiva's head is found at Asi and his feet at the confluence of Varana and Ganga. Kashi is said to remain forever in the state of golden age, although only the divine sight of a *yogi* might realize that. While time turns out to be immune to degeneration, the blissful territory — Kashi-kshetra — is continuously redefined and confirmed by the feet of pilgrims. These may come from far for the realization of a vow, preferably during the inauspicius period of an intercalendary month, that occurs every two or three years or in the days following the full moon in October. People from Varanasi itself often prefer the dark night of Shiva, *shivaratri* in February. Hordes of young men from the wrestling clubs will on that occasion cover the circuit in less than twenty hours. Pilgrims move in groups and, for most of them, it is an annual exercise. The ultimate aim is to die within the *kshetra* defined by the circuit, because death in Kashi ensures liberation, *mukti*. At the time of death Shiva whispers a *mantra* into the ear which destroys all sins.

A hierarchy of sacred spaces is prevalent in which the ultimate aim is represented by Vishveshvara. For example, those, who die in one of the other six sacred cities of India, are reborn in Kashi. Sins committed in Kashi are destroyed by the merit gained in performing the *Antargriha-yatra* encircling the inner realms, and sins committed while performing the *Antargriha yatra* are wiped out by the merit gained performing the *Panchakrosi-yatra*.

Similarly, Kashi itself contains all outer space. People residing in Kashi don't have to leave the place for other pilgrimages, as Kashi contains all other places, like the 12 *Jyotirlingas* of India and the 4 *Dhamas* that mark the four corners of the subcontinent. And, on a different scale, Kashi itself is represented in a nutshell. The act of pilgrimage circuits or routes to a set of sacred places is in such cases incorporated into an act of worship that makes any movement unnecessary. For example, the *Kashi Khanda* text has identified three clusters of 14 *lingas* which may be worshipped along a *Bayalisalingi-yatra* ("journey to the 42 *lingas*"), preferably on the days of new moon. To avoid the burden of such a procession, the 42 *lingas* are viewed in miniature form (see illustration), forming together a collective *linga*. One level of the sacred infrastructure of Kashi is thus isolated from the rest and shaped into a symbol.

There is even a temple that goes by the name of Panchakrosi Mandir. But it represents much more than the 108 places along the circuit. The frame of the temple's entrance, the side and rear walls bear altogether 272 niches (see illustration) in which stylized reliefs symbolize Kashi's sacred places in their entirety. If sculptures in the lintels and beside the main door's jambs are added, the number adds up to 289 representations of gods, goddesses and places. A circumambulation of the temple encompasses Kashi as a whole. The essence, however, is found in the womb chamber. It houses a *linga* that is named Dvadasheshvara — Shiva as manifested by 12 *lingas* — of which the central one represents Vishveshvara and 11 miniature *lingas* carved of crystal the remaining eleven of the *Jyotirlingams*.

The Panchakrosi Mandira incorporates the 108 places of the *yatra*, that have provided the name for that temple, and acknowleged the great complexity of Varanasi by adding 164 other places. On yet another level, Varanasi in its entirety is reduced to be represented by Varanasidevi, an idol found within the compound of Trilochaneshvara and Kashi is reduced to Kashidevi, a goddess found at Lalita Ghat.

A final step even does away with viewing or an emphasis of place. A *siddha*, a person who has achieved insight, will locate Kashi in his body and perform the *Panchakrosi-yatra* within himself.

Kashi is a well-defined *mandala* that incorporates other circuits. The centre consisting of Vishveshvara with Jnanavapi, the two protectors Dandapani and Dhundiraja, and the five Vinayakas that guard the inner realm, is encircled by three more circuits of ever reduced space. Vishveshvara is thus the innermost sanctuary protected by successive shells.

The *Nagarapradakshina* (see map), lit. the circumambulation of the urban Varanasi, follows exactly the route of the *Panchakrosi-yatra* between the two rivers that define the stretch of *ghats* along Ganga. From the temple of Durga the *Nagarapradakshina* parts and incorporates roughly one-sixth of Kashi-kshetra. The following shell is defined by the *Avimukta-yatra*, dedicated to the space, "that is never forsaken by Shiva." Early sources such as the ninth century *Skanda Purana* already mentioned that the territory of Avimukta "is superior to all other places, including Prayaga, because it bestows most easily release (*moksha*)" (Bakker 1993: 25). Not only "Shiva destroys all sins," but the place itself, Varanasi, "is veritably the rescuer of all beings." In a cryptic way the territory is called "the most excellent knowledge." It is probably not the place itself from which knowledge emanates, but the knowledge about the quality of place that turns into a tool on the way towards liberation. It is a vulnerable knowledge that has to be protected from the ignorant. Therefore it is called "hidden." Today, the Avimukta circuit is rarely performed, as it turns to the ancient centre, Avimukteshvara, instead of Vishveshvara. The *linga* representing Avimukteshvara has been relocated to an unconspicuous niche along the innermost circuit, hardly known or recognized by anybody. The *Avimukta-yatra* certainly represents a remnant of

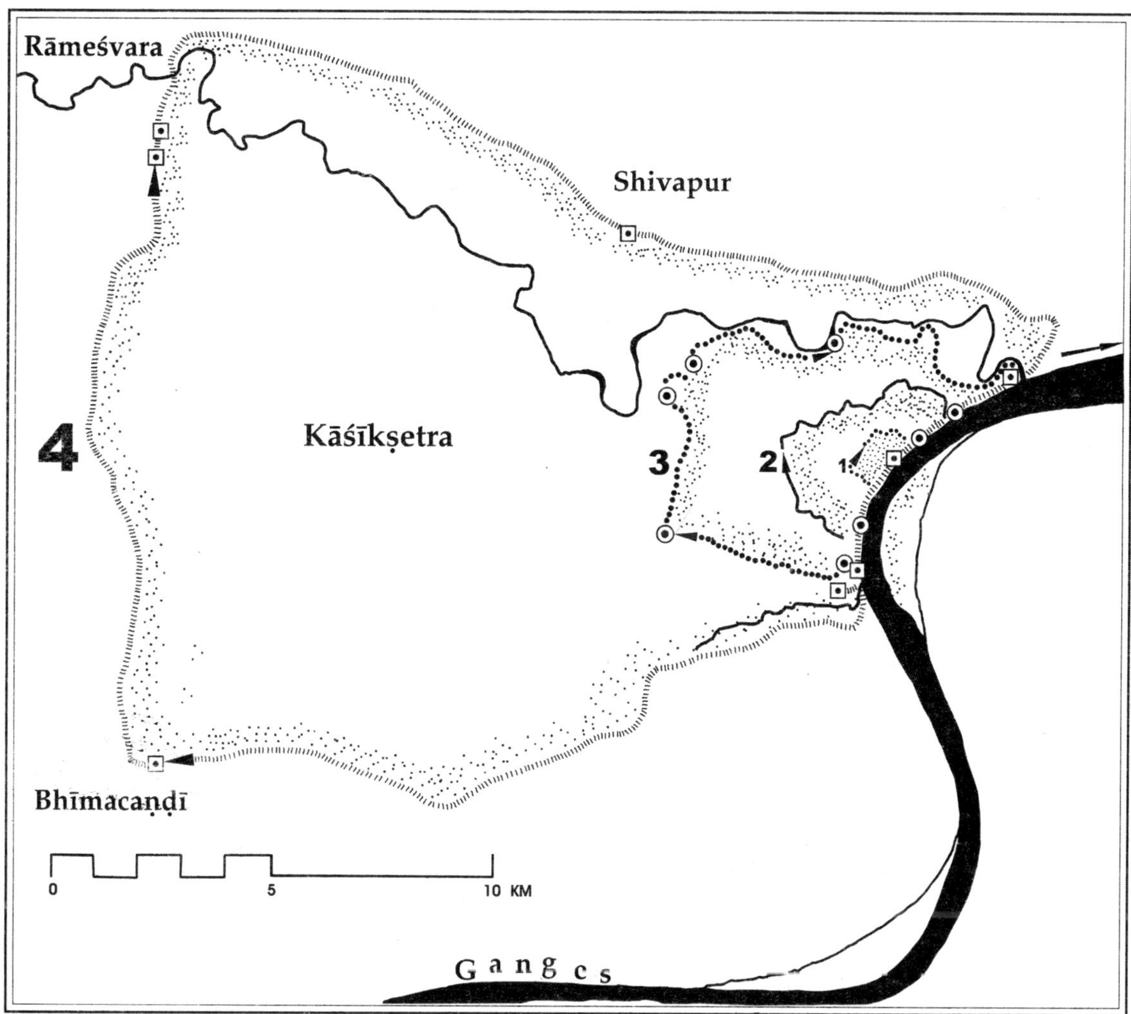

Map. 4.7. Varanasi: Four circumambulatory routes encircling an ever increasing territory: 1. Antargriha-yatra represents the innermost route that encircles the centre sevenfold before it reaches the centre, Vishveshvara; 2. Avimukta-yatra encircles "the realm that is never left by Shiva." The route is punctuated by 70 sacred places, followed by the last round that is dedicated to the four innermost shrines dedicated to Vinayaka before it reaches its destination, Avimukteshvara; 3. Nagarapradakshina encircles urban Varanasi (nagara) — it commences with the worship of Manikarnikadevi and terminates at the Jnanavapi, the entire route being punctuated by eight Vinayaka temples (as indicated on the map by circles); 4. Panchakrosi-yatra delimits present-day Kashi Mandala — the circuit starts at Manikarnikesvara and ends with the worship of Visnu, Annapurna and the five innermost Vinayakas after having reached Vishveshvara. The route is punctuated by eight Vinayaka temples, as indicated by squares on the map.

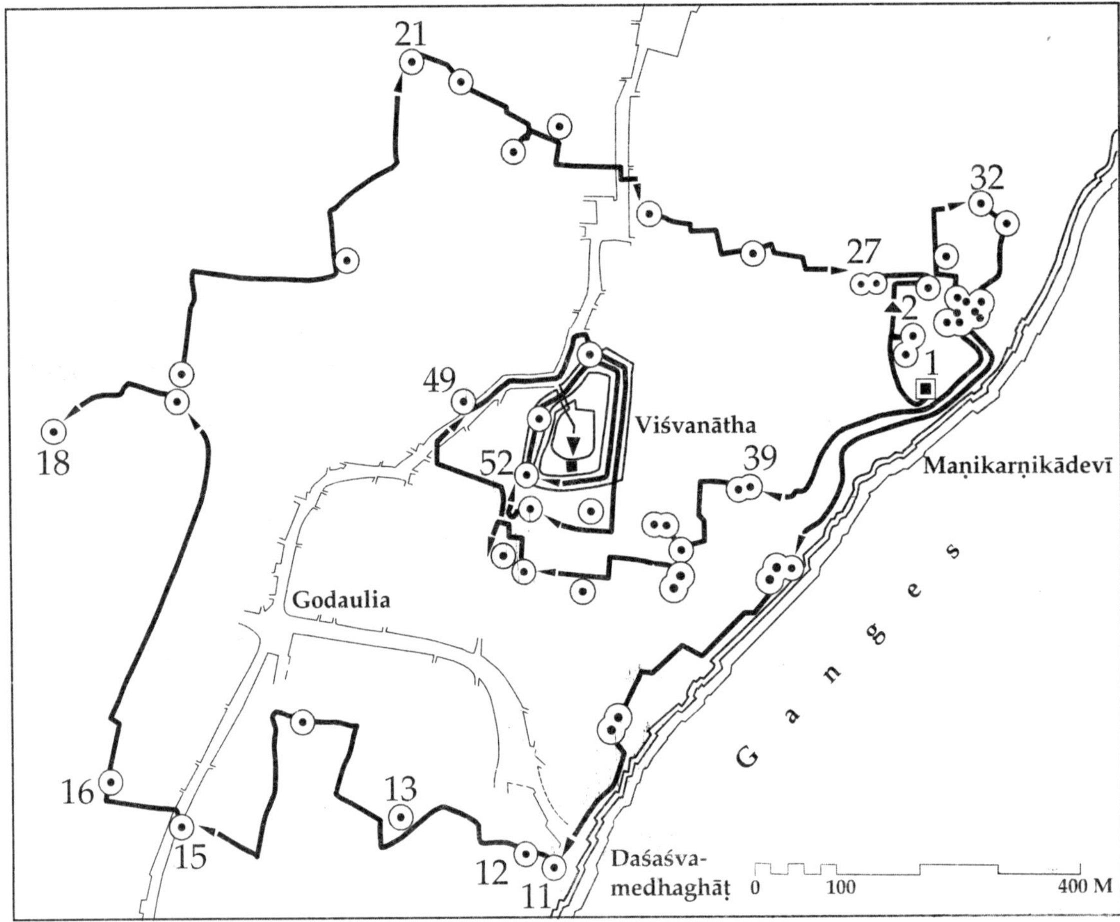

Map. 4.8. Varanasi: Processional route around the inner realm of the 'Lord of the Universe' (Vishveshvara), called Antargriha-yatra or Vishveshvarakhanda-yatra. A sevenfold circumambulation starts with the worship of Manikarnikadevi and leads towards the centre in a spiral-like movement. Altogether 76 temples and shrines punctuate the route before Vishveshvara is reached.

an ancient configuration that is superseded by the establishment of the *Panchakrosi-yatra*. The route covers only a small section of the *ghats* between Trilochana Ghat and Kedara Ghat and moves in a circle around what might have constituted the core of the early settlement of Varanasi.

The innermost pilgrimage, literally "the route inside the house," *Antargriha-yatra* (see map), encircles the inner realm of the Lord of the Universe and is thus also called *Vishveshvarakhanda-yatra*. The circuit is said to be preferably performed as a precondition of the circuit around Kashi. The procession starts with the worship of Manikarnikadevi, touches a few places near

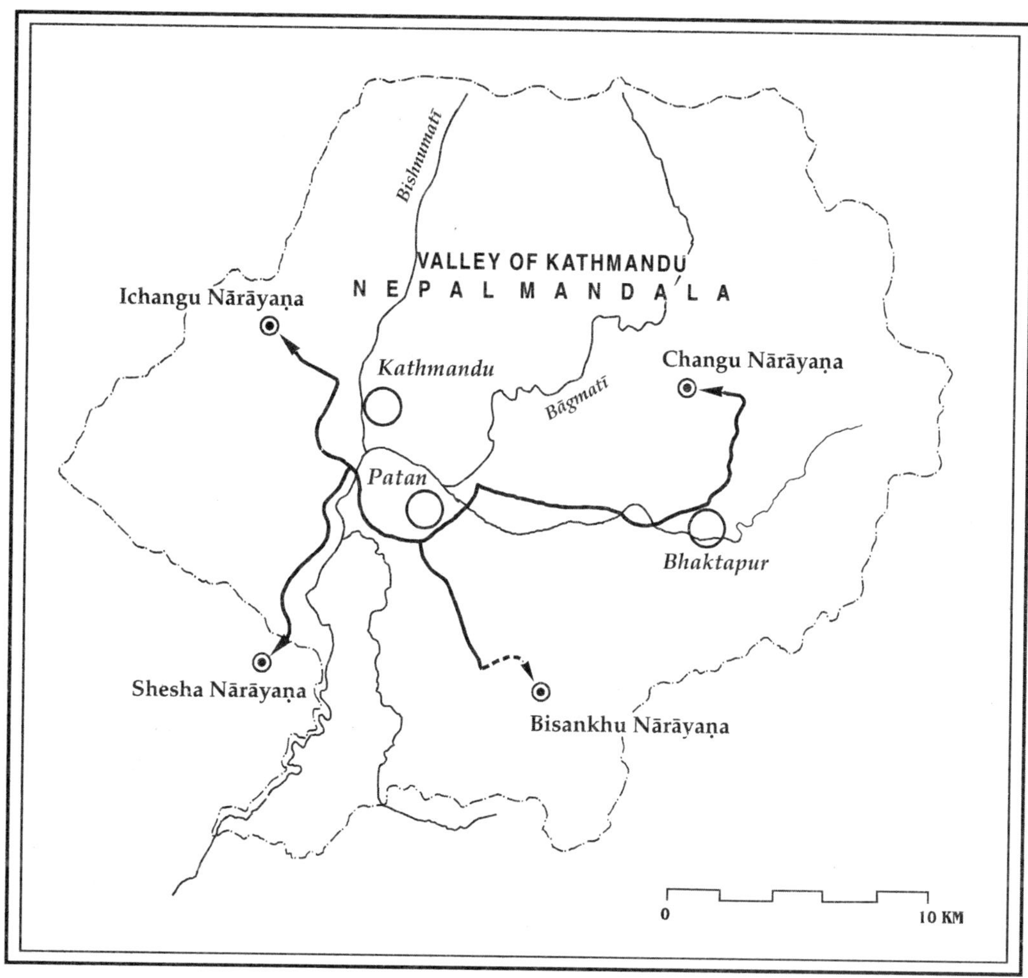

Map. 4.9. Kathmandu Valley: The pilgrimage to the four Narayana temples on the eve of Haribodhini Ekadashi, the eleventh day of the waxing moon in November. The new infrastructure of motorable roads guides the 'traffic' between the four places that punctuate the circuit of the cosmic mandala.

Sankatadevi, and then follows Ganga between Scindhia Ghat and Dashashvamedha Ghat. Seventeen *lingas* are worshipped to complete the first circuit. Six more circumambulations follow before the final destination, Vishveshvara, is reached. The spiral-like movement demonstrates perfectly the gradual approach as an ideal movement of the pilgrim. No doubt, there is an identifiable destination, a centre or navel which bestows bliss, but the movement reflects a process. It is not an outer edge that defines an inner space. The spiral rather tends to claim the entire "house" as it identifies 72 places within it.

Conclusions

TIME AND SPACE

In many cases (Bhaktapur, Varanasi, Kag) the processional path not only remains unchanged over a long period, but it is mandatory as it forms the backbone of a ritual activity. I know of pathfinding commissions, which, days in advance of processional circuits, check the accessibility of former routes. Gates have to be kept open and new walls removed not only to simply facilitate the ritual but to make it "effective." A loss in authenticity would probably harm the expression of ritual commitment and the resulting religious result or merit. Such rituals will eventually lead to a self-organization as could recently be observed on the occasion of the *Narayana-jatra* of the Kathmandu Valley (see below). Turning away from the path towards the enclosed space one would say that the microcosm is renewed or reconstructed by the pilgrim — certainly unknowingly, because the pilgrimage does not need knowledge. A pilgrim rather acts non-intentionally as in ritual he is and he is not the author of his act (Humphrey and Laidlaw 1994: 99). The route is prescribed and to follow the prescription is identical with the goal. It is the ritual commitment that elevates his action; he is not simply covering a distance in space but performs a circumambulation. The mandatory quality of the prescribed route must also be understood as a demonstration against change. The ancient path survives change and remains valid forever. The pilgrim who follows such a route is in fact, as M.C. Joshi said in the concluding discussion of the conference in Delhi, "on a journey into the realm of deathlessness." The question is, whether this notion can also be applied to space? If time is set apart from secular time and if the ritual commitment transforms a path into a circumambulatory route, is then the enclosed space sacred?

I do not think that pilgrims create personal of ritual spaces but instead they participate in collective actions in space, which in most cases were created by ritual specialists. These specialists also created meaningful *yantras* and designed *mandalas* on the basis of a geometricised or ordered landscape. The average pilgrim does not need to worry about all this; meaning or even transcendental implications belong to a realm of thought that remains with the specialist — or is reconstructed by the anthropologist.

COMPLEXITY AND SELF-ORGANIZATION

These notions are tied to certain observations that have been presented above. I am well aware that complexity and self-organization start the moment that ruthless rules are given up. This happened years ago, when the *Narayana-jatra* of the Kathmandu Valley which is annually observed on the eve of Haribodhini Ekadashi, the eleventh day of the waxing moon in November. On this very day Vishnu is said to have awakened from his four-month dreamless sleep on the body of a snake called Ananta — Infinity. For many, a period of four-month fasting comes to an end and many others observe 24 hours of fasting in honour of Vishnu or Narayana as he is usually called in Nepal. On November 14, 1998 I saw thousands of people moving as fast and as conveniently as possible from one Narayana temple to the next in order to cover all four of them in a short day (see map). Nobody followed any ancient processional route which, two generations ago, needed a long day to be covered. Instead, buses take advantage of a recently improved infrastructure of motorable roads. The pilgrimage to the four temples of Narayana at Changu, Bisankhu, Pharping and Ichangu developed into the most popular pilgrimage of the Valley within a decade. Earlier this was an event followed by Newars alone, the inhabitants who for two thousand years constitute the urban population. Since the opening up of the country at the middle of the twentieth century, the diversified bureaucracy of a modern state and educational institutions has resulted in an influx that doubled the population within a generation. Today the newcomers join the *Narayana-jatra* in order to demonstrate their integration into an emerging society beyond borderlines set by caste or ethnicity. New motifs overshadow ancient rituals and allow for self-organization that was unthinkable in an hierarchically structured society. Earlier, the occasion, participation and enactment were tied to a fixed order that did not allow for an individual performance.

References

Bakker, Hans T., 1993, "Early mythology relating to Varanasi," in: Singh, Rana P.B. (ed.), *Banaras, Varanasi: Cosmic Order, Sacred City, Hindu Traditions*, Varanasi: Tara Book Agency, p. 21.

Eck, Diana L., 1983a, *Banaras. City of light*, London: Routledge & Kegan Paul.

———, 1983b, "A survey of Sanskrit sources for the study of Varanasi," *Purana* 22 (1), pp. 81-101.

Gutschow, Niels, 1982, *Stadtraum und Ritual der newarischen Städte im Kathmandu Tal. Eine architekturanthropologische Untersuchung*, Stuttgart: Kohlhammer.

———, 1996, "Bisketjatra of Bhaktapur," in Lienhard, S. (ed.), *Continuity and change of an urban ritual, Change and continuity. Studies in the Nepalese Culture of the Kathmandu Valley*, Torino: Edizioni dell'Orso.

———, 1993, "Bhaktapur: Sacred patterns of a living urban tradition," in: Spodek, H. and Srinivasan, D. M., (ed.), *Urban form and Meaning in South Asia: The shaping of cities from prehistoric to precolonial times*, Hannover and London: University Press of New England.

———, 1994, "Varanasi/Benares: The centre of Hinduism?" in: *Erdkunde* 48 (3): 194-209.

———, 1998, "The settlement process in lower Mustang (Baragaon), Nepal. Case studies from Kag, Khyinga and Te," in: *Beiträge zur allgemeinen und vergleichenden Archäologie*, 18: 49-145.

Gutschow, Niels and Axel Michaels, 1993, *Benares. Tempel und religiöses Leben in der heiligen Stadt der Hindus*, Cologne: DuMont.

Humphrey, Caroline and James Laidlaw, 1994, *The Archetypal Actions of Ritual: A Theory of Ritual Illustrated by the Jain Rite of Worship*, Oxford: Oxford University Press.

Panikkar, Raimundo, 1991, "There is no outer without inner space," in: *Concepts of Space, Ancient and Modern*, Delhi: Abhinav Publications, pp. 7-38.

Parry, Jonathan P., 1981, "Death and cosmogony in Kashi," in: *Contributions to Indian sociology*, 15 (1-2): 88-111.

———, 1994, *Death in Benares*, Cambridge: Cambridge University Press.

Ramble, Charles, 1995, "Gaining ground: representations of territory in Bon and Tibetan popular Tradition," *Tibet Journal* 20 (1), pp. 83-124.

Ramble, Charles, 1998, "The Mustang villages of Kag, Te and Khyinga: An introduction to history, ethnicity and the idea of place," in: *Beiträge zur allgemeinen und vergleichenden Archäologie*, 18: 147-82.

Singh, Rana P.B., 1987, "The pilgrimage mandala of Varanasi (Kashi). A study in sacred geography," in: *National Geographic Journal of India* 33 (4): 493-524.

Singh, Rana P.B. (ed.), 1993, *Banaras, Varanasi: Cosmic Order, Sacred City, Hindu Traditions*, Varanasi: Tara Book Agency.

PART II

PILGRIMAGE IN INDIA, TIBET AND NEPAL

5

Kashi as Cosmogram

Panchakroshi Route and Complex Structure of Varanasi, India

Rana P.B. Singh

Introduction

"PROBABLY when people became people and they began to think, to remember, to want a deeper experience of perceived reality, pilgrimage begins" (Clift and Clift 1996: 22). According to the *Mahabharata* (13.111.18), a fifth-century BCE epic, pilgrimage places are auspicious because of the extraordinary power of their earth and efficacy of their water and because they were frequented by the sages (cf. Bhardwaj 1973: 29-42). Such characteristics are still invoked by contemporary Hindus. By journey to these places connected by sacred routes, pilgrims obtain its "fruit" (*phala*) which transform their life, give inner satisfaction and also purification and peace — as pilgrims express.

By the combined process of sacralisation, ritualisation, and deeper inter-connectedness, the place becomes a distinct "sacred place" or sacredscape. It possesses the integrative entity of eternal bond between the human psyche and nature-spirit (cf. Singh 1995: 97). Here the relationships of devotees to sacred land are expressed simultaneously in terms of myths, folk history, cultural traditions, rituals, kinship, and even politics.

Pilgrimage is a spirit — a guiding force unifying divinity and humanity; i.e., it is a search for wholeness. Ultimately the wholeness of landscape and its sacred and symbolic geography creates a faithscape that encompasses sacred place, sacred time, sacred meanings, sacred rituals and embodies both symbolic and tangible psyche elements in an attempt to realise man's identity in the cosmos (Singh 1998: 56). Through the centuries devotees have followed the sacred journeys (pilgrimages) to revive themselves and their *spirits*. The pilgrims come and find what is timeless and eternal. Millions of pilgrims had walked before and a pilgrim had a sense that s/he was in company of those people who preceded them. In Hindu religious tradition pilgrimage is a process of realising energies within — not going without the *spirit*. Without a *way* a pilgrim gets lost in the route. The *way* is an insight or a mental state from transcendent to immanent, creating a path in the right order. The key in/of the way to pilgrimage is "spirit of place," which should be realised by faith.

The present study deals mainly with the aspects of complex structure of cosmogony associated with *Panchakroshi* route. It is assumed that the landscape geometry, together with interlinking alignments and multi-layered structure, makes the web more complex. This helps to regulate its functioning simpler and easy. Elsewhere we have already dealt with the issues of mythology and spatiality (Singh 1991), and empirical and participatory experiences (Singh 1998).

Multiple territorial layers

The *Panchakroshi* route (*fig.*5.1) demarcates the territorial limit of the cosmic territory of Varanasi, referred to as *Kashi Mandala* (cf. Singh and Rana, 2002: 161-62). The *Padma Purana* (*Srishti Khanda*, 65.14-20), a seventh-century mythological book, describes its territory whose centre lies at Madhyameshvara and radial point at Delhi ("Gate") Vinayaka, measuring a distance of 5 *krosa* (i.e., 11 miles/17.6 km). Thus the covering circumambulatory circuit is 168 miles (269 km) and is known as *Brihata Panchakroshi* or *Chaurasikroshi-yatra.* During the past few centuries, this circuit has shrunk down to the present path of *Panchakroshi* (i.e., *laghu*, the shorter one) and covers a distance of 25 *krosa* (i.e., 55.2 miles/88.6 km). The third level of manifestation is marked by the *Nagara-pradakshina* (NP), marking the sacred territory of the holy city. The fourth level is symbolised as *Avimukta*, marking the inner city in which Lord Shiva, the patron deity of Kashi, moves; the name *Avimukta* means the "Never Forsaken" zone. The fifth level is marked by the *Antargriha* ("inner sanctum").

These five sacred journey routes are identified by the respective boundaries in a series, never crossing one another, and are connoted as the five *koshas*, the "sheaths." That is how *koshas* are analogous to the five gross elements of organism according to Hindu mythology and also "with human being where the outermost (*annamaya* — food-made) *kosha* being the material body and the innermost (*anandamaya* — bliss-made) *kosha* being the subtle body" (Eck, 1986: 46). By this archetypal manifestation the interconnectedness between the divine and the human realms can be perceived and expressed into the true form of natural existence (cf. Eck 1982: 30). The five sacred territories are further explained as the symbol of "gross elements" (*mahabhutas*) and compared with the corresponding body-symbols, transcendental power and the sheaths (*fig.*5.2; Table 5.1).

Like the human body, the Kashi-Mandala is the *Brahman* (the cosmos) who illumines the world and dwells inside the citadel of the above-mentioned five *koshas*, the world within. This way the pilgrimage journey completes the macrocosmic journey in the form of a microcosmos. This reflects that "man tries to integrate multifaceted nature in terms of the intuitively known unity of his body. This perception of and analogy between human anatomy and the physiognomy of the earth is widespread" (Tuan 1977: 89). Thus "the cosmos in its entirety can become a

fig.5.1. Kashi Mandala

hierophany" (Eliade 1959: 12). The revelation of hierophany gets initiated and finally completed at a fixed centre, i.e., Jnanavapi ("Well of the Wisdom"), the source of the primordial water from where life begins. In terms of area and time the coverage from higher to lower territories descends; however, the intensity of the power of revelation follows the reverse tendency. This dialectics of shrinking universe and expanding force reflect the idea of creation and existence from the opposite forces. This is being operated by the drama of divine forces (*maya* or *lila*) which, while developing in complexity, converges into a simplicity and resulting order. This metaphor is comparable to Shiva's dance symbolising the cosmic cycle of creation and destruction as the basis of all existence (cf. Capra 1991: 242).

Table 5.1: Kashi (Varanasi) : Five Layers of Sacred Territories in Varanasi

	Macrocosm	Mesocosm: Sacred route	Microcosm: Part of body	Transcendental Power	Sheath (Cakra)
1.	Sky	Chaurashikroshi	Head	Consciousness	Food
2.	Earth	Panchakroshi	Legs	Action	Mind
3.	Air	Nagar-pradakshina	Face	Cognition	Breath
4.	Water	Avimukta	Blood	Wisdom	Intellect
5.	Fire	Antargriha	Heart	Bliss	Bliss

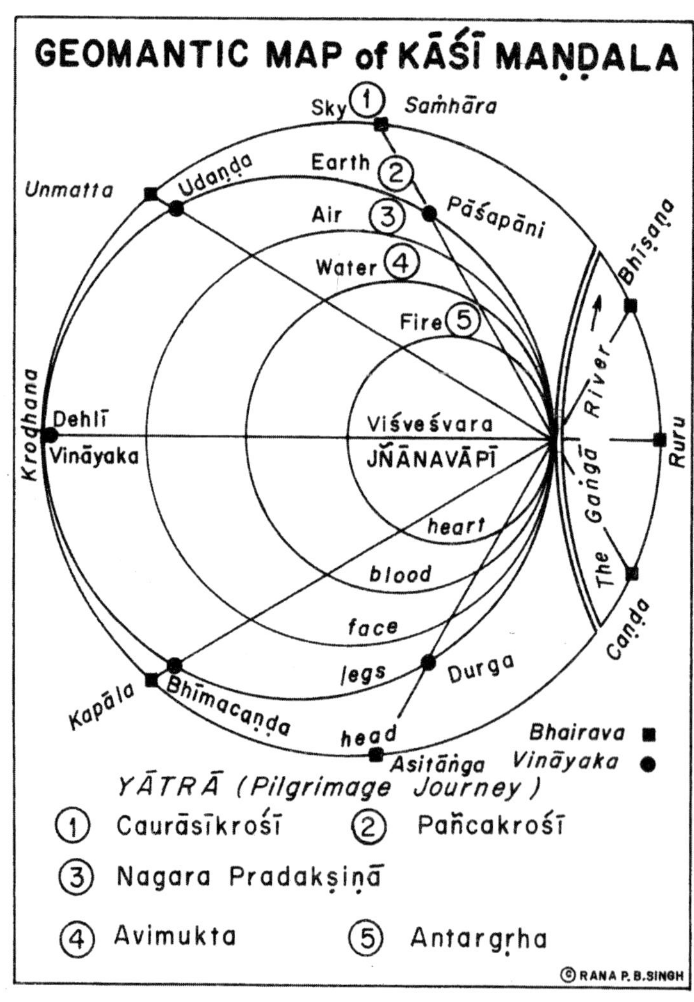

fig.5.2. Geomantic Map of Kashi Mandala

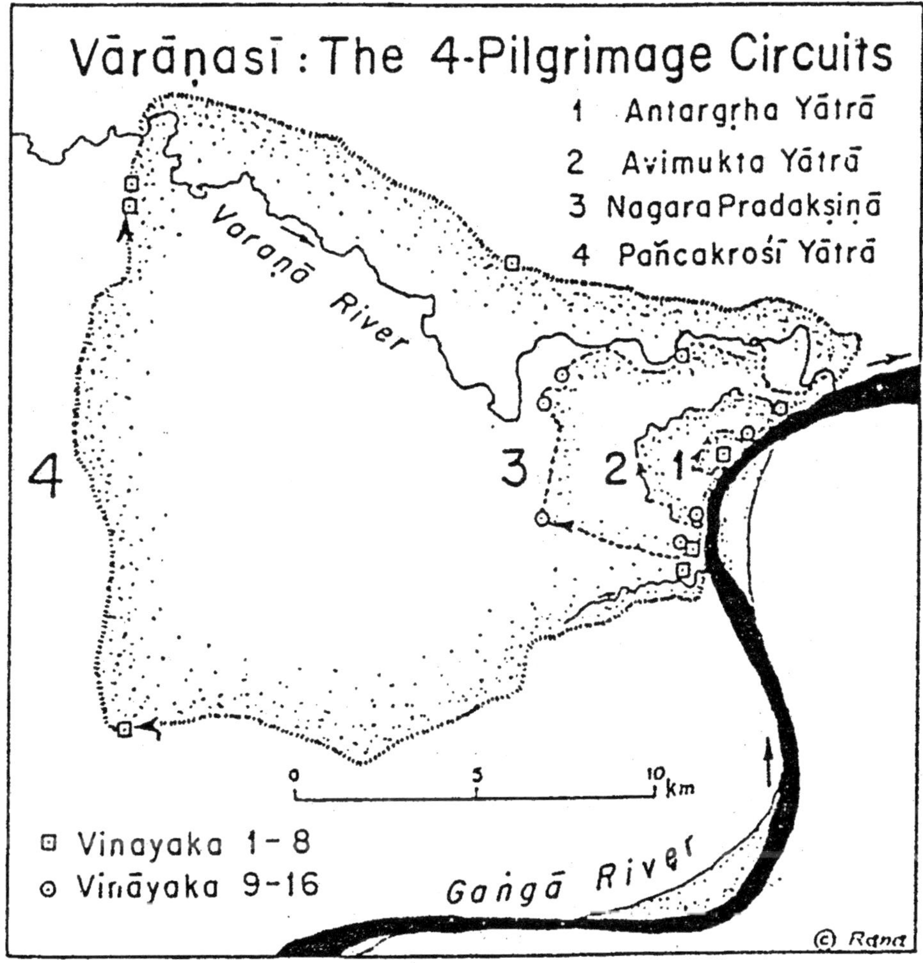

fig.5.2.A. Varanasi: The 4-Pilgrimage Circuits

These five pilgrimage circuits are like a garland consisting of different numbers of shrines in a chain, further denoting the numerical archetype symbolising universal patterns of integration among the levels of cosmic manifestation — clearly three levels are marked. The symbolisation of any number can be narrated around the cosmogonic homology, commonly connecting macrocomos (the celestial world), mesocosmos (the terrestrial world), and microcosmos (the phenomenal world/realm of consciousness). The cosmogonic sense of numbers has developed together with growth of archaic sense of human understanding and led to further promote "sacrality and spiritualism." The number attached to a particular sacred form or function also signifies the specific meaning in the formation of the pattern.

The most common numbers of archetypal connotation are 0 and 108. Zero refers to the cycle of destruction and recreation which continues together with infinity, therefore all the

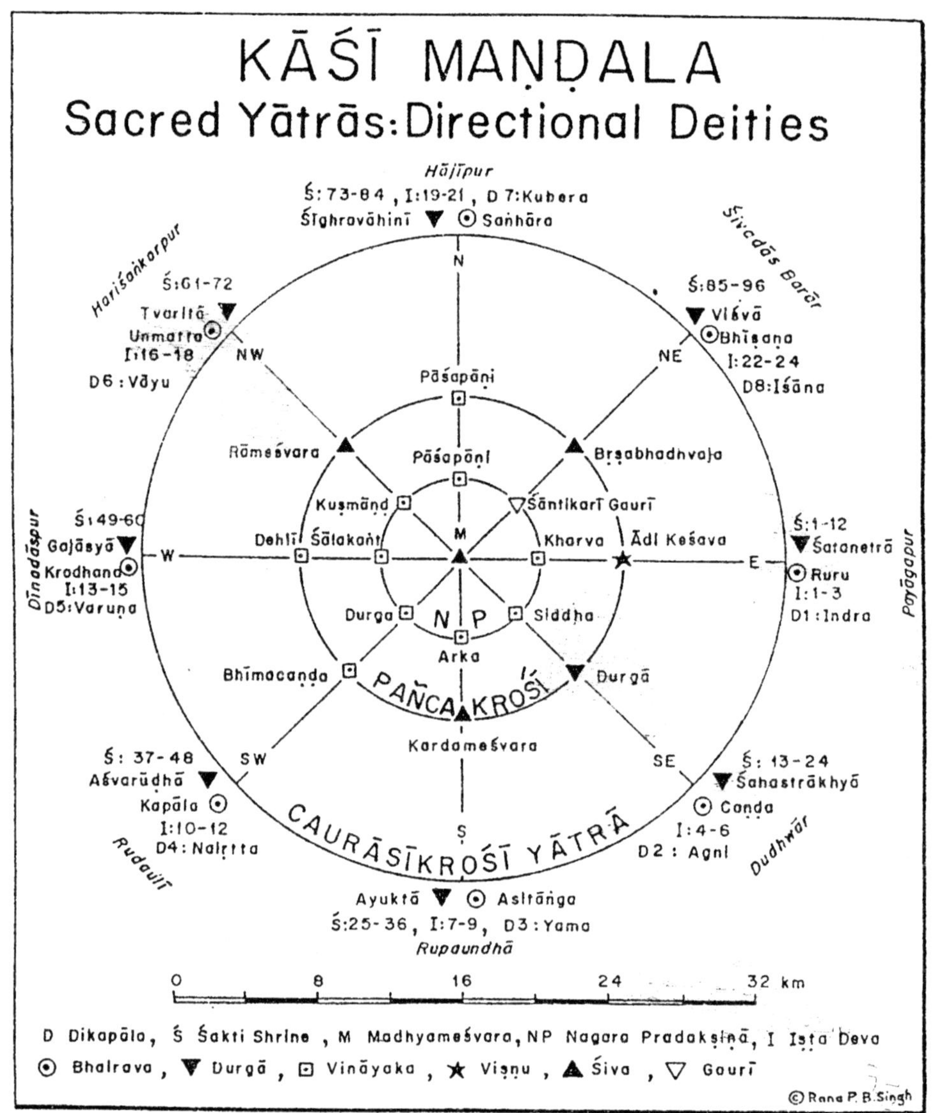

fig.5.2B. Kashi Mandala — Sacred Yatras: Directional Deities

patterns emerge within it. Thus zero symbolises the cosmic *mandala*. On the other end 108 denotes the cosmos as represented by constellations and rhythm of human cognition; this way it defines the cardinality, centrality and circulation (Singh 1994: 189-90).

Two other numbers, 72 and 144 representing shrines along the route are also common. In the case of 144 shrines (along the *Chaurashikroshi* route), the cosmic space (planets), cardinality (directions) and cognitive vision (up and down) are reflected. In the case of the three remaining circuits, on each exist 72 shrines — representing the main cardinality (directions) (see Table 5.2; Singh 1994: 197).

Table 5.2: Kashi: Pilgrimage Journey and the Cosmogonic Integrity

Sacred segment/ route of Pilgrimage Journey	1. Macrocosmos: Planet	2. Mesocosmos: Direction	3. Micro-cosmos: 3 realms/2 parts of a day	Shrines on the route = 1 × 2× 3
1. Chaurashikroshi	9	8	2	144
2. Panchakroshi	9	4	3	108
3. Nagar-pradakshina	9	4	2	72
4. Avimukta	9	4	2	72
5. Antargriha	9	4	2	72

In all the cases, Jnanavapi (together with Vishveshvara) serves as the 'centre' axis mundi. From here initiation starts by "taking the vow" (sankalpa lena) and finally by performing the completion ritual of "getting release from the vow" (sankalpa chhodana). By this symbolic behaviour of expansion (journey) and merger (returning) and in between the process of doing (rituals), the sacramental cycle completes its interconnectedness; and this is where one begins the cherishing transformation of life. This centre is the symbol of coincidential oppositorium, expressed by the zero or a "dot" and further denotes an unlimited entity, the productive point of potentiality. Nevertheless, in philosophic context, "this central point shows a mediation on the paradox of the maximum potential contained within an irreducible minimum . . ." (Lannoy 1971: 344). This numerical complexity refers to the relationship between nature and the earth and ultimately to the terrestrial unity.

The Panchakroshi-Kshetra (territory) shows an organised and meaningful archetype in the intermediate realm of integration between macrocosmos, the culturally conceived universe marking the outer edge (here it is *Chaurashikroshi*), and the microcosmic world of a closed territory forming a small compound (the area surrounding the Vishveshvara temple). In the light of ecological concept, the Panchakroshi Kshetra like a developed kingdom allowing the fulfilment of Hinduism's potentials for ordering a community, to be called as "climax communities" as suggested by Levy (1990: 28). Here developed its potential for systematic complexity, and with it a temporal stability (e.g., sacred time for pilgrimage). This idea is narrated in various mythology by referring to this sacred territory as "Light-manifested Shivalinga" (*panchakroshatmaka jyotiralinga*) and is understood by the pilgrims as they express that "while we are performing pilgrimage on the sacred earth, the divinities are also performing pilgrimage in the heavens, that is how we get merit." While walking they sing a couplet in a lyrical rhythm:

Hara Hara! Mahadeva Shambho!; Kashi Vishvanatha Gange:
Mata Parvati Sange.

Hail to our Lord Shiva, living in Varanasi together with your liquid energy the Ganga river, and your consort Mother Parvati.

They explain that by murmuring the above sacred verse, the whole area along the sacred route converges into a holy *soundscape* and it awakens the immanent spirit. The group chanting provides an energy and cohesion for peaceful journey as well as the psychic strength necessary to concentrate upon right acts, right thoughts and tight movements (cf. Singh, 1998: 66). This belief and practice provide meaningfulness to the archetypal-symbolic frame which has a multi-dimensional network.

Panchakroshi Pilgrimage (PY)

There exist 108 shrines along the PY route (*fig.* 5.3). This pilgrimage is performed according to the prescribed rule, in a period of six-days, passing nights at the five halt stations which record 44 *dharmashalas* (pilgrims' rest houses). Of the total 108 shrines and images, 56 are associated with Shiva, 11 with Vinayakas (Ganesha) and 10 with the Shiva's assistants. By the turn of the sixteenth century CE, the PY became popular. A Marathi treatise, the *Guru Charitra* (41.265-315), dated 1538, describes the details of this journey. Later the famous devotional-poet Tulasi (1497-1623) also eulogised the pilgrimage (cf. Singh 2004).

According to Hindu tradition, each month has its own merit and good for religious activities but some months are relatively more merit-giving, such as Ashvina (September-October), Karttika (October-November) and Margashirsha (November-December). For PY the most auspicious period ascribed is the intercalary month of the leap year. This is called *mala-masa*, "month of pollution" or *adhi-masa*, "extra month." According to the Hindu lunar almanac, in the period of 1945-2047 there would be 37 *mala-masas*. However, an accountable number of pilgrims also perform pilgrimage in the cold seasons (Magha-Phalguna, January-March) and the spring (Chaitra-Vaishakha, March-May), every year. Every year also holds an abbreviated pilgrimage for one day on *Maha Shivaratri*, "the great night of Shiva" (i.e., Shiva's marriage day), falling of the 13th dark-half/waning of the month of Phalguna (February-March), and marks the completion of the lunar year. According to a recent survey in a sacred Hindu month of Ashadha (June-July), 1996, (i.e., the last *mala-masa*), 48,200 foot-pilgrims and pilgrimage-tourists performed this journey. The data shows the dominance of females (66.2 per cent), and supports the perception that Hindu women are "more religious" than their male counterparts. A little over half of the foot-pilgrims followed in groups of 4-10 persons, while three-fourths of pilgrimage-tourists followed a group of 2-3 persons. From the interview of 482 pilgrims it is obvious that around half of them belong to the Varanasi district; and recorded the same share for the people belonging to the age of 40-60 years, and also the same share to the educational level between 5th and 12th grades. Brahmins and Merchant castes together share a little over half of the pilgrims (cf. Singh 1998: 78-87; also Rana and Singh, 2003).

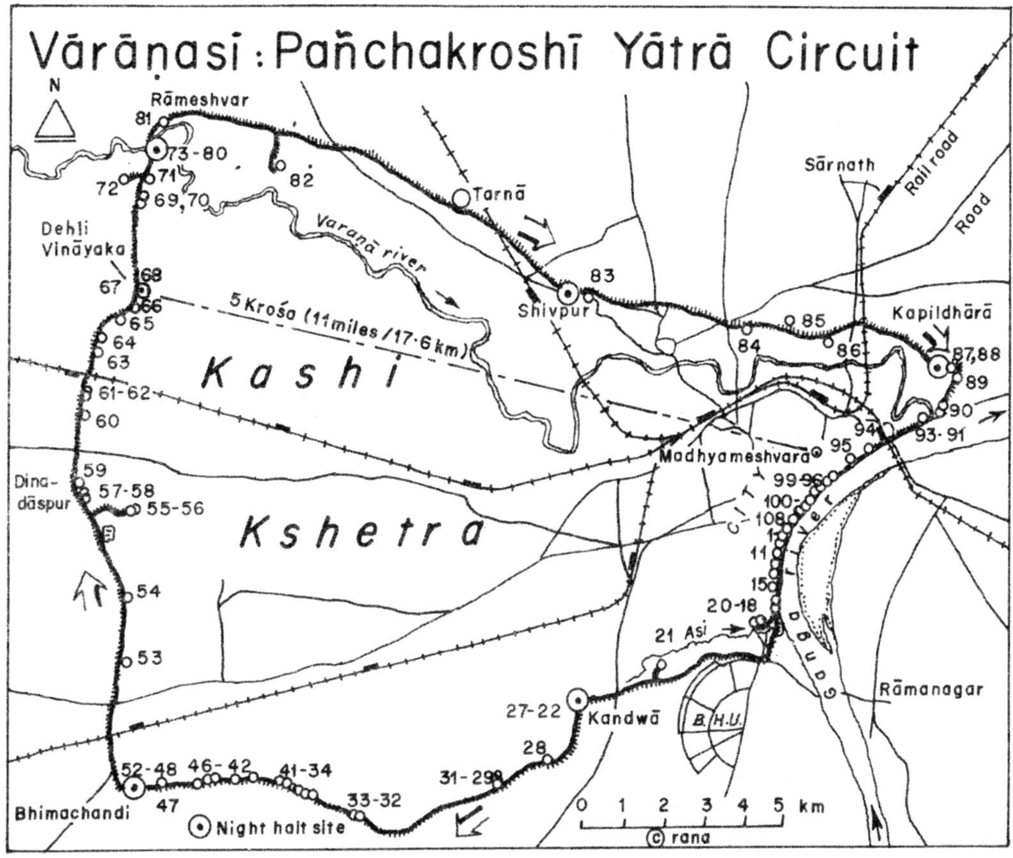

fig.5.3. Varanasi : Panchakroshi Yatra Circuit

No noticeable cultural change has occurred in the Panchakroshi pilgrimage. In fact, the cultural aspect of this sacred journey has remained basically the same, but its socio-structural aspect has undergone important changes in course of time.

The first reference of cardinality and sacred geometry was made with respect to Madhyameshvara as centre (cf. *Padma Purana, SK*: 65.14-20). However the later description refers Jnanavapi as the navel-point. The cardinal and inter-cardinal directions are referred as reference points describing routes. However they rotate at different degrees (cf. Singh, 2002:35). This can easily be explained with comparison of 56 Vinayaka shrines located on the spiral route (7 rounds) and following the cardinal bisecting points (8 directions). The exact locations have been measured with the help of GPS receivers under the direction of Prof. J. McKim Malville (cf. Malville and Singh 1998). According to Malville this is an attempt at large-scale organisation and as outer alignments do not converge upon the Jnanavapi and both the centres exist in different contexts, the whole system becomes complex. However, it works in defining the limit of outer territory (*Madhyameshvara* as centre), and the merger of the innermost segment (Jnanavapi as centre) (see *fig.* 5.4). By this one finds a state of non-equilibrium. However it is dynamic and functioning, as Cambel (1993: 4) has expressed: "Complex systems are dynamic and not in equilibrium; they are like a journey, not a destination and they may pursue a moving target."

In miniature form (*microcosmos*), the Panchakroshi temple (house No. CK 5/33 Gola Gali, Bhikharidas Lane, Chauk, Varanasi, built in early eighteenth century, possesses 100 images of the Panchakroshi path in addition to 189 other images associated with the different pilgrimage routes of Varanasi. These miniature-like stone niches (average size of about 30 × 45 cm) on the walls and at the front gate contain engraved form of names. Some of them are now ruined and poorly repaired with cement. Architect and pilgrimage scholar, Niels Gutschow (1994: 200) remarks that "as the initiated might perform the *yatra* within his own body the Panchakroshi Mandir (*temple*) serves as tool: 272 (*in fact 289!*) gods and goddesses, *ghats*, ponds and wells are visualised, worshipped and circumambulated in a single act of motion. The walls of the temple are transformed into a vast sacred scene." This temple, like other temples, visualises "the cosmic force which creates innumerable forms and these are one whole, and without the least of them the universal harmony would lack completeness" (Kramrisch 1946: 67). This temple is not so popularly visited by the foot-pilgrims of the PY rather pilgrimage-tourists and the devotees from the neighbourhood frequently pay visit to this temple.

Towards Understanding

Pilgrimage is concerned with the spirit and a deeper sense of human psyche in search of identity and interconnectedness with nature but it is difficult to say precisely how. The act of pilgrimage — journey, activities, experiences of communionship — is itself a ritual which has

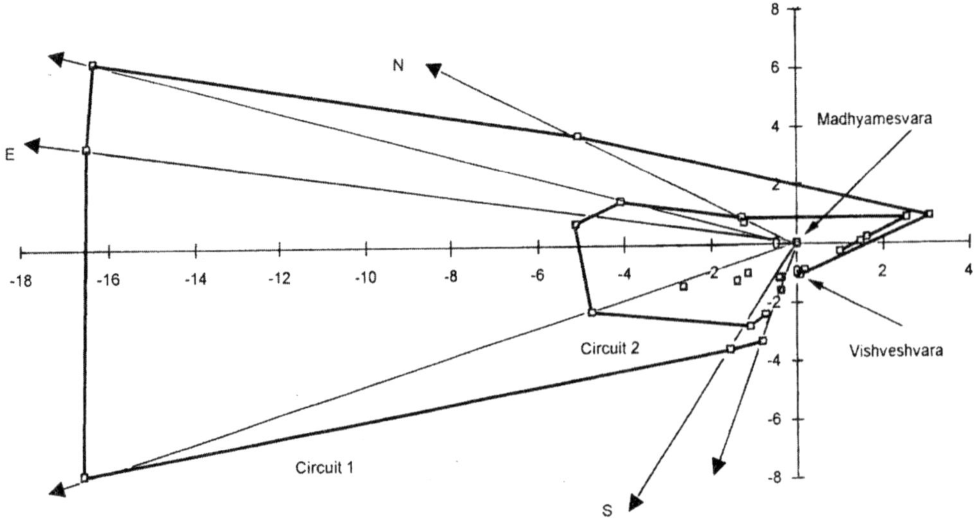

***fig*.5.4. Panchakroshi Yatra route: The alignment of the Vinayaka shrines.**

transformative value, a reinterpretation of the idea of "experience." This is where one begins. The Hindu term *Tirtha Yatra* ("crossing the ford") itself denotes this quality. Hindu devotees believe that through pilgrimage one becomes "transformed into a new life." Says Reymond (1984: 42),

> The pilgrim returns from his journey . . . strengthened by the vista of a disciplined life which is implied in the search for oneself, the attempt to live as an adult. It is a new stage of inner observation from which to approach the meeting with the Infinite.

The act of pilgrimage starts from inner space (*home*), then leads to outer territory, and later in the reverse manner, returns to the home. By this process or two forces, one moves toward wholeness — the essence of being holiness — a soul healing. Pilgrimage is a *way* of healing the body and also healing the soul through cleaning the body by walk and revealing the soul by realisation of the spirit inherent to the mother Earth.

There are shadow sides of pilgrimages related to mob psychology, chances of catastrophes in organized pilgrimages, possible use of pilgrimage camps or meetings for religious, national or ethnic prejudice, and so on. The mob psychology when moved around blind faith turns to superstition, self-gain and creates danger for the others. This can be minimized by strong wish and awareness of the deeper messages and meanings.

In terms of creating a state of equilibrium (e.g., *sacred*) in the non-equilibrium (e.g., *secular*) the dynamics of communionship and inter-connectedness are promoted by pilgrimages. A tour may be considered an outer journey in geographical space in an attempt to gain pleasure; pilgrimage is an inner journey in the outer space from where the immanent and transcendent together create a system-complex. Tour requires wish for pleasure and satisfaction; pilgrimage requires quest for revelation and peace. As human beings we need both. As Merton (1967: 92) says,

> The geographical pilgrimage is the symbolic acting out of an inner journey. The inner journey is the interpolation of the meanings and signs of the outer pilgrimage. One can have one without the other. It is best to have both.

We need religion in the form of *dharma* ("moral and natural code of conduct") but we need it freed from superstition.

References

Bhardwaj, Surinder M., 1973, *Hindu Places of Pilgrimages in India,* Berkeley: University of California Press.

Cambe, A.B., 1993, *Applied Chaos Theory: A Paradigm for Complexity*, Boston: Academic Press.

Capra, Fritjof, 1991, *The Tao of Physics*, 3rd edn., Boulder, CO: Shambhala Publs.

Clift, J.D., and Clift, W.B. 1996, *The Archetype of Pilgrimage.* Mahwah, NJ: Paulist Press.

Eck, Diana L., 1992, *Banaras. City of Light*, New York : Alfred A. Knopf, Inc.

———, 1986, "Banaras: Cosmos and paradise in the Hindu imagination," in *The Word and the World*, ed. Veena Das, New Delhi: Sage Publs.: 41-55.

Gutschow, Niels, 1994, "Varanasi/Banaras: the center of Hinduism," *Erdkunde* (bonn), Bd 48 (3), Sept.: 194-209.

Kramrisch, Stella, 1946, *The Hindu Temple,* Calcutta: University of Calcutta Press.

Lannoy, Richard, 1971, *The Speaking Tree,* New York : Oxford University Press.

Levy, Robert I., 1990, *Mesocosm. Hinduism and Organization of a Traditional Newar City in Nepal,* Berkeley : University of California Press.

Malville, J. McKim and Singh, Rana P. B. 1998, "Pilgrimage mandalas of the Gangetic plains." A paper presented at the 14th I.C.A.E.S., July 26-Aug.1, Session on *Pilgrimage: Text and Context*, Wlliamsburg, VA, U.S.A.

Merton, Thomas, 1967, *Mystics & Zen Master,* New York: Dell Publ.Co.

Rana, Pravin S. and Singh, Rana P.B. 2003, Panchakroshi Yatra of Kashi: Divine typology, and Pilgrims' Characteristics. '*Fairs and Festivals of Kashi, Seminar*' (1-3 August) *Proceedings*. Varanasi: Jnana Pravaha, 12pp + 1 map.

Raymond, Lizelle, 1984, "Intimate Journeys," *Parabola* (New York), 9 (3): 40-45.

6

Death and Transformation at Gaya

Pilgrimage, Ancestors, and the Sun

Rana P.B. Singh
John McKim Malville
Anne L. Marshall

Transformation of Gayasura

THE name Gaya is derived from a demon-king, Gayasura, who by his arduous austerity pleased the gods and received the blessing that the spirit of all the divinities would reside in his body, i.e., the territory of Gaya marked by his reclining body. One interpretation of the Gayasura mythology is that it is a metaphor for the subduing of chaos and its conversion into the sacred. Whether it is found in creation-mythologies or in thermodynamics, chaos is never destroyed or eliminated but it is transformed into a more complex and ordered state through processes of system-wide feedback loops and non-linear amplification. The submission of Gayasurya to Vishnu was that his body be used for a "higher" purpose, that it be transformed to a *veda*, altar, and *tirtha*, on which all gods and goddesses would sit for all time (see Singh, 1999: 34-36).

The result of this rather fascinating symbolic and mythic transformation of a place of chaos into an "altar" and *tirtha* is that the new system contains memory of past meanings and transformations. As a place becomes metastable, small disturbances may be amplified far beyond their initial size and may propagate through the entire system. Gaya has been a pilgrimage destination for millennia and has become a place of high spiritual energy and, we suggest, *spiritual metastability*. As a consequence, small impulses in the form of innovative rituals, ecstatic visions, or memorable individual experiences may have been amplified to cause major changes in the total system.

Sun at Gaya

Although today Gaya is predominantly a place to perform ancestral rites, perhaps the preeminence of the *shraddha* ceremony (Williams 1876; Vidyarthi 1978) over Sun worship has not always been the case. In the vicinity of the greater territory of Gaya (Gaya Mandala:

fig. 6.1), there are nine grand, architecturally significant Sun temples at Deo (Devarka), Madanpur (Umga), Hanspura (Deokunda), Madhusrava (Chyavanyashram), Ular, Belaur, Baragaon, Aungari, and Pandarak (at banks of the Ganga river). In Bihar the most popular festival is Chhath — worship of the Sun god as mother. This festival is held twice a year, i.e., in the light-half fortnights of Chaitra (March-April) and Karttika (October-November). The nine sun temples with their historical monuments, a great tank, and associated mythology attract devotees from all parts of Bihar. Even today many devotees visit sun-related sites, e.g., Surya-Kunda, Uttara Manas and the Sun Temple at Brahmani Ghat and perform special rituals associated with the sun, taking holy dips and offering items to the Sun god. In the Surya Temple a record of Vishvarupa's son, Yakshapala, mentions the homage he gave to the Sun and "draws upon solar imagery to convey a sense of the resplendent city that his father has

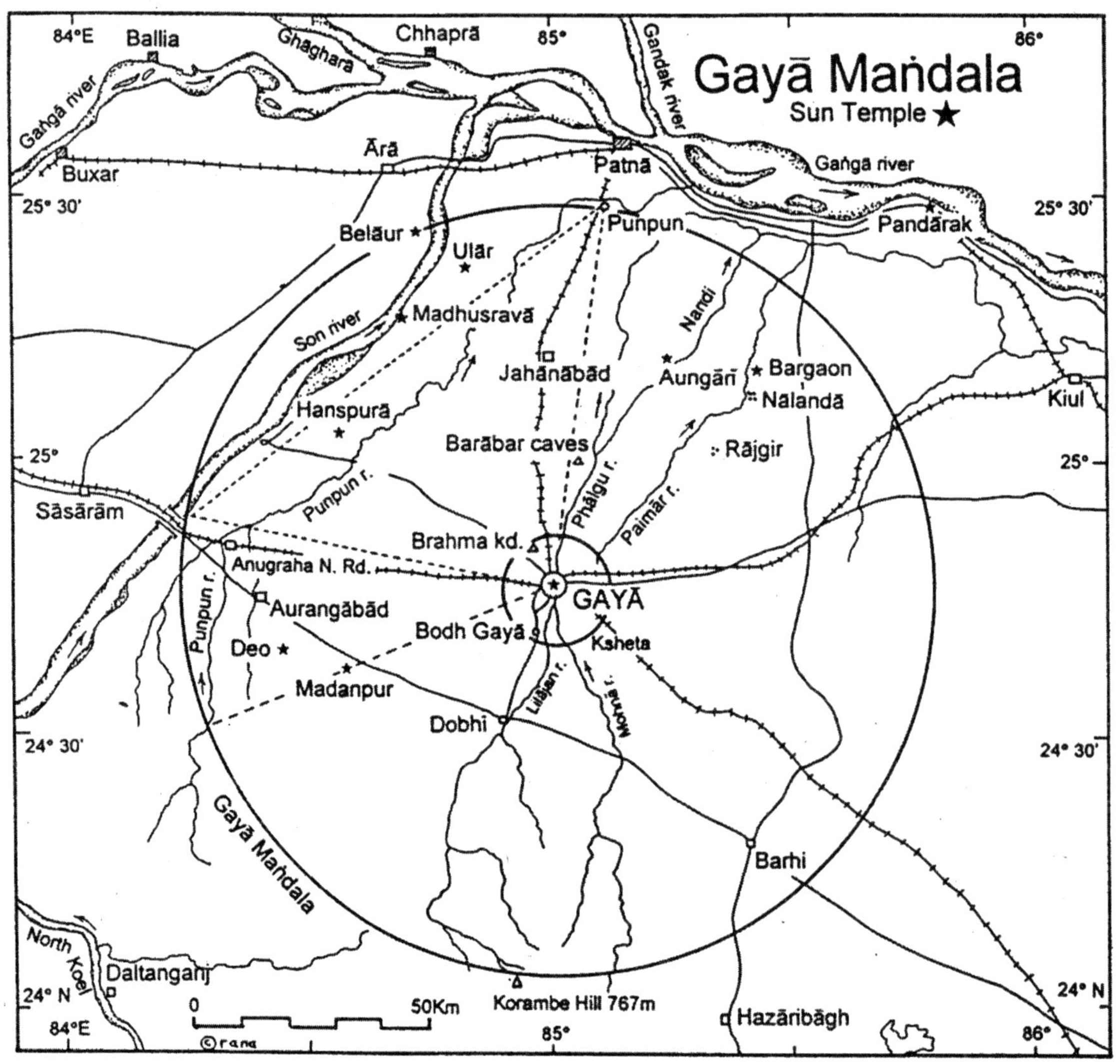

fig. 6.1: Gaya-Mandala

built" (Asher, 1989: 54, also Kielhorn, 1887). The 1.5 m high image of Surya was probably installed by Yakshapala in mid-eleventh century. The figure stands by a black slab carved with flying figures and *grahas* (planets) above his head. The largest sculpture in Gaya is also that of Surya, standing 2.44 m high at the Brahmani Ghat facing the east towards the Phalgu River now cloaked in a Vaishnava mantle (*fig.* 6.2); see Singh, 1999: 36-40).

The prevalence of Sun images in and around most of the old sites in Gaya are consistent with Barua's (1975) proposition that Gayasiras and Vishnupad were originally solar sites (Asher 1989). Prior to the importance of Vishnu and *shraddha* in Gaya, Surya worship may have been the dominant feature of the area. Such a possibility is strengthened by the large

fig. 6.2: Surya image in Brahmani Ghat shrine.

number of slabs containing images of the *grahas* throughout the city. Among the rock sites or stone slab the *VyP* (111.56) mentions sixteen sites related to different divinities, including the Sun god. The two tanks associated with the Sun god, viz., Uttara Manas and Surya-Kunda, are referred in the *VyP* (111.2,22; 111.6,8). The worship of the Sun god is described as a fasting ritual and festival in the *Mbh* (3.16-31); people believe that the tradition has been maintained since the time of the *Mahabharata*. Some of these Sun temple sites are considered to be reference points in the pilgrimage journey and delineation of the territorial boundary (*mandala*) of Gaya.

Paul (1983) provides examples of the ideological impulses that may have transformed Gaya. He suggests that the *tirtha* of Gaya first developed in association with the Vedic Sun, Vishnu, whose three strides span the universe, which also symbolizes the three positions of the sun throughout the day, i.e., dawn, noon, and dusk. The single footprint of Vishnupad, as opposed to an immobile pair of prints, suggests that Vishnu was indeed moving sun-like across the cosmos and placed his (right) foot momentarily on the head of the demon, Gaya. Surya worship, inspired by the footprint on the hill above the Phalgu River, may well have paralleled the *shraddha* ceremony for millennia in Gaya-Kshetra. Both ritual activities may have been present when the Buddha first arrived in the area, providing further ideological seeds for change (Paul 1983).

Sacred Topography

The Gaya-Kshetra (*fig.* 6.3), lies within some 8 km of Vishnupad temple and includes Preta-shila in the north-west and the Mahabodhi tree in the south. It is generally a flat area with an average elevation of 100 m out of which rises four hills, the summits of which contain holy shrines. In the past before urbanization of Gaya, the natural topography of hills, and the river would have been an impressive sight for pilgrims. Today the natural beauty and intrinsic power of the place are still accessible to visitors on the summits of the hills and along the river, especially at Sita-Kunda looking toward Vishnupad. These hills are symbolized as interlinking ladders between the earth and the heavens along which the soul may rise for final release. These hillocks — representing height, verticality, and a different realm from the earth — play a major role in the spatial symbolism of transcendence. They are also the special domain of all hierophanies of the atmosphere and therefore the dwelling of the divinities (cf. Eliade, 1958: 99). In the case of Gaya they are the homes of demi-gods or associates of the God of Death, Yama. The mythological literature mentions their roles in helping the departed soul to settle down in the abodes of divinities (see Singh, 1999: 40-45).

In addition to the enduring symbolism of the sun at Gaya, three further primal symbolic objects of nature are described and given ritual connotations: the Phalgu River, "flowing water;" Akshayavata, "the imperishable banyan tree, which is also the *axis mundi*;" and Preta-shila,

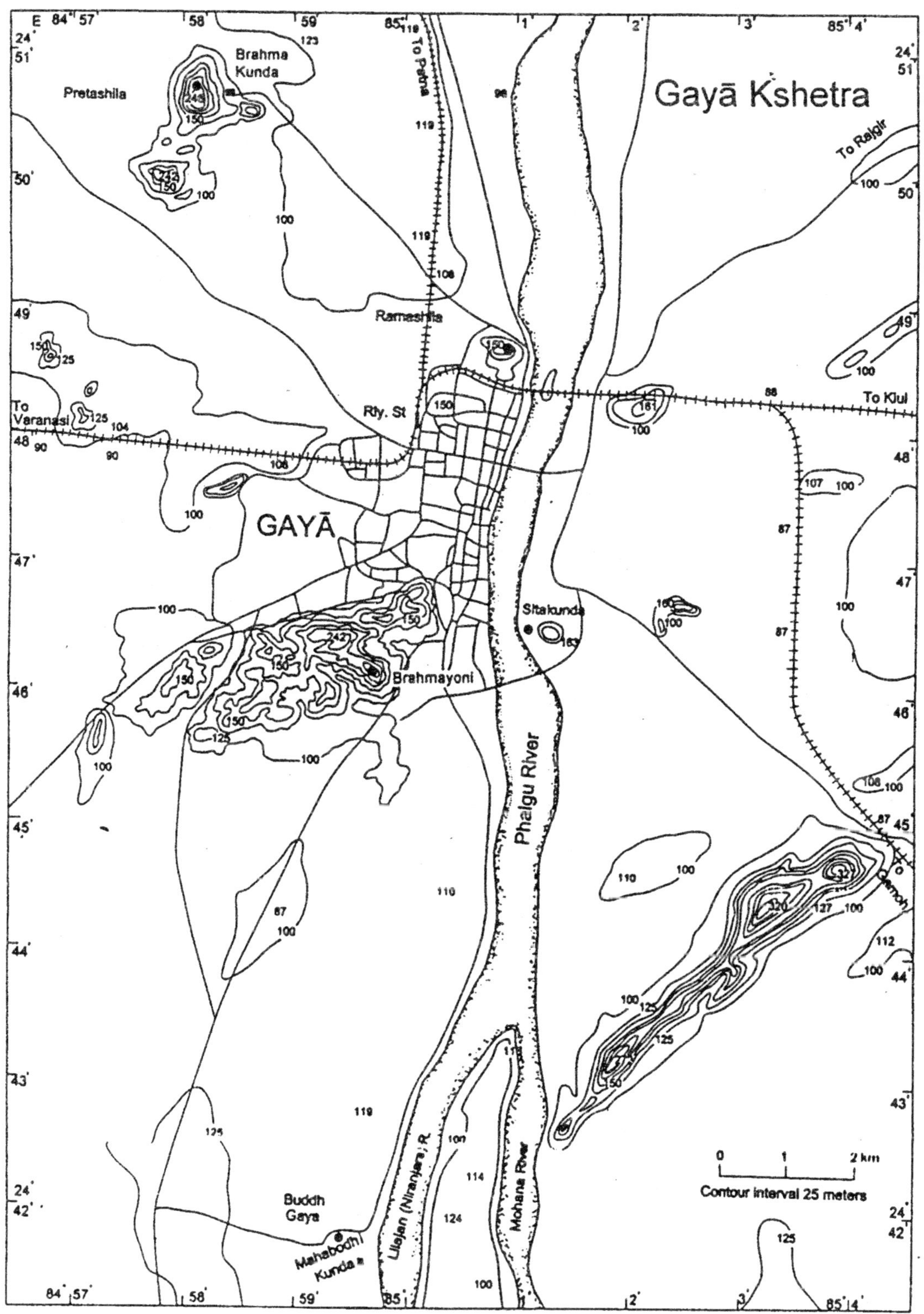
Gayā Kshetra
Pretashila
Brahma Kunda
To Patna
To Rajgir
Ramashila
Rly. St
To Kiul
To Varanasi
GAYĀ
Sitakunda
Brahmayoni
Phalgu River
Lilajan (Niranjana) R.
Mohana River
Buddh Gaya
Mahabodhi
Kunda
Contour interval 25 meters
0 1 2 km

fig. 6.3: Gaya

"the hill of the ghosts." The whole structure of time and space are thereby contained in the territory: birth, maturation and death. The Phalgu River at Gaya, flowing like the Ganga at Varanasi from the realm of death to that of birth, contains the symbols of birth and death, fertility and dissolution, and time and eternity (cf. Eliade, 1958: 193). The growth and expansion of natural elements in the symbolic manifestation of the cosmos is represented by Akshayavata, the eternal tree that pillared apart the heavens from the earth, allowing water and time to flow. The sun was released as an embryo from those moving waters, bringing light and life to the world.

The sacred topography of the "greater" Gaya-Kshetra, including Bodh-Gaya, contains another manifestation of that *axis mundi* in the form of the north-south axis established by the eternal banyan in the north and twelve km to the south, the pipal tree beneath which the Buddha attained enlightenment.

Cosmic Geometry of Gaya

"Cosmic" geometries are established by those alignments that link the microcosm with the macrocosm of the celestial sphere and the mesocosm of the terrestrial world. As we have already noted, each of the two trees, the Bodhi tree and Akshayavata represent the *axis mundi* and the centre of the universe. Each of these cosmic trees establishes fundamental cosmic geometries. Their roots sink into the earth, their trunks, bathed in the winds of the atmosphere, connect the earth and the heavens and their branches, containing the sun-bird, spread upward toward the seven realms of the heavens.

Cosmic trees, such as these two in Gaya and the Akshayavata of Prayag may have been elements of an ancient pillar cult, representing the mythical centre of the universe, where the earth and sky were pillared apart and creation began (Irwin 1983). That cosmogonic act of separation released the flowing river of time and gave birth to the sun and moon, which had been imprisoned in the dark waters. The atmospheric effect that occasionally causes a brilliant pillar of light at dawn may be one of the inspirations for the cosmogonic symbolism. We suggest that the vertical arm of Dasharatha in Sita-Kunda may have been viewed as another variation of the pillar symbolism. Furthermore, Paul (1983) has suggested that Gaya may have been the original site for the iron pillar of Qutab Minar at Delhi. Based upon the reference in its inscription to Vishnupad, he suggests it may have initially been erected in Gaya in commemoration of the ancestors of the Guptas.

Another example of cosmic geometry at Gaya may be a solar *mandala* with Vishnupad at its centre (*fig.* 6.4). If the ancient function of the *tirtha* of Gaya included sun worship, one would anticipate that in the vicinity of Vishnupad there should have existed opportunities for *darshana* of the sun at important times of the year in its movement along the ecliptic. In contrast to other sites where the dawn sun is uniquely important, at Gaya the position of the dying sun

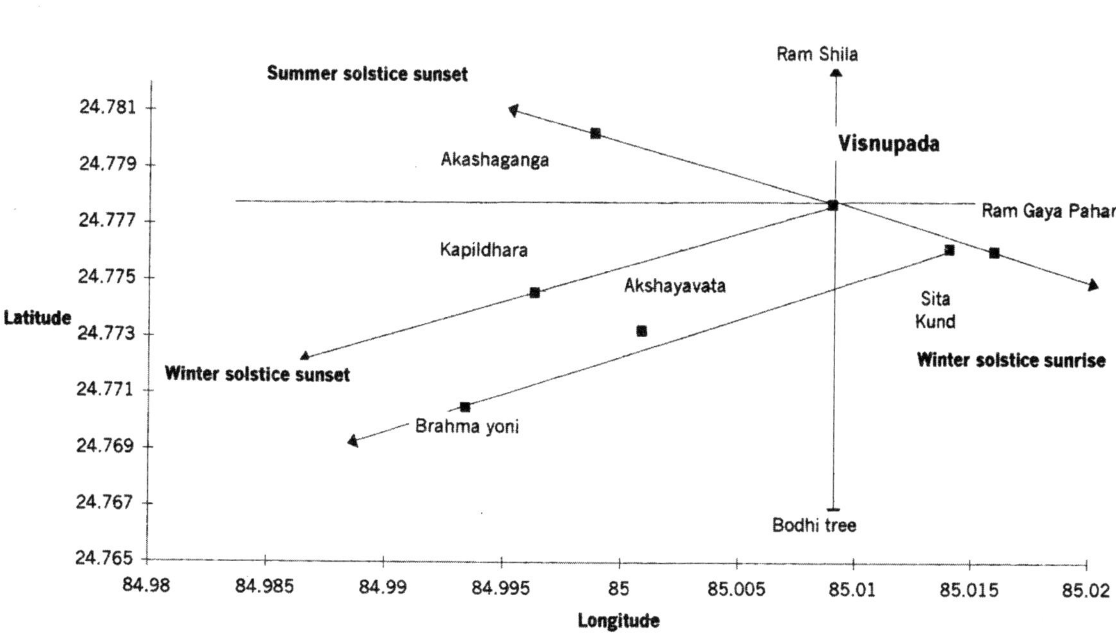

fig. 6.4: Astronomical alignments at Gaya.

on the western horizon may also have been meaningful. A suitable viewpoint for solar phenomena, with a better horizon than at Vishnupad itself, is the rocky spur that lies just west of the temple. From that point the setting sun at summer solstice sets approximately over Akasha Ganga (the ecliptic) (26.09° north of west). In the opposite direction, the sun rises at winter solstice approximately over Ramgaya Pahar (25.3° south of east). Also visible from the spur above Vishnupad almost precisely (based upon our GPS measurements) symmetrical with Akasha Ganga, the sun at winter solstice sets (dies) over Kapildhara (26.09° south of west). The solar symbolism of these two sites is notable: the Akasha Ganga is the ecliptic, the path of the sun in the sky. Kapiladhara is located where the Ganga "dies" flowing into the Bay of Bengal.

A north-south axis also passes through Vishnupad, such that, at noon, when highest in the sky, the sun is approximately in the direction of the Bodhi tree of Bodh-Gaya, 9.1 km to the south. In the opposite direction, toward the north celestial pole, lies Pita Maheshvara at 1.4 km and Rama-Shila at 3.9 km. These solar geometries involve major features of the natural landscape and suggest a long standing tradition of sun worship.

Tranformation and Self-organization of Gaya

Paul (1983) suggests that the footprint in the Vishnupad temple, identified as that of the sun god Vishnu in pre-Buddhist times, was the original impetus for the early preeminence of Gaya. Such a possibility raises the intriguing question of why sun worship has been eclipsed today by the *shraddha* ceremony. The radial lines extending from the vicinity of Vishnupad to solstitial directions are consistent with an early importance of active sun worship on the outcrop near the footprint.

The meaning of Vishnupad both as the footprint of Vishnu striding across the universe and as the morning-noon-sunset diurnal cycle of the sun may have evoked a complex constellation of symbolism involving the sun, as both creator and destroyer, the source of all life as well as the fire of the final conflagration and may have provided thereby the setting for today's emphasis on the *shraddha* ceremony. Other features of the symbolic landscape, such as the Phalgu River, the eternal banyon and Preta-shila combine with the sun as destroyer to provide the multiplicity of symbols and meaning that may have empowered the *shraddha* rituals and generated the spiritual magnetism of the Gaya *tirtha*.

We consider two models for transformation from sun worship to ancestor worship at Gaya. They differ largely in the rapidity and deterministic nature of the process.

Pilgrimage Ecosystem

The first possibility may be described as a self-organizing ecosystem. Although once a major form of worship in India, sun worship declined after the tenth century and was replaced by other forms of worship that were closer to the emotional and spiritual needs of worshippers and pilgrims. There may have been a gradual change as ancestor worship became more meaningful to pilgrims and replaced sun worship.

As we have already suggested a pilgrimage system may be viewed as a total ecosystem, which contains a multiplicity of interrelating connected elements. We employ an ecological model as a metaphor for the transformation of the Gaya *tirtha*. Within a living ecosystem a specie is characterized by a rate of birth, a rate associated with death, and the ability of the ecosystem to support the species. The population of that specie will continue to grow until the environment has reached its carrying capacity and thus becomes saturated. Restated in the context of pilgrimage, the dynamics of the system will be established by the rate of inflow of people into a pilgrimage, the rate of departure (by death, infirmity or loss of commitment), and the *tirtha*'s ability to continue to support the number of visitors. The growth in the number of pilgrims, N may be expressed as

$$dN/\,dt = (K_1 + K_2)N(M\text{-}N)\text{-}DN$$

where K_1 is a measure of the birth of pilgrims and K_2 is a measure of new commitments to pilgrimage; M is a measure of the ability of the centre to attract, support, and sustain pilgrimage. The function D is a measure of the death of pilgrims and the loss of interest in the particular pilgrimage. As it is described, this form, the growth of numbers of pilgrimage is approximately a deterministic process, which, once started, will continue until a stable state is reached (*fig.* 6.5). Over time, the pilgrimage will grow until it reaches stability established by the attractive power of the site and the relative rates of birth and death of pilgrims and their commitments. The maximum value will be achieved at a value of $N = M - D/K$.

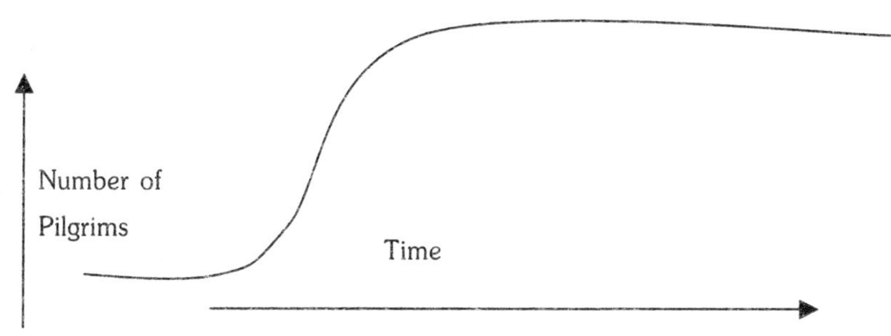

fig. 6.5: Metastablility and Transformation

Because pilgrimages are treated as interrelated parts of a total ecosystem, new pilgrimage ideologies will have to compete intellectually and emotionally with the old to acquire adherents and obtain a place in the symbolic landscape. A number of competing, alternative ideologies may appear because of the openness of the system insured by the constant flow of pilgrims from the outside and by the power of the place (the combination of the natural setting, the built-up shrines and the influences of fellow pilgrims) to inspire individual visions.

In order for a new pilgrimage to dominate over the old, it will have to have a value of M-D/K that is greater than the old one. Basically, it will have to have greater spiritual magnetism (larger M) (Preston 1992) than the old and be able to acquire adherents faster (larger K) and lose adherents (smaller D) less rapidly. M may become larger because of a more powerful vision, more appropriate to the needs of devotees or a greater number of symbolic attractors in the *tirtha*. The limiting value of M may be basically related to the success of a pilgrimage ideology to compete for the limited time and commitment of pilgrims. At Gaya the interlacing of different features of the landscape appear to have amplified the spiritual magnetism of the place and produced a coherent pilgrimage ecosystem that supports the honouring of ancestors in the *shraddha* ceremonies.

The growth of the spiritual magnetism of *shraddha* may be represented by the following diagram in which we indicate the major features of the symbolic landscape that relate to death and time (*fig.* 6.6). The presence of these symbols may have reinforced the power of *shraddha*.

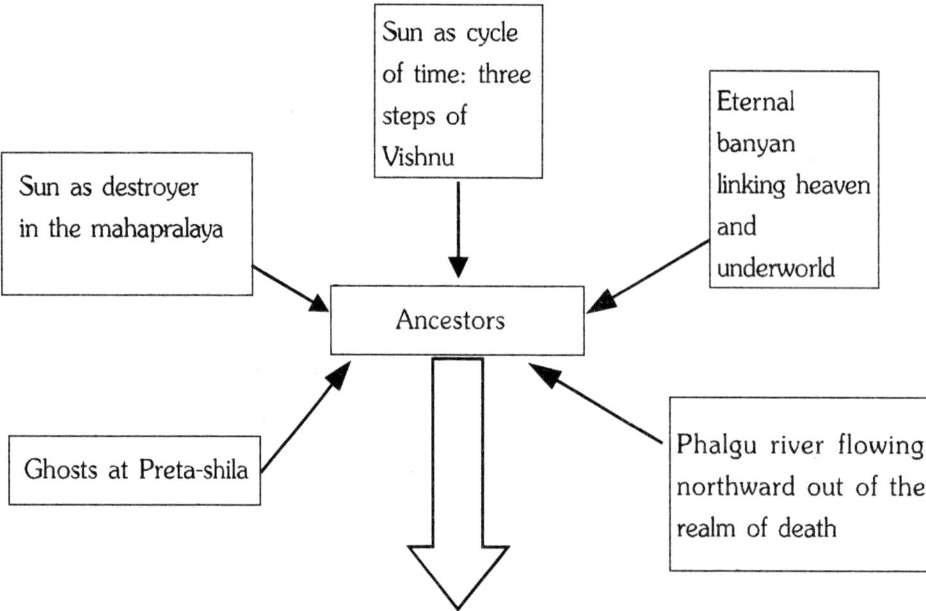

fig. 6.6: Growth of shraddha at Gaya.

The effect of the growth of *shraddha* symbolism and ritual and the consequent displacement of sun worship may be represented as follows (*fig.* 6.7).

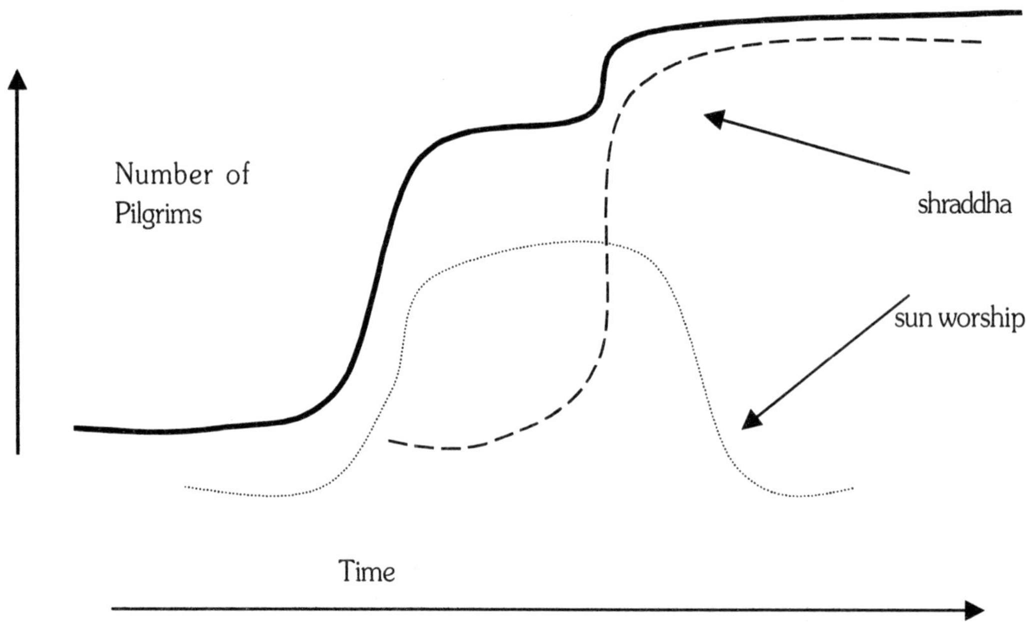

fig. 6.7: Metastablility and transformation

The alternate model involves a rapid transformation of a system due to metastability, non-linearity and positive feedback. The transformation emerges from a metastable regime in which a number of future outcomes are possible. Each differs from the other by only small degrees but diverge from each other exponentially as they evolve in time. Metastability may have been established in Gaya due to the growth of pilgrims drawn by the solar aspect of Vishnupad. The mutual interactions of many individuals may have thereby established a situation where unpredictable small chance-events could be amplified through positive feedback and non-linearity. The openness and intensity of the pilgrimage experience lends itself to those energies, sudden visions or insights that may have powerful influences on other pilgrims.

Such an event or series of events may have led to the ascendance of *shraddha* at Gaya as suggested in the following figure (*fig.* 6.8):

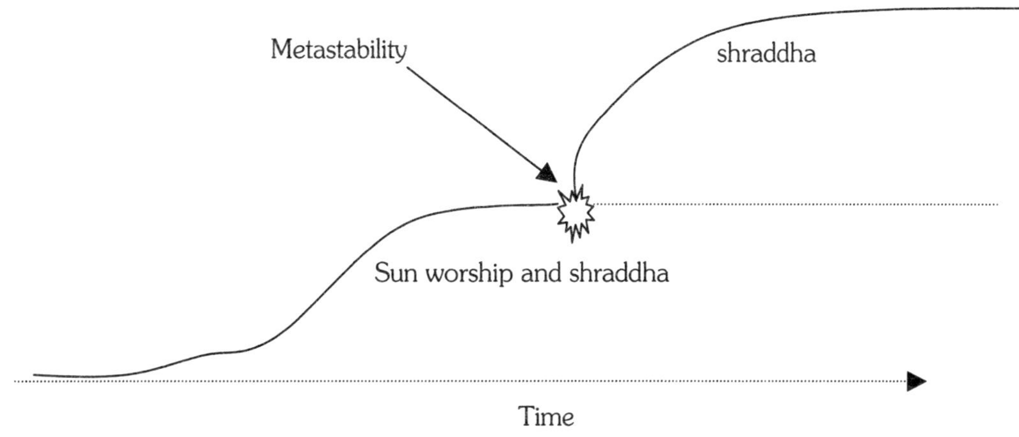

fig. 6.8: Transformation of sun worship to shraddha.

Concluding Remarks

Pilgrimage did not arrive at Gaya onto a clean slate but it developed in a place with geographic uniqueness as well as rich and deep local traditions. Hills, the north flowing river, and the natural beauty and drama of the area contributed to its attraction and power. Sun worship may have been an early source of spiritual magnetism and the primary attractor for pilgrims. The very openness of Gaya due to the steady influx of pilgrims, each with his or her own needs and spiritual inspiration, established a fertile ground for change and a form of metastability. Eventually elements of the Gaya pilgrimage landscape such as Vishnupad, Akshayavata, and Preta-shila, which may have initially developed independently of each other, appear to have come together with the pilgrims and priests to form a symbolic whole that encouraged and supported *shraddha* ceremonies.

References

Asher, Fredrick M., 1989, "Gaya: Monuments of the Pilgrimage Town," *Marg* (Bombay), vol. 40, No.1, pp. 45-60.

Eliade, Mircea, 1958, *Patterns in Comparative Religion*, London: Sheed & Ward.

Irwin, John, 1983, "The Ancient Pillar-cult at Prayag (Allahabad): Its pre-Asokan origins," *Journal of the Royal Asiatic Society*, London 1983.

Keilhorn, F., 1887, "A Gaya Inscription of Yakshapala," *The Indian Antiquary*, 16 : 63-66.

Mahabharata (*Mbh*), Critical ed. by V.S. Sukthankar and others, 19 vols., Baroda: Bhandarkar Oriental Research Institute, 1933-59. (d. *c.* fourth century BCE).

Paul, Debjani, 1983, "Antiquity of the Vishnupad at Gaya," *East and West*, N. S., 35 (1-3) : 103-41.

Preston, James J., 1992, "Spiritual magnetism: an organizing principle for the study of pilgrimage," in *Sacred Journeys: The Anthropology of Pilgrimage*, ed. A. Morinis, Wesport: Greenwood Press.

Singh, Rana P.B., 1999, "Sacredscape, manescape and cosmogony at Gaya India: A Study in Sacred Geography," *National Geographical Journal of India* (B.H.U., Varanasi), 45(1-4): 34-63.

Vayu Purana (*VyP*), Anandashram Sanskrit Series No. 49, Poona: Anandashram Mudranalaya, 1860. (d. *c.* 7th-8th century CE).

Vidyarthi, L.P., 1978, *The Sacred Complex in Hindu Gaya*, 2nd edn., New Delhi : Concept Publ. Co.

Williams, Monier, 1876, "Sraddha ceremonies at Gaya," *The Indian Antiquary*, 5 : 200-04.

7

Earthly Presence of Heavenly Bodies Navagrahas of Tamil Nadu

Marianna Kropf

THE "centre" of a pilgrimage often consists of a number of *tirthas* or holy places, to be visited following a given order with respect to specific time-periods. The core of this paper is such a pilgrimage circle (*yatra*) located in the Kumbhakonam area (Tamil Nadu) consisting of nine temples, each associated with one of the nine *grahas* or planetary deities — which are usually conceptualized as a group referred to as Navagraha.[1]

I shall draw some of the outlines which will be of importance to follow my arguments in situating the *Navagraha-yatra* within general conceptions on the complex of pilgrimage. The main focus of the *yatra*, the nine planetary deities from Surya and Chandra, the five planets up to the mathematically defined moon-nodes, Rahu and Ketu, shall be traced back to their textual origins and gradual formation into a group of nine. Some of their characteristics as given mainly within *Jyotisha* and Pauranic sources are closely related to their iconographic development — which I neglect here — and ritual integration. I shall restrict the latter to the temple ritual context, therefore, ignoring private as well as the professional *Jyotishis*' ritual practices. Within a brief description of the nine temple locations I shall point out the differences concerning the position and distinct features of the *graha*-shrines within their specific temple settlements. The amount of ritual attention given to each of the planetary deities meets with different motivations and interests towards *Navagraha-yatra* with regard to pilgrims as well as temple authorities, priestly and governmental.

Up to here one could assume to get a pilgrimage circle presented which coherently fits into a concept of self-organizing complexity outlining a process of fluid equilibrium on different levels. Instead, within a second part, I shall elaborate on reasons to contradict an underlying concept of self-organization. One point is the obvious marginality of the *yatra*-cycle as a whole; my core argument tends to demonstrate a discrepancy between ritual practice that has grown out of tradition and the *yatra* layout. I shall call back into mind a restricted selection of general features characterizing pilgrimage complexes to make some concrete observations.[2] I shall herefore refer to Preston's reflections on components of spiritual magneticism as creative for the forming of a pilgrimage centre; I shall take up the distinction of spiritual *versus* instrumental, this-world-oriented motivations guiding someone towards a pilgrimage centre (Morinis 1992: 6); I will further touch on Victor Turner's concept of communitas experience as contrasted with a stress on individual concerns following the pilgrims' path (Turner 1974).

In his recently published book on Tibetan pilgrimages Alex McKay stresses — as do other scholars with him — the need for a multiperspective approach towards pilgrimage phenomena (McKay 1998: 3):

> The individual pilgrims and their experiences and understandings of their journey as well as pilgrimage sites themselves may be seen against an ever-changing backdrop of politics and economics, sectarian and political competition and co-existence and issues of power and authority. The pilgrim is a part of a religious phenomenon but also of a socio-religious and political system in constant flux.

There is a network of relations and components that result in such a pilgrimage complex. The multiple nodes and observable phenomena may appear as having a reality on their own; in fact they are built by human thought and continual action. And this will be my point of reference to elaborate on the deficiencies of natural science-grown models to explain social phenomena. I have not yet met with all the requirements necessary to give a definitive account on my subject; still the material presented will hopefully stimulate the discussion on topics of pilgrimage and complexity.

Throughout Hindu traditions the *Navagraha*, as they are thought to manifest themselves through eternal laws of influences on terrestrial life, generally claim for paramount importance within individual as well as social processes related to time and space. The explanations of the origin of their powers are oscillating: concepts of seeing the *grahas* as a kind of messengers of some deity's will, mostly Shiva or Vishnu, are found beside those to style them as acting in their own rights. They may as well be conceptualized as parts of a self-developing, everlasting cosmic law; more recent arguments even call upon natural science-based explanations related to gravitation or magnetic fields. As a proof is beyond human tools I shall not argue further but rather adhere to the generally accepted apprehension that there is a certain kind of influence or intensified earthly presence of the planetary deities being explained in different ways according to the chains of argumentation followed.

For an understanding of what significance and conceptual status is given to the *Navagraha* let us first look at textual sources referring to their origins and constitution. Surya is already praised as a principal deity since the very beginnings of textual tradition and he has kept his paramount position, although modified, up to present time. Chandra as a clear-cut deity is not stated within Vedic sources but is gaining more and more of a deity's profile in post-Vedic times; this development includes his identification with *soma*, the Vedic nectar of immortality, his connection with fertility and medicine and his Upanishadic conception as the abode of ancestral souls. For the five proper planets in the English meaning of the term we can't find undoubted passages within the Vedas. Later on, all of them are in some way or the other included into common mythological complexes as related in Pauranic and Epic texts but, even styled as deities, they never gain a higher level of importance besides the context of *Jyotisha* (one of the Hindu scientific branches specialized in the interpretation of movements and constellations of heavenly bodies). The generic outlines of the moon-nodes, Rahu and Ketu, show specific associations: Rahu, as the ascending node of the moon, has developed from the demon who is thought to be responsible for solar as well as lunar eclipses; only from the eleventh century onwards the singular form Ketu came to designate the descending moon-node whereas ancient writers used to name all kinds of celestial optical phenomena as *ketus*.

These obviously very distinct origins are gradually brought together under the term *graha* which not exclusively refers to celestial bodies but rather stands for phenomena associated with the idea of "seizing" or "taking possession," as they appear in the context of medical treatises dealing with diseases or spirit possession. From the fifth up to the tenth century the gradual formation of a stable group of nine *grahas* as *Navagraha* took place. From that time onwards this very group is ritually adressed as one unit or entity symbolizing an all-encompassing completeness which is accentuated by their identification with the eight directions in space (including the centre occupied by the Sun) or their representation as *graha-purusha*.[3] This wholeness is obviously not challenged by later discoveries of further planets.

The oldest traceable versions of iconographic representations within Hindu temples go back to the sixth century showing the *grahas* cut out of stone on lintels and doorways. Comparing the main features of their early iconography, an influence of other than Indian cultures is quite obvious, following scholars like David Pingree (1964) and Markel (1995). A common form today of iconographic representation of the *Navagraha* is their installation as a group on an altar-like square platform (*navagraha-mandapa*) somewhere in the temple entrance area (see *Fig.* 7.1); devotees will, on their way to the main shrine, pay ritual attention to the nine *grahas* present in these *mandapas* (Türstig 1980, Pingree 1964 and 1981, Kirfel 1920, Markel 1995, Bühnemann 1989, Bühnemann 1988). Beside those iconographical depictions, different kinds of ritual manuals, not only within strictly *Jyotisha* contexts, give a number of other possible, mainly momentary, material forms to include the *Navagraha* for ritual purposes carried out privately or within temple functions.[4] Such handbooks on ritual frequently describe *yantras* or *mandalas* (geometrical designs attributed to specific deities) as well as nine symbols, nine gems, nine different plants or nine specific metals associated with the *grahas* (see *Fig.* 7.2).

The specific characteristics based on astronomical observations and calculations, as they are ascribed to each of the nine *grahas* and further developed by *Jyotisha* specialists, account

N

SHUKRA	**BUDHA**	**KETU**
MANGALA	**SURYA**	**RAHU**
CHANDRA	**GURU**	**SHANI**

S

fig. 7.1: Each of the *grahas* is associated with one of the eight directions in space. This particular arrangement is found in the Natamandir of the Sun Temple of Konarka.

for singular rituals, mainly of the pacification-type (*shanti*), for each of the *grahas* following one's own horoscope — be it of a king or, later on, of any individual bound within his or her personal, social, even cosmological environments.

One can distinguish two kinds of rituals for the planetary deities. First we find a ritual integration of the *Navagraha* as a group of nine equal parts; each of them is verbally addressed in a similar manner following a conventional order as it is given in the corresponding texts. This form is found as preliminary of a more elaborate ritual complex or it is executed in a very brief manner which can be reduced, in the course of a temple visit, to the simple offering of a butter lamp by the devotee; the ritual addressing of the *Navagraha* as a compact group is done here mainly to bestow success for the following ritual actions by keeping away possible negative influences out of planetary constellations. Additionally, in a series of priestly rituals, the *Navagraha* stand for an explicit integration of the whole cosmos, including its dimensions of space and time; here we find a more abstract level of meaning given to the *Navagraha*, their inclusion again stands for a ritual preparation of the cosmic field within which the very ritual will take place. As a second type we find rituals focused on one specific *graha*, such a ritual act is much stronger time-bound. It is motivated by one's own horoscope configuration or by a given planetary constellation or position generally viewed as problematic. This second type is again directed towards negative influences feared or already experienced — which therefore

fig. 7.2: A popular depiction of the nine planetary deities in their anthropomorphic forms, showing them with vehicle (*vahana*), specific attributes and sometimes with their symbols (square, rectangle, triangle, arrow, flag); most prominently placed in the centre figures Surya on his chariot driven by seven horses.

ask for pacification or reconciliation of the *graha* suspected of causing such troubles.

For both types, the rituals address to the whole group and the one directed towards one specific *graha*. The aim of the ritual lies mainly in appeasing rather than worshipping, executed out of respect, anxiety or even fear rather than out of devotion. The corresponding ritual actions as applied for the appeasing of the *grahas* belong to the *shanti* category. This fact actually approximates the *Navagraha* to a much wider field of celestial and terrestrial omens being interpreted and acted on; further on, *shanti* rites are an integral part of *abhichara*-practices as they are classified into six branches known as *shatkarmani*. In addition to *shanti*, those magical acts include ritually induced subordination or hate, bewitching or even the ritual killing of an enemy. Such contexts make it clear that the planetary deities are not belonging to a canon of so to say regular deities but rather occupy a ritual category of their own.

Even though the *Navagrahas* as a group nowadays regularly appear within temples, they never came to be located in the *garbhagriha*, the central shrine or inner sanctum of a temple. Few temples dedicated to Surya have survived up to our days — one of them being part of the *Navagraha* circle here discussed — only, figuring as a main deity, Surya is not put into the *graha* context but rather seen as a god in his own right (Malville 1989). Whether there ever existed, within Hinduism, a similar branch having Chandra, the moon-god, at its very centre, remains a point of controversy — in any case no present moon-temple would give evidence of such a cult. We can say for sure that neither the five planets nor the moon-nodes ever came to occupy such a position. Nevertheless, several texts list temple sites all over India having affinities for one or the other of the *grahas* and people continue to be aware of *tirthas* associated with *graha*-worship or pacification; especially *tirthas* for Shani are widely spread.

Unique is a layout of loosely connected temples by each of them housing one of the nine *grahas*. To find such nine temples conceptualized as a pilgrimage cycle in Eastern Tamil Nadu arises the question of whether this cycle, labelled as *Navagraha-yatra*, is consistent with typical features generally related to pilgrimage centres as well as to personal needs of individually motivated *graha* pilgrims. The pilgrimage setting as it presents itself to the observer consists of nine Shaiva temples, each one associated with one of the *grahas*.[5] The,"Navagraham Chart," distributed by Raya's Hotel in Kumbhakonam, gives the following order of the nine *graha-sthalas*, located at distances around 10 to 60 km from Kumbhakonam:

(1) Tirunallaru (Tirunallaru): Saturn — Shani

(2) Vaithisvaran Koil (Vaittisvaran Koyil): Mars (Tamil: Cevvay)

(3) Perumpallam (Perum Pallam): Ketu

(4) Thiruvenkadu (Tiruvenkatu): Mercury — Budha

(5) Kanchanur (Kancanur): Venus — Shukra (Tamil: Velli)

(6) Suryanar Koil (Curiyanar Koyil): Sun — Surya

(7) Thingalur (Tinkalur): Moon — Chandra

(8) Thirunageshvaram (Tirunakeccuram Koyil): Rahu

(9) Alangudi (Alankuti): Jupiter — Guru

Following local priests' information, the temples are under government control and are therefore supported by public funds. The executing priests belong to the denomination of Shivacharyas; whereas Suriyanar Koil and Tirunallaru temple occupy up to 20 and more priestly specialists, Thingalur, where Chandra resides, is run by just one single priest assisted by his son.

How and when the temples came to be connected through their respective *Navagraha* shrines is not clear, the few indications given do not allow some definite answer. The priests asked were not aware of its possible origins. Not a single reference to a textual source of the *yatra* could be found. Not even the *Sthala Puranas*, as they are available for each of the nine temples, mention the cycle as a whole. Only at two temples, at the time of my visit, an extra list indicating all nine *graha-sthalas* was distributed. However there is a recently created *Navagraha-yatra* homepage introducing its presentation as follows:

> The Tamil Nadu Tourism Development Corporation announced on June 26, 1997 in Chennai, a "Navagraha worship package Tour," covering nine temples in the State dedicated to the Navagraha deities. Pilgrims wishing to visit the temples can leave from Chennai on Friday night and return on Monday morning.[6]

This points to a promotion of the *Navagraha* pilgrimage tour within a rather touristic than religious context. The fact remains that — as the *Sthala Puranas*, the priests' interviews, the pilgrims' conceptions or local people's statements show — there is lack of a commonly shared corporate identity with regard to the *yatra*. Rather, depending on the background and personal involvement, mostly different opinions relating to the *Navagraha* pilgrimage — which will frequently include complete ignorance of the whole matter — are aired/made.

Whether the selection of the *graha*-locations out of a number of possible temple sites follows some spacial logic, is, at the moment, beyond my findings (Peston 1980). Given that all nine temples are dedicated to Shiva, who is consequently styled as being their master, we can infer that there is, at least to some extent, a sectarian motive included; out of textual tradition it becomes clear that the *Navagrahas* are not generally thought to be under Shiva's control. Most common is their submission to different deities listed as *Adhidevata*; this may underline the fact that their relevance is beyond specific Hindu denominations (see Table 7.1).

Table 7.1: The Adhidevata of the nine grahas following different sources

Graha	*Adhidevata (JaiGS)*	*Adhidevata (MaP)*	*Adhidevata (Tamil Nadu)*
Surya (Sun)	Agni	Shiva	Shiva
Chandra (Moon)	Varuna	Uma	Parvati
Mangala (Mars)	Prithivi	Skanda	Murukan (Skanda)
Budha (Mercury)	Vishnu-Narayana	Hari (Vishnu)	Vishnu
Guru (Jupiter)	Indra	Brahma	Brahma
Shukra (Venus)	Indrani	Indra	Velliammai
Shani (Saturn)	Prajapati	Yama-Dharmaraja	Yama
Rahu (ascending node)	Shesha	Kala	Bhadrakali/Durga
Ketu (descending node)	Brahma	Chitragupta	Indra

Note: Each of the *grahas* is associated with one of the eight directions in space. Depicted in their iconographic forms and joined into a group on a square platform (*navagraha-mandapa*), the Navagraha should not look at each other while they are taking up the four cardinal directions.

The placement and outlook of the *graha*-shrines within the nine temple compounds, as far as they exist at all, differ a lot; whereas Surya is given the very central position within the *garbhagriha*, the other *graha*-shrines are mostly placed within the first *prakara*,[7] in some proximity to the sanctum; the shrines of Shani (Saturn) and Rahu are majestic in size and decoration, both are given intense ritual attendance; Chandra is given a simple *mandapa* to reside; Cevvay (Mars), located at the very prominent *tirtha* of Vaithisvarankoil, the site where Shiva manifests himself as the lord of healers and which is related to the *Ramayana* epic, easily escapes one's notice being situated within plenty of other shrines; the *pranapratishtha* ceremony for the newly installed Ketu-*murti* (stone idol) only took place in 1986, after a court decision confirming that Ketu is due to have his own material "body" as a worldly manifestation. In the case of Budha (Mercury), the shrine is located in a small temple on his own at the very edge of the temple compound of Tiruvenkatu. Shukra (Venus) and Guru (Jupiter) don't even have their own shrines; they are honoured through the *murtis* of Shiva as Shri Agnishvara Svami and Shiva-Dakshinamurti, respectively.

Every temple presents a more or less elaborate list of services executed on request by the priests: They mainly consist in varieties of *archana* (offering of prayers and light), *japa* (recitation), *abhisheka* (ritual bath) and *homa* (fire offering), all of them available for one specific or all nine *grahas*. Whereas *archana* and *abhisheka* are mainly executed on the *murti* itself, for *homa* the *Navagraha* are invoked into richly decorated *kalashas*[8] (vases) placed close to the *homakunda* (fire altar for sacrifice). All the *grahas* have their own time-table for daily and weekly services in coordination with *jyotisha* calculations. Additionally there may take place festivals, including extra ritual attendance and festive processions escorted by a group of musicians and going in different circles or *prakaras* around, with the inner sanctum as the very centre. A special ritual procedure is common for Rahu: he receives mainly pure milk *abhishekas*; the milk — offered by the pilgrims and sometimes flowing in considerable quantities — is supposed to change its colour into blue as a visible sign of the strong powers emerging from that very Rahu emanation. Suriyanar Koil is designed as the very heart of the *yatra*. As *surya-kshetra* this temple is already referred to in texts from the eleventh century onwards. The other *grahas* came to be installed only some 80 or 100 years ago (following the information of a priest) around the sanctum, each one getting a small temple of his own (Figure 7.3). Pilgrims will visit all of the shrines in a

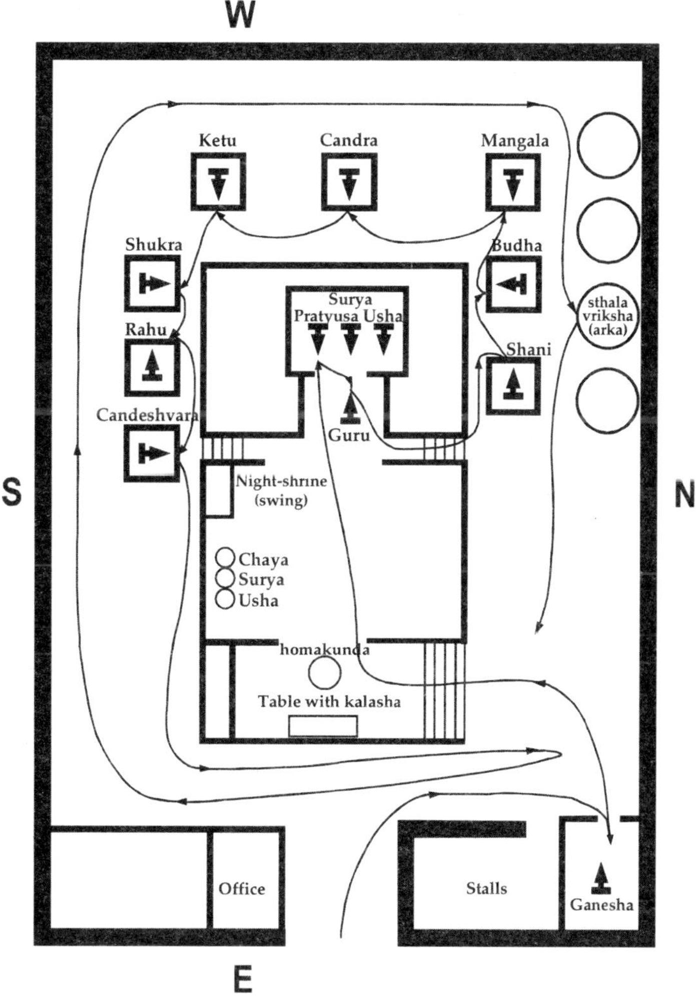

fig. 7.3: Suryanar Koil (Curiyanar Koyil); the arrow-line shows the way as it is usually followed by devotees visiting the Navagraha shrines.

given order, starting, after the worship of Ganesha, with the central shrine where Surya is installed, flanked by Usha and Pratyusha as his consorts.

With each of the *graha-sthalas* we find a more or less elaborate collection of myths referring to the origins and possible benefits of the *graha* present. As all the temples are dedicated to Shiva, mythological arguments seem to intend a clearing up of divine power-politics by explaining the relative positions of the *grahas*. One such example of locally bound myths runs as follows: Once upon a time there was a saint called Galavar who was troubled by the detection of a very bad planetary constellation within his birth chart. He consulted the Shastras but there was no advice. Hence he decided to do severe penance. In the course of time the planetary deities took note of his extraordinary efforts and finally became so much impressed and flattered that they readily accepted to fulfil the saint's wish to be freed from all negative influences caused by them. Learning about such undue highhandedness of the *Navagraha* the *Adhidevata* insulted and punished them with leprosy for having usurped their limited power as mere executors of a given divine karmic law. The *Navagraha*, soon struck with that terrible disease, begged for a remedy to get release. They were finally sent to the land of Cholas (formerly ruling dynasty in Tamil Nadu) and advised to take baths in nine different *tirthas*. So they did and at their last station, which was a holy pond close to Suriyanar Koil, Shiva accepted their remorse, freed them of the divine curse and made them his satellites again.

Another story connected with Tirunallaru as *shani-sthala* is related to a well-known episode out of the Nala-Damayanti myth. Following the local version, the demon Shani, in accordance with the gods' will, created all possible bad luck to happen to king Nala — as the heavenly males were all offended about Damayanti preferring a human fiancé to all of them. When Nala realized the inescapable real cause of all his disaster he turned to a famous saint for advice. He was sent by that wise man to Tirunallaru for penance and bath. Arriving there Nala experienced instant release from all his troubles. But as soon as he tried to leave the temple compound he was again seized by Shani's evil influences. Then Shiva intervened and asked Shani to stop his malicious game. The demon refused stating that he could not do otherwise as it was his demoniac fate to act in this way. Almighty Shiva then made him a god so that he could challenge his fate at free will. That's how Shani came to stay with Shiva at Tirunallaru and Nala regained all possible happiness with Damayanti at his side.

To a certain extent the following guidelines are taken up within all the myths: First we are given explanations for the affiliation of *graha* and *kshetra*; further on we find mythological explanations for special powers or healing effects as they are attributed to a particular place; without exception the superiority of Shiva over the *grahas* is emphasized — Shiva is their real *guru* or master, he is healer and bestower of final release and therefore he is to be worshipped above all; the myths are finally attached to episodes known out of the so-called High tradition as well as to accounts transmitted from the legendary Nayanmars, the highly valued Tamil Poet-Saints who became an integral part of the south Indian Shaiva Siddhanta tradition as it remained very popular up to our days.

We could conclude that the importance attributed to each one among the nine *graha-sthalas* is made up of three components. One is the possible influence ascribed to a specific *graha* — the amount of ritual importance is according to the negative powers feared. Therefore we find a very prominent shrine for Shani at Tirunallaru. To a similar extent for Rahu we have a shrine at Tirunagesvaram, furnished with an appropriate infrastructure to handle the crowds of pilgrims visiting those sites at corresponding dates; the ritual effort corresponding to the extent of negativity and threat of a *graha*'s specific influences supplies as well an explanation for the fact that rather positively associated planetary deities, especially Guru and Shukra, create no urge for an elaborate ritual attendance. A second component of "spiritual magnetism" related to the *graha-sthalas* results from the fame attributed to Shiva himself, binding a specific measure of power corres-ponding to his local manifestations. As the myths show, those local manifestations are interwoven with the specific *grahas* present, the latter being subdued to Shiva's will; especially Shiva's curing powers seem to be a common trait adding to the fame of the temples. Thirdly we find an additional importance given to each temple by the legendary records of the Nayanmars. Either some among them are said to have performed miracles there or they are ascribed hymns of praise addressing that very location.

The mythologically expressed tradition relates each of the *graha-sthalas* to specific results possibly attained by the execution of a number of adequate rituals. In a wider sense they may be seen as especially powerful *graha-kshetras* which will intensify the positive outputs of a pilgrim's ritual actions directed towards them. Concerning the nine *graha-tirthas*, there is no clear-cut distinction between the *graha*'s specific powers and the benefits bestowed by Shiva as their master. As we have seen, the appeasing of the planetary deities is generally acted out by addressing them as a group, having the view to keep away all possible negative influences. The inclination to undergo specific rituals is given by negatively interpreted constellations in one's own birth chart. The resulting *doshas*, bound to create troubles, may be reduced or even dissoluted by corresponding ritual measures. Those are usually advised by a an astrologer, be it the family priest or a practising *Jyotishi*. Such *doshas* are named after the troubling *graha* (*rahu-dosha, shukra-dosha* and so on) or they may denote a specific problem, say *putra-dosha* as inclination to problems with begetting children, mainly sons, or *vivaha-dosha*, which indicates problematic constellations which hinder successful marriage. The hope for cure of serious diseases is especially related to the fulfilment of pilgrimage to a specific *graha-sthala*: Angustam, a still quite common skin disease, may fade by prescribed ritual actions executed at Vaittishvaran Koil where there is a temple for Mars/Cevvay; psychological disturbances as well as leprosy are said to be conquered at *chandra-tirtha* in Thingalur, especially by taking bath in the wholy

Chandrapushkarani-pool and by worshipping Shiva-Kailasanatha, and so forth. The worship of all nine *grahas* at Suriyanar Koil is said to remove all kinds of *graha-dosha*.

By far the most feared of all the nine *grahas* is Shani (Saturn). All over India we find temples where Shani is given intensified ritual care. *Shani-dosha*, conceived as a strongly ill-influenced period in one's life, asks for intensified mesures to appease Shani, trying to avoid the worst. *Shani-dosha* covers a period of 7.5 years; it is based on Saturn crossing the zodiacal sign (*rashi*) where the moon is located in one's birth chart, including its neighbouring signs; every about 2.5 years, when Saturn is entering a new sign (*shanipeyarchi*), thousands of people dismayed by such a constellation will gather at Tirunallaru to have *shani-darshana*, they will lit oil lamps fed with black sesame to be offered to Shani and take a bath in the holy tank belonging to the temple. The moment of *Shanipeyarchi*, the transgression of that planet from one *rashi* or zodiacal sign to the next, therefore, involves the most careful ritual attendance.

Should we find some general categories of individual motivation for a procedure of *graha-shanti*, the ritual appeasing of the planetary deities, we could design a triangle field having in its extremes; first, very concrete interests concerning everyday life; second, fears and problems based on ill influences of specific *grahas* and third, the appeasing of the *Navagraha* as part of precautions to bring about successfull undertakings, ritual or otherwise. A comparison with generally stated motivations for pilgrims to head for a specific pilgrimage, scaled from purely spiritual gain to this-world-oriented instrumentality, shows a clear stress towards the latter.

As to the aspect of communitas as Victor Turner ascribed it to pilgrimage in opposition to a predominant individual experience — in contrast to everydays' constructions of self and society — *Navagraha-yatra* definitely stresses the individual aspect. Pilgrims are inclined to set-off for a specific *sthala* of the *graha-yatra* to accomplish with personal needs, suffering and desires which are given by very individual states of affair as far as they appear to be caused by planetary influences. Maybe events like *Shani* or *Gurupeyarchi* — both attracting masses of people — could be stated as including an experience of dissoluting ordinary conceptions of social position or individual inclination; but they will remain strongly time-bound.

Even though the association of *grahas* with worldly affairs seems to prevail, we should nevertheless keep in mind a higher level of cosmological implications related to the *Navagraha*. Conceptions of time and space are closely related to them. They are associated with regular movements observable in the sky (Fuller 1980; Diehl 1956). The *Navagrahas* are styled as the executors of karmic laws, binding humans' fate as it is designed in the moment of birth (Malville and Swaminathan 1998). *Jyotisha* is therefore, in one of its paramount prospects, a means to obtain sacred knowledge about divine plans or karmic rules related to human destiny.

Some specific observations rather than a definitive account on the worldly networks around the nine *graha*-temples, as they are part of the *Navagraha-yatra,* lead to the following results:

- The *Navagrahas* do not belong to a category of divine phenomena, be it deities, saints or naturally given sacred sites, that typically inject pilgrimage in one or the other way. However there are temples all over India known for their extraordinarily powerful *graha*-shrines.
- Within ritual practices towards the *grahas* dominates an instrumental means-to-ends conception alimented by time-bound astrological considerations; as the basic ritual mood is one of anxiety and fear there is no specific stress on effective spiritual growth or insight — as it is stated an integral part of classical pilgrimage concepts — but rather on the hope to effect pragmatic results.
- The conception of a *yatra* as outlined here doesn't really meet with popular demand given with singular needs, expectations and motivations of pilgrims searching for remedies to face critical situations they assume to originate from planetary influences. Such traditionally performed ritual practices, including the *Navagraha*, point either towards the group addressed as a whole or they are directed towards one specific planetary deity out of the nine; there is no such ritual tradition as to have them worshipped or appeased one by one.
- The borders between pilgrimage and tourism appear to be blurred. Within the *Navagraha-yatra* we find features pointing towards a touristic conception as well as components that generally characterize a pilgrimage. The pilgrimage tour, as it is promoted on the internet, has a fashionable touch, neglecting the aspect of proper motivations as they would emerge — strongly bound within cosmological as well as individual time rhythms — from one's own birth chart.
- The concept of the *yatra* doesn't seem to convince the priestly authorities of the temples involved; there is no intensified exchange or even cooperation among the corresponding temple trusts as it could be expected of an integral and welcomed pilgrimage concept embracing all nine temples.

The materials considered so far bring me to the conclusion that the *Navagraha-yatra* is in its essence an artificial construct designed out of other than naturally grown or self-driven motives and developments. Even though the cycle of the nine temples with the *grahas* enshrined shows characteristics of a pilgrimage centre, it doesn't really meet with the needs of pilgrims but rather seems to be directed towards increasing the popularity and fame of the sites. Neither myths nor textual references are there to connect all the *graha*-shrines — which allows one to assume that there is no given tradition or former popularity known relating to the *yatra*. Obviously the priestly authorities don't understand themselves as the promotors of the pilgrimage tour. The fact that its promotion is launched forth by governmental and private organizations rather than priestly ones might explain to some extent the proximity of the *yatra* to modern touristic sight-seeing programmes. The impulses at the heart of this pilgrimage embracing a cycle of all nine *graha-sthalas* are rather to be traced back to ideological considerations, mingled up with sectarian, economic, maybe prestige interests. There is nothing wrong about this as such aspects are known to be — in one way or the other — integral parts to any pilgrimage. Given that the concept is consistently tuned to the needs and requirements of people nothing will prevent a pilgrimage centre created out of rationally guided interests to become widely frequented in the course of time, be it — in the case here presented — by *graha*-seized pilgrims in search of relief or by distraction-seeking tourists taking advantage of a weekend coach tour — or both.

In terms of self-organized complexity we could therefore argue that within the given example there are several aspects obstructing a proper development of such a complex. The dynamics of a network of interdependent and interacting elements seem not to congregate into one single system; rather the different "components" — astrological, priestly, social, governmental, economic — are connected with divergent interests. Such an observation leads back to my initial doubt — whether social phenomena and processes, involving human's will, emotion and interest, can be fully explained alongside patterns or process models observed within fields belonging to strictly natural sciences.

Notes

1. During my stay in Tamil Nadu in 1998 I visited all nine *grahasthalas* accompanied by E. Masilamani who supported my investigations with her precious knowledge of Tamil language and local culture.
2. See the overview of possible scientific approaches given by Morinis (1984, 233–275) or the introduction in McKay (1998).
3. The Hindu concept of *purusha* is associated with different meanings all of them carrying the idea of completeness—in an organic sense related to a single human being as well as in a metaphysical or macrocosmic sense related to different levels of the universe.
4. See Türstig (1980), Pingree (1964 and 1981), Varahamihira (1987), Kirfel (1920), Markel (1995), Bühnemann (1989), Bühnemann (1988, 208–209).
5. One might oppose stating that Suriyanar Koil, the abode of Surya, is dedicated since ancient times to the sun god in his own right; I would not deny this but rather complement that Surya has been identified with Siva repeatedly.
6. A temporary internet offer was contained at http://members.tripod.com/~navagraha/navagrahatempletour.html. This site contained the names and locations of the nine temples and recommendations for hotels and car rental. A map, some brief information, and color illustrations of the nine temple sites and links for booking completed this announcement.
7. South Indian temples are, with the main sanctum as the very centre, traditionally surrounded by different numbers of circle ways (*prakaras*) which are followed by pilgrims performing *pradaksina*

or, during festivals, by the deities themselves as they are taken out for procession.

8. The use of a *kalasa* or *ghata,* a vase-like earthen or metal vessel usually filled with purified water and richly decorated serves as recipient or temporary home of a specific deity. For this purpose that very deity has to be ritually invoked and, after the accomplishment of the ritual, sent off again.

References

Bühnemann, G., 1988, *Puja: A Study in Smarta Ritual*, Wien: De Nobili, Publications of the De Nobili Research Library; 15.

Bühnemann, G., 1989, "The Heavenly Bodies (Navagraha) in Hindu Ritual," in *Sambhasa 11:* 1–9.

Diehl, C.G., 1956, *Instrument and Purpose: Studies on Rites and Rituals in South India*, Lund: CWK Gleerups.

Fuller, C.J., 1980, "The Calendrical System of Tamilnadu (South India)," *Journal of the Royal Asiatic Society*, 52–63.

Kirfel, W., 1920, *Die Kosmographie der Inder: Nach den Quellen dargestellt*, Bonn/Leizig: Kurt Schroeder.

Malville, J.M., 1989, "The Rise and Fall of the Sun Temple of Konarak: The Temple Versus the Solar Orb," in *World Archaeoastronomy*, ed. by A.F. Aveni, Cambridge: Cambridge University Press, pp. 377-88.

Malville, J.M. and R.N. Swaminathan, 1998, "People, Planets and the Sun: Surya Puja in Tamil Nadu, South India," *Cosmos and Culture*, 2, 3-15.

Markel, S., 1995, *Origins of the Indian Planetary Deities*, New York: Edwin Mellen Press (Studies in Ancient Thought and Religion; 16).

McKay, A., 1998, *Pilgrimage in Tibet*, Richmont: Curzon Press.

Morinis, A., 1984, *Pilgrimage in the Hindu Tradition: A Case Study of West Bengal*, Delhi/London: Oxford University Press.

Morinis, A. (ed.), 1992, *Sacred Journeys: The Anthropology of Pilgrimage*, Westport/London: Greenwood Press.

Peston, J.J., 1980, "Sacred centres and symbolic networks in South Asia," *The Mankind Quarterly*, 10.4: 259-93.

Pingree, D., 1964, "Representation of the Planets in Indian Astrology," *Indo-Iranian Journal*, 8: 249–67.

———, 1981, "Jyotishshastra: Astral and Mathematical Literature," *in Scientific and Technical Literature*, vol. 6, ed. by Jan Gonda, Wiesbaden: Otto Harrassowitz (A History of Indian Literature; 6.4).

Turner, V., 1974, *Dramas, Fields and Metaphors: Symbolic Action in Human Society*, Ithaca/London: Cornell University Press.

Turner, V. and E. Turner, 1978, *Image and Pilgrimage in Christian Culture: Anthropological Perspectives*, New York: Columbia University Press.

Türstig, H.-G., 1980, *Jyotisa: Das System der indischen Astrologie. Wiesbaden: Franz Steiner Verlag* (Beiträge zur Südasienforschung, Südasieninstitut Universität Heidelberg; 57).

Varahamihira, 1987, *The Brihat-Samhita of Varaha*, Delhi: Sri Satguru Publications (Sri Garib Dass Oriental Series; 43).

8

Complex Landscapes and the Ramayana Legend

Amita Sinha

Introduction

SACRED landscapes sustain and authenticate myths and legends far beyond their oral and textual traditions. The pilgrim experiences the power of the place and encounters the living presence of gods. His belief in religious texts is strengthened and his faith made stronger in the encounter with the reality of landscape, temples, rituals and fellow pilgrims. This is undoubtedly true with *Ramayana* legend as well. Ayodhya, Chitrakut, Panchavati, Kishkindha, Rameshvaram and numerous other places celebrate events in the life of Rama, enabling the devotee to get a first hand experience of the environs where, once upon a time, Vishnu's *avatara* (his re-incarnation in human form) lived. In absence of archaeological data establishing historical existence of places discussed in the epic tale, it appears probable that these landscapes were in course of time imprinted with *Ramayana*'s characters and events as the epic gathered force in its popularity and *bhakti* took a strong hold over the Indian religious imagination by sixteenth century.

This paper discusses the reification of *Ramayana* legend in Ayodhya, Chitrakut and Kishkindha, based upon the premise that the three landscapes possessed characteristics that made them inherently sacred to the folk and Brahmanical system of beliefs. Valmiki's *Ramayana* names these places and describes them in a manner much embellished by the poet's vivid imagination and style. The river valleys of Mandakini in Chitrakut and Tungabhadra in Kishkindha are painted in words as Edenic settings. In comparing the text and actual sites, as they exist today, we encounter landscape archetypes that constitute sacred *kshetra* and *tirtha*. The sites' historic veracity with respect to *Ramayana* remains to be proven. What becomes clear upon examination of shrines on the sites is their receptiveness to gods older than Rama. I argue that their landscapes constitute place archetypes, which, wherever they appear in the Indian subcontinent, often become objects of veneration. The sanctity attributed to them is inherent in their physical configuration and in natural attributes that evoke a strong charge in the believer as well as the non-believer. Their religious affiliations change over time depending upon ascendancy and decline of gods but their symbolic meanings as sites of hierophany and means of crossing over to the godly realm remain.

Ayodhya

Ayodhya, capital of the kingdom of Kosala, was the birthplace of Rama and the city from where he ruled as king-*avatara*. As such it is the most sacred site of Rama legend. Valmiki's *Ramayana* describes it as a fortified city, situated on the banks of the river Sarayu, 12 *yojanas* (42 km) in length and 3 *yojanas* (10.5 km) in breadth. It had handsome palaces (with seven courtyards) for members of royal family, wide streets for chariots, and parks and gardens. According to the *Kalika Purana*, it was laid out in the auspicious shape of a bow (as in *karmuka mandala*) along Sarayu (Bose 1942).

I have drawn upon Bakker's (1986) exhaustive study of Ayodhya and Van der Veer's (1988) introductory chapter for the following description. Presently Sarayu encircles the city on three sides. Rama's fort on elevated ground is situated north of the river. About 8 km to the west, the river fords and forms the old *tirtha* Gopratara (oxen ford) where Rama is believed to have ended his earthly life along with citizens of Ayodhya. There is now another claimant — Svargadhara consisting of a stretch of *ghats* — believed to be the spot where Rama's body was cremated. The *ghats* lie between the Shaivite temple of Nageshvarnath (associated with Rama's son Kusha) and Sahasradhara, a *naga* sanctuary on Lakshmana *ghat* (Lakshmana is said to be an incarnation of Sheshanaga, king of serpents). The banks themselves are named after Rama and Lakshmana — Ramakunda or Ramapauri, and Sahasradhara or Lakshmana-ghat where Lakshmana left his mortal body, reuniting with the cosmic serpent — Sheshanaga. The *ghats* are used for cremation rituals by the locals.There are two *ghats* named Rinamochana and Papamochana where the bather is said to be freed from debts to his ancestors and *gurus* and sheds his sins. Other *ghats* include Kaikeyi and Kaushalya *ghats*.

The excavations carried out in the fort area by B.B. Lal in 1975 and 1976 show the earliest habitation on the site dating back to seventh century BCE but the rise of Ayodhya as a major pilgrim centre occurred fifteen hundred years later. This paralleled the rise in worship of Rama as the principal incarnation of Vishnu. According to Bakker (1986):

> The tendency to reify the realm of saga occasioned a remarkable new development. It contributed to the new conception of the *avatara* of God on earth as a historical event which eventually resulted in the transformation of the site Ayodhya into a holy place. (p.11)
>
> The deification of Rama runs parallel with the reification of the city of Ayodhya. (p.61)

He traces the beginning of this process to the reign of Kumaragupta I or Skandagupta in the mid-fifth century CE when the royal court of Pataliputra moved to Ayodhya and a Vishnu temple was built at Ramjanmabhumi (birthplace of Rama). This temple was either rebuilt or renovated during the Gahadavala period in eleventh-twelfth centuries (Dubey 1995). The

Gahadavala kings of Kannauj, Chandradeva and Jayachandra built Vishnu temples — Chandrahari and Dharmahari on the bathing *ghat*, Svargadvara. A sky line of temple spires along the river banks began to emerge. In the twelfth century there were at least five Vishnu temples in Ayodhya — on Janmabhumi, on east and west sides of Svargadvara *ghats*, at Chakratirtha *ghat* and Gopratara *ghat*.

The oldest version of *Ayodhyamahatmya* belonging to the Vaishnava-Khanda of *Skanda Purana* was compiled in the thirteenth century. The *Ramayana* legend was now grounded at specific locales — Dantadhavan-kunda where Rama would brush his teeth, Maniparvata where he created a pleasure grove for Sita, Yajnavedi where he performed sacrifices, Kanakamandapa as the site of Rama and Sita's palace, Ashokavatika with Sita-Kunda on the northern banks of the river Tilodaki near its confluence with Sarayu and Bharatkunda where Bharata stayed in Nandigrama during Rama's exile.

The legend of Vishnu's incarnation began to grow into a religious cult in the period of Islamic depredations. For a period of five centuries Islamic rule precluded the buildings of Hindu temple of any repute in Ayodhya, now the capital of Avadh province ruled by Muslim governors. The Ramjanmabhumi temple was destroyed on Mogul prince Babur's orders in 1528 CE and a mosque (Babri Masjid) was built. That this mosque was itself destroyed on December 6, 1992 by Hindu *kar-sevaks*, reveals in part the deep significance of the very exact location of Rama's arrival on earth. The twin temples on Svargadvara *ghats* were replaced by mosques in Mogul Emperor Aurangzeb's reign (CE 1658-1707). This however did not stop the 'rediscovery' of legendary sites — on the contrary, the process gathered force in sixteenth century with the rise of *bhakti* movement.

The temples in Ayodhya date from eighteenth century during the liberal rule of Shia Nawabs. Their Hindu ministers constructed shrines — Naval Ray, Safdar Jung's (CE 1739-54) minister built temples along Svargadvara *ghat* and Tikayat Ray, Asaf-ud-daulah's (CE 1775-97) minister constructed Hanumangarhi, temple to Hanuman, on the eastern gate of the ancient fort of Ramkot. Bakker (1990) has traced the transformation of *yaksha*/Bhairava shrine guarding the eastern gateway of the ancient fort, into a Hanuman temple. By sixteenth century Hanuman was being worshipped at Ramachaura under a tamarind tree on the top of a mound Hanumantila. This mound formed the remains of the old guarded entry to the fort. The earlier place-deities (*yakshas* — Ajita, Mattajajendra and Bhairava) had given way to Hanuman, *Ramayana*'s celebrated monkey-warrior. The significance of Ramkot as ancient Ayodhya's royal fortress was by now well established. The mounds on the south-west and south-east are called Kuberatila and Sugrivatila with Nal and Nila (who had built the bridge to Lanka) *tilas* between them. Kanakbhavana, a small temple at the site of the golden palace of Rama and Sita, was enlarged and embellished by Rani Krishnabhanu Kunwari of Orchcha in CE 1891. The new Janmasthana temple founded by *sadhu* Ramdas, shortly after destruction of the old by Babur, includes Sita *rasoi* (kitchen). Sumitrabhavana (birthplace of Lakshmana and Shatrughna) and Kaikeyibhavana (birthplace of Bharata) are shrines as well. *Ghats* were built by Raja Darshan Singh (CE 1827-51) and new ones were built after 1964 when Sarayu had to be diverted for building a new bridge.

Ayodhya is now a city of temples — reputedly 5,000 and is believed to draw as many as 400,000 pilgrims for its main festival, Ramanaumi, birthday of Rama (Dewan 1990). The major pilgrimage circuit, *chaurasi kos parikrama* (84 *kos*) lasts for twenty-five days, taking the pilgrim to the major shrines along Sarayu's banks and concluding on Janakinaumi, birthday of Sita. Shorter circumambulatory routes are *chaudah kos* (14 *kos*) and *pancha kos parikramas* (5 *kos*). In the month of Shravana, idols of Rama and Sita are brought out of the temples and placed in swings for the celerbration of *jhula* festival. Other festivals are celebrated at their respective sites — Ramanaumi in Ramapauri and Ramjanmabhumi, Janakinaumi in Kanakbhara and Sita-Kunda, *Nagapanchami* and *Maha Shivaratri* at Nageshvarnath temple, and *Sarayu-jayanti*, celebrating the descent of the river from the heavens, with a dip in the waters.

Ayodhya shares certain topographic features with Varanasi and Mathura. The three are part of "seven cities" (*saptapuri*) which includes Ujjain, Dwarka, Kanchi and Haridwar, and where death brings *moksha*. The gods have made these cities their homes. Their landscape plays no small part in establishing them as sacred *kshetras*. Mathura is said to be laid out in a crescent shape along the banks of Yamuna by Rama's brother Shatrughna after slaying the demon Lavana. The *ghats* stretching 2 km along the riverfront bring a large number of pilgrims for the numerous fairs, festivals and *parikramas*. The *ghats* of Vrindavan curve convexly towards the river (Ray 1989). *Karmuka mandala* is evident in Varanasi as well — the city rises from the western bank of the river Ganges flowing northwards in a broad crescent sweep (Eck 1982). There are seventy bathing *ghats* on the stretch of land bordered by Ganges between the rivers Asi and Varana. The temples extending along the *ghats*, 50 to 70 ft above the river, make a magnificent skyline. The oldest part of the city was on Rajghat plateau at Varana-Ganges confluence with the rivers on its east, west and northern sides.

What these cities have in common is a location in a peninsular region, surrounded by water on three sides. Marcus (1993) in discussing an alternative community similarly located in Findhorn, Scotland, traces its power of place to the many positive influences of the surrounding water. The ancients in India chose these locations perhaps for similar reasons — presence of water in swift currents of river, lowland basins and river confluences, which provided a "ford." Coupled with plateau or hilly terrain, these sites provided a combination of natural features favoured by gods of epic and Puranic mythology. That these sites also formed strategic locations for forts and defensible settlements added to their attraction and importance. It is probable that in Ayodhya, as in Braj-*kshetra*, local gods and goddesses were overtaken by supreme gods of

Hindu religion. Mt. Govardhana and Manasi Ganga in Vrindavan were earlier worshipped as nature-deities of hills and water, later incorporated into Krishna-*bhakti*. Could Ayodhya's deities have suffered the same fate, like those of Nageshvarnath temple and Hanumangarhi which represented earlier shrines and were later co-opted into *Ramayana* legend?

Chitrakut

Chitrakut was their first sojourn in Rama, Sita and Lakshmana's wanderings in the wilderness during their fourteen-year exile. The *kshetra* is named after Chitrakut hill, part of the Vindhyan spur. The hill forms the centre of the holy region. The rivers Mandakini and Payasvini carve a valley in this hilly landscape, meeting near the town Sitapur. The two landscape elements considered most sacred in Hindu tradition — river confluence and hills, are present in the region. Their significance to the pilgrim undoubtedly derives from events narrated in *Ramayana* — from Rama, Sita and Lakshmana's stay in a thatched cottage on Chitrakut hill, their meetings with sages Atri and Valmiki at their respective *ashramas*, Bharata's arrival with news of their father Dasharatha's death and his coronation of Rama. Chitrakut had attracted ascetics before Rama's arrival. Lalapur hill, 25 km east of Chitrakut is considered to be the site of Valmiki's *ashrama* and Atri's *ashrama* is 8 km south of the hill. Atri's wife Anusuya is believed to have brought the river Ganges, known as Mandakini here, by force of her *tapas*. Bharatkupa, 7.7 km west of Chitrakut, reputedly contains the waters of all holy rivers brought by Bharata for Rama's consecration. Ramaghat marks the place of Rama's bathing, Raghava Prayaga — the confluence of rivers Mandakini and Payasvini — is where Rama performed the rites of his father's death; Sphatikashila is the stone platform on the river bank where Rama and Sita sat, admiring the landscape; Ramashayya where the couple had slept one night; Sita-Kunda where the couple sported, and Sitarasoi was Sita's kitchen. Other significant places include Kotitirtha, hallowed by penance of sages; Siddhashrama, a natural cave with a spring; Gupta Godavari, a number of limestone caves, one with a stream; and Hanumandhara, shrine of Hanuman bathed by a stream, on a hill.

Though Kalidasa describes Chitrakut in *Raghuvamsha*, as was the case with other Rama sites, it attained popularity only in the sixteenth century (Dubey and Singh 1994). Tulsidas (CE 1540-1623) extolled its virtues in his *Ramacharitmanas*. With the compilation of *Chitrakut Mahatmya* in the eighteenth century, more sites were added to the list of sacred places. The temples of Chitrakut were mostly constructed in eighteenth and nineteenth centuries. Sites on the edge of *kshetra* such as Gupta Godavari and Bharatakupa are sacred to Shiva. Raja Aman Singh of Panna established a *linga* at Gupta Godavari in CE 1754. Before sixteenth century, Bharatakupa was referred to as Jyesthasthana, sacred to Shiva in *Mahabharata*, *Padma Purana* and *Bhushundi Ramayana*. Worship at the shrine of Mattagajendranath, which is Shiva as the *kshetrapala* or "territorial guardian" at Ramaghat initiates the pilgrimage of Chitrakut

(Eck 1991). Shiva guards the sacred *kshetra* on its margins at Siddhashrama, Kotitirtha, Bharatakupa and Gupta Godavari. He could rightfully be called the ancient deity of Chitrakut. There is yet another and older tradition of worshipping Chitrakut as Kamnath or Kamatnath who is not identified with Rama, Shiva or the Goddess. Eck (1991) suggests that this represents an ancient *yaksha* cult incorporated into Vishnu-*bhakti* similar to worship of Mt. Govardhana in Braj.

Dubey and Singh (1994), Singh and Malville (1997), and Dubey, Malville and Singh (2000) have studied the spatial alignments in the landscape and have called "the intersection of mytho-historic traditions with the natural landscape to be of great interest and continuing puzzle." The sacred sites of Chitrakut fall into a pattern of three interlocking isosceles triangles. Their alignments mark the sunrise and sunset on solstice. Singh (1994; 1997) calls them 'cosmic geometries' since they connect different levels of the cosmos — macrocosm of stars, planets, moon and sun; mesocosm of the natural landscape; and microcosm of city, temple, home and body. The largest triangle is formed by Valmiki *ashrama*, Atri-Anusuya *ashrama* and Bharatakupa. Bharatakupa, Sphatikashila and Balaji constitute another triangle in turn containing the innermost triangle formed by Kamadagiri (Chitrakut mountain), Balaji and Sphatikashila. The arms of the largest triangle are roughly equal — the distances between Valmiki *ashrama* to Atri-Anusuya *ashrama* and Bharatakupa are 29.4 km and 32.15 km respectively. The second isosceles triangle has sides of 9.3 km and 9.6 km while the third isosceles triangle has sides of 2.4 km and 2.7 km. Nine sites lie on the bisector of the largest triangle, stretching for 30 km between Valmiki *ashrama* and Gupta Godavari. It aligns with the direction of sunrise on summer solstice. The bisector of the second triangle, extending from Bharatakupa to Hanumandhara aligns with the sunset on summer solstice.

Are the triangles, constituted by visual axes, intentional *yantras* inscribed on the landscape for the purpose of gathering sacred spots in a meaningful pattern? *Chitrakut Mahatmya* describes the triangles as Rama's bow and arrow. Singh (1997), in another context, that of Vindhyachala hills, shows the *yantra* embedded in three goddess shrines of Lakshmi, Kali and Ashtabhuja (Sarasvati). Here the triangle is the Goddess' aniconic form and her *yantra* is perhaps a mystical diagram used for concentration. It is likely that the "discovery" of these sacred sites was aided by a pre-existing, extraordinary configuration of natural features established by sight lines and equivalent distances.

At Chitrakut, the pilgrim's belief that he is indeed at the centre is strengthened by his experience of sunrise and sunset on hills. On Kamadgiri hill, centre of the *kshetra*, he would see the summer solstice sunrise near Balaji and the winter solstice sunrise near Hanumandhara. On the summit of the hill at Sitarasoi, near Hanumandhara, he would see the summer solstice sun rise near Valmiki *ashrama* hill and set above Kamadgiri hill. Indeed the hill summits appear to graze the skies and bring about the symbolic birth and death of the sun. Of these, Kamadagiri — "hill which grants desires" — derives its power from being the location of Rama, Sita and Lakshmana's huts and is therefore, the *axis mundi*. The stone-paved circumambulatory pathway around the hill (4.5 km long and constructed by queen of Bundela chief, Chhatrasal in CE 1725) takes the pilgrim to 56 temples, four of which called *mukharavinda*, are located in cardinal directions. In doing so, he retraces the steps of Bharata. In five days he completes the pilgrimage circuit by visiting all the sites in Chitrakut that Bharata had visited before leaving for Ayodhya (Tripathi 1990). While it may never be proven beyond doubt that Rama, Sita and Lakshmana, did ever stay here or that they were historical personages, the spirit of the site is undeniable.

Kishkindha

The ruins of Vijayanagara in central Karnataka are spread over landscape of the famed monkey-kingdom, Kishkindha of *Ramayana* legend. Like Chitrakut this is a hilly and dramatic area; to the north of the city the river Tungabhadra makes a northward turn similar to that of the Ganga at Varanasi. Here Rama and Lakshmana arrived searching for Sita; here they met Sugriva, Hanuman and other monkeys; here Rama killed Vali; and here the brothers waited out the monsoons before embarking upon the journey southwards to rescue Sita with the army of monkeys and bears. The landscape is viewed as the site of these major events and is an ever-present, physical reminder of the narrative. Yet there are other and older narratives associated with the site that appear to make its particular geography myth-prone. The river valley of Tungabhadra, like that of Godavari and Mandakini, possesses the combination of hill crests and meandering river that make it a sacred place archetype in folk and Brahmanical traditions. Here myths of succeeding epochs are validated by power of the place.

Wagoner (1985) points out that the Sanskrit text *Hemakutakhanda* and the Kannada *Pampamahatmya* describe the site as Hemkuta *kshetra* named after the sacred hill, Hemakuta. The hill was the home of Virupaksha (one of Shiva's forms) who married Pampa, the daughter of sage Matanga. The sage's hermitage was located on another hill named after him and it was on this Matanga hill "where hares chased hounds" that Sugriva found protection from his brother Vali in *treta-yuga*. According to *Rayavacakamu*, a Telugu historical text dating from the sixteenth century, sage Vidyaranya founds a city on this hill and installs a king named Harihara on its throne in *kali-yuga* (Wagoner 1993). The city is named Vijayanagara and becomes the capital of a medieval Hindu empire, which collapsed in CE 1565 with the invasion of the city by armies of adjoining Muslim kingdoms. The power and authority of its kings are derived from the city's site as much as its structure of temples and palaces. Shiva's fierce warrior form, Virabhadra, protected the city and temple on the summit of Matanga hill.

Malville (1994) has studied spatial alignments of the site's landscape features using data from GPS (Global Positioning System). While there are no triangular *yantras* formed by visual axes as at Chitrakut, natural features and their architectural embodiment (temples) are consistently aligned with each other, establishing strong visual axes that provide for a spectacular experience. The building activities of Vijayanagara kings sought to accentuate the sacred features of the landscape and refied the *Ramayana* saga as Gahadavala kings did in Ayodhya on a smaller scale. The temples strengthened the impact made by the already existing unusual visual coincidence of hilly crests.

Matanga hill lies at the intersection of at least three visual axes — between Ramachandra temple (royal shrine of Vijayanagara kings), Kodandarama temple (where Lakshmana crowned Sugriva king of Kishkindha) and Hanuman temple on the summit of Anjenadri hill (where Hanuman was born); between Raghunatha temple on Malyavanta hill and Virupaksha temple on Hemkuta hill; and between Prasanna Virupaksha, Sugriva's cave (where jewels dropped by Sita were hidden) and Pampa Sarovara (by Shabari's *ashrama*). It is also the centre of other radial lines that extends outwards to other natural and built features.

A major north-south axis links the royal centre, Matanga hill and the lake at its base, Kodandarama temple, Chakratirtha on the northward turn of Tungabhadra river and Anjenadri hill with a Hanuman shrine at its summit. The *shikhara* of Virabhadra temple on Matanga hill is only 0.8 arc minutes from true north when viewed from the centre of gateway to the royal enclosure. Matanga hill is framed in the doorway of Ramachandra temple. From the entry avenue of Ramachandra temple, the devotee sees its *shikhara* and that of Anjenadri temple separated by only seven minutes of an arc. Kodandarama temple also faces Anjenadri hill. The *shikharas* of Virupaksha and Raghunatha temple lie on a straight line, differing by only a minute of an arc from 180 degrees. The visual superimposition of temple spires has a powerful effect. The natural landscape is enhanced by architecture and its most prominent hill framed in openings — its sacred energies, its munificence and its powers of protection — are forever kept in view.

Fritz and Mitchell (1987) describe the three phases in the sacred site's transformation into a royal capital and the assimilation of local deities into the *Ramayana* tradition. Temples were built in the tenth and eleventh centuries CE in Hemakuta *tirtha* famous for its legend of Virupaksha and Pampa, whose symbols were Hemakuta hill and Pampa Lake.

The boundaries of the *tirtha* are ritually verified by taking the god and goddess in a circumambulatory tour (*giri-pradakshina*) twice a year even today (Wagoner 1985). The Vijayanagara kings built the huge Virupaksha temple complex and Manmatha tank, down the hill and on its north, making it the sacred centre of the city. In the final phase around the beginning of fifteenth century, Rama gains ascendancy and the Vijayanagara kings began to identify themselves with the king-*avatara*. *Ramayana* themes began to be depicted in sculpture and Ramachandra temple was built in the centre of royal enclosure (Dallapiccola 1993). It was visually aligned with Rishyamukha hill (an island in Tungabhadra) on the north and Malyavanta hill on the north-east, points of Rama's arrival into Kishkindha and departure to Lanka (Fritz

1986).

As in Chitrakut and Ayodhya, a process of transformation in site and temple worship can be discerned. The sacred site's god and goddess were local and assimilated into Shiva mythology. According to legend, as in Chitrakut, Shiva was worshipped by Rama at Kishkindha. He continues to preside as *svayambhu* (self-manifested) *linga* in Virupaksha temple and at Raghunatha temple (Eck 1991). The pilgrims worship him in visiting the landscape sanctified by Rama and Lakshmana's stay. When Vijayanagara kings styled themselves in the image of the divine king of Ayodhya, the sacred centre of the city shifted from Virupaksha temple complex to their royal chapel and pilgrimage to Kishkindha sites became popular.

Conclusion

Clearly all three sites are not sanctified exclusively by Rama legend. In fact, Rama appears to be a late arrival in terms of temple building and worship. In the beginning of second millennium, the dormant *Ramayana* tradition was revived and it gathered force with royal patronage and as *bhakti* gained ground as the predominant religious sensibility of the masses. Accordingly landscapes discussed in the epic were "re-discovered" — their mythic existence now became a physical reality. In the absence of material evidence going back to sixth century BCE when events in *Ramayana* would have taken place, this is a plausible conclusion. The controversy surrounding *Ramayana* sites lends support. Some scholars argue, as Singh (1991) points out, that Panchavati, Kishkindha and Lanka were within the Vindhyan range, in close proximity to Chitrakut. The existence of numerous Sita-Kundas, Sitarasois and Hanumandharas in north and central India shows that claimants to sites of the *Ramayana*'s unique events are more than one, lending credence to the notion that landscapes absorbed parts of the *Ramayana* tradition over time and were accordingly remade into the shape of myth. Eck (1981) calls the incorporation of a local *tirtha* to an all-India tradition as the geographical equivalent of Sanskritization.

What do Ayodhya, Chitrakut and Kishkindha have in common that attracted the worshipper's of the gods, Shiva and Rama, over time? Was there something inherent in their landscapes that invites myths and attracts *sadhus*, preachers, devout followers, royal patronage and pilgrims? For the Rama-*bhakta*, of course, this is hallowed ground where, once upon a time, Rama, Sita and Lakshmana walked and where *Rama-rajya* — utopia on earth — flourished. The faithfuls are nourished in their belief by the physical environment as much as by the vows they make, by the rituals in which they participate and by presence of fellow devotees. This physical environment is not only the holy mountain or the confluence of holy rivers; it is temple spires that create a skyline on the *ghats*, spires that accentuate summits of hills and spires that coincide with the appearance and disappearance of the sun. The environment includes *kundas* (water reservoirs), bathing *ghats* and circumambulatory paths that take one on a journey to spots already made familiar with the daily reading of *Ramayana*.

Underlying the complex, self-sustaining systems that pilgrimage complexes are today, there are certain topographic features that have lent themselves continually over millennia to sacred meanings. They are spatial archetypes in the sense that their physical configuration has been associated consistently with the encounters with numinous and transcendence in Hindu thought. Eck (1981) and Bharadwaj (1973) have drawn attention to natural features that have become symbols for the Hindu to climb and cross the mundane world of existence to *moksha* and liberation from the cycle of birth and death. To the believer the river ford is a physical image for the spiritual journey of the *atman* (individual soul) to the *Brahman* (universal spirit). A dip in the flowing waters is a metaphor for moral cleansing and shedding of *papa* (sins). The rivers, believed to have fallen from heaven to the earth, are flowing *axis mundi*, in the same way that mountains thrust themselves from the earth's bowels into the rarefied realm of the gods and are perceived as centres of the universe and its borders. In Puranic cosmology, Mt. Meru is conceived as the centre of the universe, surrounded by four island-continents. The river Ganga falls from the heavens directly above Mt. Meru. In Valmiki's *Ramayana*, mountains rim the known world.

It is not surprising that river confluences are *tirthas* and mountains are homes of ascetics. The combination of hilly terrain and river(s), in a valley landscape, would therefore be of added significance. The mountain-river dyad constitute an archetypal place that forms the structure of sacred sites in Indian geography. Are they also natural symbols of masculine and feminine archetypes and therefore represent a complementary totality, a wholeness found in the natural landscape? Mt. Kailasa and Lake Mansarovar are home of Shiva and Parvati respectively and are prototypes of similar configurations revered beyond Himalayas. Numerous holy sites display this complementarity in the naming and worship of natural features — Mt. Govardhana and Manasi Ganga in Braj, Kamadagiri and Mandakini in Chitrakut and Mt. Hemkuta and Pampa *sarovara* in Kishkindha. Chitrakut, Panchavati and Kishkindha have Mandakini, Godavari and Tungbhadra rivers coursing through a hilly terrain. In Ayodhya, there is Maniparvata and Sita-Kunda and the fort itself on a plateau with Sarayu flowing below it.

According to Eck (1981), India's *tirthas* are grounded in the folk tradition of groves, pools and hillocks. The *yakshas* and *nagas* as spirits of the place were, and still are, worshipped for guarding off evil and as benefactors. Epic mythology with its cosmography, its notions of duality of *prakriti* (nature) and *purusha* (divine essence), of *atman* and *Brahman*, treated the natural world as a vehicle for transcending *samsara*. The ancient sacred sites were perfect locales for practising the evolving metaphysics in rituals that included the worship of more powerful gods who descend to earth periodically for setting the moral order right. The choice of sites in folk and later Brahmanical traditions is not an accident — their selection is an example of geomancy. It can be compared with *feng-shui* stemming from Taoist tradition in East Asia, which favours sites with a balance of *ch'i*. At these sites, mountains and rivers are interdependent and complementary landscape features, expressive of passive and active energies, whose balance is a key to Tao-like harmony. I believe Hindus also sought harmony in the landscape and found it conducive to thoughts of liberation from the cycle of birth and death. They duplicated this harmony in architecture of temple *shikharas* (spires) and stepped tanks, creating *tirthas* out of built form. There are perhaps psychological and physiological explanations behind what causes such places to be so powerful. Science may hold some clues for their nature, but it is mythology that provides us with symbols upon which the pilgrim's faith rests.

References

Bakker, Hans, 1986, *Ayodhya*, Egbert Forsten.

———, 1990, "The History of Hanumat Worship at Ayodhya," in D.P. Dubey (ed.), *Pilgrimage Studies: Text and Context*, Allahabad: The Society of Pilgrimage Studies.

———, 1991, "Ayodhya: A Hindu Jerusalem," *Numen*, vol. XXXVIII: 88-109.

Bose, Atindra Nath, 1942, "Oldest Indo-Aryan Cities," *Journal of Indian History*, Madras. XXI: 60-82.

Bharadwaj, Surinder, 1973, *Hindu Places of Pilgrimage*, Berkeley: University of California Press.

Dallapiccola, Anna, 1994, "The City of Vijayanagara: Kiskindha, the Monkey-Kingdom," in Vidya Dehejia (ed.), *The Legend of Rama: Artistic Visions*, Marg Publications.

Dewan, Jatin, 1990, *Development of Land-Water Interface: Ayodhya*, Unpublished B.Arch. Thesis, Chandigarh College of Architecture.

Dubey., D.P., 1995, "Ayodhya: Where History Stands Abused," in Dubey, D.P. (ed.), *Sacred Places, Sacred Traditions*, Allahabad: The Society of Pilgrimage Studies.

Dubey, D.P. and Rana P.B. Singh, 1994, "Chitrakut: The Frame and Network of the Faithscape and Sacred Geometry of a Hindu Tirtha," in Rana P.B. Singh (ed.), *The Spirit and Power of Place: Human Environment and Sacrality*, National Geographic Society of India, 41.

Dubey, D.P., J.M. Malville and Rana P.B. Singh, 2000, "Chitrakut: A Hindu Tirtha and its Cosmic Geometry," in J.M. Malville and Lalit M. Gujral (eds.), *Ancient Cities, Sacred Skies: Cosmic Geometries and City Planning in Ancient India*, New Delhi: Aryan Books International.

Eck, Diana, 1981, "India's Tirthas: Crossings in Sacred Geography," *History of Religions*, 20, no. 4.

———, 1982, *Banaras: City of Light*, New York: Alfred Knopf.

———, 1985, *Darsan: Seeing the Divine Image in India*, Chambersburg: Anima Books.

———, 1991, "Following Rama, Worshipping Rama," in Diana Eck and Francoise Mallison (eds.), *Devotion Divine: Bhakti Traditions from the Regions of India*, Egbert Forsten.

Fritz, John, 1986, "Vijayanagara: Authority and Meaning of a South Indian Imperial Capital," *American Anthropologist*, 88, no. 1.

Fritz, John and George Mitchell, 1987, "Interpreting the Plan of a Medieval Hindu Capital, Vijayanagara," *World Archaeology*, 19: 105-29.

Malville, John McKim, 1994, "Astronomy at Vijayanagara: Sacred Geography Confronts the Cosmos," in Rana P.B. Singh (ed.), *The Spirit and Power of Place: Human Environment and Sacrality*, Varanasi: National Geographical Society of India, pub. 41.

Malville, John McKim and Rana P.B. Singh, 1997, "Pilgrimage Cosmologies at Chitrakut and Vijayanagara: Emergent Geometries and Self-Organization," paper presented at the 26th Annual Conference on

South Asia, Madison, Wisconsin.

Marcus, Clare Cooper, 1993, "Designing for a Commitment to Place: Lessons from the Alternative Community of Findhorn," in David Seamon (ed.), *Dwelling, Seeing and Designing: Towards a Phenomenological Ecology*, New York: State University of New York.

Ray, Rajat, 1989, "Ghats of Mathura and Vrindavan," *Architecture+Design*, Nov.-Dec.: 61-69.

Sankalia, H.D., 1978, "Ayodhya of the Ramayana in a Hisorical Perspective," in R.N. Dandekar (ed). *Annals of the Bhandarkar Oriental Research Institute*, vols. LVIII and LIX, Poona.

Singh, Rana P.B., 1991, "Rama's Route After Banishment: A Geographic Viewpoint," *Journal of Scientific Research*, Banaras Hindu University: 39-46.

———, 1994, "Varanasi Cosmic Order and Cityscape: Sun Images and Shrines," in *Architecture+Design*, Nov.-Dec.: 75-79.

———, 1997, "Sacredscape, Faithscape and Cosmic Geometry: Goddess Territory of Vindhyachal, India," Paper presented in the *Sixth International Conference on Built Form and Culture Research*, University of Cincinnati.

Tripathi, G.C., 1990, "Chitrakut and its Mahatmya," in D.P. Dubey (ed.) *Pilgrimage Studies: Text and Context*. Allahabad, The Society of Pilgrimage Studies.

Van der Veer, Peter, 1988, *Gods on Earth — The Management of Religious Experience and Identity in a North Indian Pilgrimage Centre*, London School of Economics Monographs on Social Anthropology, no. 59.

Wagoner, Philip, 1985, "Architecture and Mythic Space at the Hemakuta Hill: A Preliminary Report," in *Vijayanagara: Progress of Research, 1985-87* :142-48, Mysore: Directorate of Archaeology and Museums.

9

Traces of Buddhist Pilgrimage in Ancient India

Kurt Behrendt

IN this paper, I examine some of the broad parameters that governed early Buddhist pilgrimage until *circa* the seventh century CE, focusing on two main categories, local and distant pilgrimage as documented in inscriptions, art and early textual sources. The Buddhist tradition originally rooted in the Ganges basin spread to outlying regions and, as a result, the Buddhist world can be viewed as a wheel with the homeland of Shakyamuni at its hub and distinct communities radiating outward like spokes. This centre-periphery model will be crucial for understanding the dynamics of pilgrimage as in many cases we know more about the periphery than we do of the centre.

Starting with the life of Shakyamuni a geography associated with his quest for enlightenment emerges. Later artistic evidence from Bharhut, Sanchi and the regions of Gandhara and Andhra would lead us to believe that the most important life events took place at Bodh-Gaya (*fig.* 9.3). the place of enlightenment, and Sarnath where he taught his first sermon (*fig.* 9.8) When Shakyamuni is depicted in ancient sculpture he is most often represented with reference to these locations. Both sites are adjacent to already established Brahmanical sacred places — Gaya and Banaras. As Surinder Bhardwaj (1973: 33, 50-51) has pointed out, Shakyamuni's own path to enlightenment can be viewed as a pilgrimage to places already considered sacred (*tirthas*). From a religious perspective, one could argue that the Buddha's access to such nexi of power led to his enlightenment or, to take the more pragmatic view, these sites were chosen to make the ideas of Buddhism available to people already engaged in a cycle of pilgrimage. Syncretism probably explains this commonality, but whatever the motivation, the physical locations of Bodh-Gaya and Sarnath worked in effect to spread this new doctrine along a web of pre-existing *tirthas*. Thus, from the inception of Buddhism, the geographical locations of significant actions performed by the Tathagata functioned to define the nodes of pilgrimage.

While this emphasis on sacred geography can be compared to the Hindu *tirtha* tradition, it is important to stress that with Buddhism the places are associated with a historic individual, who carried out certain actions, possessed tangible objects and ultimately died leaving his body behind. This last point is of great relevance to us, as the portable bodily relics of the

Buddha make the power of enlightenment accessible even in the most remote places. They provide an efficacious alternative to sacred geography and their importance to the Buddhist community should not be underestimated (Strong: 2004). The early Brahmanical practices lack a comparable relic tradition. Even later, when the Buddhists started to develop a notion comparable to the *svayambhu* or self-made images, there is always the idea that they indeed reflect a true likeness of the living man, Shakyamuni. In this sense certain images attain the status of being relics.

Origins of Buddhist Pilgrimage

The question then arises — was there pilgrimage during or immediately after the time of the Buddha in about the 6th century BCE? In fact, it is not until the third century BCE with the Mauryan emperor Ashoka that we have epigraphical and sporadic archaeological evidence of Buddhist activity (Falk: 2006). Many early texts tell us that Ashoka divided the Buddha's relics and placed them in "84,000" *stupas* throughout his realm. In association with a few surviving Mauryan monuments we find inscribed pillars and edicts (*fig.* 9.1) — which may have worked to mark Asoka's territory and unify his subjects under a common religion. While the extant evidence is thin, it is feasible that his use of relics provided him the opportunity to establish potent religious centres throughout the northern half of the subcontinent. Ashoka's redistribution of relics is in some cases associated with pre-existing sacred geography, as the edicts at Sarnath and Girnar testify. Over time, the religious centres established by Ashoka drew Buddhist pilgrims, Lumbini or Sanchi being good examples. However, there is no compelling evidence to suggest that Buddhist pilgrimage was occurring during the Mauryan period. In fact, so little is actually known about this time that these observations should be taken simply as possibilities.

At Bharhut and Sanchi, two Buddhist centres that bear no connection with the historic life of Shakyamuni, nearly 750 donative inscriptions suggest for the first time the existence of an established pilgrimage network. These inscriptions dating to the beginning of the current era were incised on the crossbars and pillars of the *vedikas* surrounding these *stupas*. Typically they give us the donor's name along with both his or her occupation and most significantly the place of residence. At Bharhut 129 donative inscriptions show that the site attracted lay and monastic devotees primarily from the Ganges area — notably Pataliputra and Kaushambi. There are also records of donors coming from more distant areas, such as Nasik, which is mentioned once and Vidisha, which occurs four times (Barua 1926: 1-38). In the Sanchi Bhilsa area, more than 600 inscriptions indicate that the site relied on pilgrims coming from the modern region of Malwa, with the cities of Vidisha and Ujjain mentioned most frequently (Schopen 1996: 60; Bajpai 1981: 14). Here, hundreds of individual gifts from monks, nuns and lay people financed the construction of the *stupas* (*fig.* 9.2).

How can we interpret this evidence in light of pilgrimage? People were drawn to both sites by powerful relics that, in the case of Sanchi, could have been installed by Ashoka. Both lay people and monks travelled to make donations; as pointed out by Gregory Schopen, 40 per cent of Sanchi *stupa* I's donors were monks and nuns and in the case of *stupa* II, this number rises to 60 per cent (Schopen 1996: 60). The same pattern of donations is repeated at Bharhut though here lay followers predominate. Thus, at the beginning of the Common Era, it is clear that both monastic and lay pilgrimage was crucial to the support and establishment of these major Buddhist centres. Finally, while both sites attracted pilgrims from several distant Indian cities, they did not receive international patronage. Bharhut and *Sanchi* appear to have basically served a local population and can be classified as regional pilgrimage centres.

The sculpture on the *toranas* at Sanchi and Bharhut also provides insight into early pilgrimage practices. At both sites we find depictions of enshrined Bodhi trees (*fig.* 9.3) and temples housing *chakras* surrounded by worshippers, perhaps, referring to Bodh-Gaya and Sarnath. While the exact reading of these reliefs has been the subject of a debate between Susan Huntington and Vidya Dehejia, it seems clear that the sacred geography of the Buddha was already important to devotional practice (Dehejia 1991; Huntington 1985). These depictions, whether representations of worship or narration of events from the Buddha's life, speak of making the sacred geography of the Tathagata manifest to the regional devotee. For instance, at both Bharhut and Sanchi the ladders of Sankasya are shown surrounded by adorants (*fig.* 9.4). While the reliefs could depict either the miraculous descent of the Buddha from Trayastrimsa heaven or a monument erected to commemorate it, these images suggest that Sankasya was important to the regional communities of Sanchi and Bharhut. In any case by CE 400 when Fa Xian visited India, this site had become a significant centre of pilgrimage (Beal 1983: xxxix-xli).

On the basis of Sanchi and Bharhut, one might be inclined to conclude that all early Buddhist sites were patronized through a process of popular pilgrimage but this is not always the case. The many early rock-cut caves on the Deccan, dating to the first centuries BCE-CE, such as Junnar, Nasik, Karle or Ajanta, show little trace of a pilgrimage tradition. The community as a whole is not represented in the inscriptions, which record elite donations of kings, ministers, guilds, merchants and the monastic community. Thus, unlike Sanchi and Bharhut, we do not find popular patronage by pilgrims at the Deccan Buddhist outposts, which appear to have catered more to the needs of itinerant traders as Himanshu Ray (1986) has pointed out.

Surprisingly, these same sites in the fifth to seventh centuries show considerable traces of regional pilgrimage. At this time inscriptions tell us that the Buddhist centres, such as Ajanta or Kanheri, continued to be built with dynastic and mercantile support. However, literally thousands of votive images were haphazardly painted or sculpted into these caves by individual patrons (*fig.* 9.5). This devotional practice had a popular basis, which we know from the numerous donors shown within the reliefs as well as remembered in the attached votive inscriptions. At

Ajanta at least 17 inscriptions survive (Burges and Indraji 1976: 80-88) recording the offerings of monks and nuns. However, the many sculpted plaques for painted inscriptions, now empty, could well have recorded lay offerings. While many donor figures are clearly monks or nuns, lay followers also occur frequently. The images were only added to finished caves under worship and typically consist of single Buddha or Bodhisattva figures or standardized depictions of the "Miracle of Shravasti". There is a clear pattern indicating that individual patrons tried to have their votive panel placed in visible places as near as possible to the objects of devotion, such as key image shrines or relic *stupas*. All this evidence points to regional pilgrimage, repeating the pattern of donations observed at Sanchi and Bharhut.

Pilgrimage on the Periphery of the Buddhist World: Importance of Relics

Between the fifth and seventh centuries a variety of literary and archaeological sources begin to shed light on the practice of pilgrimage. Most useful for this endeavour, are the accounts of the Chinese pilgrims Fa Xian (CE 399-414) and Xuanzang (*ca* CE 630). The fact that they came to India as pilgrims and left us written record of their travels shows us that pilgrimage at this point of time was a popular phenomenon within the Buddhist world. These monks travelled from outlying regional centres to the Buddha's homeland and thus, by following their itineraries, insight can be gained into the active regional and long distance pilgrimage networks.

While these two pilgrims are crucially important, their accounts must be treated with caution. As T.H. Barrett (1990: 99) has pointed out, they came to India with the main goal of bringing texts back to China and thus are not to be seen as typical pilgrims. Fa Xian and Xuanzang travelled extremely long distances, spent considerable time and had solid financial support for these undertakings, while most common pilgrims, lay or monastic, would have visited nearby centres that would have been logistically practical and inexpensive. Therefore, in using Chinese pilgrims accounts as primary sources it should be remembered that they had somewhat different interests, destinations and goals then Indian pilgrims would have had. Some inaccuracies in these narratives must also be the result of later compilation by disciples upon their return to China. Still for the study of early Buddhist pilgrimage these sources give us a broader context for understanding the complex dynamics of this practice.

Both Fa Xian and Xuanzang crossed central Asia, traversed the Himalayas and entered the Indian subcontinent through Gandhara. In this frontier territory of north west Pakistan, numerous well-preserved *stupas*, shrines and monasteries are extant, which together with a large corpus of sculpture, helps to corroborate the observations of the Chinese travellers.

In Gandhara, the main foci of pilgrimage were either significant possessions of the Buddha, such as his alms bowl, staff and robe or important body relics. In other words, like the other above-mentioned regional sites, highly portable relics charged with the power of enlightenment served as the focus of pilgrimage.

One of Fa Xian's companions, Hui-ying, returned to China after "fulfilling his destiny" of visiting the Buddha's alms bowl, making offering at Hadda to the Skull-bone and tooth of the Buddha, and visiting the Shadow of the Tathagata. (Beale 1983: xxxiii) This mention of "fulfilling his destiny" suggests that he knew, prior to visiting Gandhara, that these relics were there, and visiting them exhausted the goal or vow of his pilgrimage. *The Gaosengzjuan* (The lives of Eminent Monks), edited in CE 519, records the accounts of 96 Chinese monks, half of whom travelled to Gandhara to worship the alms bowl (Kuwayama 1987). It is interesting that this relic alone was significant enough to warrant crossing central Asia and traversing the Himalayas to reach Gandhara from China. The alms bowl appears repeatedly within the corpus of Gandharan sculpture (*fig.* 9.6), confirming its importance as a devotional object not only for foreigners but also for the local community.

It is remarkable that very few of the Chinese pilgrims chose to push on to the Ganges basin after having completed the most difficult part of the journey. Apparently, the alms bowl and other significant relics of the Buddha available in Gandhara, held more importance for the Chinese travellers than did the sacred geography of Shakyamuni in the Ganges basin. Perhaps these foreign pilgrims were drawn by the power of relics, which can also be found in China and they did not fully understand or where uninterested in the South Asian tradition of sacred geography common to the Vedic religion, Hinduism, Jainism and Buddhism.

A relic to which Fa Xian and Xuanzang devote considerable attention is the skull-bone of the Buddha from the site of Hadda on the Western edge of modern Afghanistan. Xuanzang writes:

> All who wish to see the skull-bone of Tathagata have to pay one gold piece; those who wish to take an impression pay five pieces. The other objects in their several order, have a fixed price [the robe, the walking staff, the tooth and more body relics]; and yet, though the charges are heavy, the worshippers are numerous.
>
> — Beal 1983: vol.I, 97

It would appear that pilgrimage allowed Hadda to garner considerable wealth from the worshippers who travelled to this centre. The practice of charging admission rather then accepting donations would seem surprising but later in reference to the north Indian site of Shiladitya, speaking of another tooth of the Buddha, Xuanzang says:

> People assemble from far and near. . . . Every day hundreds and thousands come together . . . those wishing to see the tooth of Buddha must pay one great gold piece. Nevertheless, the followers who come to worship are very numerous and gladly pay the tax of a gold piece. — Beal 1983: vol. I, 222

These passages are particularly revealing of the financial significance that a powerful relic had both on the frontier and at the centre of the Buddhist world. Such a financial concern also works to legitimize the importance of the site as it forces the devotee to acknowledge monetarily the power of the object at the nexus of the pilgrimage. The system of charging to see the relic also suggests that a local audience probably supported these sites. The long distance travellers, visiting a great number of Buddhist centres, would not have been in a position to make substantial contributions everywhere. In fact, the reverse was probably true; in most cases the religious establishment would have provided them with shelter and food. The foreign pilgrims would have made offerings only at most significant sites like Bodh-Gaya, where many inscriptions testify to this practice.

The archaeological evidence from Gandhara also indicates that pilgrims and lay devotees might have played an important role as patrons. Today more than a dozen large first to seventh-century complexes survive and despite a lack of inscriptional evidence, a consistent pattern of patronage can be deduced. Typically, a large *stupa* containing relics was built first and subsequently it was surrounded by a heterogeneous assemblages of votive *stupas*, relic shrines and images. These smaller structures were given over time by individual patrons with varying financial resources. Thus, we find a situation not so different from Sanchi or Bharhut and remarkably in line with the offering of votive images found at the many west Indian cave complexes.

Long Distance Pilgrimage and the Ganges basin

Fa Xian and Xuanzang next travelled to the Ganges basin to visit the many outlying pilgrimage sites and ultimately to retrace the historic actions of Shakyamuni that led to his enlightenment. Due to a scarcity of other sources, it is hard to assess how common long distance pilgrimage was among both monastic and lay followers. Nevertheless, one cannot help but think of the hundred million pilgrims that visited Rome to celebrate the 2000th year since Christ's birth, again in a relic oriented tradition. A similar desire may have motivated more Buddhists than we think, even if the goals of the pilgrimage differed.

The *Mahaparinirvanasutra* has the Buddha say:

> After I have passed away, monks, those making the pilgrimage to the shrines, honouring the shrines, will come [to these places], they will speak in this way: "Here the Blessed One was born," "Here the Blessed One attained the highest most excellent awakening," etc.
>
> — Schopen 1987:195

This passage, demonstrating that monastic long distance pilgrimage was an active practice, goes on to tell us that monks were also given honorific titles such as the "one who makes the pilgrimage to the Shrines." Similar appellatives appear as monastic titles in the inscriptions of

Amaravati (Schopen 1987). Also in the *Mahaparinirvanasutra* the Tathagata says:

> After I have passed away, monks, those making the pilgrimage to the shrines. . . . Those who during that time die here with believing mind [in my presence], all those who have karma still to work will go to heaven. — Schopen 1987: 195

Here the inherent danger of long distance pilgrimage is legitimized, since even if you die in the process you will be rewarded with a favourable rebirth.

Difficulties and hardships were integral to the pilgrimage process. The Chinese pilgrims make interesting references to networks of facilities established for the aid of travellers. We know from the account of Fa Xian that the Buddhists were, at times, supported by the "ninety-six heretical sects" of central India. He writes:

> They build hospices by the side of solitary roads for the shelter of travellers, where they may rest, sleep, eat and drink, and are supplied with all necessaries. The followers of Buddha also, as they pass to and fro, are entertained by them, only different arrangements are made for their convenience.
>
> — Beal 1983: xlviii

Monks could also seek refuge at the many Buddhist monasteries. Near Ramagrama in north India Xuanzang notes:

> When any priests come from distant regions, they entertain them with the greatest courtesy and liberality; during three days they keep them in their society and offer them the four necessary things [food, drink, clothing, and medicine].
>
> — Beal 1983: vol. II, 26

However, such examples of hospitality were not always the case. Xuanzang at Bodh-Gaya recounts the exploits of a pilgrim from the country of Tu-ho-lo (Tokhara in Central Asia):

> Formerly there were two or three Sramanas, passionately fond of learning, who lived in the Country of Tukhara, to the north of the Snowy Mountains, . . . [who desired to see]. The sacred relic shines with their own peculiar splendour; let us go together from place to place and tell our faithful friends what sacred relics we ourselves have seen. On this the two or three associates, taking their religious staves, went forth to travel together. Arrived in India, at whatever convent gates they called, they were treated with disdain as belonging to a frontier country and no one would take them in. They were exposed to the winds and the rains without and within they suffered from hunger [and so on] . . . [the king noticed them and asked of their plight and the Sramanas respond] we have come to see and adore the sacred relics . . . [but] the Sramanas of India deign not to

> give us shelter and we would return to our own land but have not yet completed the round of our pilgrimage. [the account ends with the king saying] I have built this sangharama for the special entertainment of strangers.
>
> — Beal 1983: vol. II, 63

It appears from this passage that the travellers had a predetermined itinerary to follow, which suggests that established pilgrimage routes existed. Clearly, these foreign Shramanas encountered less hospitality than the previous passages would indicate. Xuanzang tells a second story. The protagonist here is a monk, the brother of the king of Sri Lanka, who was travelling to Bodh-Gaya.

> At all the convents he visited, he was treated with disdain as a foreigner . . . [Upon his return he asks his brother the king to build monasteries throughout India and the account continues with the king saying] . . . I desire to build in all the Indies a convent for the entertainment of such strangers, who may have a place of rest between their journey there and back. Thus the two countries will be bound together and travellers be refreshed . . . [a monastery is built at Bodhgaya that] entertains many priests of Ceylon.
>
> — Beal 1983: vol. II, 136

Of great relevance is the fact that international patronage existed at Bodh-Gaya in 630 CE and a significant community of Sri Lankan monks was resident. Both accounts suggest that support of foreign pilgrims was an issue that warranted the construction of special housing. Further, *sangharamas* were built for outside visitors both with international and local patronage.

In the Ganges basin there is also mention of a miraculous well to aid travellers. Both Fa Xian and Xuanzang mention at Kapilavastu, that Shakyamuni as a boy shot an arrow which pierced the ground creating a well for the use of travellers. (Beal 1983: xlix; vol. II, 23-24)

This introduces us to a sacred geography marked by miracles, which characterized, in a different way, both the periphery and the hub of the Buddhist world. While relics are crucial to the Gandharan tradition, miraculous events also empowered centres of pilgrimage. For example, it was at the site of Hadda where Shakyamuni in a former rebirth venerated the past Buddha Dipankara and vowed to pursue the path to Buddhahood (Beal 1983: xxxv).

Fa Xian also maps a local pilgrimage tradition in Gandhara that had miraculous geography at its core rather than relics. Along a route that took him fourteen days to traverse, there were four sites — each linked to one of the past lives of the Buddha: the first was related to the *Sibi Jataka*, with a *stupa* marking the place where the Buddha sacrificed his flesh in substitution of a dove. Following were the places where he sacrificed his eyes, where he gave his severed head in multiple rebirths and finally, the site where he offered his body to feed a starving tiger (Beal 1983: xxxi-xxxii). Fa Xian ends his discussion writing:

> The kings, ministers, and people of all the surrounding countries vie with each other in making religious offerings at these places, in scattering flowers, and burning incense continually . . . men of that district call these four the four great Stupas.
>
> — Beal 1983: xxxii

Here, the participants in the pilgrimage are the people of the surrounding countries who are visiting geographic centres made sacred by the past actions of the Buddha. It is noteworthy, that these *stupas* were not the focus of Fa Xian's travels, but rather those of local people, ministers and kings — thus not the goal of either monastic or foreign pilgrims. Judging from the visual evidence the miraculous geography of the Buddha appears less relevant to the Gandharan community than the relics. The alms bowl relic left a clear trace in the sculptural record while only the *Sibi Jataka* appears occasionally within the corpus of Gandharan narrative reliefs.

This regional itinerary is known only from Fa Xian account. Hardly two centuries later, when Xuanzang visits Gandhara, he only finds ruined *stupas* marking the places of the sacrifice of the eyes and the severing of the head (Beal 1983: vol I, 138-39). This is just a single example, but I think indicative of how fragile and transient many of the regional pilgrimage systems must have been.

As Xuanzang and Fa Xian move closer to the Buddha's homeland, the pilgrimage sites are increasingly legitimized by the sacred geography associated with the miraculous power of the enlightened Buddha. For instance, both Chinese pilgrims stress the significance of Sankasya. As I briefly mentioned above, it was here that the Buddha went up to Trayastrimsa heaven to preach the Law to his mother. Fa Xian records that three ladders made of precious substances could be seen to the seventh step. Apparently they had largely disappeared into the earth after Shakyamuni's descent. Before him, three previous Buddhas had done the same thing leaving traces of their passage nearby. Furthermore, at Sankasya, a pillar stood with a lion capital that miraculously roared giving supernatural proof to some "heretics" that the place belonged to the Buddhists.' It was also here that the Buddha cut his nails and hair, leaving a few body relics (Beal 1983: xxxix-xli). Thus, at the threshold of the territory where Shakyamuni lived, is a powerful site associated with prodigious actions of the Enlightened One and his predecessors. Here the relics, although present, are overshadowed by the miracles performed at the site. Moreover, the large number of significant events speaks of the desire to give Sankasya a status rivaling that of other centres like Bodh-Gaya, Sarnath and Kushanagara.

At Shravasti, again located on the edge of the Buddha's homeland, the Tathagata performed a series of miracles (Brown 1984; Rhi 1991: 207-315). These particular miracles had great resonance in the art and became a popular theme. Unlike Sankasya, the Buddha actually lived here. It was in Shravasti that Shakyamuni spent the rainy seasons after his enlightenment at the very first monastery established in the Jetavana garden (*fig.* 9.7). Upon arriving at the

Jetavana *vihara* Fa Xian and his associate Chi-un were:

> much affected to think that this was the spot in which Buddha had passed twenty-five years of his life. Around them stood many strangers, all occupied in similar reflections. They had traversed a succession of strange countries. Perhaps they might be spared to return home, perhaps they would die. — Beal 1983: xlv

The narration emphasizes how "wonderful!" it was that these men of Han (China) had come from such a remote corner of the earth to search for the Law (Beal 1983: xlv). This passage is particularly significant as it makes a very clear reference to other pilgrims, with special regards to the ones coming from distant places.

Shravasti acquired enormous popularity due to the miracles and the prolonged residence of the Tathagata. In the early reliefs, such as those from Bharhut, it is Jetavana's garden that is represented, whereas, by the time of the Chinese pilgrims the miracles of Shravasti acquired greater importance.

Once we enter the region in which Shakyamuni lived prior to enlightenment, the nature of pilgrimage seems to be transformed. Both the relics of the periphery and the miracles at the threshold of the Buddha's area of action are no longer of importance. Now the emphasis revolves around retracing the actions of Shakyamuni that led to his enlightenment. He followed the path of the past Buddha Dipankara who in turn performed the same set of actions as the Buddha before him. Walking in the Buddha's footsteps was a proven path to enlightenment and an obvious goal for pilgrims who were physically able to reach these places. To stand before the Bodhi tree — the cosmic axis of the world — was to be at the very nexus of enlightenment and potential enlightenment.

Relics, nevertheless, remained important in the homeland of the Buddha, but now they are associated with the life and death of the Buddha, in particular the *parinirvana* at Kushanagara where all the relics trace their origin.

Fa Xian and Xuanzang began their pilgrimage in the heartland by visiting Kapilavastu, where Shakyamuni grew up. All of the events of his childhood leading up to his departure were marked by traces or by *stupas*. Fa Xian tells of monuments erected at the sites where the young prince's horoscope was calculated and where the first meditation at the plowing ceremony occurred. Towers were also built where Shakyamuni saw the sick man and at the gate and where the Great Departure took place (Beal 1983: xlix-l). In other words, the geography of the Buddha prior to his enlightenment had in its entirety become sacred by CE 400, when the earliest account was compiled. These events were also quite commonly represented in the art of Sanchi, Amaravati and Gandhara.

Approaching Bodh-Gaya, Fa Xian and Xuanzang describe the sites where Shakyamuni fasted for six years and, after his decision to renounce extreme asceticism, where he bathed, received milk and rice and finally, where he broke his fast. Then they visit several places that had been rejected by the Buddha as seats of enlightenment, and yet, were sanctified by some sort of manifestations of Shakyamuni's passage. Finally, the pilgrims arrived at the Bodhi tree. Surprisingly, both Fa Xian and Xuanzang devote little attention to the place of enlightenment and quickly proceeded to other shrines commemorating where the Buddha walked in meditation, where he received the alms bowl, where merchants presented him wheat and honey and so forth (Beal 1983: xlix-lxii; vol. II, 123-32). Miraculous images, relics, monasteries and other worldly institutions further augmented these key places. In the end, the Bodhi tree appears not to be the climax of pilgrimage but just one step in a complex itinerary that involves a myriad of sites, events and relics.

Summary and Conclusions

The following conclusions might be drawn from this survey of Indian Buddhist pilgrimage in ancient times. Ashoka may be the first historical figure who can be associated with pilgrimage. While his role as a pilgrim is unclear, he probably established a series of pilgrimage centres that acquired importance through time. Beginning in the first centuries BCE-CE several self-contained, interlocking circuits of pilgrimage can be defined. The first evidence available from the sites of Bharhut and Sanchi points to the existence of popular and regional traditions centred on relics. Most pilgrims came from nearby areas with the goal to pay homage to the specific relics and offer donations. Thus, it appears that the primary patrons of these sites were in fact the lay and monastic pilgrims.

Later, in Gandhara and on the Deccan plateau we find a similar pattern of individual donations of shrines, images and *stupas*. The proliferation of small votive structures at sites like Takht-i-bahi in the Peshawar basin or Ajanta on the Deccan is certainly an indication of involvement and patronage by local communities. The pilgrim in these peripheral areas did not retrace the Buddha's path, but rather travelled to be in the presence of powerful relics like the skill bone at Haddha or those housed in Sanchi's main *stupa*. Such relics were physical pieces of enlightenment and at the same time they functioned to establish a re-created cosmic axis at the nodal point of the *stupa*. Thus, the centre of the Buddhist world, Bodh-Gaya, was effectively available in the provinces. In Gandhara, in addition to the importance of body relics, miracles associated with the Buddha's past lives play a role in legitimizing pilgrimage centres.

The consistent pattern of pilgrimage and lay donation that occurs within the independent peripheral Buddhist communities appears to confirm the applicability of models of self-organization (Malville 2004) to pilgrimage systems. In other words, while each system is distinct,

fig. 9.1: Inscribed base of the Ashokan pillar from Sarnath, mid 3rd century BCE (photo Kurt Behrendt)

fig. 9.2: Sanchi Stupa I, probably established by Ashoka in the mid 3rd century BCE, gateways and last encasement date to *ca* 25 BCE – 25 CE (after J. Marshall. vol. III, plate IIIb.)

fig. 9.3: Bodhi Temple from gateway of Sanchi Stupa I, *ca* 25 BCE – 25 CE (after Marshall. vol. III, plate LI)

fig. 9.4: Sankasya from gateway of Sanchi Stupa 1, *ca*. 25 BCE - CE (after Marshall. vol. III, plate XXXIV)

fig. 9.5: Façade of cave 26 Ajanta, late 5th century CE (photo Kurt Behrendt and Nicholas Morrissey)

fig. 9.6: Alms bowl of the Buddha flanked by worshippers, Gandhara, *ca* 3rd century CE (after Foucher, A. 1905. L'Art Greco-Bouddhique Du Gandhara. Paris: Imprimerie Nationale. fig. 211)

fig. 9.7: Donation of the Jetavana garden from the vedika of the Bharhut Stupa, *ca* 2nd century BCE (after Cunningham plate XXVIII)

fig. 9.8: Buddha preaching the first sermon, Sarnath, late 5th century CE (after H. Zimmer, 1955. *The art of Indian Asia.* New York: Pantheon Books. plate

fig. 9.9: Buddha preaching the first sermon, Ajanta cave 19, late 5th century (after Zimmer plate 179)

fig. 9.10: Buddha sitting in meditation, Anuradhapura Sri Lanka, 6th-7th century (after Zimmer plate 457)

the communities of Bharhut and Sanchi, as well as Gandhara and west India, share a similar set of structures and meaning.

As we approach the Ganges basin, the miracles of the Buddha seem to acquire more relevance. They appear to bridge the relic-focused pilgrimage network of the periphery with the sacred geography defined by the historic life of Shakyamuni at the centre.

In the land associated with the life of the Buddha, miraculous events give way to a sacred geography that the pilgrim follows in order to re-enact Shakyamuni's quest for Enlightenment. The goal here is not to visit one single powerful centre, as was the case in peripheral systems, but rather to pass through an itinerary of greater and lesser sites. At the time Fa Xian and Xuanzang visit the subcontinent, long distance pilgrimage by Buddhist devotees coming from China, Central Asia and Sri Lanka existed. This extended pilgrimage network functioned to link regional centres not so much with each other but with the heartland of the Buddhist world. It is significant that during the fifth and sixth century CE the style of the Sarnath Buddha image (*fig.* 9.8) spread to the peripheral regions of the Buddhist world. Long distance pilgrimage seems to have provided the means of communication that brought this style to places like the Deccan (*fig.* 9.9), Sri Lanka (*fig.* 9.10), Nepal and Central Asia.

The Chinese pilgrims remain, in any case, our main source for understanding early Buddhist pilgrimage practices. They passed down to us vivid pictures of what pilgrimage centres were like in the fifth to seventh century AD. I end my paper with this passage describing the popular practice that occurred at the Jetavana *vihara* in Shravasti every year when the rains end:

> Religious persons come here from every quarter in thousands and myriads, and during seven days and nights they scatter flowers, burn incense and sound music.
>
> — Xuanzang, vol. II, 135-36

References

Agrawal, R. C., 1995, "Stupas and Monasteries: A Recent Discovery from Satdhara, India," in *South Asian Archaeology*, ed. R. Allchin and B. Allchin, Cambridge: Science Publishers Inc., USA.

Bajpai, K., 1981, "Some Place-Names of the Sanci Inscriptions," in *Studies in Indian Place Names*, vol. 2, ed. M. Katti & C. Srinivasan, Mysore: Geetha Bookhouse.

Barrett, T.H., 1990, "Exploratory Observations on some Weeping Pilgrims," *The Buddhist Forum Volume I: Seminar Papers 1987-88*, ed. Tadeusz Skorupski, New Delhi: Heritage Publishers.

Barua, B., 1926, *Bharhut Inscriptions*, Calcutta: University of Calcutta.

Bhardwaj, S.M., 1973, *Hindu Places of Pilgrimage in India: A Study in Cultural Geography*, Berkeley: U.C. Press.

Beal, S., 1983, *Si-Yu-Ki Buddhist Records of the Western World*, rpt., New Delhi: Munshiram Manoharlal.

Brown, R., 1984, "The Sravasti Miracles in the Art of India and Dvaravati," *Archives of Asian Art* 37: 79-95.

Burgess, J. & B. Indraji, 1976, *Inscription from the Cave Temples of Western India*, rpt., Delhi: Indian India.

Cunningham, A., 1854, *The Bhilsa Topes; or Buddhist Monuments of Central India: Comprising a Brief Historical Sketch of the Rise, Progress and Decline of Buddhism; with an account of the Opening and Examination of the Various Groups of Topes around Bhilsa*, London: Smith, Elder and Co.

Dehejia, V., 1992, "The collective and Popular Basis of Early Buddhist Patronage: Sacred Monuments, 100 BC-AD 250", in *The Powers of Art: Patronage in Indian Culture*, ed, B.S. Miller, Delhi: Oxford University Press.

———, 1991, "Aniconism and the Multivalence of Emblems", *Ars Orientalis* 21: 45-66.

Falk, H. 2006, *Asokan Sites and Artefacts*, Mainz: Von Zabern.

Huntington, S., 1985, "Early Buddhist Art and the Theory of Aniconism", *Art Journal*: 401-8.

Kuwayama, S., 1987, "The Buddha's Bowl in Gandhara and Relevant Problems", in *South Asian Archaeology*, ed. M. Taddei, Rome: IsMEO.

Malville, J.M., 2004, "The Geometries of Self-organizing Systems: From Chaos to Pilgrimage", in *Rita: The Cosmic Order*, (ed.) Madhu Khanna, New Delhi: D.K. Printworld.

Marshall, J. & A. Foucher, 1940, *The Monuments of Sanci*, 3 vols, Calcutta.

Rajanubhab, D., 1973, *Monument of the Buddha in Siam*, tr. S. Sivaraksa, A.B. Griswold, Bangkok: The Siam Society.

Ray, H., 1986, *Monastery and Guild: Commerce under the Satavahanas*, Delhi: Oxford University Press.

Rhi, J., 1991, *Gandharan Images of the Sravasti Miracle: An Iconographic Reassessment*, University of California at Berkeley Dissertation.

Schopen, G., 1987, "Burial "Ad Sanctos" and the physical presence of the Buddha in early Indian Buddhism: A study in the Archaeology of Religions," *The Archaeology of Religions:* 193-225.

———, 1996, "What's in a Name: The Religious Function of the Early Donative inscriptions," in *Unseen Presence: the Buddha and Sanci*, ed. V. Dehejia, Bombay: Marg Publications.

Strong. J., 2004, *Relics of the Buddha*, Princeton: Princeton University Press.

10

Pilgrimage Places and Sacred Geometries

Robert H. Stoddard

PILGRIMAGE flows, often involving millions of people, attract the attention of scholars seeking to explain these patterns of movement. A multitude of explanations have been attempted, but none has provided an entirely satisfactory understanding about why certain sites attract worshippers to undertake the sacrifices of pilgrimage. It is recognized that, from the perspective of many religious traditions, Earth space is not homogeneous – that specific places are sacred and different from the surrounding profane land. The reasons certain locations are holy and attract pilgrims from afar have long evoked the geographic question: Why are pilgrimage places distributed as they are?

The potential answers discussed here focus on general principles of location — rather than on ideographic descriptions of particular pilgrimage places. Specifically, this paper reviews some of the previously proposed answers to the question, concentrates on one locational hypothesis as it applies to a setting in the Kathmandu Valley of Nepal, and considers the more recently suggested theory of self-organized criticality.

Proposed Explanations for Distribution of Pilgrimage Places

An early attempt to formulate a general locational principle for pilgrimage places was theorized by Stoddard (1966; 1968), who examined the distribution of Hindu holy sites in India. He hypothesized that a specified set of holy sites would be located in an arrangement that would minimize the aggregate travel distances to the sites from the dispersed Hindu population. After generating several theoretical distributions, based on different sets of major pilgrimage places and varying definitions of the potential pilgrim population, he compared the resulting patterns with that of the actual sites. None of the theoretical distributions matched the actual one — thus indicating a less than optimal arrangement of pilgrimage destinations; but several matched better than a random pattern of points would predict.

Later the anthropologist Victor Turner (1973) suggested that pilgrimage sites occur at locations around the periphery of the pilgrim population. He did not formally test his hypothesis, but he cited a few examples to substantiate it. However, Sopher, after testing Turner's contention in India, found only 38 per cent of the pilgrimage places in peripheral locations (paper presented in 1981 and published posthumously in 1997: 185). Cohen (1992) also rejected the contention that pilgrimage sites tend to be in peripheral locations because of pilgrims' attachment to the socio-cultural core of their society.

Nolan and Nolan (1989) examined the same Turnerian thesis in their study of more than three thousand Catholic shrines in continental Western Europe. They compared centrally located ones (i.e. those situated in the urban area of cities with 25,000 or more persons) with remote shrines (those more than 50 km from a city and 10 km from any settlement). They noted that "34 per cent of the central shrines draw large numbers of pilgrims from extensive catchment basins, as compared to 16 per cent of the remote shrines" (299). When this observation is added to previous doubts about peripheral locations, the Turnerian hypothesis must be rejected as a satisfactory answer about the distributions of pilgrimage places.

A slight variation to the core *versus* periphery debate concerns a possible association of pilgrimage sites with major cities. In his 1966 study, Stoddard tested the geometric relationships between the 45 major pilgrimage sites in India with the 45 largest cities. He concluded that the generalized arrangements of the two distributions did not match well. Nolan and Nolan (1989) examined this same issue by noting the spatial proximity of many European shrines to settlement sizes. They observed that "about 18 per cent of the shrines are located in or near cities of 25,000 or more" (294), a proportion giving only limited support for associating pilgrimage places with urban centres.

Other attempts to establish locational relationships with pilgrimage places have commenced by observing their site features. According to Nolan and Nolan (1989: 303), "between 33 and 42 per cent of Europe's current shrines are associated with environmental features." Similarly, Bhardwaj, in his intensive study of Hindu places of pilgrimage, states (1973: 95): "Our study shows a fairly strong association of Hindu sacred places with certain elements of the physical landscape, namely, flowing water and hilltops . . ." But as Sopher replies (1997: 184): "[These physical features] do not tell us which places associate with water and which particular hills will acquire special sanctity." Certainly a topographic map alone will not produce a good predictor of pilgrimage sites.

In an attempt to generalize locational relationships for all religions throughout the world, Stoddard (1994) looked for areal associations with the 33 major pilgrimage places. He was able to conclude that "major pilgrimage places are located in areas of low altitude and moderate climate, where large rural populations have low incomes" (34). However, he utilized rather weak measures of association at a broad areal scale, so his results are not sufficient for predicting precise distributions of pilgrimage places.

Although these attempts to understand the locations of pilgrimage places have provided some tentative answers, no encompassing principle of location has been accepted and the search for alternative hypotheses continues.

The Role of Sacred Geometry

It is well known that the arrangement of many sacred places reflects the geometry of a cosmogram, such as the *mandala*. For many societies throughout history, the *mandala* or *yantra* has been regarded as a graphic representation — or map — of the cosmos. This geometric projection of the universe consists of a pattern that surrounds and shapes the lives of inhabitants. By representing characteristics of the universe, the diagram structures religious activities, including movements to specific places.

Certainly in South Asia, Hindu and Buddhist cosmological ideas have influenced the arrangement of the built environment and associated activities for centuries. These range in scale from the arrangement of rooms to the layout of towns (Dutt 1925; Malville 1998). In Nepal, for example, visual evidence of the *mandala* as a pervasive model in the design of the built environment is common, especially in Newar settlements. At the scale of an individual house, its siting, orientation and relative proportions are based on the same geometric principles as expressed in a *mandala* (Vogt 1977).

At a different scale, the arrangement of buildings within and around a Nepalese town may also manifest a *mandala* (Gutschow and Kolver 1975; Pieper 1973; MacFadyen and Vogt 1977). At yet another scale, the importance of sacred geometries is clear in the discussion by Gutschow and Bajracharya (1977: 4) about sets of *Matrika* shrines that encircle inhabitants' sacred space:

> In the case of Kathmandu, the first of these circles . . . surrounds the city, the second encompasses the valley and the third at times transcends the boundaries of the valley proper to include places traditionally under the spiritual . . . domination of Newar kings.

The next section of this paper, therefore, concentrates on the spatial arrangement of pilgrimage places in the well-defined region of the Kathmandu Valley of Nepal.

Evaluating the Cosmological Model in the Kathmandu Valley

The setting in which data were collected is the Kathmandu Valley. The Valley, which is almost circular, with a diameter of approximately 25 km, is a fairly discreet region because of the surrounding mountains. The location of several temples within this region may be best understood when they are considered as members of a set, with each position corresponding to a part of a Valley-sized *mandala*.

The study was guided by three questions:

(1) Are there sacred sites within the Valley that are members of an intentional set? That is, do several places constitute parts of an overall unit of sacred space?

(2) Are the sacred sites actually located in a geometric pattern? That is, does each place in a set have spatial significance in terms of an overall religious design?

(3) Do most persons living in the Valley actually perceive specific sacred places as parts of a set? That is, do residents of the Valley perceive an enveloping cosmogram that determines the arrangement of pilgrimage places?

If persons intentionally make pilgrimages to replicate or to reaffirm the sacred geometry of the *mandala*, their actions will affect which shrines are considered to be important pilgrimage places today. This, in turn, will lend support to the contention that the distributions of at least some pilgrimage places in the world result from particular sacred geometries.

To answer the first two questions, this author consulted several experts and relevant publications. The experts were local persons who have studied the ancient religious texts and have specialized in understanding Hindu-Buddhist Tantricism. The publications were ones readily available in Kathmandu and written in English.

According to these sources, the answer to the first question seems clearly to be that, indeed, several religious sites do exist as sets. The experts and various publications generally agreed with what has been summarized in the monumental inventory of cultural features in the Valley, namely, the Protective Inventory (Prusha 1975). The Inventory lists several religious sets, including those of the Chara Ganesha and the Chara Narayana.

The answer to the second question about whether the sets of four sites form a meaningful pattern is not a clear-cut "yes." The lack of an unequivocal affirmation is partly because there is not complete agreement about which Ganesha and Narayana shrines are members of each set. The Ganesha shrines and their locations according to one page in the Protective Inventory are Surya Vinayaka (south of Bhaktapura), Jala Vinayaka (at the Chobar gorge), Rakta or Chandra Vinayaka, and Karya Vinayaka (*fig.* 10.1). However, elsewhere in the same publication, Ashok Vinayaka in Kathmandu replaces Karya Vinayaka; and Auer and Gutschow (1974) list a Ganesha shrine in Sankhu instead of Rakta Vinayaka.

Likewise, the four Vishnu shrines are usually, but not always, given as Changu Narayana (south-west of Sankhu), Ichangu Narayana (near Halchok), Sekh Narayana (near Pharping) and Bisankhu Narayana (midway between Lubhu and Godavari). As exceptions, Pandey and Prusha state that Buddha Nilakantha is even more important than these other four Vishnu temples; and Auer and Gutschow (1974) include a sixth one at Macchegaon.

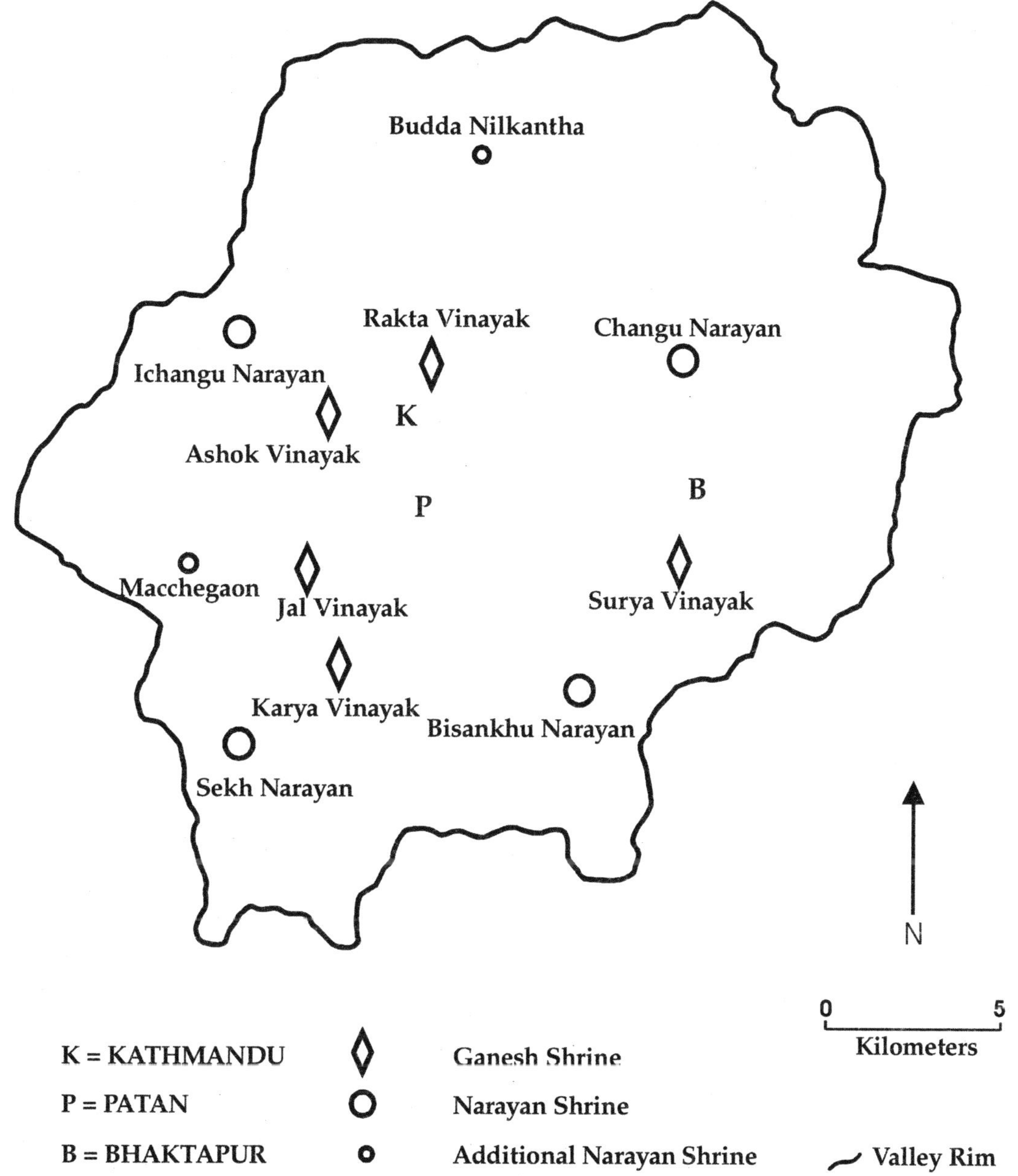

fig. 10.1. Ganesha and Narayana shrines in the Kathmandu Valley.

With this diversity in enumerating which places actually constitute the set, it becomes a little difficult to discern whether either set does form a regular pattern that conforms to a Valley-sized *mandala*. Generally, the experts who commented on the geography of religious sites agree with the Gutschow thesis: sets of sites are theoretically positioned in the Valley in the cardinal directions. Nevertheless, the writers recognize that topographic features and ancient religious structures have modified a perfect north-south and east-west orientation, and these locational deviations from the ideal make it difficult to determine visually which of the conflicting sites are most likely members of the set. This is especially true in the case of the Ganesha shrines because there was less agreement about which four of five major Ganesha shrines constitute the true set and their locations deviate from a square. In contrast, there was greater unanimity about the four Narayana temples. When Buddha Nilakantha and Macchegaon are omitted, the remaining four do display a certain spatial regularity with the Valley.

Perceptions of Sacred Sites in the Kathmandu Valley

The third question deals with how inhabitants perceive the geography of sacred sites in the Valley. Information about perceptions was acquired by asking selected villagers and townspeople about the major Ganesha and Narayana shrines. Fieldwork consisted of going to 25 sites scattered throughout the Valley during a month's period to interview 114 laypersons. A heterogeneous sample of persons was contacted, with the respondents representing a variety of ages (Table 10.1), schooling levels (Table 10.2) and occupations (Table 10.3). Respondents were asked to name the four main Ganesha shrines and then the four Narayana sites to describe the locations of all those sites and to show their locations on a large-scale map. Then they were asked why the sites are located as they are.

Table 10.1: Ages of respondents

Age group	*Number*
18 - 31	24
32 - 41	23
42 - 51	26
52 - 61	20
62 - 78	21
	114

Table 10.2: Schooling levels of respondents

Schooling	*Number*
None	36
Read & Write	28
Elementary	22
SLC	12
College	14
Unknown	2
	114

Table 10.3: Occupations of respondents

Occupation	*Number*
Farmers	30
Shopkeepers	25
Teachers	19
Government & Military personnel	11
Retired & non-farm wives	10
Misc./Others	19
	114

Table 10.4: Frequency of Ganesha shrines named, mapped and visited by respondents

	(a)	(b)	(c)	(d)
Place	*Named*	*Named and Mapped*	*Named, Mapped and Visited*	*Visited*
Surya Vinayaka	92	74	49	54
Ashoka Vinayaka	85	74	50	60
Jala Vinayaka	71	55	21	30
Rakta Vinayaka	63	49	20	29
Karya Vinayaka	50	39	16	19

Table 10.5: Frequency of Narayana shrines named, mapped and visited by respondents

	(a)	(b)	(c)	(d)
Place	*Named*	*Named and Mapped*	*Named, Mapped and Visited*	*Visited*
Changu	97	75	21	28
Ichangu	85	60	7	9
Sekh	83	64	24	28
Bisankhu	83	57	11	16
Buddhanilakantha	27	15	11	19
Macchegaon	7	3	3	5

The answer to the question about the perceived sacred geography of the Kathmandu Valley is based on their responses. First, the extent to which respondents identified sets of Ganesha shrines is noted in Table 10.4. From Column (a), it appears that the interviewed laypersons — like the experts — were uncertain about which of the five Ganesha shrines constitute the actual set of four. This uncertainty is evidenced by the gradual decrease from 92 to 50 in the frequency the top five places were named — rather than a sharp break after the mentioned top four.

In contrast, respondents were more certain about which of the four Narayana sites form a distinct set, as revealed by the fairly obvious break in frequencies between the fourth and fifth listed shrines (Table 10.5, column (a)).

It is possible that persons might perceive a spatial regularity in sacred places even though they might not give such an explanation verbally. In an attempt to detect whether respondents visualize a *mandala*-like pattern in the positions of Ganesha and Narayana shrines, the interviewed persons were asked to show the locations of these shrines by placing stones on a large cloth-map placed on the ground. This base-map included the Valley rim, along with a few of its demarcating peaks, all the main streams, the major surfaced roads and a few landmarks — but, of course, no shrines. The responses are summarized here by both a frequency table and a map. Column (b) of Table 10.4 shows the number of respondents who mapped, as well as named, each of the five main Ganesha sites. It is evident that a strong majority of those who identified specific shrines were willing to indicate where they thought the Ganesha sites are located.

All of the locations marked on the field map of the Valley by respondents have been transferred to the map shown at *fig.* 10.2. This technique does not display the locational perception of each individual, but it provides a clue to the collective concepts. The general impression conveyed by this map is not one of greater regularity than displayed by the actual sites. That is, if respondents truly envisioned the temples situated according to the regularities of the *mandala* then they might be expected to place stones on the map in a more regular arrangement than the true geographic positions. Instead, the dots seem to cluster around the actual sites, especially the best-known ones.

The same procedures were followed for the Narayana shrines. Column (b) of Table 10.5 again signifies that a large majority of those who named a particular Narayana shrine also indicated on the map their answers about its position in the Valley. Respondents' perceptions about the locations of Narayana shrines are shown in *fig.* 10.3. The collective perceptions indicate some regularity but this could well be because the actual sites are, in fact, situated in a fairly regular pattern. Consequently, the results may reflect good mapping skills rather than a tendency to place the markers according to a perceived *mandala* pattern.

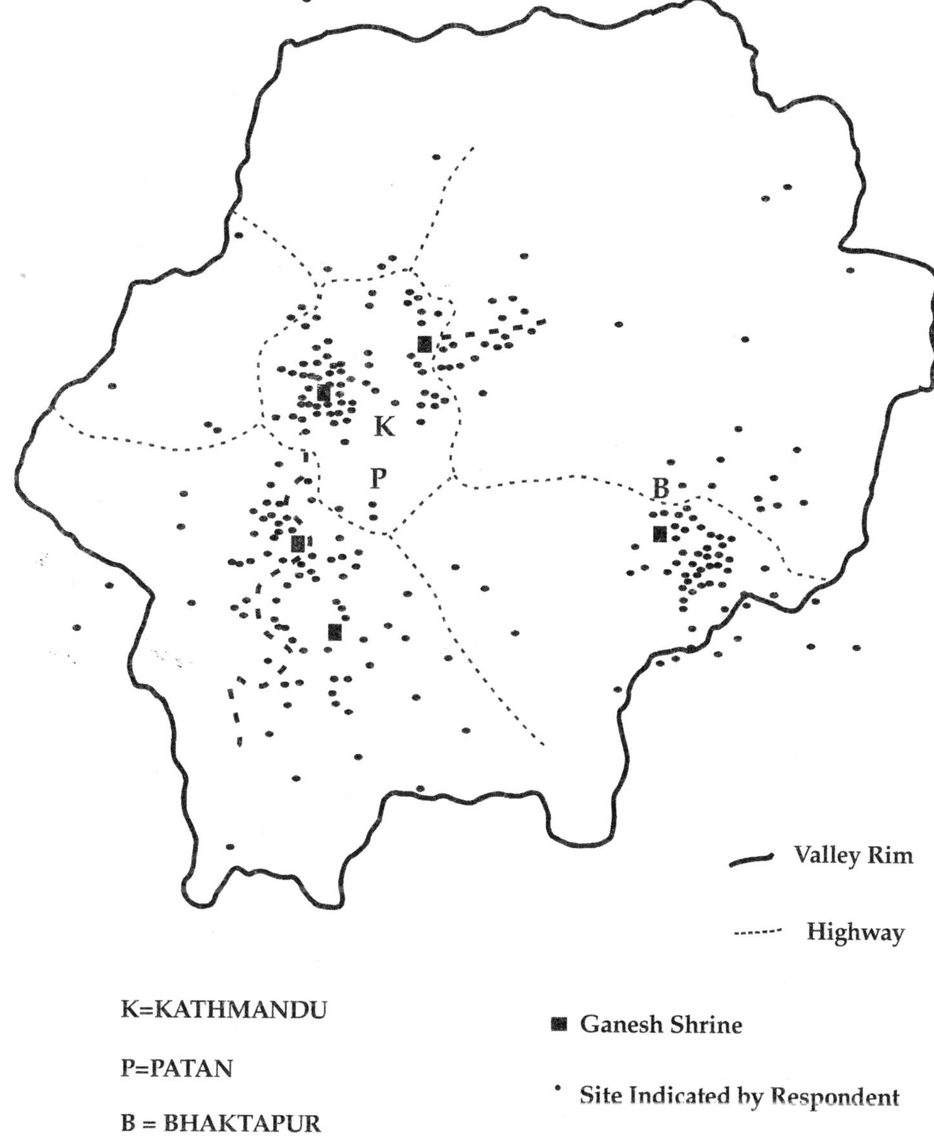

fig. 10.2. Perceptions about the locations of Ganesha shrines.

In reply to the question about why Ganesha and Narayana shrines are located as they are, only two persons pointed out that the sites are located in the four directions; two others regarded the shrines as protectors for the Valley; and three interviewees specified that the four shrines were situated to serve the entire Valley. Four persons declared that the position of Surya Vinayaka in the east is significant, but they did not mention the other three as having similar locational importance. Another thirteen told a specific story about why a particular location is sacred. Approximately 80 per cent of those who answered this question, though, did not provide any reason for the spatial distribution of sacred sites.

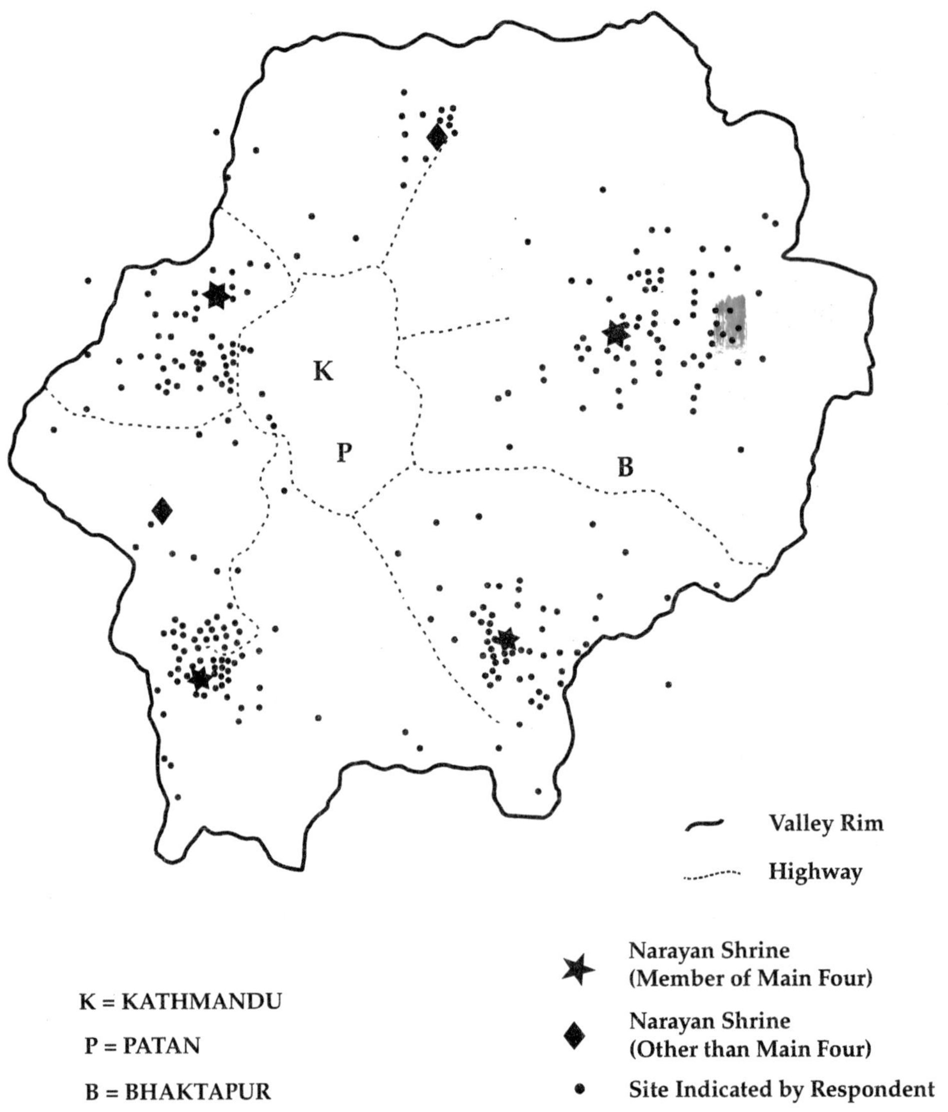

fig. 10.3. Perceptions about the locations of Narayana shrines.

Admittedly, there may be some problems with these data. For one, respondents were not selected by a statistically random procedure. That is, no prescribed method for using a sampling frame was employed and thus the respondents cannot be regarded necessarily as an unbiased subset from the general Valley population. However, if there is any bias, it is probably that persons having more information about places away from their immediate vicinity were over-represented. For example, a higher percentage of school teachers were interviewed than their proportion of the total population (see Table 10.3), thus producing a sample of persons who undoubtedly leave their home-village more frequently than do farmers. It is reasonably safe to assume that persons not chosen for interviewing were even less aware of religious places outside their immediate locality. Therefore, this possible source of error would not jeopardise a negative conclusion about perceptions of patterns in the locations of Valley sites.

Secondly, respondents may not have given correct information. It is recognized that, in any technique that depends on the co-operation of others, people may deliberately choose to mislead the interviewer. However, the percentage of persons in the Kathmandu Valley willing to answer questions compares very favourably with other parts of the world and indicates a positive attitude about giving valid answers.

Respondents may have given incorrect information unintentionally. This problem could arise from faulty communication. Under the best of conditions it is possible that an interviewer and interviewee misunderstand what the other person is trying to say. The possibility of such misunderstanding is increased if the information must be communicated through a third person, especially when the conversation must be translated into another language. Fortunately many of the questions and answers were fairly factual, so these data were probably communicated satisfactorily; but the attempt to learn about respondents' beliefs about regularity in religious sites undoubtedly was less successful.

Incorrect information could occur from memory lapses or similar mistakes. This situation is illustrated by those who were not able to remember names or places or to use the map. Some persons knew where a Ganesha or Narayana temple was located but could not remember its name. Others knew a name but forgot the location. And, of course, people vary in their ability to understand and communicate an isomorphic relationship between earth locations and map positions. Analysis of the data, however, does not suggest any major sources of limited knowledge. Columns (c) and (d) of Table10.4 provide information about the level of mapped replies by those who visited each Ganesha shrine within the previous 12 months. The percentage of those who had visited the sites and also mapped them was high — not only for the frequently visited Surya Vinayaka and Ashoka Vinayaka shrines but for the other three also. Although the number of respondents who visited the Narayana shrines was generally lower than the Ganesha shrines (Table 10.5, columns (c) and (d)), the percentage of visitors who also mapped the shrine locations remained high.

The possibility that a correlation between responses and characteristics of the interviewees was checked by examining the locations of respondents, their gender, and their ages. No correlations were significant enough to alter the basic conclusion: Valley residents generally are not conscious of an enveloping cosmogram.

Although residents of the Valley may view the various shrines as belonging together in one of the two sets, very few respondents gave any reason for the locations of the shrines. In contrast to the experts, who usually related the positions of the shrines to the cardinal directions in the Valley, the laypersons seldom mentioned any overall pattern. Many respondents did answer queries about local shrines around their own village or town in terms of protective positions, but they rarely applied the same kind of locational model to the sets of shrines in the entire Kathmandu Valley. Consequently, it seems safe to conclude that, although inhabitants regard spatial regularity as very important in the sacred space of their local vicinity, they do not necessarily perceive a similar geography of sacred sites at the scale of the Kathmandu Valley.

This absence of a perceptual sacred geometry, however, does not necessarily determine pilgrimage behavior. Most respondents did consider four specific shrines as belonging to a set (i.e. one set for Ganesha and one for Narayana), and each set was identified as distinct. Further evidence that the four Narayana shrines are regarded as members of a unique set was acquired when two dozen respondents reported that, during the last ten years, they had made the special circular pilgrimage to all four of these.

The lack of awareness about concepts held by religious leaders, however, does not necessarily negate a type of geometric regularity in their pilgrimage behavior. For example, each year at the time of Haribodhini Ekadashi, pilgrims make a one-day 40-km journey to the set of four Narayana shrines in the Kathmandu Valley. More than one in five respondents reported that, during the last ten years, they had made the special circular pilgrimage to all four Narayana shrines. Thus, even though many pilgrims may not be consciously aware of an encompassing sacred geometry, their aggregate pilgrimage flows perpetuate the importance of these regularly spaced pilgrimage-places.

These results suggest at least three avenues for additional inquiry. One concerns the areal scale of study. Although the spatial isomorphism between a conceptual sacred geometry and actual religious movements is fairly well understood within homes and temples, it is less apparent for an area the size of the Kathmandu Valley. This outcome leads to the need for extending the study geographically by looking at other regions where similar cosmological geometries are known to exist.

A second evenue opens the search to the entire Earth over long periods of time. Although much insight can be gained from restricting studies to short timespans and to small areas where variables are limited, broad patterns of behavior may be missed.

A third observation is that an inventory of reasons given by individual worshippers to a particular pilgrimage site does not necessarily reveal the patterns produced by a multitude of pilgrims. Plotting the paths of individual grains of sand may not detect the configuration of a large dune. Looking at major pilgrimage flows may yield insight not detected by examining the details of only a few sacred sites.

Consideration of Self-organized Criticality

The foundation for additional comments here consist of (1) observations about places on the Earth exerting perpetual sacred power combined with (2) the theory of self-organized criticality. Discussion about places of sacred power is provided by Gray (2007), who has visited and experienced, as well as interacted with worshipping pilgrims, at pilgrimage sites throughout the world. He states (2007: 9):

> Over the long pageant of civilizations – endlessly rising, falling, and rising again – one phenomenon has remained constant in the background of continuing use of power places by one culture after another. Prehistoric and historic cultures keep coming and going, yet the power places have exerted a spiritual magnetism that transcends human time. The great religions of the historical era – Hinduism, Taoism, Buddhism, Judaism, Christianity, and Islam – have each taken over the sacred places of earlier cultures and made them their own.

According to this perspective, various sites across the Earth have attracted worshippers in prehistoric and historic eras because they experienced enlightenment, a healing of their bodies, a burst of creativity, and similar life-changing transformations. This is not to deny that particular religions may attribute a specific meaning to selected sites; but concurrently it declares that certain places are inherently prone to attract humans with spiritual aspirations. Sacred scriptures and religious leaders may promote worship at specific sites during long periods of time, but this does not deny the existence of universal power points. As stated by Malville, 1999: 10):

> As self-organizing systems, the complexity of the pilgrimage landscape may be natural and internal, and we do not need to look for the evidence of structure imposed by decree or by a city planner, pundit, or priest when encountering complex geometries and complex ritual.

Furthermore, according to Gray, the sanctified power of places is amplified by the intensity of religious energy exerted by millions of worshippers over long periods of time. This intensification of sacred power creates a dynamic system that is both self-fulfilling and evolving. Pilgrimages may be generated by specific religious beliefs in events that occurred and/or continue to occur at particular sites, but these places have attracted, and will continue to attract, pilgrims from other religious traditions at other times in history. It is this characteristic of a natural system – one not in equilibrium – that provides the basis for embracing the theory of Self-organized Criticality.

The concepts of Self-organized Criticality are discussed more thoroughly elsewhere in this volume (Malville: Chapter 2); but some of the system's characteristics are applicable here. One concerns the value of studying phenomena comprehensively. Bak and Chen state (1991: 46):

> Self-organized criticality is a holistic theory: the global features, such as the relative number of large and small events, do not depend on microscopic mechanisms. Consequently, global features of the system cannot be understood by analyzing the parts separately.

A second characteristic is its dynamic nature. The "composite systems never reach equilibrium but instead evolve from one metastable state to the next" (Bak and Chen, 1991: 46). The ebb and flow of pilgrimages to certain places over eons of time, irrespective of particular religious beliefs about the uniqueness of a site for a period of time, inevitably substantiates a perspective of change among its constituents.

A companion factor relates to the incremental impact of pilgrims' journeys on future pilgrimages. Whether it results from an increase in site energy, as proposed by Gray, or primarily from the effects of pilgrimages' popularity, the results may contribute to the critical state that is an important component of a system of Self-organized Criticality.

Although these similarities do not demonstrate the applicability of the concepts of Self-organized Criticality to understanding pilgrimages and the distribution of sacred sites, they certainly provide another insightful direction for further study.

Acknowledgement

Gambhir Bahadur Hada from the Centre for Nepal and Asian Studies, Tribhuvan University, was the research assistant for this project.

References

Auer, Gerhard and Niels Gutschow, 1974, *Bhaktapur: Gestalt, Functionen und Religiose Symbolik einer Nepalishchen Stadt im Vorindustrielien Entwicklungsstadium*, Darmstadt: Technische Hochschule.

Bak, Per and Kan Chen, 1991, "Self-Organized Criticality", *Scientific American*, 264: 45-53.

Bhardwaj, Surinder M., 1973, *Hindu Places of Pilgrimage in India: A Study in Cultural Geography*. Berkeley: University of California Press.

Cohen, Erik, 1992, "Pilgrimage Centers: Concentric and Excentric", *Annals of Tourism Research*, 19: 33-50.

Dutt, Binode B., 1925, *Town Planning in Ancient India*, Calcutta: Thacker, Spink.

Gray, Martin., 2007, *Sacred Earth: Places of Peace and Power,* New York: Sterling.

Gutschow, Niels, and Bernhard Kolver, 1975, *Ordered Space. Concepts and Functions in a Town of Nepal,* Wiesbaden: Steiner Verlag.

Gutschow, Niels, and Manabajra Bajracharya, 1977, "Ritual as Mediator of Space in Kathmandu", *Journal of the Nepal Research Centre*, 1: 1-10.

MacFadyen, J. Tevere and Jay W. Vogt, 1977, "The City is a Mandala: Bhaktapur", *Ekistics*, 44: 307-9.

Malville, J. McKim, 1999, "Complexity and Self-Organization in Pilgrimage Systems", Paper at Pilgrimage and Complexity International Seminar, New Delhi.

———, 1998, "The Symbolic Landscape of Vijayanagara", *The Pennsylvania Geographer*, 36: 30-54.

Nolan, Mary Lee, and Sydney Nolan, 1989, *Christian Pilgrimage in Modern Western Europe*, Chapel Hill: University of North Carolina Press.

Pandey, K.R., and Carl Prusha, eds., 1969, *The Physical Development Plan for the Kathmandu Valley*, Kathmandu: His Majesty's Goverrment of Nepal.

Pieper, Jan, 1973, "Three Cities of Nepal", in Paul Oliver, ed., *Shelter, Sign & Symbol*, London: Barrie & Jenkins, 52-69.

Prusha, Carl, ed., 1975, *Kathmandu Valley. The Preservation of Physical Environment and Cultural Heritage. A Protective Inventory*, Vienna: Anton School & Co.

Sopher, David, 1997, "The Goal of Indian Pilgrimages: Geographical Considerations", in Robert H. Stoddard and Alan Morinis, eds., *Sacred Places, Sacred Spaces: The Geography of Pilgrimages*, Baton Rouge: Geoscience Publications, 183-90.

Stoddard, Robert H., 1966, "Hindu Holy Sites in India", Ph.D. dissertation, Department of Geography, University of Iowa, Iowa City.

———, 1968, "An Analysis of the Distribution of Major Hindu Holy Sites", *National Geographical Journal of India*, 14: 148-55.

———, 1994, "Major Pilgrimage Places of the World", in Surinder Bhardwaj et al. (eds.), *Pilgrimage in the Old and New World*, Berlin: Dietrich Reimer Verlag, 17-36.

Turner, Victor., 1973, "The Center Out There: Pilgrim's Goal", *History of Religions*, 12: 191-230.

Vogt, Jay W., 1977, "Sacred Space, Architectural Tradition and the Contemporary Designer", *The Himalayan Review*, 14: 41-53.

11

Complexity and Economy in Pilgrimage Centres of the Vijayanagara Period

Alexandra Mack

ECONOMY is often overlooked as an element that is essential to the complex system of pilgrimage. Although economy is part of the mundane world and appears to lie far from the spiritual, emotional and symbolic world of the pilgrimage journey, spatial arrangements of pre-colonial south Indian temple centres indicate that the economic considerations of pilgrimage are inextricable from the ritual and cosmological aspects of the journey. This paper will explore the confluence of spatial arrangements and economic transactions at pilgrimage centres using archaeological evidence from the area surrounding the Vitthala temple at the precolonial south Indian imperial capital city of Vijayanagara.

Economy of Pilgrimage

The spiritual journey of pilgrimage is, in fact, often structured around debt relations. The debts are most frequently associated with pilgrimage centre on the relationship between the pilgrim and the deity. Appadurai and Breckenridge describe the reigning deity in a south Indian temple as a sovereign who "stands at the centre of a set of moral and economic transactions which constitute . . . a redistributive process" (Appadurai and Breckenridge 1976: 190). This concept is not limited to Hinduism. Catholics visiting the Bom Jesus shrine in Brazil make the journey primarily to pay *promessas* offered in exchange for healing (Gross 1976). Other similar exchanges occur throughout the world at shrines visited by followers of numerous religions. During the journey, these relationships of spiritual exchange are mirrored in the physical world by transactions that are dominated by human economics in the form of money and goods.

Although many aspects of an overall economic system are controlled through hierarchical systems, there is an economy of pilgrimage that lies outside the control of the dominant forces and is driven largely by the pilgrims themselves. This is an interlinked part of the overall experience of pilgrimage; economic transactions are conducted within both the spatial and temporal realms of pilgrimage. If pilgrimage is a liminal experience, then perhaps these transactions, too, are liminal. However, the end products of these transactions may be worldlier and may come in a form that can be carried home with the pilgrim, providing tangible reminders of a spiritual journey. These ritual souvenirs can be shared with villagers at home who did not, or could not, make the journey, thus extending the impact of the pilgrimage to others. The economy of pilgrimage is undeniably complex and self-organizing and must be understood within the overall context of the pilgrimage experience.

In developing guidelines for an interdisciplinary study of pilgrimage Preston (1992: 43) mentions the economic dimension as one of the key methodological issues, noting,

> Virtually every pilgrimage is associated with a field of economic exchange, as in fairs, carnivals and permanent or temporary marketplaces. Materials are redistributed as pilgrims enter sacred centres and then disperse. A relationship of debt between deity and pilgrim, institution and begging, and the temporary incorporation of peripheral tribal peoples in the process of exchange are examples of secondary (in some instances primary) motives for pilgrimage behaviour.

In his study of Bom Jesus de Lapa in Brazil, Gross noted the dominance of pilgrimage on the town's economy. Pilgrimage is such a dominant force that many residents move away during the rainy season when muddy roads prevent visitation. Those who stay are underemployed or unemployed. Pilgrimage prevents the development of other economies in the town; for instance, the coincidence of the pilgrimage season with the planting season discourages investment in agricultural pursuits. However, he counted "at least 50 permanent stores and hundreds of tiny stalls set up during the festival" (1971: 132).

Pilgrimage can encourage overall economic prosperity. Michell (1993: 10) notes that in southern India

> the simultaneous growth of pilgrimage and trade is an outstanding feature of urban life in the region. Kanchipuram provides an excellent example of a significant religious-commercial centre dealing in locally woven textiles and other goods. Festivals in temple towns are generally sensational events that also benefit business. (1993:10)

That this pattern was established in pre-colonial times is clear from inscriptions. Stein (1982: 121) notes that

> fairs augmented urban trade . . . Regular and periodic fairs were established on the main roads to great temples during the times of major festivals.

Indian Temple as Economic Centre

Indian temples serve as important economic centres. Temples were, and are, landholders, employers and consumers. In some cases, an entire town's socio-economic structure may be entirely dependent on the temple (Jindel 1976: 6). Jindel recorded that the temple at Nathdwara, Rajasthan provided work to as many as 1000 families, with the rest of the population subsisting on industries which were at least indirectly associated with either temple functions or the needs of pilgrims (Jindel 1976: 177-78). The types of people needed to keep the household of the temple running included suppliers of food, flowers and baskets, potters, carpenters, blacksmiths, leather-workers, sweepers, tailors, bamboo workers, painters and washers. Arts surrounding the temple and its festivals included music, dance, drama, painting, calligraphy and cottage industries such as enamelling, dyeing, pottery, tailoring, embroidery, and the manufacture of bangles, glass-frames, snuff boxes and toys.

The economic role of the temples was far more complex than simply that of an employer. In his work on the Tirupati temple, Stein concluded that temples became centres through which state resources were redistributed during the pre-colonial periods (Stein 1958: 127). This redistribution has a moral component as well, with shares received from the deity in exchange for donations to temples. As Appadurai and Breckenridge note,

> the deity . . . commands resources (i.e., services and goods) such as those which are necessary and appropriate for the support and materialization of the ritual process . . . [These resources] are redistributed in the form of shares to the royal courtiers, the donor and the worshippers at large. — Stein 1958: 195

However, the select group of those wealthy enough to make large donations to the temple are in the minority of those who visit a shrine. Most pilgrims may be able to afford some small gift for the deity, if anything. Nonetheless, this does not exclude them from the larger redistributive process. Food, that was presented to the deity and was thus consecrated as *prasad*, became an important commodity for pilgrims. It conferred additional merit for the traveller either through consumption on-site or by bringing it home for others to share (Stein 1958: 100). Although in theory this food should have been provided as a freely given service to pilgrims, it was regularly sold by temple functionaries. Pilgrims regularly paid for such food, setting up an important exchange system that was maintained by their demand for the sacred product (Stein 1958: 115). Consecrated food was not the only commodity of exchange for pilgrims; trade in tangible goods took place in the bazaars surrounding the temples. People bought offerings, purchased food and even obtained souvenirs which would remind them of the trip and which could be shown to others at home when the pilgrim returns.

Pilgrimage and Space

These economic transactions take place within the spatial and temporal realms of pilgrimage. The sacred journey to the home of a god or other holy sites takes the traveller out of the context of daily life and into a new realm where ordinary physical and social boundaries no longer apply. While quotidian boundaries may be broken, new patterns become part of the experience that will shape the individual during the journey. Some of these patterns are spiritual and others are part of the physical world and at times these two realms cross.

In India, this experience is fueled on the more mundane levels by the ways in which temple towns are planned to direct movement and direct lines of sight. Starting in the medieval period, particularly the Vijayanagara era, the spatial arrangement of a temple town was aimed at enhancing perceptual importance of the place (Pieper 1980). Ideally, the temple complex was placed at the centre of the town. While this may not always have been possible due to topography or other factors, the temple complex did become the conceptual centre of the town, if not the physical centre. Today temple centres are recognizable as a set of monumental structures covered with ornate sculpture and highlighted by tall gateways. This set of structures creates a landmark visible from many miles away, which dominates its immediate vicinity. The pattern of movement through temple towns creates spiritual links and enhances the emotional experience for visitors. Paths of movement are directed and lines of sight are concentrated on particular features to emphasize the monumentality of temples and their ornately decorated facades (Michell 1993; Pieper 1980). Directed routes control access in the city, separating public from private space, or one part of the city from another. Circulation and circumambulation are fundamental elements of Hindu pilgrimage (Bhardwaj, Chapter 3 of this book). Particular routes are followed both to journey to holy sites and also to move around those sites. Thus the pilgrim may experience a sense of awe that is engendered in part by the journey itself and in part by the physical aspects of the place and the perception of the pilgrimage centre as transcending ordinary places. The spiritual impressions of the journey and the perceptions of the pilgrimage centre are inextricable from the economic transactions that take place there.

Vijayanagara

The remainder of this paper will focus on the archaeological evidence from the Vitthala temple and its surrounding neighbourhood at the pre-colonial imperial capital city of Vijayanagara in order to explore the ways in which the spatial arrangement of pilgrimage influences the economy of pilgrimage. The Vijayanagara Empire flourished in south India from the fourteenth to the sixteenth centuries AD (*fig.* 11.1). The emergence of the empire was made possible by political fracturing and upheaval within the Delhi Sultanate, which allowed Hindu rulers to establish a new polity. The capital was established in the mid-fourteenth century on the southern bank of the Tungabhadra River in the northern Deccan, in what is now central Karnataka. Although there had been settlement in the area for hundreds of years, Vijayanagara was the first city at the location (*fig.* 11.2). However, the area had spiritual connotations long before it became the centre of an empire. The village of Hampi at the heart of Vijayanagara was also home of the local river goddess Pampa. In local tradition, she became a consort to Virupaksha, an incarnation of Shiva. The large Shaivite shrine in Hampi continues to be actively visited by pilgrims each year. In addition, Vijayanagara lies at the centre of what is locally believed to be the mythical kingdom of Kishkindha, the home of Hanuman and the setting for much of the *Ramayana*. These Vaishnavite associations became especially important as the empire matured and later emperors primarily endowed Vishnu shrines.

The physical structure of the city may reflect complex spiritual meanings. Fritz (1985, 1986, 1987) argues that Vijayanagara is an example of a cosmic city and argues that the deeper structural levels of the city reflect the relationships between the celestial and the terrestrial. Much of the internal structure is focused on the areas of performance of the *mahanavami* rites, which took place in the Royal Centre on a high platform facing audience halls. This performance area was separated from the royal residence area by a large north-south wall that lay on the

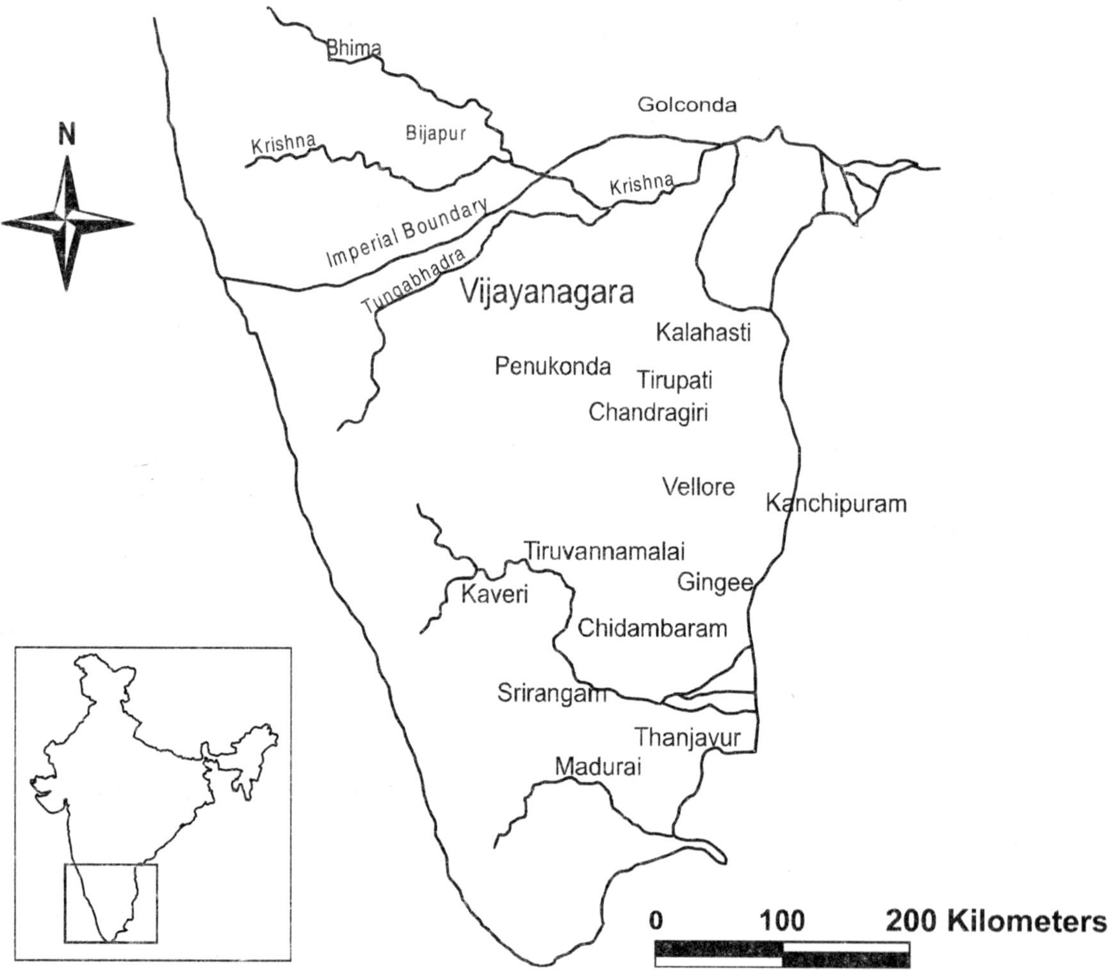

fig. 11.1: Vijayanagara Empire

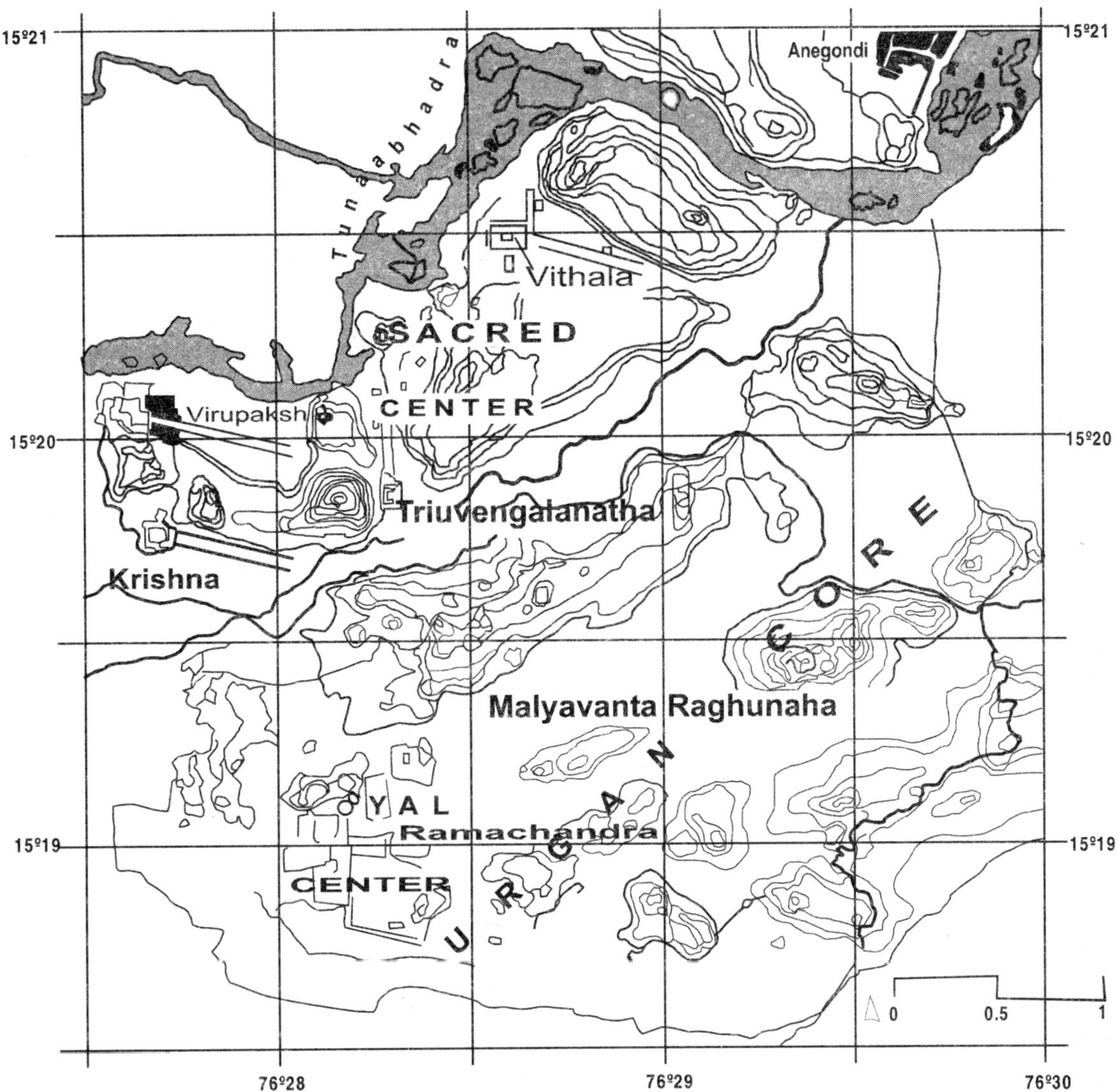

fig. 11.2: City of Vijayanagara, showing major temples.

same axis as the Ramachandra Temple. Routes of movement in the city were directed towards the royal centre, and once in the centre, attention was focused on this temple. Fritz proposes that these geometric similarities created a pattern of analogies that related the temple to the city and the empire as a whole. He has observed related structures in the layout of the architectural elements involved at these higher levels and argues, "that particular qualities of religious experience in sacred buildings were projected to larger scales" (Fritz 1987: 332). More recently, Malville (2000) has used the Geographical Positioning System (GPS) to measure with high precision the locations of the major temples in the city. His findings show that north-south alignment connects the Royal centre, Matanga Hill and the North Celestial Pole and he concurs with Fritz (1987) that that the sacred space in the city as a whole was shaped by both cosmological alignments and the movement of pilgrims.

Temples played an important role in the economic and political structure of the Vijayanagara Empire. Although temple towns and temples existed for hundreds of years before the empire, Vijayanagara rulers embarked on a systematic programme of temple construction and renovation throughout south India (Michell 1993; Appadurai and Breckenridge 1976). Nag and Reddy note that at Tirupati "the colony around the Govindaraja temple expanded over a period of centuries, particularly during 1336-1680 coinciding with the rule of the Vijayanagara dynasty" (1994: 118-19). This support of these rulers is evident in the extensive number of inscriptions on both the Govindaraja and Venkateshvara temples, which date to the sixteenth century.

Vijayanagara rulers endowed temples within the city walls of the capital as well. The Krishna temple was constructed by Krishnadevaraya to commemorate a military victory in 1515. The Tiruvengalanatha temple, constructed with funds donated by Hiriya Tirumala, the brother-in-law and chief minister of Achyutadevaraya, who ruled from 1530-42, was consecrated in 1534 (Fritz and Michell 1991: 92). Today the complex is commonly referred to as Achyutaraya's temple. The Vitthala, Malyavanta Raghunatha and Ramachandra complexes were also constructed during the Vijayanagara period. The areas surrounding the temples at Vijayanagara are often called by the temple name plus the suffix *puram* which translates as town. Thus, the area surrounding the Vitthala temple is known at Vitthalapuram.

It is also important to note that pilgrimage to the city of Vijayanagara was not likely on the same scale as pilgrimage to towns such as Tirumala or Srirangam whose primary focus was (and still is) the temple. Vijayanagara was the centre of government; the locus of imperial power and therefore a visit to a temple in the capital was a visit to the capital itself. Likewise, those visiting the capital for business or political purposes may have also visited the city's temples, even if they did not come on a pilgrimage, as such. As with other temples of the period, or the Virupaksha temple in Hampi today, the major temples in the city had a steady stream of visitors throughout the year, with peaks at times of festivals.

The city of Vijayanagara was abandoned in 1565 after the empire was defeated in war by a confederacy of northern states. Although a Vijayanagara ruler tried to reoccupy the city in 1567, his attempt was unsuccessful, leaving the area largely depopulated. Only small villages occupy the area today. This shift of power is visible at temples throughout the Vijayanangara imperial region: there was a sharp drop in donations to temples after 1565.

Spatial Studies at Vitthalapuram

Because the pilgrims' movement through the space of the pilgrimage centre forms such a fundamental part of the pilgrimage experience, the primary component in this study consists of understanding the patterns of movement through the areas immediately surrounding a large temple complex. The plans of temple towns throughout south India provide evidence of directed access and flow of people through space, directed lines-of-sight and physical changes in these pathways as people moved through them in ritualized patterns. One of the most notable features of Vijayanagara is the topography. The city is set in a landscape of rocky granite outcrops emerging from the Deccan Plateau. This landscape is spectacular visually and strongly dictates settlement patterning in the area. Although there are monuments strewn across the north ridge in the centre of the city, few archaeological remains are otherwise found on the ridges. Almost all the settlement of the city is found in the valleys as are all the major temple complexes. This topography, in itself, undeniably controls spatial patterning and the flow of movement inside the city within the temple districts.

The first part of the study was aimed at reconstruction and visualization of these routes in order to recreate the experience of the pilgrim's circulation at Vitthalapuram. Although the initial construction of the Vitthala temple may date to the latter half of the fourteenth century (Filliozat 1988: 28), numerous inscriptions dating from 1513-54 indicate that it was extensively renovated in the sixteenth century (Fritz and Michell 1991: 93). Vitthalapuram contains the remains of a substantial bazaar as well as residential structures (*fig.* 11.3).

During the 1996 field season the Vijayanagara Research Project recorded the archaeological remains at Vitthalapuram and base maps showing major remains and topography were drawn at 1:400 scale by professional surveyors from Bangalore. Archaeologists conducted surveys in the areas covered by the maps, noting additional remains and numbering and describing all features. In order to perform the following analyses, these maps were placed in ArcView, a Geographical Information System (GIS), and the relevant databases were converted to Microsoft Access in order to link them to the GIS.

In order to assess the probable routes of movement through the city, a least cost path through the area was calculated. The least cost path is the one that utilizes the least amount of energy in order to traverse a given area. The resulting map fits expectations based on what is known about circulation through pilgrimage centres. The easiest route follows the car path through the bazaar and towards the temple and apparently went around the temple complex before entrance into the complex could be made. The map also highlights several important features of the spatial characteristics of pilgrimage (*fig.* 11.4).

First, the prime area of spatial focus was the Vitthala temple complex itself. It was the major feature on the landscape and the routes easily lead towards it. Pilgrims would have been drawn through the bazaar and towards the temple, with its tall gateways drawing visitors closer while also looming overhead. This must have had quite a strong psychological effect

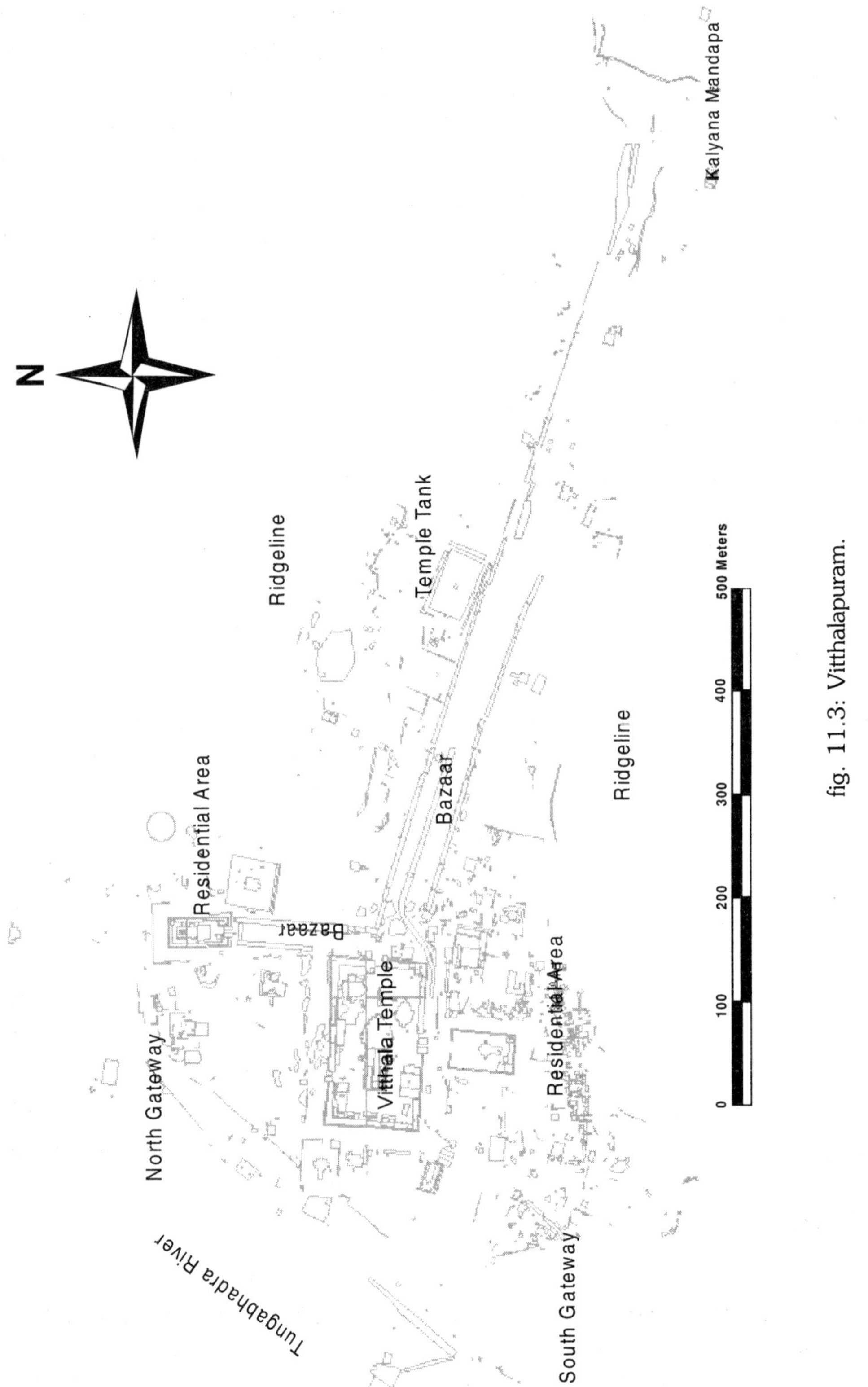

fig. 11.3: Vitthalapuram.

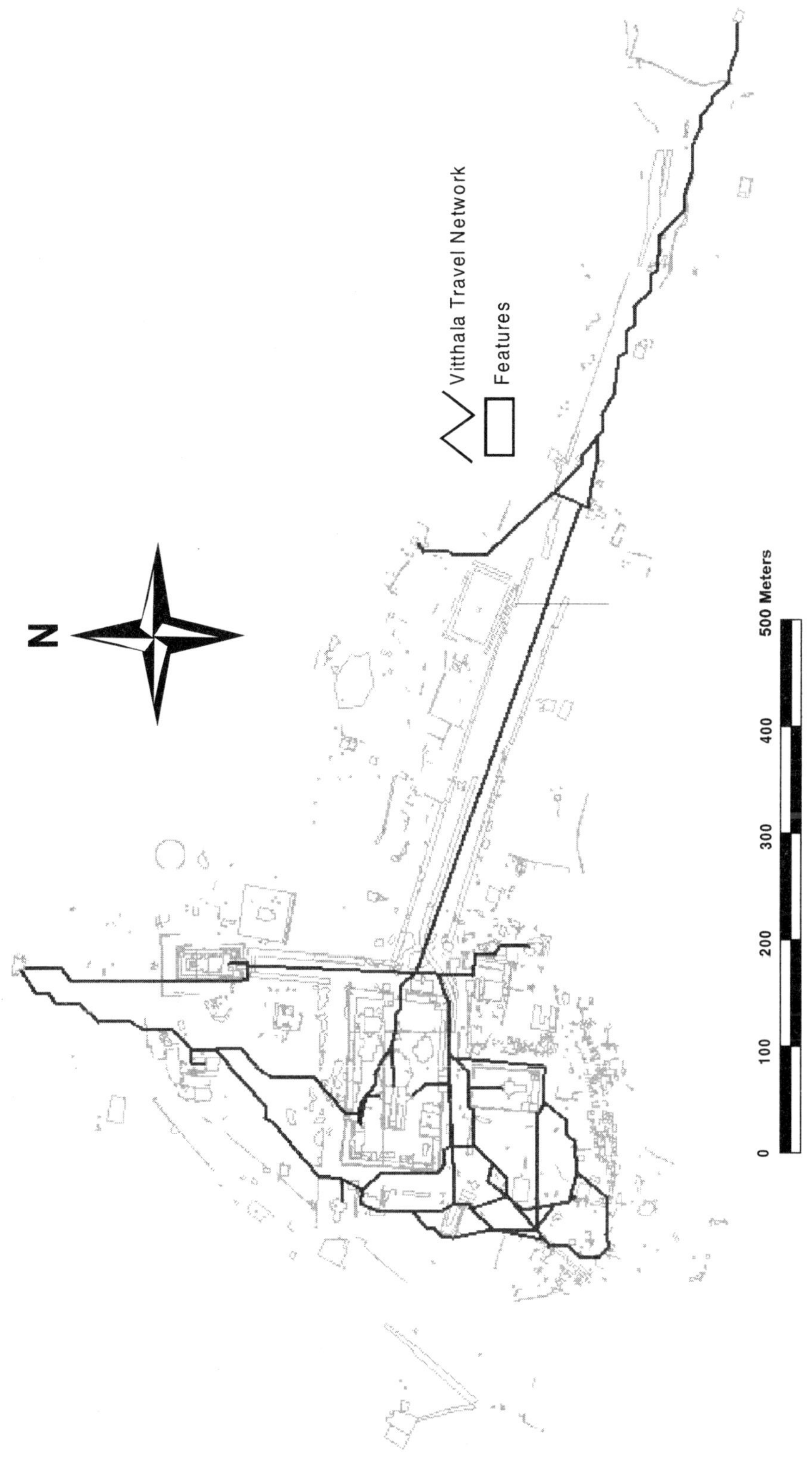

fig. 11.4: Vitthalapuram travel network.

before a pilgrim even entered the temple complex itself. Second, there was a clear spatial emphasis away from residential areas. Pathways appear designed to keep outsiders out. The pathways to and from the residential areas were limited and more restricted than those around the bazaar and temples. While outsiders thronged in the public areas, the roads and paths were planned to keep residential areas private and outside the realm of a pilgrims visit and experience of the city. A corollary to this is the third point, which is the fact that travellers were herded through the bazaar, which was the main focus of commercial transactions. Although there was access to the district from along the river, this route may have been a secondary route used primarily by city residents. Since there are clear patterns that separate public from private space within the district itself, it is reasonable to assume that this separation of public and private carried over to the city as a whole. In fact, in a network analysis of the known Vijayanagara era roads (Dunham concluded that the sacred centre, while relatively well connected in its own sub-network of roads) was not very accessible to the rest of the city network system (Dunham 1995: 136). This could indicate that although access between temples was kept open pilgrims were discouraged from venturing into other parts of the city, such as private residential areas.

Economy of Pilgrimage at Vitthalapuram

The archaeological remains at Vijayanagara do not reveal all the economic activity that must have occurred around the major temple complexes. Based on what is known ethnographically, it is reasonable to assume that most of the residents of Vitthalapuram were employed in the service of the temple, were merchants or otherwise provided services to the temple or its visitors. As at other temples, the goods sold most likely consisted of flowers, incense, textiles, jewellery and food. Service guilds, such as tailors and artists, probably also had space in the main bazaar. It would have been difficult for pilgrims to avoid these goods and services, even if they did not partake of them.

Another important economic aspect of pilgrimage is the provisioning of the travellers, who must sleep, drink and eat. Often these processes are economized, as for instance, pilgrims may avoid the costs of a room by sleeping outside. Water is usually free, procured from rivers and streams or strategically placed troughs and wells found along roadsides. Several inscriptions from Vijayanagara and the immediate vicinity record the construction of wells and troughs. One such inscription was found on a rock by a road near Anegondi, which lies across the river from Vijayanagara. It dates to 1551 and mentions a land-grant that was specifically for the purpose of granting water to travellers (Patil and Patil: Inscription 2). Ethnographic studies (Gold 1988; Lynch 1988) indicate that pilgrims often carry food with them and prepare it as needed, and in some cases food may be provided for pilgrims at various points on the journey. Many of the major south Indian pilgrimage temples today provide food and lodging for pilgrims. This practice may have occurred at Vitthalapuram, as indicated by an inscription on the temple that records, among other things, a donation to a *ramanujakuta* or pilgrim's feeding house (Filliozat and Filliozat: Inscription XVI). In addition, there are three possible large kitchens remaining in the district, identified by high double roofs (*fig.* 11.5). One is in the south-west corner of the arcade surrounding the inside of the enclosure wall, inside the temple complex. Another lies inside the enclosure walls of a smaller temple just west of the main complex. The last is part of a *mandapa* that surrounds a small temple near the old Shiva temple, south of the main Vitthala complex. These kitchens may have primarily fed temple functionaries but if there was a main supply kitchen for pilgrims, only the largest would have been sufficient for the task.

None the less, observations of the archaeological remains at Vitthalapuram show that food items were also bought and sold in the district. Artefact distributions suggest that a variety of provisioning activities were occurring around the temple. The distribution of artefacts between the public and private areas of the district is distinctive. The most visible and numerous archaeological artefacts were grinding stones, which can be further classified as slicks or mortars. Mortars are individual blocks of granite, square or rounded, generally no longer than 50 cm on a side. They have spherical basins cut into the middle to make room for the material to be ground and a handstone, such as a pestle. Slicks are worn, smooth areas on sheetrock or floors of buildings. Analyses of the distributions of the grinding stones show high densities of grinding stones around the main temple complex, and at important *mandapas* (*fig.* 11.6). In addition, visual analysis indicates a distinction in the distribution of types of groundstone artefacts in the district, with more mortars in the residential areas and more slicks in public areas such as the bazaar and temple (*fig.* 11.7).

These observations are supported by statistical analyses, which have also shown that there were differences in the types of activities occurring throughout the districts. Statistically significant differences can be seen in the artefact distributions in different regions of the district. Overall, preliminary analysis indicates that the differences in groundstone types may also indicate differences in public *versus* private provisioning. Artefact distributions in three areas classified as Residence, Bazaar and Temple were mapped, and a chi square analyses was run on the distribution of slicks and mortars in these three areas (*fig.* 11.8). The chi square statistics was 25.4 with 2 degrees of freedom, with a probability of this distribution occurring by chance less than one part in 1000. The bazaar has a relatively equal mix of groundstone of both types, with slightly more mortars than expected. Around the temples, almost no mortars are found. The groundstone in the residential area consists entirely of mortars and a single grinding slab on legs was also found in this area but not included in the analysis. Although the archaeological materials in Vitthalapuram have been subject to centuries of disrepair and more recent tourism does not bode well for preservation, the distinctions in these distributions are clear enough to be considered reflective of the different types of activities that took place in these separate areas of the districts. Further analysis is necessary to determine the distinct uses of mortars *vs.* slicks. However, based on the size and distribution of these stones, it is likely that mortars were

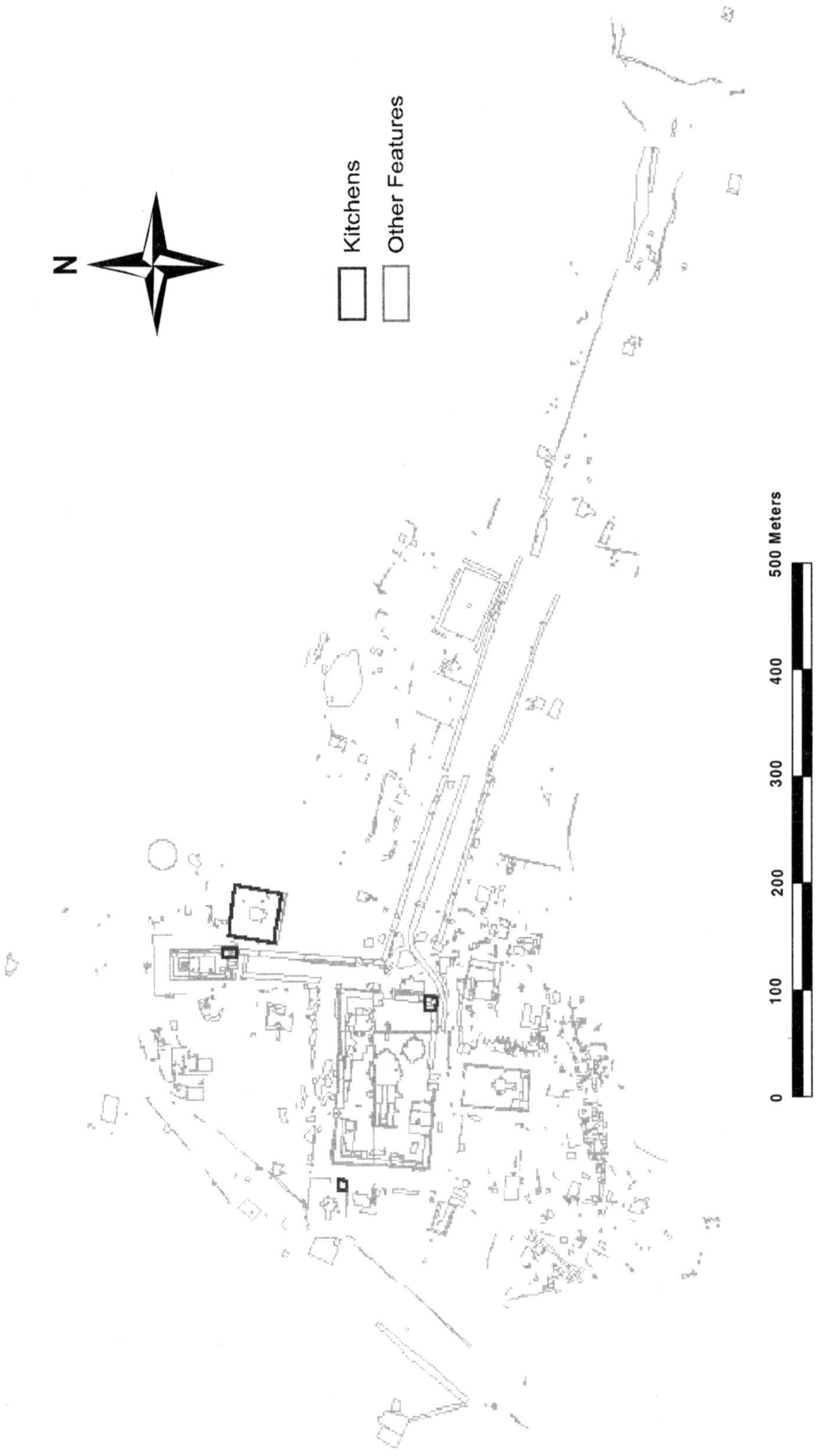

fig. 11.5: Vitthalapuram kitchens.

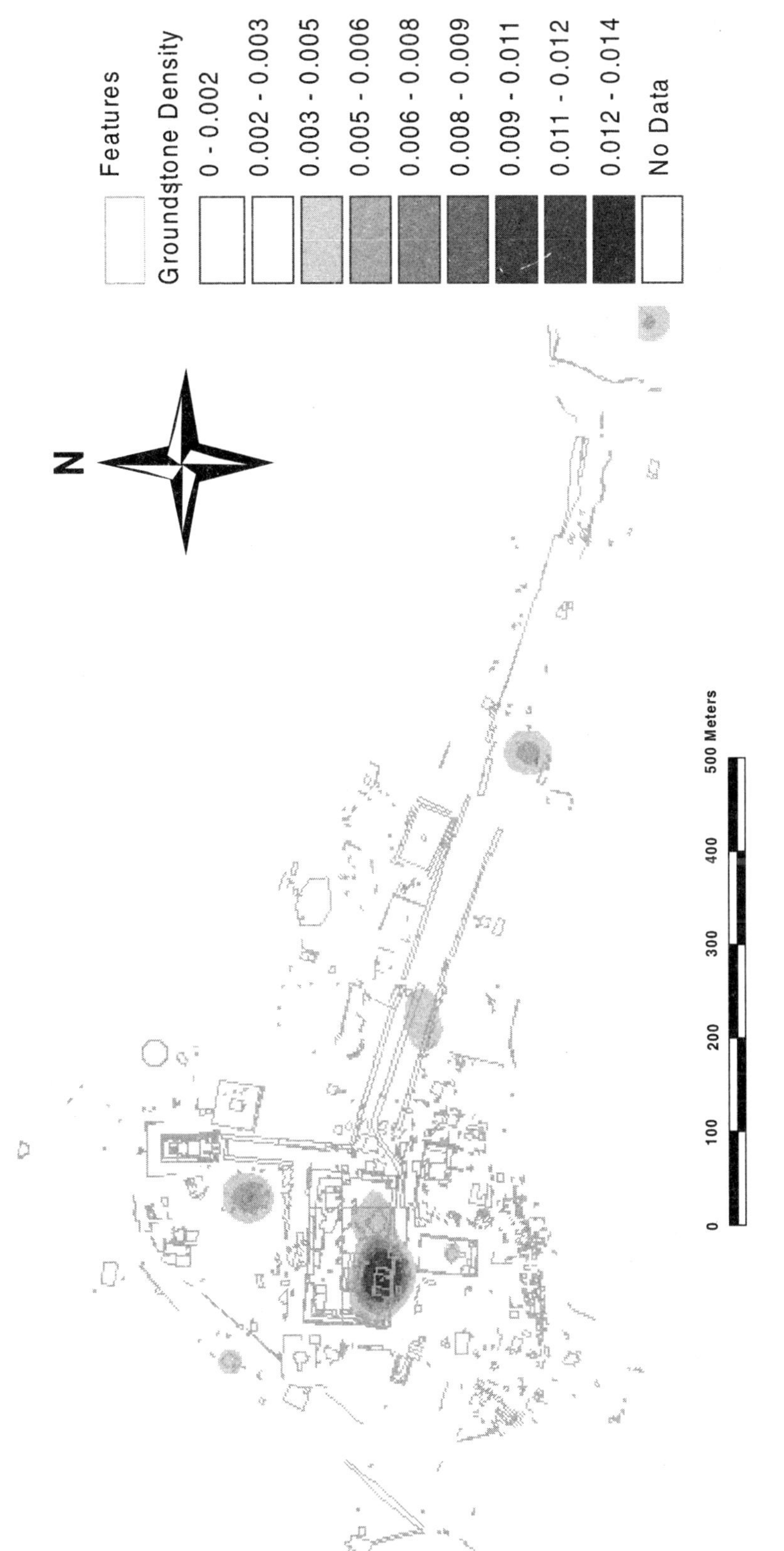

fig. 11.6: Extrapolated groundstone density map, darker areas show higher densities.

fig. 11.7: Distribution of grinding stones.

	mortar	slick
Bazaar	31	28
exp.	*28.3*	*32.7*
Residence	13	0
exp.	*6.1*	*6.9*
Temple	7	28
exp.	*16.6*	*18.5*

fig. 11.8: Observed and expected artefact distributions.

more commonly used for small-scale grinding, while slicks were used for faster, larger scale food processing. In the residential area, where food preparation would be for single families, mortars or similar stones are found exclusively. Slicks are more common in the public areas of the district. John Fritz estimates that some of these slicks, especially around the temple, may have been used in plaster production (personal communication). Further analyses are planned in order to make more accurate comparisons.

There are other artefactual indicators of differences in public and private space. Basins and troughs are both water-holding features, relatively shallow and smaller than a meter long. On visual inspection it appears that most of the basins and troughs are in the residential area, as are most of the wells and larger reservoirs (*fig.* 11.9). Basins and troughs would have been used primarily for short-term water storage. The water in these small tanks was likely used soon after it was placed there for uses such as cleansing and food preparation. It is interesting to note that based on their relative inaccessibility, certain water supplies may have been kept private at Vitthalapuram. Some wells and the Tungabhadra river (considered holy by many) were accessible to the public and travellers such as pilgrims but once again it is clear that there are places and things to which pilgrims do not have free access.

Other artefacts than those previously mentioned were found in the area. These included celts, lamps, mauls, quernstones and ceramics. They occurred in such low densities that they were unreliable for chi square analysis. However, visual inspection of the distributions of all these artefact types indicates that the temple has a low artefact diversity, while the residence and bazaar both seem to have an assortment of artefacts, indicating a greater variety of activities, including economic activities, taking place in these areas (*fig.* 11.10).

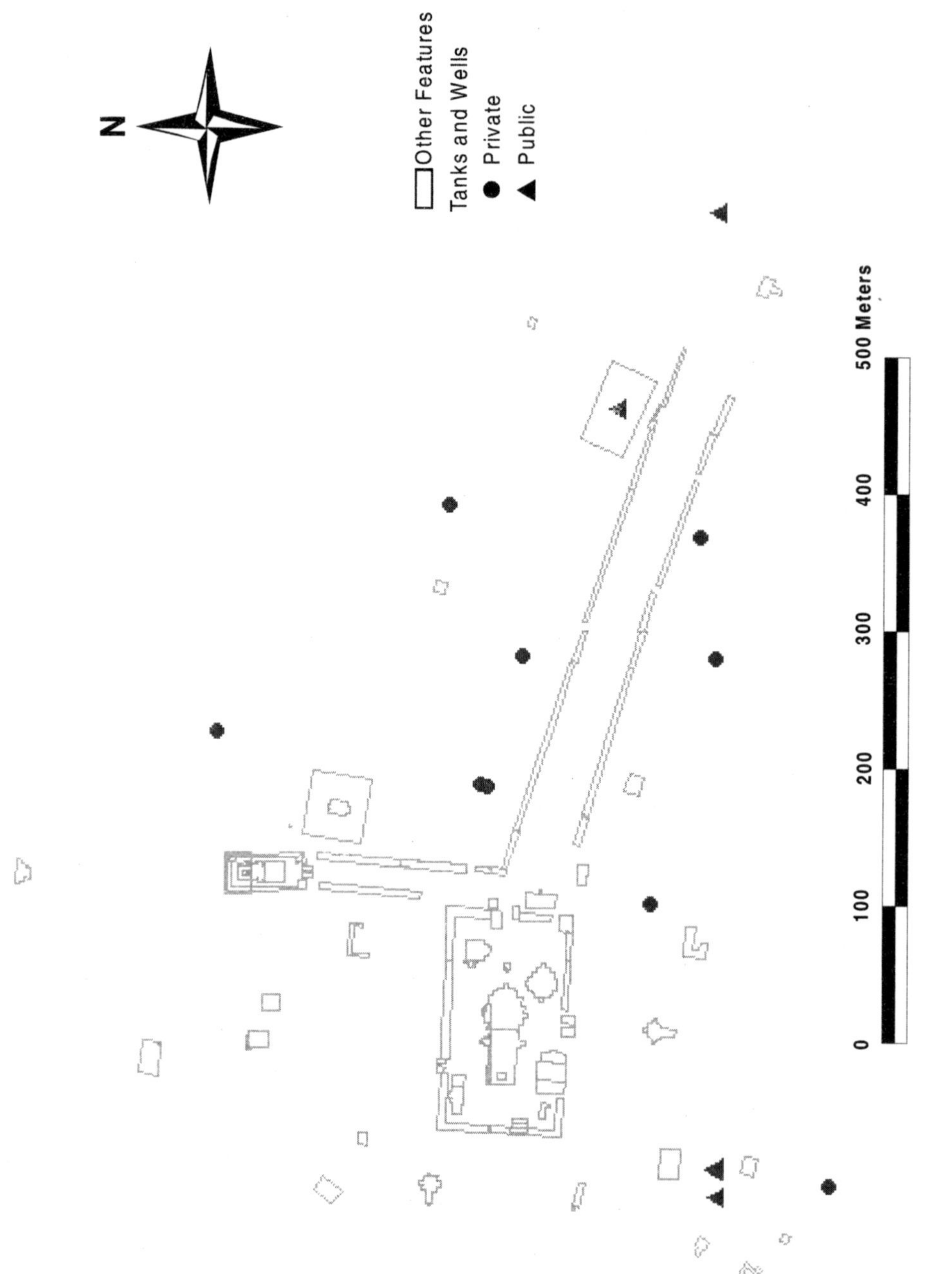

fig. 11.9: Distribution of water features.

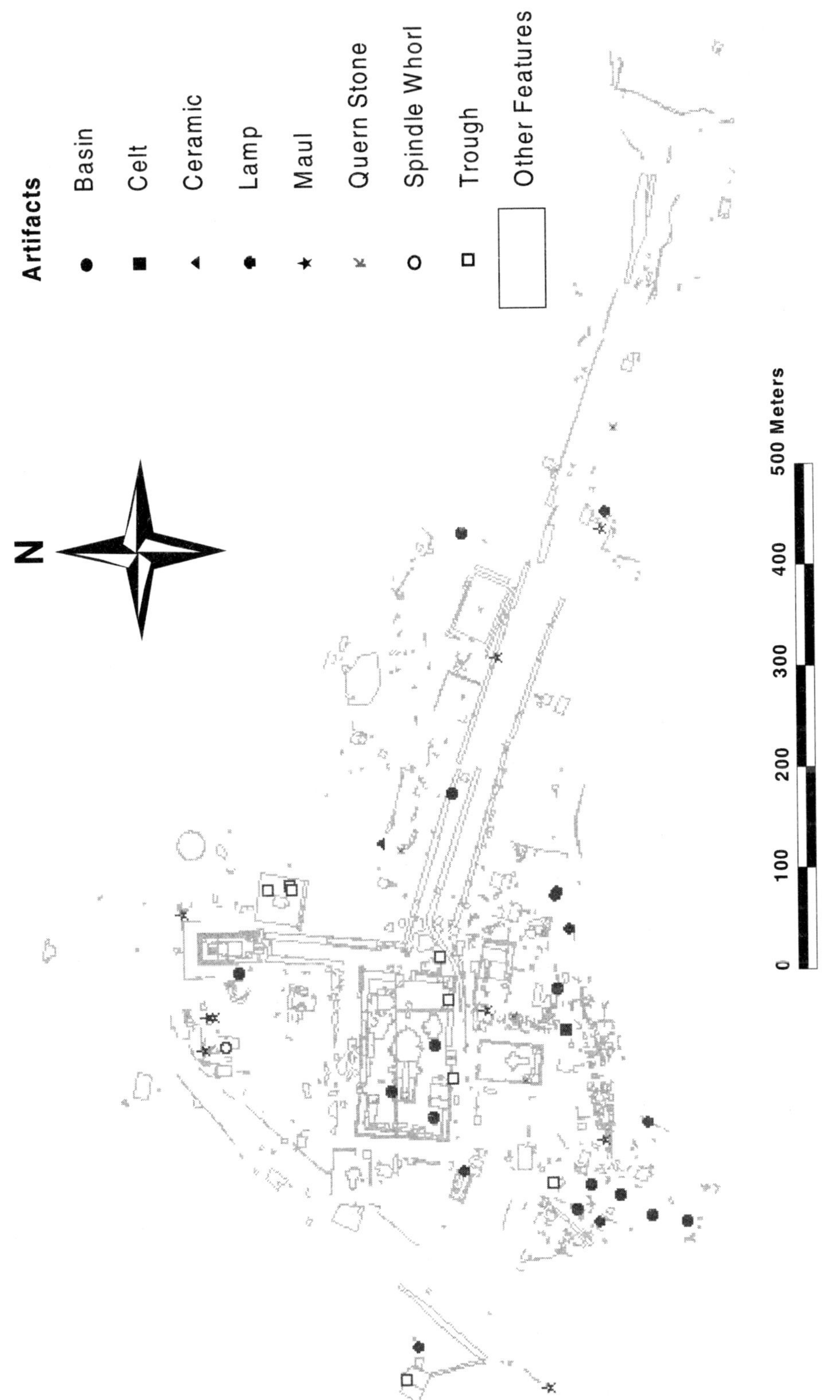

fig. 11.10: Vitthalapuram artefact diversity.

Conclusions: Space, Economy and Complex Systems

The economy of pilgrimage is intricately connected to the spatial aspects of pilgrimage. As this small study of the uses of space at Vitthalapuram has shown, the layout of the temple district reflects the economic uses of the area, through distinctions in public and private space and in provisioning activities. Pilgrims are directed through the district along particular routes, which emphasize the intended role of the pilgrim in the town. They are outsiders; separate from residents and potential customers and trading partners.

The spatial arrangement of the temple town is much more than an economic filter. These arrangements have a great emotional and psychological effect on pilgrims. The directed routes emphasize the greatness of the temple and the holiness of the place, imbuing the pilgrim with a sense of the sacred. The spatial arrangement of the town is an integral part of the overall pilgrimage experience and the spatial connection between spirituality and economy makes it clear that economy cannot be separated from the spiritual experience.

References

Appadurai, A., and C.A. Breckenridge, 1976, "The South Indian Temple: Authority, Honor, and Redistribution," *Contributions to Indian Sociology* (ns) 10:187-211.

Bhardwaj, S.M., 1997, "Circulation and Circumambulation. Paper presented at the *26th Annual Conference on South Asia*", Madison, WI, October 16-19, 1997.

Dunham, P. S., 1995, "Spatial Hierarchies and Activity Foci within Nuclear Vijayanagara: A Network Analysis of the Internal Roads and the Royal Centre," in *Sri Nagabhinandanam: Dr. M.S. Nagaraja Rao Festschrift*, ed. L. K. Srinivasan and S. Nagaruju, Bangalore: Dr. M.S. Nagaraja Rao Felicitation Committee.

Filliozat, P. and V. Filliozat, 1988, *Hampi-Vijayanagara: The Temple of Vitthala*, New Delhi: Sitaram Bhartia Institute of Scientific Research.

Fritz, J.M., 1985, "Was Vijayanagara a "Cosmic City?"," in *Vijayanagara — City and Empire: New Currents of Research*, ed. A.L. Dallapiccola, Stuttgart: Steiner-Verlag.

———, 1986, "Vijayanagara: Authority and Meaning in a South Indian Capital," *American Anthropologist* 88: 44-55.

Fritz, J.M., 1987, "Interpreting the Plan of a Medieval Hindu Capital," *World Archaeology* 19:105-29.

Fritz, J.M., G. Michell and J. Gollings, 1991, *Vijayanagara: City of Victory*, New York: Aperture.

Gold, A.G., 1988, *Fruitful Journeys: The Ways of Rajasthani Pilgrims*, Berkeley: University of California Press.

Gross, D., 1971, "Ritual and Conformity: A Religious Pilgrimage to Northern Brazil," *Ethnology* 10: 129-48.

Jindel, R., 1976, *Culture of a Sacred Town: A Sociological Study of Nathdwara*, Bombay: Popular Prakashan.

Lynch, O., 1988, "Pilgrimage with Krishna, Sovereign of Emotions," *Contributions to Indian Sociology* 22:171-94.

Malville, J.M., 2000, "The Cosmic Geometries of Vijayanagara", in *Ancient Cities, Sacred Skies: Cosmic Geometries, and City Planning in Ancient India*, eds. J.M. Malville and Lalit M. Gujral, New Delhi: Aryan Book International.

Michell, G., 1993, "Introduction," *Marg* XLIV: 2-17.

Nag, S.C. and M.V. Reddy, 1994, "The Urban Origin of Tirupati Temple Town," *National Geographer* 29: 115-20.

Patil, C.S. and V.C. Patil, 1995, "Inscriptions at Vijayangara (Hampi)," *Inscriptions of Karnataka*, Vol. 1, Vijayanagara Research Centre Series Number 8, Mysore: Directorate of Archaeology and Museums.

Pieper, J., 1980, "The Spatial Structure of Suchindram," in *Traditional Concepts of Ritual Space in India: Studies in Architectural Anthropology*, ed. J. Pieper, London: Art and Archaeology Research Papers.

Preston, J.J., 1992, "Spiritual Magnetism: An Organizing Principle for the Study of Pilgrimage," in *Sacred Journeys: The Anthropology of Pilgrimage*, ed. A. Morinis, Westport: Greenwood Press.

Stein, B., 1958, *The Tirupati Temple: An Economic Study of a Medieval South Indian Temple*. Unpublished Ph.D. Dissertation, University of Chicago.

Stein, B.,1982, "Vijayanagara c. 1350-1564," in *The Cambridge Economic History of India*, vol. I: c. 1200-1750, ed. T. Raychaudhuri and I. Habib, Cambridge: Cambridge University Press.

PART III

WORLD PILGRIMAGE

12

Continuity and Adjustment within a Representative Japanese Pilgrimage System

Hiroshi Tanaka Shimazaki

Introduction

BUDDHISM shares with other great religions the practice of pilgrimage to sacred places both for spiritual benefit and to render homage, although it was not advocated by Gautama Buddha. It was not until after the death of the Buddha in the sixth century BC that the practice emerged, as his followers began visiting those places associated with him. Whatever its origin, the practice of pilgrimage has been widespread in Buddhism over many centuries in both of its main branches, Hinayana in southeast Asia and Mahayana in east Asia (Geden).

The earliest known reference to *junrei*, the Japanese word for pilgrimage, appears in *Nitto Guho Junrei-goki* written by Priest Ennin after he travelled to China in 838 to study Buddhism. It is thought that the practice of pilgrimage was introduced to Japan in the middle of the Heian period (794–1192) by Buddhist priests who, during periods of study in China, made pilgrimages to various sacred places and, on their return, were instrumental in establishing the practice in Japan. Today, pilgrimages to Buddhist sites are but one of several types. Others are made to sacred mountains, to sites of historic events, and to scenic wonders, some of which have strong connections with Shinto (Reischauer, Kitagawa, Reader & Swanson, Hoshino 1981).

A dominant characteristic of Japanese pilgrimage is the inclusion of multiple sites. The Shikoku pilgrimage, the focus of this paper, encompasses 88 temples and its circular route extends over 960 miles (1,385 kilometres), making it one of the longest pilgrimages in Japan (*fig.* 12.1). Associated with the Buddhist priest, Kobo Daishi (774–835), this pilgrimage has been popular since the 17th century and today attracts upwards of 80,000 pilgrims annually. Firsthand observation coupled with information gleaned from the literature reveals the dynamic nature of the pilgrimage, a characteristic shared by pilgrimages worldwide.

Underlying the dynamic processes are ongoing adjustments occurring in response to inescapable tensions between tradition and modernization. These adjustments, manifest in almost every aspect of the pilgrimage, are the outcome of the attempt to reach a compromise between, on the one hand, the acquisition of religious merit and, on the other, expediency. Conflict between the attainment of religious merit and externally imposed restrictions and pressures symbolizes the larger set of incongruities associated with the increased physical pace of life in the secular arena and the yearning for the security of some sacred absolute.

This paper examines the emergence and evolution of various aspects of the Shikoku pilgrimage, both as a system and as a practice, and explores the roles played by various individuals and organizations (pilgrims, pilgrim leaders, priests, scholars, Buddhist association, area residents, transportation providers, government) in its longevity. The data on which this paper is based were first collected during 78 days in the fall of 1972 when I participated in the pilgrimage on foot. Since then I have returned to Shikoku numerous times and have had the opportunity to augment and update the data. In the preparation of this paper, I have drawn on information contained in my earlier publications on various facets of the pilgrimage with regard to its traditional aspects. Prior to 1991, my publications appeared under the name Hiroshi Tanaka.

Formative Stage

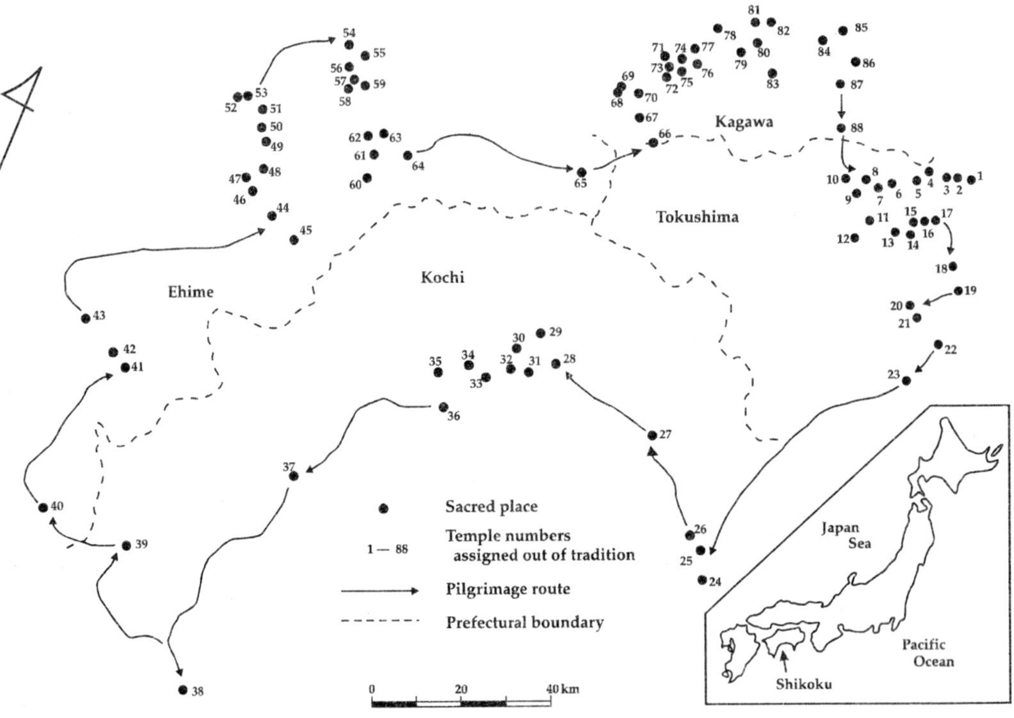

fig. 12.1. Locations of 88 Buddhist pilgrim places on Shikoku.

KOBO DAISHI: SPIRITUAL FOUNDER

Tradition holds that the Shikoku pilgrimage was established by Kobo Daishi, a late eighth/early ninth-century priest who founded the Shingon Mikkyo sect of Buddhism and introduced many new ideas, technologies and practices after a period of study in China (Hasuo). The significance of the association of the pilgrim places with Kobo Daishi manifest in artificial and natural features, together with the acknowledgement of this association by pilgrims through their behaviour, is a distinctive feature of this pilgrimage. Pilgrims carry staves that symbolize Kobo Daishi. Written on them are the words *dogyo ninin*, meaning "together with Kobo Daishi," whose presence is acknowledged through pilgrim behaviour at each of the 88 sacred places. Today, *daishido*, the building dedicated to Kobo Daishi, are found at all 88 temples and statues of Kobo Daishi and trees, stones, cliffs, caves and waterfalls with which legend has associated him are also frequently found within the compounds and along the pilgrim path.

Shikoku being the birthplace of Kobo Daishi, it is not surprising that it was here that a pilgrimage associated with him developed. In the existing records left by Kobo Daishi, however, there is no reference to a pilgrimage to the 88 places although in *Sango Shiiki* written in 796, he does mention three places on Shikoku (Mount Tairyu, Cape Muroto and Mount Ishizuchi) where he went to seek religious revelation (Y. Kondo 1971, Miyazaki). As well, in *Konjaku Monogatari*, edited by Minamoto in 1106-08, there is reference to Kobo Daishi visiting Manno and reconstructing the irrigation pond there.

Temple records indicate that all 88 temples were established before 835, the year of Kobo Daishi's death, giving credence to the notion that he could have visited the sacred places. These 88 temples, however, were not the only temples on Shikoku during Kobo Daishi's lifetime. There were at least 165 temples of which, today, 130 claim a strong association with Kobo Daishi, citing him as founder, consecrator, or sculptor of their *honzon* (chief deity) or claiming association with his activities (Hori, Tanaka 1983).

PILGRIMAGE TO SHIKOKU

That it would have been possible to make a pilgrimage on Shikoku as early as the ninth century is apparent from the earliest known map of Japan drawn by Priest Gyoki in 805. This map shows that Shikoku, literally four countries, was divided into four administrative regions, now known as prefectures, and that there was a road leading from Kyoto, then the nation's capital, across Awaji Island to Shikoku and around the periphery of the island (Akioka).

Priest Jakuhon, in *Shikoku Henro Kudoku-ki*, suggests that Shinzei, a follower of Kobo Daishi, may have been the first person to make the pilgrimage (Jakuhon 1690), visiting those places with which Kobo Daishi was believed to be associated, immediately after Kobo Daishi's death in 835. The validity of this suggestion is questioned by Maeda, though, as there is no reference in Shinzei's biography to such a journey to Shikoku (Maeda). Maeda also draws attention to Hasuo's statement that the possible visit to Shikoku by Shinzei would have been of a personal nature and that of greater public significance and more likely to have been imitated would have been the probable journey to Shikoku by Shinnyo Shinno, a member of the Royal family, in 861. That Shinnyo Shinno did visit Shikoku is supported by the fact that his grave, constructed prior to his death, lies within the compound of Kiyotakiji (temple 35). Whether Shinnyo Shinno actually made a pilgrimage on Shikoku and visited other sacred places besides Kiyotakiji, however, is not definitely known.

Other documents concerning the origin of the pilgrimage suggest beginnings that have no apparent association with Kobo Daishi. *Konjaku Monogatari* contains an account of three Buddhist priests who travelled along the difficult terrain on the fringe of Shikoku, but it does not relate this journey in any way with Kobo Daishi. A similar reference to priests travelling around the coast of Shikoku is found in *Ryojin Hisho* (Goshirakawa Tenno). Other accounts suggest that one of the reasons that pilgrimages were made to Shikoku was that certain places such as Ashizuri Cape and Shido were considered to be departure points for *Fudaraku Jodo* or the "Pure Land" which was believed to lie to the south across the sea.

The Japanese term used to refer exclusively to the Shikoku pilgrimage is *henro. Hen* is usually interpreted as "to go around" and *ro* as "road." Within the existing records, for example in the above mentioned *Konjaku Monogatari* and *Ryojin Hisho*, there is repeated reference to journeying to the *henchi*, or *hendo* of Shikoku (Y. Kondo 1971). Although the pronunciation is the same, the Kanji character for *hen* used in *henchi* and *hendo* is different from that presently used for *hen* in *henro* and is interpreted as "fringe". *Chi* and *do* both refer to place or area. These early references to *henchi* and *hendo* and the present use of the term *henro* suggests there is a relationship between the present pilgrimage and the early practice of travelling around the fringe of the island. Like pilgrimages elsewhere, the Shikoku pilgrimage has a "peripheral" character.

EMERGENCE OF THE 88 SITES

When and how did the pilgrimage come to encompass the present 88 places? These questions were raised as early as the late 17th century by Buddhist priest Jakuhon in his guidebook to the Shikoku pilgrimage, *Shikoku Henrei Reijoki* (Jakuhon 1689). The answers were not known then nor are they now although there has been considerable speculation (Shinjo). Y. Kondo (1971) suggests that the number 88 had come to be associated with the Shikoku pilgrimage by 1471 based on inscriptions found on temple statuary. Jakuhon provides descriptions of 92 sites without reference to assigned numbers. The list begins with Zentsuji, widely recognized as the birthplace of Kobo Daishi and today temple 75.

Temple numbers did not come into usage until sometime after the seventeenth century, when the pilgrimage gained popularity. Today the first temple in the circuit is Ryozenji. Since it is the first temple to be reached by pilgrims coming from central Japan via Awaji Island, the temple is a convenient starting point for the pilgrimage. Ryozenji is also a convenient starting point for pilgrims who come to Shikoku after visiting Koyasan, the headquarters of the Shingon Mikkyo sect and the place where Kobo Daishi died.

Over the years, repeated practice of the pilgrimage starting at Ryozenji and continuing in a clockwise direction, reinforced by constant reference to this order in pilgrim guidebooks and maps, cemented the sequence. Thus it could be said that, from the outset, the Shikoku pilgrimage assumed a convenient circuit for pilgrims, at least for those approaching the island from central Honshu.

Elaboration of the Pilgrimage System

ADDING MEANING

The historical process through which the 88 sites came to be included in the pilgrimage is uncertain. Nor can it be ascertained if the number 88 played a role in the selection process or was imbued with meaning as a result of its association with the pilgrimage. Whatever the case, inspired by Buddhist writing and folk tradition, several illustrations of the importance of the number 88 to the Shikoku pilgrimage have emerged, indicative, perhaps, of a desire to anchor an otherwise loosely coordinated system and synthesize the pilgrimage (Tanaka 1983).

In 1690, Jakuhon equated the 88 sacred places with the 88 kenwaku or illusions of the mind that distort the truth (Jakuhon 1690). To visit the temples is to eliminate the illusions one by one. In 1763, Hosoda, on an early pilgrimage map, suggested that the distribution of the 88 sites over the four prefectures of Shikoku symbolized a fourfold mandala situated among ten worlds on each of the eight petals of a lotus altar and shining incessantly over the Buddhist world (Hosoda 1972). To make the pilgrimage is to unite with the universe.

The numbers four and eight have long been important in Buddhist thought. Four sites marking the birth, training, enlightenment and death of Gautama Buddha as well as the division of his ashes into eight parts and their initial enshrinement in stupas are widely known. Japanese folk tradition holds that ashes from one or all of the eight Indian stupas are buried within the compound of each of the Shikoku 88 temples. The significance of the number 88 has also been linked to the fact that the Kanji characters for 88, when combined, form the character for rice, the most important staple in Japan. Reference is frequently made, especially on Shikoku, to the fact that 88 is also the total of the three dominant *yakudoshi* or "calamity years": 42 for men, 33 for women and 13 for children.

For pilgrims, the clear declaration of 88 as the number of stages within the "closed spatial entity" provides confirmation that the pilgrimage has culminated when the assigned temples have been visited. Maintaining the number at 88 over the centuries has given the temples a strong collective identity, while reinforcing their special religious significance. Acting as a consistent binding force, it has contributed to the integration of the Shikoku pilgrimage as a spatial and symbolic system. This pilgrimage, however, is not a closed system.

Along the Shikoku path, pilgrims encounter, and often visit, a multitude of temples and wayside shrines known as *Bangai* ("out of number of sites") and/or *Okunoin* ("inner temples affiliated with one of the 88 temples"). These are not within the designated 88 but many claim a strong connection with Kobo Daishi as in the case of Kaiganji (a contestant, along with Zentsuji, for Kobo Daishi's birth place) and Dogakuji (where Kobo Daishi studied in his youth). Twenty of these temples known as *Bekkaku Nijukka-ji Reijo* are engaged in a collective effort to strengthen their links with the official pilgrimage (Tanaka 1983). Headed by *Kaiganji*, they have united into a sub-pilgrimage. Official sanction of this sub-pilgrimage would bring the combined number of sacred places to 108, widely recognized as a significant number in Buddhism as well as in Hinduism (Singh).

SHIKOKU AS A SYMBOLIC IMAGE

The distribution of the 88 temples over Shikoku's four prefectures has fostered the development of the concept of Shikoku as a Buddhist dojo or holy place of learning and practicing The Way. "In the religious world the metaphor of the "way" (*do, michi*) is used to refer to situations such as seeking the way or seeking the law" (Hoshino 1997: 297). Traversing the island in a clockwise direction, it is believed that pilgrims are travelling the path to enlightenment.

Each of the four prefectures represents a stage along this path and symbolically constitutes a smaller *dojo* serving a specific purpose reflected in its name. *Hosshin no Dojo* (Tokushima Prefecture) is the *dojo* in which it is determined that supreme enlightenment will be obtained; *Shugyo no Dojo* (Kochi Prefecture) is the *dojo* for the religious practice required to attain enlightenment; *Bodai no Dojo* (Ehime Prefecture) is the *dojo* for the attainment of wisdom and understanding of life necessary for enlightenment; and *Nehan no Dojo* (Kagawa Prefecture) is the *dojo* in which the satisfactory completion of all that has gone before will lead to enlightenment (Tanaka 1981).

Within each *dojo*, one temple functions as *sekisho*, or "checkpoint," which "sinners" cannot pass. Their locations do not follow any particular rule with respect to their spatial relationship to other sacred places within the *dojo* but, with the exception of the *sekisho* (Tatsueji) in the first *dojo*, the sekisho is one of the most physically challenging sites to reach within each *dojo*. In addition to Tatsueji (temple 19), Konomineji (temple 27), Yokomineji (temple 60) and Unpenji (temple 66), the four prefectural *sekisho*, there is also the *ura-sekisho*, a fifth *sekisho* for the four *dojo* together. Kanjizaiji (temple 40), located approximately halfway along the circular route from Ryozenji (temple 1), was chosen to fulfil this role. It is the first sacred place pilgrims visit after crossing into the third *dojo*.

The process through which the notion of Shikoku as a Buddhist *dojo* emerged is not clear, although it was likely to be initiated by Buddhist priests/scholars who wished to illumine the deeper and transcendental dimensions of the pilgrimage beyond the pragmatic realm.

LANDSCAPE AND RITUALS

Each sacred place is a geographic complex encompassing a multiplicity of concrete "physical features," both artificial and natural, each of which possesses a unique character. What were the distinguishing features of the 88 temple landscapes centuries ago? The earliest surviving comprehensive written and pictorial description of the pilgrimage sites is contained in Jakuhon's *Shikoku Henro Reijoki* published in 1689. From Jakuhon's data I have attempted to reconstruct the 17th century temple landscapes (Tanaka 1977).

Examination of Jakuhon's records reveals that the 88 temples had six "common" (occurring at more than 44 temples) structures: *hondo* (main hall), *yashiro* (Shinto structure), *kuri* (priests' residence), *mon* (gate), *shoro* (belfry) and *hei* (wall). At the end of the 17th century, 85 temples had a *hondo* in which the temple's chief deity was enshrined, 77 had *yashiro*, the dwelling place of various Shinto deities, indicative of the strong connection between the early temples and Shintoism and 76 had *kuri*. However, *daishido*, the building enshrining Kobo Daishi's image and currently found at all 88 temples, was present in only 35 temple compounds in Jakuhon's time. The dramatic increase in *daishido* over time suggests a deliberate strengthening of the association of the pilgrim places with Kobo Daishi on the part of the Shingon sect, with which 80 of the 88 temples are affiliated.

SUPPORT SYSTEM

As the pilgrimage increased in popularity the custom of *settai* developed. Local residents along the pilgrim route endow pilgrims with gifts of food, money, accommodation and sometimes transportation. Such actions not only help pilgrims but are considered to bring merit to the donors. Over the time this custom expanded into the development of *settai-ko*, voluntary groups who provided *settai* on a large scale (R. Kondo 1999). Participants often come from outside Shikoku and spend several weeks during the pilgrimage season in a temple.

Another avenue of support stems from the substantial network of legends associated with the pilgrimage. For example, the legend that has grown up around Emon Saburo has caused many to consider him to be the originator of the pilgrimage. It is recorded in the temple history of Ishideji (temple 51) that Emon Saburo visited the 88 sacred places 21 times as penance for his refusal to assist Kobo Daishi and the resulting death of his eight sons. In 831, on his 22nd time around the island, Emon Saburo died near Shosanji (temple 12) and his grave may still be seen there today. The graves of Emon Saburo's children, on the other hand, are located near Ishideji in Matsuyama city at the opposite end of the island. Thus the legend functions as a bond between these three sites to further strengthen their spatial interaction within the pilgrimage.

Expansion, Stability, and Changes

REPLICATION OF SHIKOKU PILGRIMAGE SYSTEM

To make the pilgrimage to the 88 sites on foot requires 50 to 60 days, longer for the sick or crippled. A pilgrimage of two months duration, after possibly travelling to Shikoku from other parts of Japan, for many was a difficult task. Personal considerations of finances and time were barriers to participation in the pilgrimage, as were political constraints during the Edo period (1600–1868) when movement from one prefecture to another was regulated. In response to these difficulties and to endorse the worship of Kobo Daishi, the process of pilgrimage replication in miniature emerged.

These miniature pilgrimages have generally been instigated by the head priest of the core temple where they emerged, either at his initiative or in response to congregational demand. Many, if not all, seem to share the process where soil from each of the original places was embedded in its counterpart in the miniature pilgrimage. Of at least 41 such miniature pilgrimage systems established outside Shkoku, many are still active today (Shinjo 1979). I have compared three imitative pilgrimages, Shodo, Chita and Sasaguri, with the original model elsewhere (Tanaka 1981).

Miniature pilgrimages cover a shorter distance, although there is considerable variation in circuit length; if made on foot, some take up to two weeks to complete. Like the original Shikoku sites, the miniature pilgrimage places are circular in arrangement, although the assigned temple numbers do not always conform to the sequential-spatial order of the sites. While the original sites contain a variety of built structures, their miniature counterparts are marked by smaller structures with limited variety, or, in some cases, by natural features, such as caves or waterfalls. Each pilgrimage site, whether original or imitative, has an association with Kobo Daishi and one or more Buddhist deities. In the miniature pilgrimages, however, the association with Buddhist deities differs from the Shikoku model with regard to the range and frequency of occurrence of images enshrined. In the Shodo pilgrimage, for example, variations among the deities are particularly great, with a number of Shinto deities included.

In addition to the miniature pilgrimage systems, the sacred places of which are primarily marked by temples, there are, throughout Japan (including Shikoku), numerous replicas of a much smaller scale. In these, the 88 sites are represented by a set of stone markers each of which has carved on it the name of one temple and the figure of the *honzon* of that temple. These stone markers are placed side by side in a row within a temple compound or at the side of the road leading to a temple and can be visited in a matter of minutes. They particularly attract the local residents of the area (Tanaka 1983, Hoshino 1984).

Replicated pilgrimages of various geographic scale have been established for the convenience of those who wish to make the original pilgrimage but are unable to do so. The opportunity provided for symbolic participation in the Shikoku pilgrimage affords the participants at least some religious merit. Such pilgrimages may also stimulate the desire to make the Hon-Shikoku, or "Real Shikoku," pilgrimage at a later date. In both cases the establishment of replicated pilgrimages increases awareness of the Shikoku pilgrimage.

RELOCATION OF SACRED PLACES

In inquiring into the stability of the 88 places over the time, I have examined published sources and temple records. Since the middle of the 16th century, the earliest period for which records exist, the exact positions of at least 14 temples have changed (Tanaka 1983). Six were originally located within Buddhist/Shinto complexes. Changes in their locations occurred when Buddhist temples and Shinto shrines were forced to separate in the early 1870s under Haibutsu-kishaku, the nationalist policy of the Meiji Government that declared Shinto to be the state religion and attempted to weaken externally introduced Buddhism. With regard to the eight remaining site changes, priests made the decision to relocate the complexes in each case after the temple structures were destroyed by fire during a succession of feudal wars. The most recent relocation occurred in 1921 when Hojuji (temple 62), forced to move in 1636 by the ravages of war, altered its location again, this time to accommodate the building of the national railway.

With the exception of Jurakuji (temple 7), which moved 3 km from its mountain site to the plain, all the moves have been less than 2 km. Thus, the general locations of the sacred sites have not changed and neither have their positions within the sequential order of the pilgrimage. By undergoing minor positional adjustments, the temples have been able to maintain their traditional relative position within the pilgrimage system.

CHANGE IN MODE OF TRANSPORATION

Modern modes of transportation have affected pilgrimages everywhere by continually expanding their catchment areas and altering the way pilgrimages are made. Many of the changes the Shikoku pilgrimage has undergone in the last century have stemmed from the development of alternative modes of transport.

In the 1920s, some pilgrims began to use local rail facilities where they were available.

As a rail system encompassing the entire periphery of the island, where most of the temples are found, has never been built, today, the most common form of transport is a chartered bus. Private bus companies within Shikoku and other parts of Japan have developed all-inclusive "pilgrim packages" in which transportation, accommodation and meals are included in the price.

Pilgrims also travel by taxi, private car, motorcycle and bicycle, with the result that the required time to complete the pilgrimage has been reduced from two months to about two weeks. With that has also come a reduction in the overall cost of accommodation until today, to make the pilgrimage on foot as the most expensive way.

The reductions in time and cost have opened the possibility of making the pilgrimage to almost everyone. With this, the line between the religious pilgrimage and the recreational journey has blurred. Meeting and mingling with other pilgrims as equals regardless of social position, a characteristic of pilgrimage in general (Turner 1978), was one of the great pleasures of the journey. The chance to interact with people from other walks of life and from other parts of the country, however, has been greatly diminished now that pilgrims travel in large groups, the members of which often belong to the same social unit, propelled around the island at breakneck speed in order to complete the pilgrimage in the minimum amount of time.

When I made the pilgrimage in 1972, the immediate access to one temple in each prefecture was by mountain footpath only — deliberately left this way to give pilgrims some sense of the traditional pilgrimage. All but one of these footpaths lead to *sekisho* temples. In the intervening years, however, paved roads and cable cars have been introduced to provide alternate access to all of these temples. The most recent innovation in pilgrim transport came in 1998 with the advent of charter helicopters for "flying visits" to the sacred sites. These helicopters belong to Shikoku Koku, a company engaged in the transport of construction materials to the remote mountain sites of a variety of hydro projects. The intention of the company is to serve physically handicapped individuals who wish to make the pilgrimage. Six pilgrims at a time can be accommodated on this four-day pilgrimage. Sixty-seven temples are visited from the air, the helicopter hovering above each sacred place while the pilgrims chant and pray. Due to their urban locations and subsequent air traffic restrictions, the remaining 21 temples are visited by van.

ADJUSTMENT IN CIRCULATION

The circular arrangement of the temples makes it possible for the pilgrimage to be initiated at any point. The contemporary trend is for pilgrims to begin at the most readily accessible temple. The recent construction of bridges linking Shikoku to Honshu has increased access to the pilgrimage circuit. The first, opened in 1987, was the Naruto automobile bridge connecting Sumoto, on Awaji Island, and Naruto City, in Shikoku. Its completion had little impact on the pattern of traditionally prescribed circulation, as pilgrims using it continued to arrive on Shikoku at a point close to Ryozenji (temple 1). The second, the Seto Bridge, opened 1988, is an automobile and railway bridge connecting Kojima, on the mainland, and Sakaide, on Shikoku. It brings pilgrims close to Zentsuji (temple 75), the birthplace of Kobo Daishi. The third, the Imabari Bridge for vehicular traffic, opened in 1999 linking Onomichi, on the mainland, with Imabari, on Shikoku, bringing pilgrims close to Nankobo (temple 53) upon arrival on the island.

Since the opening of the Naruto and Seto bridges, a new and unexpected pattern of pilgrimage circulation has emerged. Arriving via the Naruto Bridge, pilgrims visit Ryozenji (temple 1) then, travelling counter clockwise, go directly to Okuboji (temple 88) and leave the island via the Seto Bridge. Despite the fact that, "in the Shikoku pilgrimage one can never say one has completed the pilgrimage just by visiting the first and last temples on the route" (Hoshino 1997: 280), "this highly abbreviated circuit has been recognized as a distinctive pilgrimage and named, accordingly, *tobashi henro* or "Skipping Shikoku Pilgrimage."

As more and more pilgrims use some form of transportation, fewer and fewer follow the prescribed sequence exactly. Because it was originally designed for the walking pilgrimage, it is not always well suited to vehicular travel and access to some temples from the preceding temple in the sequence does not always make good sense "economically." These changes in sequence are relatively minor though, occurring only within small groups of temples in each prefecture. Prefectural boundaries are never crossed out of sequence, no matter how the order of the sacred places is altered and the overall clockwise direction of the pilgrimage remains. Despite the minor changes, the traditional spatial symbolic organization of the Shikoku system is still essentially intact.

Visiting the 88 sacred places in sequence in a clockwise direction, following the route believed to have been designated by Kobo Daishi, gave rise to the term *junrei* or "sequentially ordered visit." Although the pronunciation is the same, this term is different from *junrei* meaning pilgrimage. The difference is evident from the Kanji for each term. Many pilgrims believe that Kobo Daishi made the pilgrimage in a clockwise direction and that they are following in his footsteps. But visiting the 88 places in sequence in a counter-clockwise direction is not prohibited and is done occasionally, often by pilgrims who believe that by travelling in the opposite direction they will meet Kobo Daishi coming towards them.

Another accommodation of pilgrims unable to make the pilgrimage in its entirety has been the recognition of segmental pilgrimages. Traditionally, the practice of visiting only the temples in one prefecture (*Ikkoku mairi*) and returning to Shikoku four times in order to complete the pilgrimage was common. With the completion of each segment, certain religious merit is believed to have been attained and when all segments of the pilgrimage have been completed the religious merit is almost equal to that gained when the pilgrimage is made all at once. Today, starting at any point, pilgrims make whatever segment of the pilgrimage is convenient at one time.

RITUAL ADUSTMENTS

As the pilgrimage gained popularity, the temple priests united to form Shikoku Reijokai or Association of Shikoku Sacred Places. Formally established in 1956, the aim of the association is to maintain clear lines of communication among the priests as they collectively meet the challenges of contemporary pilgrimage. These may include the setting of accommodation and temple stamp fees and the timing of increases, the process of pilgrim leader nomination and recognition, and appropriate temple landscape changes. In addition, priests and pilgrim leaders meet annually at the birthplace of Kobo Daishi to exchange ideas and information with respect to new regulations, financial concerns and matters related to pilgrim ritual.

Over the centuries, pilgrims have ranged from the poor and infirm to royalty. They have come from every corner of the nation and from all economic, social and religious backgrounds to engage in a variety of ritual activities. In order to standardize pilgrim behaviour along the route as well as at each sacred place, the association has introduced a prescribed ritual model supported by the publication of a pilgrim handbook (Shikoku Reijo-kai) and the licensing of pilgrim leaders. Within the guidelines provided, a pilgrim leader will make appropriate adjustments to accommodate the needs of his particular group. For the pilgrim travelling alone, pilgrimage guidebooks offer information on conduct.

Despite the intention to give a definite structure to pilgrim behaviour, the reality of the ritual landscape is diverse. Today pilgrims have only a short time to spend at each temple if the pilgrimage is to be completed in the time available. In order to complete the set of rituals at each temple as quickly as possible, contemporary pilgrims often abbreviate the rituals (Tanaka 1977) especially if they have to wait for the pilgrim group ahead of them to finish before they can begin.

In order to minimize the time spent chanting at the *hondo* and *daishido*, for example, pilgrims mumble the words at top speed. In extreme cases, individual pilgrims glance at the *hondo* and/or *daishido*, bow in its general direction and hurry to receive the temple stamp, omitting most other ritual activity.

The *honoin* or temple seal was given originally in exchange for handwritten *okyo* (Buddhist scripture) but now pilgrims pay a prescribed sum and get the seal which signifies that the pilgrim has visited the temple. In the height of the pilgrim season, in spring and fall, the *nokyosho* is very crowded and stamping is seldom completed in the time it takes pilgrims to complete the rituals. At these times it is not uncommon for the stamp books to be driven around the island in a separate vehicle and the stamps to be collected independently of the pilgrims' visits. Busloads of pilgrims entrust their stamp books to the drivers and/or someone employed especially for the purpose who will receive stamps at the *nokyosho* on their behalf. In the meantime the pilgrims proceed with other ritual activities. Pilgrims travelling singly will often observe the *nokyosho* upon entering the compound and, if it is not crowded, will go there immediately. Such activities as these have brought about considerable variation in the traditional, ideal pilgrimage ritual process.

MANAGEMENT OF SACRED PLACES

Pilgrim places are centres of meaning and the focus of human endeavour to foster their special significance. The temple landscape is an expression of the priests' intentions, managerial abilities, and the accommodation of pilgrims' needs. The tasks related to site maintenance are diverse.

Proper maintenance of the temple complex is an important issue facing priest managers concerned with the maintenance of the forms and functions of the temple as a site of pilgrimage ritual. Priests must identify those features which should be replaced or added to the compound and set priorities within the financial limitations of the temple. The central debate often revolves around the decision concerning building materials. Tradition has given rise to a prescribed correspondence between the function and form of the structures and to replacement buildings that closely resemble the "original." However, materials traditionally used in temple construction such as *keyaki* (zelkova) and *hinoki* (Japanese cypress) are becoming scarce and expensive; carpenters skilled in temple craftsmanship have almost disappeared. Three courses of action present themselves: construct the structure of wood; build only a wood facade with the remainder of the structure being concrete; construct the structure entirely of concrete.

Priests favouring structures made of wood maintain that the prevailing atmosphere of the temple must be one in which the worshipper can communicate with the sacred beings. Compared to wood which creates a soft, warm and authentic atmosphere, concrete buildings, some priests feel, are bleak and without comfort, tending to shut off the human mind. On the other hand, those who have used concrete point to its durability, fire resistance, lower cost, and lower maintenance. Priests who favour building with concrete emphasize the economic factor while priests who choose all wooden structures emphasize authenticity. Priests who seek a compromise position do not escape the problems. Here the main concern is the successful integration of the two materials, physically and aesthetically.

The financing of building and reconstruction projects is an ongoing concern. There are three primary sources of revenue available. The first is the temple congregation, the size and affluence of which varies. About one third of the 88 temples do not have a local congregation. Pilgrim contributions are another important source of funds. The third source of revenue is the national and/or prefectural government. This funding is only available, however, to those temples at which particular buildings have been designated "Important Cultural Assets" or " National Treasures". If a particular statuary is so designated, government funding is also available for the upkeep of the building in which it is housed. If, however, the *hondo* no longer provides the *honzon* (principal image) with the protection it requires, government funding is available for the construction of a concrete, climate-and security-controlled storehouse for the statue but not necessarily for the construction of a new *hondo*, a very expensive undertaking.

With the increasing number of pilgrims, problems related to "mundane" aspects of the pilgrimage multiply. Priests must concern themselves with such things as the provision and maintenance of parking, toilet, and garbage facilities, not to mention the daily upkeep of the grounds: raking, sweeping, watering, pruning. Beyond the temple boundaries they must concern themselves with the upkeep of the traditional pilgrim walking path leading to the temple including the maintenance of traditional and contemporary route markers. Recently, there has been an effort on the part of the Japanese government to preserve historical pathways throughout Japan. On Shikoku, these pathways are primarily those of the original pilgrimage route. Government interest as well as grass roots volunteer movements dedicated to the upkeep of the traditional walking path are helping to ensure the continuity of this centuries-old pilgrimage for future generations.

Conclusion

Focusing on a representative popular multiple-site Buddhist pilgrimage in Japan, this paper has identified the changing nature of the Shikoku pilgrimage. The Shikoku pilgrimage has witnessed dynamic change in spatial setting, symbolic meaning, temple landscapes and pilgrim ritual and movement. Despite the increasing secularization of Japanese society, the popularity of the Shikoku pilgrimage shows no signs of waning. Changes are ongoing to accommodate the modern pilgrim and his/her fast-paced, affluent lifestyle.

Is the fact that some of the world's age-old pilgrimages have survived and continue to serve important functions due in part to their having been able to accommodate those changes necessary to keep pace with modernization, while not abandoning traditional ties? This case study focusing on a Japanese example supports the notion that pilgrimage is an inherently dynamic self-organizing system accommodating internal and external factors inducing necessary transformations: pilgrimage sites emerge and evolve and the spatial patterns of pilgrimage circulation and ritual activities at specific locations change over the time.

Exploration of transformations initiated by individuals and organizations in the attempt to participate in the resolution of the conflict between tradition and modernization reveals the underlying strength of the ongoing popularity of this pilgrimage that has evolved over the time. The nature, intensity and focus of the roles played by those individuals and institutions central to the foundations and practice of the pilgrimage have shaped the direction and texture of the evolution of this pilgrimage. The successful adaptation of the Shikoku pilgrimage to "contemporary society" down through the centuries is indicative of the remarkable metamorphic ability of Japanese society.

References

Akioka, T. (ed.), 1971, *The Collection of Old Maps of Japan*, Tokyo: Kashima Shuppan.

Geden, A.S., 1918, "Pilgrimage (Buddhism)," *Encyclopaedia of Religion and Ethics*, 10, New York: Scribner.

Goshirakawa Tenno, ed., Ryjin Hisho (1171) reprinted in Ryojin Hisho-ko, ed. by Junichi Konishi, Tokyo: Sanseido, 1941.

Hosoda, S., 1972, "Shikoku Henrei Ezu," *Monumenta Cartegraphica Japonica*, Tokyo: Kodansha.

Hasuo, K., 1931, *Kobo-Daishi-den*, Koyasan: Kongobu-ji.

Hori, Y. (ed.), 1966, *Dai-nihon Jiin Soran*, Tokyo: Meicho Kankokai.

Hoshino, E., 1981, *Junrei: Sei to Zoku no Genshogaku*, Tokyo: Kodansha.

Hoshino, E., 1984, "Shin Shikoku reijo no tenkai katei: Fukuoka-ken Sasaguri reijo no baai," in Shukyo bunka no shoso, Takenaka Shinjo Hakase Beiju Kinen Ronbunshu Kankokai, ed., 619-35, Tokyo: Sankibo Busshorin.

Hoshino, E., 1997, "Pilgrimage and Peregrination: Contexualizing the Saikoku Junrei and the Shikoku Henro," in I. Reader & P. Swanson (eds.), *Pilgrimage in Japan*.

Jakuhon, 1689, *Shikoku Henrei Reijoki reprinted in Shikoku Reijo-ki-shu*, 1973, ed. by Y. Kondo, Tokyo: Benseisha.

Jakuhon, 1690, *Shikoku Henrei Kudoku-ki reprinted in Shikoku Reijo-ki-shu*, 1973, ed. by Y. Kondo, Tokyo: Benseisha.

Kitagawa, J.M., 1967, "Three Types of Pilgrimage in Japan," in E.E. Urbach, et al. (ed.), *Studies in Mysticism and Religion*, Jerusalem: The Magnes Press.

Kondo, R., 1999, "Miniature Pilgrimage System and Community in Japan," Paper presented at the seminar Pilgrimage and Complexity, Indira Gandi National Centre for the Arts, New Delhi, January 5-9, 1999.

Kondo, Y., 1971, *Shikoku Henro*, Tokyo: Ofusha.

Maeda, Taku. 1972, *Junrei no Shakaigaku*, Kyoto: Mineriba Shobo, 1972.

Miyazaki, N., 1977, *Chozen: Shikoku Henro Nikki*, Tokyo: Daito Shuppansha.

Reischaer, E.O., 1955, *Ennin's Diary, The Record of a Pilgrimage to China in Search of the Law*, New York: Ronald Press.

Reader, I., and Swanson, P. L., 1997, "Pilgrimage in Japan," *Japanese Journal of Religious Studies* 24: 3/4: 225-452.

Shikoku Reijo-kai, 1977, *Sendachi Gongyo Shidai*, Shikoku Reijo-kai.

Shinjo, T., 1979, "Junrei no Rekishi," *Dento to Gendai*, 59: 28-36.

Singh, R.P.B., 1991, *Panchakroshi Yatra, Varanasi: Sacred Journey, Ecology of Place and Faithscape*, Varanasi: Tara.

Tanaka, H., 1977, "Geographic Expression of Buddhist Pilgrim Places on Shikoku Island, Japan," *The Canadian Geographer*, 21: 2: 111-32.

Tanaka, H., 1981, "The Evolutioin of a Pilgrimage as a Spatial-Symbolic System," *The Canadian Geographer*, 25: 3: 240-51.

Tanaka, H., 1983, *Junreichi no Sekai*, Tokyo: Kokon Shoin.

Turner, V. and E., 1978, *Image and Pilgrimage in Christian Culture*, New York: Columbia University Press.

13

The Pilgrim in an Individualistic Context

Kaj Noschis

Summary

TRADITIONAL pilgrimage may be compared to migratory bird movements: a collective, repetitive and unquestioned urge to travel long distances with considerable effort. Among Christians, some Catholic groups still experience pilgrimage in this way today, with annual journeys to holy places like Lourdes, Fatima and Compostela. Among other Christians such as European Protestants, where the relationship to the spiritual dimension is predominantly individualistic, pilgrimage lost its collective appeal after being disallowed by the Reformation in early sixteenth century. Yet the effort of travelling (and particularly walking) long distances towards a spiritually significant place while surrounded by nature, its beauty and challenges has recently gained attractiveness for numerous non-practising people, generally of Christian and particularly of Protestant origin. The paper considers this phenomenon and discusses possibilities for a systematic review. A correspondence might be suggested between moments of an inner (or searched for inner) journey and those of an outer journey such as an effort-demanding, spiritually oriented trek. In 1997, on the occasion of the 1000 years celebrations of Trondheim, efforts were made to reactivate the ancient pilgrim's route from the South to the North of Norway. Pilgrim journeys to St. Olav's shrine in Nidaros — built into a Gothic Cathedral (Trondheim's Cathedral is the most Northern in the world) in the twelfth century — began shortly after St Olav's death in 1030, and lasted up to the Reformation in 1537. Today, with more touristic ambitions than religious ambitions, the project of reopening the pilgim route has again become a reality in this Protestant country. This case is discussed in some detail.

Introduction

Within Christianity, pilgrimage has through the centuries been a popular expression of belief, periodically at odds with the Catholic Church. Pilgrimage grows spontaneously from hearsay — people being attracted in large numbers to places where miracles have been heard to have happened. Such a place becomes like a magnet. The Church will follow by canonizing and eventually declaring the sanctity of the person involved, and confirming the miraculous nature of an event that gradually and often very rapidly enter popular belief as an extraordinary phenomenon demonstrating the tangible presence of the divine. When the Church is slow to follow, a conflictual situation may arise with pilgrims, a disagreement between religious authorities and the popular generating basis of the importance of the event.[1] In entering popular history, pilgrimage to a given place will continue from generation to generation, usually strengthened by new miraculous events. Particular paths will become "the right way" to reach the goal. So not only reaching the place but also following a definite path will become conditions for fulfilling a given pilgrimage.

The spiritual motives of Christian pilgrims, undertaking very often long, arduous and demanding journeys, have been varied: penance pilgrimage to forgive former sins, in the Middle Ages given explicitly as a form of punishment, votive pilgrimage with the hope of being cured of disease, thanksgiving pilgrimage for having been exhausted, to mention only a few most common ones. Pilgrims would mostly travel together on foot or on horseback, blessed by the priest before departure and with instructions about prayers and rituals to be performed during the pilgrimage itself.[2] Each pilgrimage has its own calendar, a date or a period of the year when it is considered most favourable to undertake it.[3] In any circumstance, the trip is a physical effort subject to nature's conditions, believed to favour an explicit quest for contact with God or his representatives. In fact the pilgrim's path itself becomes the occasion for other miracles. In turn, this becomes evidence for it being "the right way" for the pilgrim, being "in the right place at the right time," part of a larger context of "being in accordance with God." Many of the major pilgrim paths in Europe have witnessed the building of important churches, monasteries and even cities as consequences of pilgrims' gratefulness for such events.[4] Here, clearly a systematic view on pilgrimage is appropriate; paths and stops along them have developed into a network of buildings and cities. On a psychological level, this has been accompanied by pilgrims feeling themselves part of such a growing system. Apart from such remarkable and tangible evidence of pilgrim activity through the centuries, the social dimension of pilgrimage itself, feeling part of a group, sharing fears and joys as well as exchanging information has always been very important. The stories related to miracles would find here their amplifiers and channels for diffusion. Among pilgrims and along the pilgrim's path would also hide thieves and other malevolent people who would represent a concrete danger for wanderers. Escaping the dangers of difficult natural conditions and such predators would become reasons for gratefulness and signs of having passed successfully the pilgrims' trials.[5]

In the Christian tradition, Jerusalem — connected with the life of Christ — became the first and foremost destination for pilgrimage from the fourth century CE onwards, that is, once it was believed that excavations had brought to light the cross that Jesus was crucified on. Rome, where Saint Peter was buried and which soon became the centre of the Christian world, would also become a goal for pilgrimage at approximately the same time. With Europe becoming Christian, other places would also become pilgrimage sites as soon as events of a miraculous order were seen to have manifested themselves. From the eleventh century, reaching St. James de Compostela would be established as the most important pilgrimage aim in Europe; paths from all over Europe would soon be leading to this place in northwestern Spain.[6] We might add that at that time it was also believed to be "the end of the (known) world." Through the centuries, the Catholic Church in particular has cultivated the importance of such places.

On the other hand, even as recently as 1981, a new and major pilgrimage has been imposed by popular belief in former Yugoslavia. People from all over are coming to Medjuvorjde where, according to the tales, the Virgin Mary appeared to three young girls. However this site has not yet been officially endorsed by the Catholic Church, so it remains for the time being, although very popular, a pilgrimage that is adopted only by some communities within the Catholic Church.[7] This is just an example of how pilgrimage often begins outside the official Church before being recognized as part of the Church's activities.

If we were to define stages in the appearance of a pilgrimage site we may consider the following ones:

- an extraordinary event takes place (vision of Godly figure, miraculous cure, etc.); this is the hierophany, the place becomes sacred — of special respect;
- the event becomes a story that is widely circulated, with the mention of the particular spot where it took place;
- people start coming to the spot in order to "see the place where the extraordinary event took place" — and to establish a personal connection with this event;
- a territory (e.g. a fountain, cave, field) is marked, and eventually an altar, a chapel or another religiously connotated construction is built on the spot;
- the place becomes an "official" pilgrimage site, with pilgrims travelling there as an expression of their faith, with the eventual hope of another miracle happening;
- by being commonly used, specific paths become "the pilgrim's way." In walking along these paths towards the site, the pilgrim knows that he is "on the way," establishing a connection with the Godly, recognized as such by fellow wayfarers and others along the way; and
- other "extraordinary events" might take place along this path, creating other sacred spots and reinforcing the importance of this particular pilgrimage.

Such a sequence describes the reinforcement of the sacred character of a site by adopting a systematic view where pilgrimage is instrumental in affirming a connection between a locale and something supra-human.

Certainly pilgrimage existed also before Christianity, but it has been massively adopted and incorporated into its practices. Probably, some places for pilgrimage were recognized as such even before Christianity took them over. Be this as it may, there have been two periods in the Christian history of Europe when pilgrimage has lost its attraction. After the Reformation in the 1530s, pilgrimage became ill considered in the parts of Europe that adhered to Protestantism. The father of Reformation, Luther, suggested the suppression of pilgrimage because it had men leave their tasks and families, often meeting illicit temptations and making them spend their savings on the way.[8] In Luther's fight against indulgences as practiced by the Church — inasmuch as the Church forgave sins when it received appropriate gifts associated with religious rituals such as pilgrimages — these were probably also seen by Luther as inappropriate. He had, before becoming the initiator of the Reformation, himself made a pilgrimage to Rome, and he had direct experience. So Protestants, following Luther, would deny pilgrimage as an expression of faith; rather it was to be seen as lost working time for society. On the other hand the Counter-Reformation would set out rules for acceptable pilgrimages, admitting implicitly that excesses had been committed. Thus the Catholic Church in the late sixteenth century would still encourage pilgrimages although their importance with respect to indulgences was lessened. Practically, this meant that, while the North of Europe would stop pilgrimage, the South and generally Catholic Europe would continue to practise it. The late seventeenth and eighteenth centuries again saw a crisis in pilgrimage when the Enlightenment was accompanied by an important loss of interest in religion and the supernatural generally. Then, in the nineteenth century, with the advent of Romanticism and travelling, spiritual preoccupations were again in the forefront and pilgrimage "was back." Now nature itself had a major role as the place for visions and emotions. Today we are still in the aftermath of this historical period. Yet, with greatly facilitated group transportation, there has been a tremendous quantitative increase in very organized forms of group pilgrimage that have almost taken over. Travelling by air, train, bus and car are more common today than walking. In this perspective — although preparation for arrival may take place during the travelling — it is no longer the journey itself and its events that are central to the pilgrimage but visiting the site, reaching the goal.

In considering Northern Europe, let us be reminded that even the official banning of pilgrimage did certainly not mean that the populations converted to Protestantism would immediately give up practices that had existed for centuries. But among Protestants, pilgrimages would lose their officially recognized character and become individual or small group travels. Gradually, pilgrimage would thus lose its collective appeal and be perpetuated through more informal and isolated ritual journeys. Only during this century, in parallel with a tremendous increase in popular tourism among Europeans, have Protestants again started to consider pilgrimage as a form of religious practice. This means that in an ecumenical spirit, a pilgrimage by a Protestant to a non-Protestant destination is seen as an expression of Christian faith. But because, within Protestantism, faith is basically an individual matter — of a personal relationship with God — pilgrimage is first of all an individual search. Hence the notion of effort and contact with nature are of importance.

It should be added that during the last 30 years, Europe has collectively witnessed the birth and strengthening of an ecological consciousness — a concern with the conservation of nature. This entails a major change of attitude. Over the previous centuries, the general attitude of Christians towards nature had been to submit it, to exploit its resources for the betterment of human living conditions. There has been little regard for the consequences of this exploitation of natural resources on nature itself. Human beings were there to dominate and use nature for their purposes. The recent realization that some natural resources might run out and that, on the other hand, human beings are capable of doing so much harm to nature as to make some places uninhabitable and dangerous for man himself, has now compelled Europeans to look at their relationship with nature in different terms. Instead of dominating nature, the issue is gradually becoming how to live in accordance with it, to reduce or avoid pollution, to renew natural resources. This change of attitude also had an impact on Christians' search for a closer relationship with nature. While, since the rise of Romanticism in the early nineteenth century, there has been an interest in travelling through beautiful natural landscapes and in enjoying mountains or sea, forests or natural parks among people having such opportunities, this interest is today much more general. Escaping inhabited and polluted cities during weekends and vacations in private cars or public transportation has become almost a mass movement. Besides, physically quiet demanding walks in nature have also become popular among all age groups, in particular the young.

Trekking as a Form of Pilgrimage?

Trekking might be defined as "travelling by foot using as much as possible old tracks, paths and passages."[9] The chosen path is then the trek itself. Practised often with sophisticated, light and practical equipment, as well as following pre-defined paths indicated on special maps, it is today a well-established form of free-time activity with shops, magazines and travel agencies catering to its adepts. These paths are ancient ones that have "traditionally" been used by travellers, generally joining small villages to each other, reaching places of particular interest for a group or community, or being paths through hunting, forest fruit or fishing areas. Today, when such paths are found to be along or close to highly trafficked or inhabited areas, new paths will be established to keep trekkers in the realm of wilderness. Trekking is certainly a way of getting away from harassing urban life, but it is, in its more devoted forms, quite demanding itself as a physical effort. The point is to spend time in an uncontaminated nature, while carrying in a backpack all that is needed for sustenance during the wandering. The challenge is in distances to be covered daily, in the difficulty of the paths, in facing climatic and weather conditions, while the pleasure is in meeting untouched and unspoiled nature, its flora and fauna, in encountering unique views and good company. When deciding on a trek, considerations on the path's characteristics are predominant; the aim and pleasure is the travelling and what happens during the walk. A plan for distances to be covered, for resting points and meals is generally pre-established and then followed. The goal of the path is not itself to be considered of major importance except for being the end of the effort, the endpoint of the trek.

As its main point is to get away from the daily urban environment, its buildings, rhythm, demands and offers, a trek is generally away from man-made environments. On the other hand, constructed and protected rest places, or human help in crossing watercourses or difficult mountain passes are acceptable. These are generally occasions for meeting other trekkers, sharing experiences and asking questions.

Nature dictates the rhythm for the trek; changing weather conditions as well as the difficulty of the path to be followed will decide the progression. This is an important aspect to trekking and directly invites the trekker to be in dialogue with nature and himself. In fact, although the term inner dialogue is not necessarily evoked in discussing trekking, these wanderers will acknowledge that they are also experiencing a confrontation with themselves.[10]

Although trekking is primarily walking towards nature, looking for nature and finding harmony in it, there is also an inner dimension, one that can be phrased using the same terms: walking towards oneself, looking for oneself and finding harmony in oneself. This is often related to what happens during the trek: encounters, escaping dangers, being taken by nature's beauty, etc. Many trekkers will explicitly say that wandering is of spiritual significance for them.

In fact, the description that we have just given comes close to what has always been happening in pilgrimage except for a lack of overt religious intention. Prayers and other explicitly religious rituals are substituted by lay practices: writing a journal, astonishment in front of a natural spectacle, sharing emotions around a campfire. During a trek, these moments are very meaningful for the participants; they "connect" them with nature and themselves. Thus, a good trek is to find oneself in harmony with nature and its events: to "be connected," to be "on the right path," to "feel in syntony" with the surroundings. Although these terms apply to trekkers as well as to pilgrims, the notion of "miracle" seems specific to the pilgrim. A miracle is an event that cannot be understood in only rational terms, it is something favourable and highly improbable outside the normal course of events. For the person experiencing it, a miracle is evidence of a supra-human intervention, that of a saint or of God himself. The event that has saved, cured or helped the persons makes, him or her feel especially privileged in his or her connection with God, and makes him or her particularly grateful. If a miracle takes place pilgrimage has more than responded to expectations. As we mentioned, churches, monasteries and even cities have grown, as expressions of gratefulness, on spots where pilgrims witnessed miracles, for instance on their journeys to Compostela. Trekkers will not talk about miracles, nor construct churches or shrines on the spots where they feel particularly touched by nature, but they might still talk about overwhelming outer and inner experiences. A fundamental aspect of trekking, unlike pilgrimage, is not to leave traces in nature, but to keep nature "untouched."

In comparing trekking to the sequence in pilgrimage that we described above, the difference might not be so large. Trekkers will not mark a territory or construct a chapel on an impressive location because of their respect for nature, but to talk about hierophany might still experientially be the best way to describe the power of such a site, and, as such, it might enter the shared knowledge of trekkers. A systematic view on trekking does recognize many similarities with pilgrimage, but also pinpoints a fundamental difference that we may call ideological; pilgrimage pays tribute to God through civilization of the world — by building a church or a monastery, trekking pays tribute by preserving nature. Yet, in practice, the difference might be more negligible. Furthermore, not all trekkers are so respectful to nature while some pilgrims today consider as a priority the preservation of pilgrimage paths that are not contaminated by traces of our industrialized world.

Nidaros

Let us now consider in some detail one of the high places of Christian pilgrimage in the Middle Ages but where, due to Reformation's impact, pilgrimage was no longer allowed after 1537. We will then see how trekking is today contributing to the comeback of this pilgrimage, and speculate on how these two practices are to be related. The cathedral of Trondheim, officially named Christ's Church in Nidaros (the former name of the Trondheim region), is the most northern cathedral in Europe. It is located in the northern part of Norway, a country that was progressively converted to Christianity after the year 1000 and where Protestantism was imposed soon after the Reformation in 1537. Trondheim is covered by snow for approximately half the year. Even today it is extremely impressive to arrive, no matter what season, in front of the huge Gothic cathedral in a small city where many of the other buildings are wooden. Nidaros Cathedral's history goes back to the eleventh century. In 1070, a small wooden chapel was demolished and work began on the construction of a stone church on the spot where, according to tradition, Norway's patron saint, King Olav Haraldsson, was buried after his death in a battle in 1030. The coffin was brought from the distant battleground to Nidaros — name of the town at that time — and buried in the sand beside the river. Olav had allegedly been baptized in Rouen (France) during one of his Viking expeditions and, as he gained power in Norway in 1016, he actively tried to convert Norwegians to Christianity. In 1028, Olav had to flee the country, chased by a Danish invader king, and he died in a battle while trying to return and re-establish his power. Yet the country became totally Christian soon afterwards.[11] Only short time after his burial, people started talking about miracles which were brought about with the help of the king. In the sand where he had first been buried, a spring appeared. It was water that would cure its drinkers of disease. He was soon declared a saint. His coffin had by then been moved to what was also the first church built in town, the already mentioned wooden chapel. Nidaros Cathedral's high altar today stands in this place. Soon, great numbers of pilgrims flocked to Olav's shrine in Nidaros. Across Europe, other churches were dedicated to St Olav; for instance, in London six churches were dedicated to St. Olav before the end of the eleventh century.[12] There are innumerable accounts of miracles in places where Olav had been during his lifetime travels across Europe, and there are many springs connected with his name. The saint's day of martyrdom — his death in battle — is July 29, and impressive numbers of pilgrims would invade Nidaros on that date. In the Middle Ages, on that day, there was also a procession carrying the saint's reliquary, so that all those in attendance would have a chance to glimpse it — a chance for a miracle.[13]

During the thirteenth century, the town, due to increased pilgrimage and the establishment of an archbishopric, also became an important commercial centre. The great cathedral builder was Nidaros' second archbishop, Erlendsson, from 1161 to 1188. He introduced Gothic architecture to Norway. In the following century, Nidaros retained its position as the country's religious and cultural centre but dramatic events took place. In the fourteenth century, when the nave and most of the church had been completed, plague reached the country and it is estimated that 70% of Nidaros' 3000 inhabitants died. The situation remained difficult for two centuries — admittedly pilgrimage also diminished — and construction of the cathedral was interrupted. The Reformation was imposed to Norway in 1537 by the Danish-Norwegian king ruling over the country at that time and against the will of the Norwegian archbishop. The king took over as the head of the Norwegian church. With the Reformation, an end was also put to the cult connected with St Olav. Pilgrimage was not allowed anymore. Nidaros Cathedral would further decline in importance and the construction itself would suffer. It was only in the nineteenth century, corresponding with Norway's new independence, that restoration work began on the cathedral. Yet there would not be talk anymore about pilgrimage in this Protestant country.

Follow the Pilgrim's Footsteps

In 1997, the city of Trondheim celebrated its 1000th birthday. On that occasion, a pilgrims' route for travellers was "reopened." It was the result of an important public effort which made it possible to walk from the capital city, Oslo, to Trondheim and cover the almost-1000 kilometers separating the two cities on mainly mountain paths. During the preceding years, efforts had been made to rediscover the old pilgrim roads and they were now proposed for journeys toward Nidaros. As part of Trondheim's millennium celebrations, there were again groups of Christians explicitly carrying out a pilgrimage. But given the Protestant context and country, the insistence is on a journey through impressive natural landscapes "that might also become an innerly significant experience." The emphasis for the larger potential public is more on trekking than pilgrimage. The "recreational and touristic" character of the wandering is stressed.

On reading a leaflet produced in Trondheim on this occasion, a brochure called "Follow the pilgrim's footsteps,"[14] it becomes clear that the question is foremost about a "souvenir" relationship to ancient pilgrimages; to wander today is a way of getting closer to the pilgrims of old times, to ultimately share what they saw and to experience places they wandered through. This difference is emphasized: to wander to Nidaros today is to do it "in the pilgrims' footsteps," not as pilgrims.

The leaflet tells about wanderings along pilgrim roads. "The outings will give a historical retrospective view upon the first wanderers and settlements. Discoveries of sites and graves are visited. The guides give information about the multitude of nature, e.g. flora and fauna, species of stone and minerals in the mountains. The wanderers will be people interested in nature, cultural history and joint activity."[15] The leaflet will then give details about the hiking: daily stretches, equipment needed, provisions and lodging conditions.

In fact along the path to Trondheim today you will meet many trekkers, and only few of them will even mention that this was formerly an important pilgrimage. What makes the pilgrim's route from Oslo to Trondheim particularly attractive is its location, partly in almost untouched nature offering spectacular scenery and a great variety of natural surroundings. Nordic countries are in this respect particularly favoured, as there are still very large territories that are in the wilderness. So, given what we said above about trekking, is not the route to Nidaros an interesting example of how, by following ancient paths, wayfarers could be having experiences and emotions very similar to those of their forefathers almost 1000 years ago, although this is not explicitly thought of in such terms? When the pilgrim or the trekker feels that he or she is "on the right path," that is, they feel connected with the Godly or with nature, are these two figures not superimposable?

Inner and Outer Journey

The Old Testament is replete with images of travel, to be in search of the Promised Land, to leave for an unknown destination because this is asked by God. In fact, life on earth is described as a journey toward the celestial kingdom. Christ in the New Testament is similarly described as travelling to Jerusalem, as wandering in the desert and suffering in carrying the cross for his own crucifixion on Golgotha. These are all very important scriptures in the Christian tradition and suggest, when interpreted more symbolically, parallels not only with our outer life but also with our inner search.

To engage in a search through the unconscious suggests the image of a journey, of travelling along unknown paths, meeting unknown forces and having unknown experiences within ourselves. It is an inner journey in search of better knowledge of oneself. Now, an outer journey can connect the wanderer with his inner journey, when, for instance, she or he feels that she or he is "on the right path." Psychologically this is probably a very meaningful aspect. It is not specific to Christianity.

For instance, at the Eranos Conference of 1933,[16] a paper by Rousselle (1980) entitled "Spiritual guidance in contemporary Taoism" comments, among other points, on a stone tablet to be found in the Monastery of the White Clouds (Po-yun-kuan) near Beijing. This is an example, from Taoism, of an inner journey completed by a map of the human body that insists on geographical parallels — to be viewed symbolically but nevertheless expressed geographically. It is an inner meditational journey with a description of its "regions." It is at the same time a representation of the path of life.

On the other hand, real pilgrimage may be viewed as parallel to the inner journey, an occasion to reflect on life's meaning, that what I am doing is the right thing to do, if where I am is "the right path at the right time," a feeling of syntony with my surroundings.

Psychologically, the aim of pilgrimage is probably still today fundamentally very similar to what it was centuries ago. The question has been and is about experiencing a wandering where outer reality speaks to and awakens inner reality. I undertake a pilgrimage when I have lost the contact with myself — or when I want to explore it further or reinforce it. Travelling towards the end-point of the pilgrimage is an image of reaching the centre, "the centre of the world," and, symbolically, it might thus reconnect us with the centre in ourselves. It "works" because I share with others the conviction of "contact with God" and its power of "regeneration" by moving towards a specific place.

As we discussed above, trekkers will talk about their experiences in similar terms, although avoiding explicit references to Christian religion. If we use psychological terminology, the search and meaningfulness of trekking becomes almost identical with pilgrimage: the image of an outer journey as related to an inner journey. Specifically, by deciding to do a trek we embark on a journey that is an end in itself, a wandering *per se*. This characteristic probably opens the symbolic parallel between inner and outer journey. As the point is the wandering itself, I to some extent "become one with the surrounding world"; what my eyes see helps me to see deeper in myself, what I feel inside helps me to see further with my eyes. Eventually I can feel and understand that "I am on the right track." And this is a theme that seems universal for spiritual traditions: to be in syntony with the surrounding world. It might also be one meaning of the above-mentioned stone tablet; to travel inside oneself is like travelling in the outside world. In discussing trekking, we should also remind ourselves of the physical characteristics of its environment. Located in nature away from places transformed by men, the paths offer trekkers encounters with nature as such in conditions where human beings have to accept that they are greatly dependent on whatever nature's forces decide to confront them with. These might again symbolically be viewed as encounters with deep instinctual and or spiritual aspects of oneself, particular emotions that open specific venues for inner search.

Conclusion

Viewed systematically, the pilgrim exists in a religious context where you are supposed to express your faith and experience contact with God by following a path towards a place where God's presence has been proved. In following this path the pilgrim can feel that he or she participates, is part of a system ruled by God. If he or she has lost contact with God, this is "a way" for finding it again. Particularly during the Middle Ages, this would be a guarantee for a good after-life. Today, pilgrimage for believing Christians has still the same meaning although the concern is primarily with life on earth and feeling that one's life is in accord with what is expected by the Church and oneself. Thus the value of pilgrimage in bringing the pilgrim into closer contact with God is particularly stressed. Psychologically, this can be phrased as "being on a meaningful path," where one is in harmony with oneself and one's surroundings.

In Western Europe religious pilgrimage is still extensively practised today, but due to modern means of transportation, the travel itself has lost its previous importance. Some of the essential components of pilgrimage, when viewed psychologically, are therefore lost, such as a parallel between an outer and inner journey. Hazardous meetings with nature's forces were the unpredictable lot of pilgrims through the centuries. In fact, it may be argued that when pilgrimage loses such encounters with nature — as when buses or trains are the means of transportation — the spiritual meaning is no longer the same. It becomes impossible to get confirmation from the environment that "this is the right journey for me." In this major respect, trekking is closer to the old forms of pilgrimage than modern mass pilgrimage with public means of transportation, and may be viewed as its inheritor among groups of people who are of Christian tradition but who do not recognize religious practices.

The paths to Trondheim's cathedral may be a good example of this situation. There is hardly any talk today in Protestant and largely laic Norway about restoring pilgrimage as such, but when one has a closer look at what walking in the "pilgrim's footsteps" entails, at least on a psychological level, the meaningfulness of what is today named trekking is almost strictly superimposable on ancient pilgrimage. To be a trekker is to be looking for "the right path," to feel that one is connected, that "my life is in syntony with the forces around me."[17] In the case of trekking, God is not named but the experience is certainly of a spiritual order, wandering to explore and feel parallels between our outer and inner journey. The trekker's assumption is that miracles are not needed, that nature as such is enough or perhaps that it is the only miracle.

Notes

1. For a discussion on such issues within the Catholic Church see for instance (in French) Laurentin (1985). As long as the conflict over the divine nature of the miraculous event has not been solved, the Church will consider it superstition instead of an expression of Christian faith.
2. There were also cases where the pilgrimage was done by someone for someone else who would be unable to do it him or herself, or who would pay for it to be done. Long distances would eventually be covered by sea — these were, however, quite adventurous trips during the Middle Ages.
3. In the following pages I will repeatedly refer to the two major pilgrimage sites in Western Europe from the twelfth to the fifteenth century: St. John of Compostela and St Olav of Nidaros (Trondheim). The major dates for these pilgrimage sites were (and are) July 25 for Compostela and July 29 for Trondheim. People would thus be crossing Europe in large numbers at the same period of the year, some going South to Spain (Compostela) and others going North to Norway (Trondheim).
4. For the impressive amount and importance of religious construction connected with the nine major pilgrim paths from all corners of Western Europe to Compostela, see, for instance, Bourdarias & Wasielewski (1996).
5. For a general introduction to the social dimension of pilgrimage, see, for instance, (in French) Laurentin (1983).
6. Today there are considered to be nine main historical paths leading to Compostela from different parts of Europe: from the Netherlands, Denmark, Poland, Hungary, Croatia, Austria, two from Italy (all these through France) and from Portugal. See Bourdarias & Wasielewski (1996).
7. See, for instance, Laurentin (1985) cf. supra.
8. See, for instance, by Luther "Call to the Christian nobility of the German nation" (1520)
9. See, for instance, Corbellini & Figari (1990) page 6 (our translation from Italian).
10. I have been able to discuss this issue informally with about a dozen trekkers.
11. For a brief historical account of St Olav's life and the Nidaros Cathedral (in English), see, for instance, Ekroll, Lohre Krokstad & Soreide (1995).
12. See, for instance, Kollandsrud, M (1997) page 192 (in Norwegian).
13. There are many historical works on these events. As an introduction, refer to Krokstad & Soreide (1995) cf.supra. A historically accurate but romantic account in a very captivating format is to be found in Hansen (1997) (in Norwegian, however). The author relates the supposed journey to Nidaros of two young pilgrims through Norway by foot in approximately 1300.
14. Several guides for wandering from Oslo to Trondheim have been published lately. The most complete and impressive guide (although in Norwegian) seems to be: Kollansrud (1997), with clear maps and indications for travellers. The introduction and the text generally stresses the historical interest of the re-constructed paths, being thus foremostly a guide for the trekker interested in the history of the path. The same can be said about the leaflet "Follow the pilgrims's footsteps" (1997) (in English), published by an agency specialized in accommodating the needs of such travellers.
15. Leaflet "Follow the pilgrim's footsteps," p. 3.
16. These yearly conferences in Switzerland by Lake Maggiore were organized around the Swiss psychologist C.G. Jung with a wide intercultural scope exploring shared religious themes and saw the participation of many of the most prominent historians of religion of that time.

17. If psychologists discuss pilgrimage — or trekking for that matter — out of their own experience or more generally, they will talk about "a journey of transformation," how it changes oneself, how to the outer journey corresponds an inner transformation. Although a psychologist, I do not view it in this way. The central point is about "feeling connected," "being on the right track," not about transformation. For what I call the psychologist's view, see, for instance, Bacchetta(1986). This book (in French) is an excellent account of an inner and outer journey to Compostela by foot from Puy-en-Velay, with beautiful pictures, by a Jungian psychoanalyst.

References

Bacchetta, F., 1986, *En marche vers Compostelle — Un chemin de transformation*, Geneve: Editions du Tricorne.

Bourdarias, J., & Wasielewski, M., 1996, *Guide Européen des chemins de Compostelle*, Paris: Fayard.

Corbellini, G., & Figari, F., 1990, *Europa — I grandi itinerari di trekking*, Milano: Modadori.

Ekroll, O., Lohre Krokstad, J., & Soreide, T., 1995, *Nidaros Cathedral and the Archbishop's Palace*, Trondheim, Nidaros: Cathedral's Restoration Workshop's Publishers.

"Follow the pilgrims's footsteps, Pilgrimsleden Dovrefjell, Nidaros og Storlien." 1997, Trondheim: Nidaros, Trykkeri.

Hansen, K., I., 1997, *Pilgrimsgang til Nidaros*, Oslo: Gyldendal.

Kollandsrud, M., 1997, *Pilegrimsleden til Nidaros*, Oslo: Gyldendal.

Laurentin, R., 1985, *Multiplication des apparitions de la Vierge aujourd'hui*, Paris: Fayard.

Laurentin, R., 1983, *Les routes de Dieu*, Paris, O.E.I.L.

Rousselle, E., 1934, *Seelische Fuhrung im Lebenden Taoismus*, Zurich: Eranos-Jahrbuch 1933, Translated as: *Spiritual guidance in contemporary Taoism*, published in Spiritual Disciplines, Papers from the Eranos Yearbooks 4, New York and London: Bollingen Series XXX, 1980.

14

Basilica of La Madeleine, Vézelay

Spatial and Symbolic Narratives in the Medieval Western Christian Church

Thomas Barrie

Introduction

THE spiritual path and place is a recurring theme in mythology and world religions. From Christ's journey along the Via Dolorosa to Theseus and the Minoan Labyrinth, heroic trials and quests are found throughout religious and mythological traditions. The "hero's journey," as documented by Joseph Campbell, is an enduring mythic theme and its narrative patterns appear trans-historically and pan-culturally. The Way, the spiritual path and the sacred journey are all terms used to describe the process of spiritual development. Not only do they describe spiritual and psychological journeys but they imply physical landscapes as well.

A rich spatial sequence and symbolic narrative that symbolizes the spiritual path and its goal have typically been central to sacred architecture. In this context its peregrination by the religious aspirant and pilgrim is a recapitulation of the spiritual quest — a symbolic journey from the profane outer world to the sacred inner world. This paper argues that the architecture often symbolizes the religious quest through enclosures, thresholds, gateways, spatial sequence and a clearly articulated inner sanctum. Patterns of the psyche, mythology, religious beliefs and pilgrimage are central to the argument that architecture is essentially "built myth," that symbolizes religious beliefs and accommodates the enactment of shared rituals.

Background

PATTERNS OF MYTHOLOGY, RITUAL AND ARCHITECTURAL EXPRESSION

The use of symbols has played an important role in the unique human need to define our place in the world. Most commonly, symbols have been used to express what might have otherwise been inexpressible religious and mythological themes. According to Carl Jung,

> Because there are innumerable things beyond the range of human understanding, we constantly use symbolic terms to represent concepts that we can't define or fully

comprehend. This is one reason why all religions employ symbolic languages or images.

— Jung 1968: 3-4

Jung's "archetypes of the collective unconscious," Claude Levi-Strauss's "structural anthropology", and Joseph Campbell's "universal mythic themes," are explorations in psychology, anthropology and mythology that establish repeating elements and patterns in each discipline. For example, Jung defined "archetypes of the collective unconscious" as shared elements of the human psyche and argued that there is a psychic "strata" or archetype that all humans share. Furthermore, according to Jung, the psyche, most of which lies in the realm of the unconscious, expresses itself through mythology and myths are an "expression of the archetypes" (de Laszlo 1959: 288).

Claude Levi-Strauss, a key figure in the development of structuralist theory who studied the mythology of cultures around the world argued that there was an "astounding similarity between myths collected in widely different regions." Additionally their underlying structure was consistent, something that could be proved by diagramming the myths by means analogous to an orchestra score (Strauss 1963: 206-51). The repetitive nature of myths served "to render the structure of the myth apparent" (Strauss 1963: 229), and Levi-Strauss saw the examination of patterns to be the primary task towards their understanding. "If there is meaning to be found in mythology," he argues, "it cannot reside in the isolated elements which enter into the composition of the myth but only in the way those elements are combined" (Strauss 1963: 210).

Similar to Jung, Joseph Campbell described myths as "spontaneous productions of the psyche," each bearing "within it, undamaged, the germ power of its source" (Campbell 1949: 4). Campbell found patterns in mythology, which he termed "universal mythic themes," and argued that there are repeating mythic themes, which appear pan-culturally but find unique expression in each particular culture.

Campbell (1949: 30) argues that the mythic quest or "hero's journey" is an enduring theme in world religions. He characterized the hero's journey as a sequence of "separation, initiation and return," where the pilgrim experiences a rite of passage and emerges in most cases spiritually transformed. The journey typically comprises four segments: the finding of the path, trials along the path, the attainment of the spiritual place, and the return; which suggest a physical as well as psychological distance. The finding of the path and a challenging journey along it appear in the myths, religious texts and folk tales of cultures around the globe and throughout history. Campbell argues "there is but one archetypal mythic hero whose life has been replicated in many lands by many people" (Campbell 1988: 136). The hero's quest is a journey from the known to the unknown and its ritual enactment, as found in the act of pilgrimage, symbolizes the spiritual quest and recapitulates the original spiritual trials and journey of the deity.

PILGRIMAGE

The rite of pilgrimage, analogous to the spiritual journey, is found in all the world's major religions. Moreover, the characteristics that define the act of pilgrimage are strikingly consistent across all the faiths. Though pilgrimage often involves large groups of pilgrims, the essential act is an individual one — a spiritual quest as a test or affirmation of one's faith. It was, and still is, both an outer and an inner journey, a physical journey to distant locations, that leads the pilgrim to a deeper spiritual understanding. Most writings on pilgrimage describe journeys *to* the sacred site but rarely *through* the sacred architecture where the pilgrim's journey was created by the spatial sequence and symbolic narrative of the architecture. The goal, the sacred place — be it an oracle or holy person, a healing site or a reliquary — through its architecture, often created a microcosm of the pilgrimage. An internalized world was created in which the pilgrim's journey is re-enacted in the architectural setting and its spatial sequence.

Most religious pilgrimage is a mimesis of the universal myth of the "hero's journey," a re-enactment of the hero-redeemer's spiritual journey and trans-formation. Pilgrimage typically entails the following: ritual preparation for the journey, separation from society, trials and rituals along the pilgrim's way, arrival at and passage through the sacred place, and the return to society in a changed state — each of which correspond to Campbell's pattern of the mythic quest.

The act of separation is perhaps one of the most significant components of the pilgrim's journey. Similar to ancient initiation rites, the pilgrim is separated from society and placed in a marginal state (Barber 1991). This intermediary zone acts as a bridge between the pilgrim's old life and the hoped-for healing cure or spiritual transformation; it is both a physical path and an emotional state. Physical and spiritual trials and specific rituals in part define the act of pilgrimage. Practices range from crawling on one's hands and knees to the sacred spot to extreme acts of self-mortification.

After the journey there is the arrival at the sacred place, the goal of all pilgrimage, both physically and symbolically. In Christianity it might be the crypt underneath the choir of the cathedral that contained the relics of a saint that were possessed with prayer-granting powers. In Mecca it is the Great Mosque and the Ka'aba, the sacred black stone, around which the pilgrims ritually circumambulate. Even on arrival within the sacred precinct, the sacred place was not easily accessible and the pilgrim's journey continued with gateways, thresholds and paths that had to be passed before the inner sanctum was attained. At some Gothic cathedrals, labyrinth patterns were set into the floor of the knave through which penitents would crawl on their hands and knees, a miniaturized journey to the sacred place. The 660-foot labyrinthine circumambulation at Chartres, which recreates the pilgrimage to Jerusalem, is an excellent example of self-similarity in the ritual landscape.

In some cases the "holy of holies" was attainable only to the "initiated" — only the Pharaoh and high priests entered the inner sanctum at the Temple of Amun-Re at Karnak; the *garbha-griha* of the Hindu temple can only be entered by priests; or it is unobtainable to all — the central *stupa* at the Buddhist temple at Borobudur cannot be viewed or entered into. Rites performed within the sacred place often mirror the pilgrim's journey — Christians walk along the ambulatory of the cathedral and pray at the Stations of the Cross; Buddhists and Hindus circumambulate *stupas* and temples. At the rock-cut tombs at Ajanta, an ancient Buddhist pilgrimage site, pilgrims climb steep, narrow steps to enter into their dark recesses. With the cave wall on their left and the stone colonnade on their right, they circumambulate in a clockwise direction, spinning around the "cosmic egg" of the enclosed *stupa* (Kostof 1985: 237). Acts such as these serve to mark each of these places as a sacred centre, an *axis mundi* and the centre of the world (Eliade 1959: 182). Each is a microcosm that mimics the macrocosm.

Observances at the sacred site precede the hero's eventual return and reintegration into society. The return is an integral part of the journey though its importance varies between religions. In all faiths the common theme is of spiritual transformation and increased status within the society. One rejoins the family, the village, as a new person, spiritually reborn by the trials and knowledge of the pilgrim's way.

The preparation, act of journey and attainment of the spiritual place, all put the pilgrim outside of everyday life, in an intermediary zone where contact with god is possible. This act not only celebrates the deity and the pilgrim's faith but also mirrors the god's own spiritual journey. In this way the pilgrim performs a mimesis of the god, the archetypal hero's journey common to the world's religions and mythology. Architecture has traditionally consecrated sacred places — the goal of pilgrimage — and articulated the path to attain it. This is a role it still performs today. Sacred architecture, through its entrance, articulation and spatial sequence creates at a smaller scale, the pilgrim's way, symbolizing this essential religious act.

SPATIAL SEQUENCE AND SYMBOLIC NARRATIVES IN SACRED ARCHITECTURE

Sacred places, according to Mircea Eliade (1958: 367-85), all share one common trait, "there is always a clearly marked space which makes it possible (though under varied forms) to communicate with the sacred." The path to the sacred place is typically a "hard path, sown with obstacles," which in part underlines its separateness but also "serves the purpose of preserving profane man from the danger to which he would expose himself by entering without . . . having gone through the gestures of approach." The path in essence symbolizes a spiritual journey with its attendant risks, gates and trials, which leads to the sacred place.

Myths are particularly potent symbolic vehicles because of their ability to weave symbols into a narrative. In sacred architecture, however, we find the most potent use of symbolism, because here symbols are not only representational but spatial and temporal as well. Consequently, the totality of the architectural experience is a powerful synthesis of the various media used to communicate symbolic themes. In essence, the symbolic content is represented by the orientation, plan, surfaces, geometry, form and spaces of the architecture. Moreover, it is not a static activity, such as the viewing of art nor a passive one such as listening to a folk tale but a dynamic experience — the inexpressible expressed three-dimensionally and experienced totally.

Examples of sacred paths and places are found throughout the world and many exhibit the characteristics of a clearly articulated entry, a spatial sequence that leads to the sacred place and a symbolic story expressed by the path and place. For example, the axial path and inner sanctum of the Late Kingdom Egyptian Temple of Amun-Re at Karnak created a symbolic journey from the west to the east along a path that grew increasingly more enclosed and sacred until the final goal of the sanctuary was reached. At the "sacred way" at Delphi the path first entered the sacred precinct through the temenos wall then wound up the hillside passing the monuments and treasuries that lined the path until it reached the inner sanctum of the Temple of Apollo. At Koto-in, a sub-temple of Daitoku-ji Zen Buddhist Monastery in Kyoto, the entry path sequence symbolizes the journey to the hermit scholar's retreat celebrated in Zen stories and landscape paintings and the ideals of Zen practice and the path to enlightenment. Borobudur is a massive *stupa* built in a *mandala* pattern, which physically mirrors the stages of spiritual passage. Pilgrims circumambulate through each of its concentric, image-laden galleries before finally arriving at the centre and peak of this sacred mountain.

The approach, entry and passage through sacred architecture to the sanctuary is typically a rich spatial sequence and symbolic narrative that symbolized the spiritual path and its goal. Religious beliefs and myths are often symbolized through ritual and typically there is a close correspondence between the rituals and the architectural setting. This correspondence is not simply functional but operates at a deep symbolic level in which belief, ritual and architecture are firmly interwoven. In other words, religious architecture is fundamentally "built myth," that both symbolizes a culture's belief systems of its time and accommodates and facilitates the enactment of shared rituals. Moreover, the entry, path sequence and sanctuary of sacred architecture often symbolized the spiritual path and its goal and its ambulation by the religious acolyte recapitulated the spiritual quest. As religious pilgrims traversed the spatial sequence, its symbolism unfolded as a narrative and their journey served as a mimesis of the hero's journey to apotheosis.

This paper suggests that the psyche is the source of mythological and religious expression and that it is composed in part of certain shared archetypes. It proposes that an essential quality of sacred architecture is that it is "built myth" which symbolizes cultural beliefs and facilitates the enactment of shared rituals. If one accepts that there are common elements that religion and mythology comprise and that architecture is a spatial and temporal symbolization of myth and religion; then it can be argued that there are shared architectural patterns in sacred architecture. Specifically, I argue that there is a corollary between the myth of the "hero's journey" and the path and place in sacred architecture. In other words, from the psyche the myth of the hero redeemer arises and from this an architectural setting is created to symbolize the spiritual quest. Consequently, the path and place in sacred architecture in its many forms from a wide range of historical settings suggests an archetypal pattern in architecture (*fig.* 14.1).

In this context, this paper argues, the architecture of the Western Christian church exhibits strong path and place characteristics, typified by the pilgrimage path which leads to the western doors and tympanum and the axial path which continues through the nave and ends at the sacred domain of the sanctuary; all of which had significant symbolic content and power. I use the church of Sainte-Madeleine to demonstrate these themes.

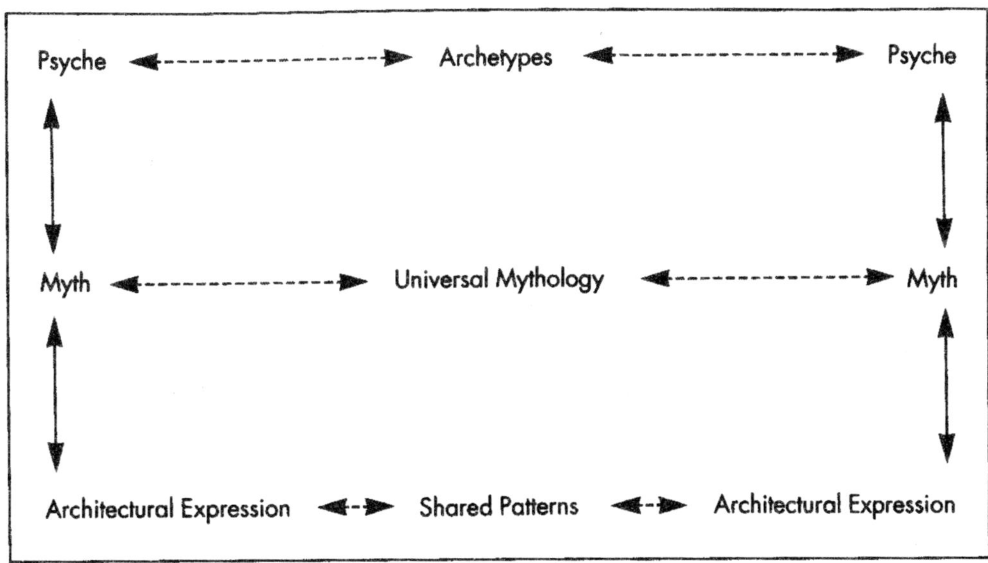

fig. 14.1: Architecture as built-myth.

Basilica of La Madeleine, Vézelay

The Romanesque pilgrimage church of Sainte-Madeleine is located in the Burgundian village of Vézelay, an area that has long been held as sacred. The present-day cathedral was first begun during the Carolingian Era and the first structure to be built was a crypt reputed to contain the relics of Mary Magdalene. This early reliquary plus its geographic location, established Vézelay as an important pilgrimage church. (It was located at the head of the Limoges-Perigueux road, one of four pilgrimage routes that led to Santiago de Compostela.) In the Middle Ages, Vézelay was a religious and monastic centre and its community of monks at one time numbered 500. Today, little remains of the monastic buildings outside of the church itself. The town at its height had a population of over 10,000 and as an obligatory pilgrimage destination as well as an important political and economic hub it became very prosperous. The result was a series of ambitious building programmes that built and rebuilt the church over a number of years, most of which occurred during the early twelfth century.

As a pilgrimage site, an active monastery, and a significant economic and political centre, Vézelay had many functions. However, among the plethora of functions it served, its symbolic content was arguably of primary importance. For the largely illiterate populace of the Middle Ages, religious architecture performed the role of communicating shared meaningful ideas and concepts. Similar to religious texts and rituals, the architecture was didactic — it served to communicate religious and social beliefs and enforce codes of behaviour.

The early Christian church appropriated the Roman Basilica and gradually transformed its organization to accommodate its liturgy. The word basilica is derived from the Greek *basileus*, which meant "king" and thus denoted the "king's house," and in Roman times it was a hall of justice (Whone 1977). In the early Christian church the apse of the basilica, formerly the place for the Roman Tribunal, became the seat of authority of Jesus Christ. Just as the young Christian faith subsumed pagan rituals and practices, it also took over its architectural forms for its own uses. In Roman times sacrifices were made on an altar in front of the apse and in the Christian Church this was transformed into the symbolic ritual of imbibing the blood and body of Christ.

Many elements of Christianity distinguished it from its "pagan" predecessors. One of the most outstanding aspects of its belief system was the concept of man's personal relationship to God through the intermediary of Jesus Christ. This was to have profound architectural implications because now the architecture was not only for the deity but also for its worshippers as well (Davies 1982: 91), which demanded particular spatial and symbolic responses. This was in striking contrast to sacred spaces such as the inner sanctum at Karnak or the *cella* and *adyton* at Delphi, which were reserved only for the gods and the priesthood. The basilican model, as it came to be developed by the Western church after the Great Schism of 1054, proved especially fertile for the creation of a symbolic path sequence. It richly and dramatically utilized the basic spatial components of the axial path and its destination to create a symbolic pilgrimage path from the secular to the sacred, from sin to salvation, from death to life (Norberg-Schulz 1974: 119). The path passed through a sequence of portals and spaces along the way to the goal of the sanctuary: the place of meeting between man and God.

Vézelay was a pilgrimage church but because it lacks significant transepts, its plan does not correspond to the typology of pilgrimage churches, such as those found at Tours, Limoges and Santiago de Compostela. The plan of Sainte-Madeleine is axially symmetrical and is aligned E-W (*fig.* 14.2). The linear path travels from the west to the east, from the more public foyer of the narthex, through the nave to the sacred centre of the sanctuary and crypt. The pilgrimage path led through the crowded main street of the medieval village to a forecourt fronting the church's imposing western facade. Three sets of doors establish entry at the western front. Inside, the dark constricted space of the narthex leads to the nave and side aisles. The linear orientation of the nave establishes the path to the sanctuary, which is placed above the crypt. Over time its form and organization synthesized a complex spatial composition and sculptural motifs to create its sacred setting and symbolic content.

The path and place of the original Roman and Christian basilica provided a simple and direct route to the powerful and sacred altar. The path and place at Saint-Madeleine, a product of its time and influenced by the demands of pilgrimage, has more depth and complexity. The

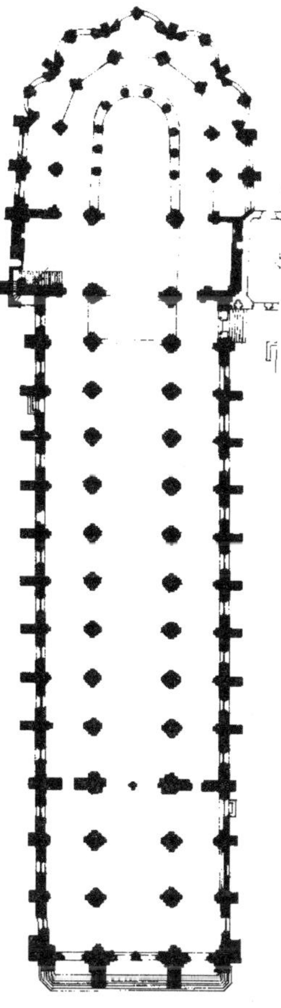

fig. 14.2: Floor plan Cathedral of Sainte-Madeleine, Vézelay, France (twelfth century).

exterior mass and scale of the building contributes to its sense of place and was derived from Roman precedents as well. Two towers flank the entry doors to La Madeleine, the southern one, named for St. Michael, rises to a height of 120 ft (*fig.* 14.3).

Gateways in many ancient cultures expressed the power and omnipotence of their god-rulers. Often palace gateways were the only places where the populace would see their rulers as they emerged in a royal procession or looked down upon them from a raised arcade and, consequently, gateways were symbolic of either the departure or return of the god-ruler. For example, the Egyptian gateway of pylon and trabeated entry portal had powerful symbolic meaning related to the pharaonic gods. Here ceremonial rites took place where the pharaoh would appear in the "golden loggia" or "window of appearances" as a sun god. Subsequently, the "emperor cult" in Imperial Rome adopted certain Ptolomaic pharaonic rituals and architectural devices. Imperial Roman city and palace gates were typically a combination of towers and gateways and symbolized an "imperial stronghold." Triumphal arches similarly consecrated the return of the god-rulers of Imperial Rome. According to E. Baldwin Smith (1956: 10-11), as a result, "the gateway became a kind of architectural ideogram denoting a *sacrum palatium* as the seat of government and the place from which emanated the divine wisdom of the state."

At La Madeleine the towers and west front were heir to the symbolic content of the "city-gate" and depicted both the gravity and security of the entrance to the *civitas dei*. The interior of the church also replicated the Roman fortified city or Imperial palace, implying communal habitation and political authority. According to Karsten Harries (1998: 103), "The church building signifies a quite specific ideal of communal dwelling, even as it signifies the journey character of life, speaks of both path and goal." The arcaded nave recalled the cardo and decamanus of a provincial capital and its fortified western front protected it from malevolent forces. The church became a haven where the devil is warded off by gods who guard its portals and reside within.

In its medieval setting Saint-Madeleine had a number of uses: fortress; place of solitary pilgrimage; a religious community of monks; a setting for processional and religious celebrations; and a place for civic and political events. For each its path and place both symbolized shared beliefs and accommodated communal acts. The predominant experience facilitated by the architecture was that of journey. For the pilgrim, this journey would have begun miles away, the church first becoming visible from a promontory 12 miles distant. Pausing here they would shout Montjoie! ("Mount of Joy!") when the sacred acropolis came into view. Next there was the passage through the crowded medieval town, a steep ascent up the hill through the secular world of man. Next the towers and entrance doors would be visible, the marking of the beginning of the sacred passage.

The tympanum above the central doors, with its iconographic and allegorical figures, marked the first threshold of the path similar to guardian deities common in other religious sites (*fig.* 14.4). The west front and its flanking towers underline their importance as the threshold to God. The tympanum of the central door shows "Christ in Judgement" a warning and an encouragement to the uninitiated as well as the laity. As we find in *Matthew 7.13-14*, "Enter by the narrow gate; for the gate is wide and the way is easy, that leads to destruction and those who enter it are many. For the gate is narrow and the way is hard, that leads to life, and those who find it are few." Its timeless message demands a commitment to die to the ways of the world and submit to God and the salvation promised by Christ.

The east-west axis of the church established the path as a journey from the west to the east. The relationship of the Christian path to the rising and setting sun most likely has pagan roots, as do many of the symbols and rituals of Christianity. The east, the place of the rising sun, symbolized the resurrection of the son of God and the Christian goal of salvation. The west, where the sun died each day, was the place of death and darkness, to be guarded against. The Western front provides a bulwark against the west, and beyond it one enters the narthex, a nodal point along the path. Here there was holy water and a place for ritual purification before entering the sacred space of the nave.

In the past the interior of Sainte-Madeleine was more colourful and decorated than it is today. However, decoration still remains in the form of sculptural reliefs. The most distinctive and symbolically rich carvings at Vézelay appear at the tympana inside the narthex that not only contained religious messages but also served to mark a threshold to the space beyond. At the aisle entrances tympana show biblical scenes; the southern one is called the "Child Jesus" tympanum and shows the annunciation and the nativity flanked by guardian angels. The central narthex tympanum is the most notable and shows Christ in a *mandorla* ("almond" in Italian, which describes its shape) passing his teachings on to his twelve disciples (*fig.* 14.5).

The solidity of the massing of the church and the compression of the narthex dramatically dissolve as one enters the nave (*fig.* 14.6). Here through proportion, articulation, repetition, rhythm and light is a new world, self-contained and static, but also compelling one forward to the goal beyond. The nave, volumetrically the most significant space, is principally formed by a repeating bay system of composite columns, spanned by cross-vaulting. The segments of the columns thrust uninterrupted to the cross-vaulting, which accentuates the repeating unit of the bay. Additionally there is the distinctive red and white banding on the nave vault arches and incised chevrons which appear at the aisle arches. The bays therefore appear, at least at one level, as separate repeating volumes. A marching rhythm of A-B-A-B is established by the vaults and the columns and arches which accentuate the linear spatial orientation of the nave. The repetition and cadence of the arcading relates the longitudinal axis to movement along it. Further emphasizing the directionality of the space are horizontal bands that appear at the column capitals and a string-course above the arcade. Additionally, the flanking side aisles are composed of repeating spatial modules, which form two longitudinal arcades and further reinforce the axiality of the nave and orient the path to its goal in the east (*fig.* 14.7).

The sanctuary is raised above the level of the ambulatory, which provides openings that offer light for the crypt below. This, along with enclosure screens, established it as a sanctified space, a place apart, obtainable only by the initiated. This was both a symbolic and practical device to separate the monks and priests from the laity (*fig.* 14.8).

The interior of Sainte-Madeleine exists as a living Bible and stories from the Old and New Testament along with morality scenes are depicted in sculptural carvings. The scale of this space is both monumental and personal. The space in its totality dwarfs the individual, an effect heightened by the diaphanous east end. However, the scale is also personal with messages contained within each column capital which spoke directly to the individual. Column capitals contain different scenes, pedantic lessons for the throngs of pilgrims. One capital depicts the story of David and the Lion from *The First Book of Samuel*, a message of patriarchal authority, where David says to Saul, "Your servant used to keep sheep for his father; and when there came a lion or a bear and took a lamb from the flock, I went after him and smote him and delivered it out of his mouth; and if he arose against me, I caught him by his beard, and smote him and killed him" (I Samuel 17:34-35) (*fig.* 14.9).

An adjacent column capital depicts the fate of the "evil rich man", a New Testament morality lesson about the damnation of a greedy man. In the sculpture he is shown lying over his sacks of gold while devils snatch his soul with hooks to carry it to hell (*fig.* 14.10). Another sculptural morality lesson warns against pagan rituals and customs — practices that Christianity both subsumed and attempted to eradicate. The scene depicts a woman, intoxicated by the music played by a man with a horn (symbolizing paganism), allowing herself to be fondled by a grotesque devil.

When one enters the nave and sees its myriad of symbolic messages, its intentions are unambiguous; repent and submit to God or suffer eternal damnation. As one walks down the nave and aisles, repeating the act of the generations of medieval villagers and pilgrims, a didactic narrative unfolds. Symbolic lessons confront one along the journey from the gloom of the narthex and nave, to the glory of the choir, from sin to salvation.

The symbolism of trial and redemption is a strong Christian concept, one that appears throughout the Old and New Testaments. The architecture expresses this through the elongation and segmentation of the path and the creation of a clearly defined goal at the end of the path. According to Norberg-Schulz (1974: 74).

The following of Christ does not imply that the centre is reached at once. The way is

fig. 14.3: View of the west front of the Cathedral of Sainte-Madeleine.

fig. 14.4: The west front tympanum showing Christ in Judgment.

fig. 14.5: The narthex looking toward the central tympanum, which depicts Christ in Majesty. Beyond the central post of the entrance is the nave.

fig. 14.6: The nave looking east; the rhythm of the arcading accentuates its longitudinal axis.

fig. 14.7: The north aisle looking west.

fig. 14.8: The ambulatory and choir with crypt below.

fig. 14.9: A column capital depicting the story of David and the Lion.

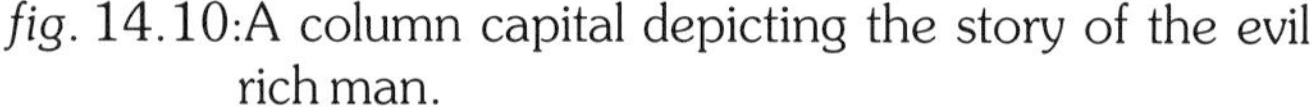

fig. 14.10:A column capital depicting the story of the evil rich man.

long and in architectural terms it was concretized as a longitudinal axis, as a path of salvation leading to the altar, the symbol of communion with Christ.

The plan of the Christian church has been equated to the proportions of the human body and as a symbol in plan of the cross. This image is symbolized by the path, a journey from the base desires of man, the feet being the part of the body in contact with the earth. The crossing is at the heart, the point of decision of whether to submit to God or not. Past this gate one journeys to the *chevet*, the root of which means head, the place of spiritual enlightenment (Whone 1977). Along the path a pantheon of warnings and encouragement concerning the secular and sacred is expressed by the sculpture.

Originally, stained glass in the nave made it dark in comparison to the choir beyond, a feature that was elaborated upon in the Gothic that followed. It was a journey from dark to light, which, along with its linear spatial organization, served to compell one forward to the chancel beyond. The nave, a word derived from the Latin "navis" meaning ship, symbolized a contained vessel, ferrying souls from damnation to redemption. For the medieval mind the spaces of the church were physical manifestations of images of heaven, the desired state of grace. Otto von Simpson (1956: xvii) states that, "Within its walls God himself was mysteriously present. The medieval sanctuary was the image of heaven." Theologians of this time were concerned with questions concerning transubstantiation, alchemists were trying to change one material to another and the architecture aspired to change physical stone to a divine paradise. According to von Simpson (1956: 50), "For the twelfth and thirteenth centuries light was the source and essence of all beauty." The rarefied light of the Medieval Cathedral served as a medium where God was revealed and through which man and God were joined.

According to Eliade (1954: 17),

> The very ancient conception of the temple as the *imago mundi*, the idea that the sanctuary reproduces the universe in its essence passed into the religious architecture of Christian Europe: the basilica of the first centuries of our era, like the medieval cathedral, symbolically reproduces the Celestial Jerusalem.

The macrosocm and microsocm were intertwined through architecture. The medieval masons knew well the structural demands placed upon them. Through the structural organization, surface treatment and a sophisticated control of light, the constructive elements dissolved, re-forming in the image of an ethereal sacred spiritualized space. It was an internalized world, separate from the secular world, and attained only through the trials of the path. Unlike pagan religions, Christianity did not directly respond to the natural world. Instead its interior spaces created a hermetic, self-referential place, the primary symbol of which was the path to the redemptive sacred place.

The pilgrimage road which led to the west front and the axial path that attained the sanctuary, communicated through numerous symbolic and iconographic means the journey of trial and redemption. Jesus says in the Gospel of St. John, "I am the way, and the truth, and the life; no one comes to the Father but by me." At Vézelay the architecture expressed and facilitated this journey to God, beginning with the distant view of the church perched on fortified acropolis, and concluded with passage through the internalized world of the church itself. The enclosed hermetic space of the church synthesized a plethora of potent symbols and represented the *civitas dei* or the "Heavenly Jerusalem" described in *The Revelation to John*. The path sequence was a spiritual journey to a place of sacrality and authority.

Conclusions

The Basilica of La Madeleine comprises a well-defined path and its goal: a consummate example of Christian symbolism rendered spatially, formally and sceno-graphically. Through the case study of Vézelay, repeating motifs of the Western Medieval Christian church are revealed. In most, powerful interplays of good and evil; solidity and dematerialization; static and dynamic; heaven and earth are communicated by the form, spaces and surfaces of the architecture. All contain, to varying degrees, a rich path sequence and symbolic narrative that leads to a sacred centre. Central to the Christian belief system and the buildings built to serve it is a clearly defined place where man and God were joined by the celebration of the Eucharist; a threshold between earth and heaven (von Simpson 1956: xv). Perhaps it can be described as a crossing-over point, similar in meaning to the Hindu *tirtha*. The sanctuary in essence was a specific location where God was present. Its images of perfection embodied Christian ideals of purity and sanctity.

To the religious pilgrim, the world was a treacherous labyrinthine path that negotiated between evil and good, sin and salvation. The pilgrimage path provided a clear route to salvation — which was then replicated by the form, space, organization and surface decoration of the Medieval cathedral. The pilgrim's journey to this sacred centre was a mimesis of the "original deed" of Christ. The Fourteen Stations of the Cross which typically marked passage along the aisles or ambulatory, were the most overt representation of "Everyman's" Via Dolorosa. Passage through the thresholds and spaces of the cathedral symbolized the spiritual path that leads to its goal; the sacred place and its promise of redemption and apotheosis. In the sacred enclosure of the cathedral, the "perspective" of the linear path marching towards the altar, was also emblematic of the Medieval desire for *perspective* (Harries 1998: 106), a looking through to reveal the truth within. In this aspect, the church was a rarefied place, the house of God, where truth was revealed and souls redeemed.

The Christian cathedral "can be understood as an architecture of representation" (Harries

1998: 103). It was declarative architecture that expressed symbolic themes and social dictates directly and abstractly. Its form, organization, surface imagery, spatial sequence and symbolism communicated a fortified stronghold and place of authority and divinity and throughout the architecture themes of pilgrimage, spiritual path and sacred centre dominated.

References

Barber, R., 1991, *Pilgrimages*, Woodbridge, Suffolk, England: Boydell Press.

Campbell, J., 1949, *The Hero with a Thousand Faces*, New York: Princeton University Press, Bollingen Series XVII.

Campbell, J., and Bill Moyers, 1988, *The Power of Myth*, New York: Doubleday.

Davies, J.G., 1982, *Temples, Churches and Mosques: A Guide to the Appreciation of Religious Architecture*, Oxford: Basil Blackwell.

Eliade, Mircea, 1959, *The Sacred and the Profane: The Nature of Religion*, London: Sheed and Ward.

Eliade, Mircea, 1958, *Patterns in Comparative Religion*, London: Sheed and Ward.

Eliade, Mircea, 1954, *The Myth of the Eternal Return. Cosmos, and History*, New York: Arcana.

Harries, Karsten, 1998, *The Ethical Function of Architecture*, Cambridge, Mass: The MIT Press.

Jung C.G. (ed.), 1968, *Man and His Symbols*, New York: Dell Publishing.

Kostof, Spiro., 1985, *A History of Architecture, Settings and Rituals*, New York/Oxford: Oxford University Press.

Laszlo, de., 1959, *The Basic Writings of C.G. Jung*, ed. Violet Staub, New York: Modern Library.

Norberg-Schulz, C., 1974, *Meaning in Western Architecture*, London: Studio Vista.

See Fox, Robin Lane, 1986, *Pagans and Christians*, Hammondsworth: Penguin Books Ltd.

Smith, E. Baldwin, 1956, *Architectural Symbolism of Imperial Rome and the Middle Ages*, Princeton: Princeton University Press.

Strauss, S. and Claude-Levi, 1963. *Structural Anthropology*, New York: Basic Books Inc.

von Simpson, Otto, 1956, *The Gothic Cathedral*, Princeton: Princeton University Press.

Vorreux, D., 1988, *The Story of Vezelay*, Ouest France.

Whone, H., 1977, *Church Monastery Cathedral: An Illustrated Guide to Christian Symbolism*, Shaftsbury, Dorset: Element Books

15

Pilgrimage and Ritual Movements in Cuzco and Inca Empire

R. Tom Zuidema

THE central concern of this paper will be a pattern of ritual movements on which we have excellent concrete evidence from Cuzco, the capital of the Inca Empire. Following a description of the setting of the problem, I will indicate the importance of that information for an understanding of the attraction once exercised by the two most famous pilgrimage centres, *Pachacamac* and *Titicaca*, in the pre-Hispanic central Andes, on which places we have little concrete evidence. Thus I can explore the tradition of pilgrimage in pre-Inca and Inca cultures and reflect on the significance of the concepts of pilgrimage and self-organizing systems both then and in colonial and modern *Peru* and *Bolivia*.

When Spanish chroniclers and missionaries, some time after the conquest of the Inca empire and its capital of Cuzco in 1533, began to think more systematically about the subject of Andean culture in previous times, they discovered or developed the idea that since long ago two poles of religious attraction had existed in the country: the island of *Titicaca*, in the highland lake of the same name and the temple-city of *Pachacamac* at the border of sea and desert coast just south of *Lima*, the modern capital of Peru (map 15.1). Once, in *Titicaca*, the Creator god, *Viracocha*, had called forth from the Underworld the Sun and the Moon as well as the first ancestors of the royal dynasty in Cuzco and of other peoples (Betanzos 1987:11-15; Molina 1989: 50-52). These ancestors were sent underground from Titicaca near the places where they were going to live and here, they emerged a second time. According to the mythology of the central Peruvian province of *Huarochiri*, *Pachacamac*, "He who animates the World," was the Underworld god who caused earthquakes. His wife, *Urpihuachac*, had thrown the first fishes into the Ocean (Taylor 1987: 68-71). In their relationship on Earth, Titicaca and Pachacamac symbolized an opposition of Heaven to Underworld. Both places had been the most important pilgrimage centres in the Andes since the time, some 500 years before the rise of the Incas in Cuzco, when two other cities had ruled the country: *Huari*, near modern *Ayacucho* in southern highland Peru and *Tiahuanaco*, near the lake and island of Titicaca (Isbell & McEwan 1991; Kolata 1993, 1996). Their memory was not lost after their empires had disappeared.

Map 15.1. Inca empire.

Pachacamac and Tiahuanaco-Titicaca are of foremost interest not only to Archaeology and Ethnohistory but also to Anthropology. For instance, the town of *Copacabana* on the shore of lake Titicaca where Inca pilgrims departed when going to the island, became the most important pilgrimage centre in viceregal Peru (Ramos Gavilán 1988; Calancha 1974; MacCormack 1984; Salles-Reese 1997). Today, the Virgin of Copacabana is worshipped all over Bolivia on February 2 and August 5, dates that may derive from Inca and even pre-Inca times: the first marks the time when in Titicaca and Tiahuanaco the sun goes through zenith and the second was used to mark the time of planting, when the sun goes through nadir half a year later. The worship in Pachacamac to the Lord of Earthquakes is now taken over in Lima by the popular cult of Christ as the Lord of Miracles (Rostworowski de Diez Canseco 1992). Still, the three disciplines have contributed to each other's questions only in a limited way. Let me explain this situation briefly with respect to our study of pre-Hispanic Andean civilization.

In terms of its accomplishments, Andean civilization is clearly comparable to other ancient civilizations since about 1000 years BC, despite the fact that it never made use of inventions like of writing or the wheel. Devices to record information did exist but none that might have kept alive into colonial times and of use for our inspection, precisely memorized texts including, i.e., genealogical accounts. One possible exception is the system of 41 directions called *Ceques*, as these were viewed in Cuzco from the temple of the Sun toward its horizon. A topological interest in 328 shrines called *huacas* ($8 \times 41 = 12 \times 27(1/3) = 328$) was mapped onto the valley, of use for government, agriculture, state rituals, astronomy and the calendar. I will make use of some of this information later (Zuidema 1990b).

Given the way in which the Inca state collapsed under the Spanish onslaught, we hardly know how it actually operated when it was still in power, except for some eyewitness accounts by its conquerors. The first two chroniclers who tried to re-imagine Inca history for the purpose of describing Inca culture, did not write until some 20 years after the conquest, followed by others up to 80 years later. Meanwhile, the Catholic Church had made major strides in abolishing "pagan" indigenous religion, myths and rituals. Chroniclers based their interpretations on fading and coloured memories of informants, using Western concepts for their ever-changing focusses of interest. Gods like Pachacamac and Viracocha, once including characteristics of Tricksters, became "Creator" gods comparable to the Christian one. Most chroniclers had a genuine interest in Andean culture but their data can be handled critically only if, in some way, these can be checked against information of proven pre-Hispanic origin. Here I aim to compare Spanish opinions with descriptions of acceptable Inca customs. Thus I approach the problem of pilgrimage to Pachacamac and Titicaca to be introduced first, from the point-of-view of our information on the system of ritual movements in Cuzco.

One of the first acts of Francisco Pizarro in *Cajamarca* after the fatal hour in which he defeated *Atahuallpa*, the last Inca king, was to send his brother, Hernán Pizarro, to Pachacamac

(Pizarro 1938). The fame of this largest and richest of all "mosques", attracting pilgrims from all over the empire, had reached him already. Hernán Pizarro and some other early visitors report that there were two major temples erected on pyramids in Pachacamac: one dedicated to the god *Pachacamac*, himself, and the other to the Sun god. The first temple dated from long before the Incas and with its position at the border of land and sea, its cult may always have represented an opposition of above and below, of Heaven and Earth. Some cult of the Sun may also have existed but the Incas instituted that only their king, as lord of all other kings, could be worshipped as "Son of the Sun" (Zuidema 1990a). As such, the cult in the temple of the Sun reflected recent, imperial strategy.

The ruins of both temples still exist and around them are found various compounds, each containing a small pyramid (Shimada 1991). Based on some evidence from chroniclers, these compounds have been interpreted as belonging to local lords who visited Pachacamac or who sent there their emissaries (Jiménez Borja 1985). Gaining access to the most sacred part of the temple obliged a person to be present in Pachacamac for at least a year. The visit would have involved the sacrifice of children, called *capac hucha* "offering to the king". Pachacamac not only received pilgrims but myths additionally suggest that it also would have sent out its own representatives or missionaries (Rostworowski de Diez Canseco 1992; Santillán 1968).

The situation with respect to Lake Titicaca is somewhat different. Tiahuanaco had been a large capital, fallen into ruins in Inca times. The Incas still revered it for its antiquity, though we don't know if they sent pilgrims there. The island of Titicaca, also known as "Island of the Sun" and the nearby smaller island of Coati, known as "Island of the Moon", both contained an Inca temple. But the goal of worship on the first island was a rock at its highest point (Cobo 1956: 189-94), a late chronicler, but informed by early sources, mentions that pilgrims were first screened in Copacabana and that on the island road leading to the rock there were three walls with guardians. Only the most select people could pass all three walls.

How can we imagine the actual movement of pilgrims to and from Pachacamac and Titicaca? Travel was highly regimented by the Inca government. Ramos Gavilán (1988: 84-85), recording the later Catholic importance of Copacabana, includes information on its use for pilgrimage in Inca times. People from Cuzco and 40 other locations had been relocated around Copacabana. Together, they represented 41 provinces of the empire from where people were ordered or allowed to visit the island. This imperial organization is reminiscent of the local one in Cuzco with its 41 directions or *ceques* leading to so many locations in its province.

One document, written some 90 years after the conquest and dealing with the "extirpation of idolatries" in a highland village of central Peru, suggests how pilgrims' travel might have occurred in Inca times (Zuidema, 1973, 1989: ch. 3). Each of four *ayllus*, social divisions in the village, had kept a list of the child sacrifices it had been obliged to make at special occasions in its past. The first *ayllu* had sent children to Cuzco, the capital, from where they were returned in order to be sacrificed at home. The second *ayllu* had sent them to Cuzco to be sacrificed there and the third *ayllu* to different important places in the empire including Titicaca. The last *ayllu* of potters had kept and sacrificed children at home in order to obtain good clay for making pots. The children travelled for their solemn missions following *ceques* in directions as straight as possible (Molina 1989:120-28; Murúa 1964: 110-11); their attendants followed by way of normal roads. As these other people would return, we may assume that they were pilgrims of the kind that the early chroniclers heard about. However, no Spaniard had actually seen pilgrims or pilgrimages or the use of pilgrimage sites in pre-Hispanic times. We are warned that the use in Inca times of, for instance, Copacabana may have been totally different from what it was in colonial times.

Notwithstanding the conditions and limitations of our research, we can come to a clearer concept of what pilgrimage meant in Inca times by including into our view another corpus of data. This information does not deal directly with Titicaca or Pachacamac but the hypothesis to which it leads has clear implications for understanding their place in Inca cosmology and their ceremonial use. The data to be brought to the fore are especially important as their pre-Hispanic existence and way of use can be checked out well. I will concentrate on a system of ritual movements from Cuzco to the borders of its local province and back again; that is, in the province from where later the empire had been conquered. The system was more elaborate than I can describe now. Thus I concentrate on three movements that were highly interrelated and that included capac hucha sacrifice (Molina 1989: 66-71). I call the first movement a "procession," the second a "pilgrimage" and the third a "race;" later I will conclude to what extent all three included aspects of pilgrimage (Maps 15.2, 15.3).

The first two movements were carried out by priests, called *Tarpuntay*, during the Incaic month around the June solstice; the king himself then went to a temple north of Cuzco to observe the sunset of this event. The name of the priests means "planter" and their various subsequent rituals were of concern to all phases of agriculture, from before irrigation, through plowing, sowing and planting (= *tarpuy*), to harvesting and storage of the crops. Their selection involved a previous discovery as "sons of the Thunder" (Cobo 1956: 224-25). But the chroniclers called them "priests of the Sun" as their first calendrical role involved the observation of the June solstice and their later rituals marked other times of the solar calendar.

The first movement, the procession, was repeated daily by some of the *Tarpuntay* priests, going from the sacred mountain *Huanacauri* on the horizon south-east of town over *Coricancha* "the Golden Enclosure" or "Temple of the Sun" in Cuzco to *Quiancalla* as part of the sacred mountain *Senqa* on its north-western horizon. At sunrise, the priests sacrificed a first llama at Huanacauri, at noon a second llama in Coricancha and at sunset a third llama in Quiancalla.

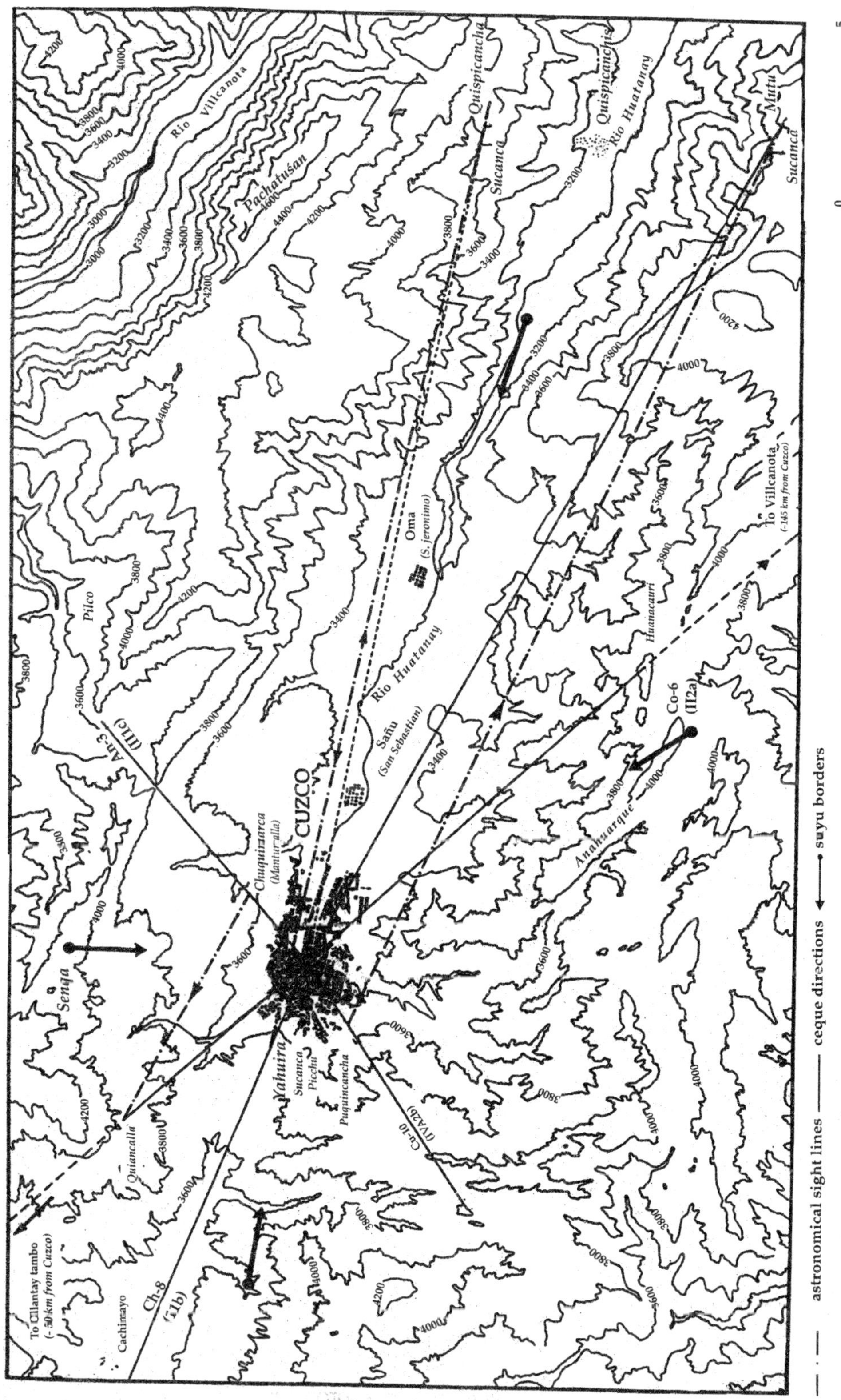

Map 15.2. Cuzco valley.

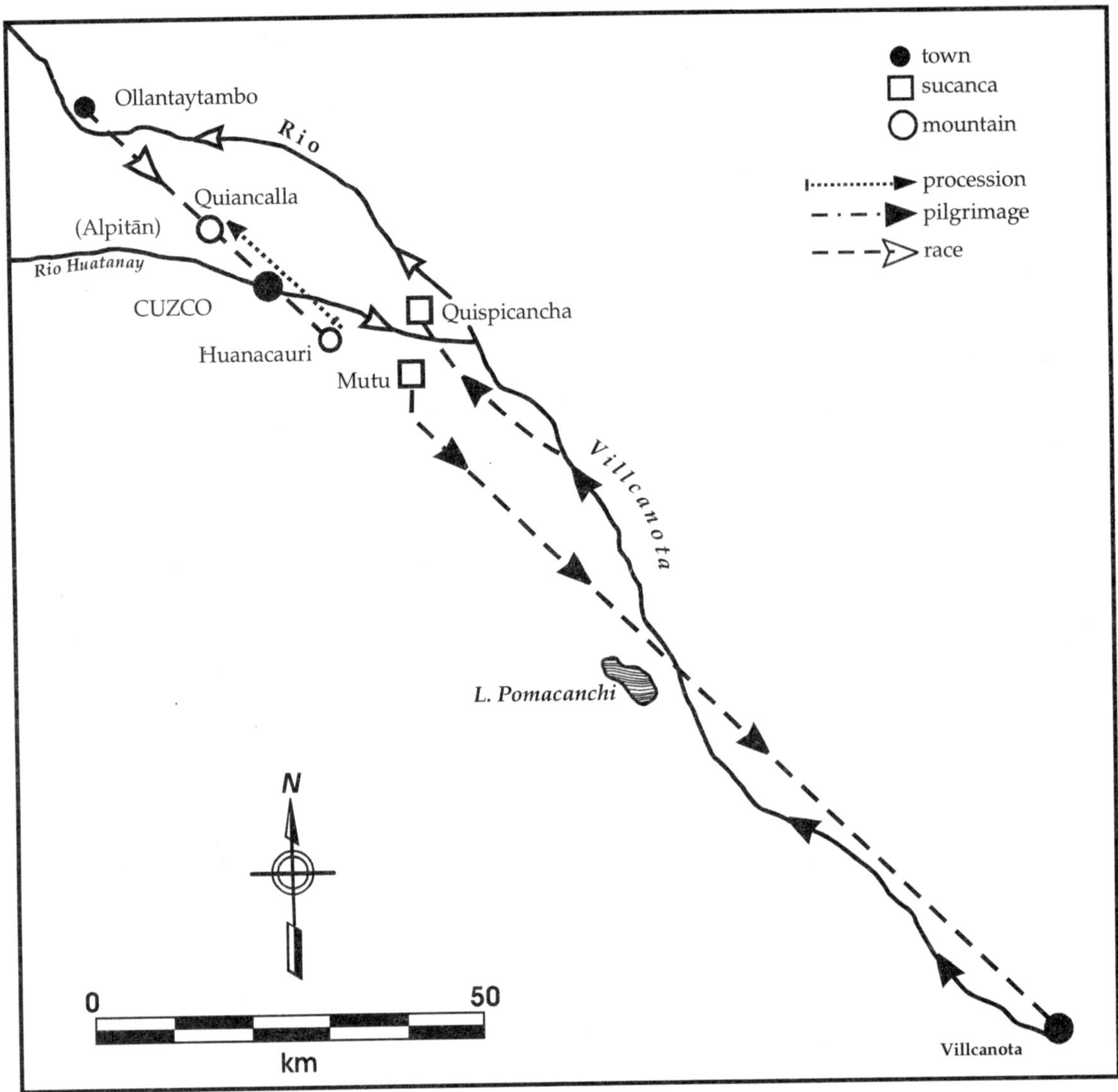

Map 15.3. Solsticial axis.

As its projection onto earth, the procession imitated the daily course of the sun through the sky and it ended at the place where the Inca actually saw the sun set (Zuidema 1981).

The goal of the second movement, the pilgrimage of other Tarpuntay priests, was another Temple of the Sun, in the same south-eastern direction from Cuzco as Huanacauri but far outside the valley (Zuidema 1982; 1989: ch. 13). It took them the same entire month to go and return from that temple, called *Villcanota* "House (*nuta*) where the Sun had been born at the beginning of time during a December solstice (*villca*)." Today, the place is called, in Spanish *La Raya*, "the borderline," as it constitutes the continental divide between Cuzco and Lake Titicaca. Here starts the river, also called *Villcanota*, which approaches Cuzco and then continues towards the tropical lowlands. The pass of Villcanota separates the river valley with maize agriculture from the high grasslands towards Lake Titicaca, mostly dedicated to the cultivation of potatoes and llama herding (Gade 1975).

The purpose of the pilgrimage was to go straight through the mountains to Villcanota and to return following the river. Molina specifies ten daily stopovers on the way down, in each of which the priests stayed overnight and worshipped the rising sun. On the way back they stopped at ten other places along the river. I assume that the pilgrimage took the whole month to complete and that the priests extended their stay in Villcanota for all the days that the sun would not visibly move from the solstice points of sunrise and sunset when, as the Incas said, "the Sun was sitting in his seat."

In various respects, the third movement, the race, was the exact and complementary counterpart of the pilgrimage (Cobo 1966; Molina 1989). The date was calculated from the December solstice and first new moon, four days after the next full moon. The ashes of all sacrifices in the previous year were thrown into the river. Runners with burning torches in their hands followed the ashes down the river of Cuzco to where it flowed into the Villcanota River. From here they continued to the town of *Ollantaytambo*, where the river approaches its subtropical part, located in the same north-western direction from Cuzco as Quiancalla and exactly opposite the direction of Huanacauri and Villcanota. From Ollantaytambo back, the men raced in competition through the mountains and we may assume that this occurred again in a direction as straight as possible. They entered the Cuzco valley at or near Quiancalla.

Comparing the race and the pilgrimage to each other, we observe that the participants in the race were not old priests but competing young men. The first part of the race was not in the daytime but took a whole night. This night was not calculated by the sun only but also by the moon. The ritual expressed wishes for the end of the rainy season. If the moon came early, the race fell in the first Incaic solar month after the December solstice, but if late, in the second. The last possible day for the return of the participants coincided with the passage of the sun through zenith on February 13.

In the pilgrimage and the race, we are dealing with two distinct movements, each carried out at different times of the year. None the less, we clearly can consider them as each other's complements in one overarching, annual ritual. Together, they had in mind that section of the Villcanota River of primary use for maize agriculture. While the pilgrimage first went out following a road through the mountains and returned along the upper part of the river and the race first took the lower part of the river and returned by a road through the mountains, the use of both parts of the river complemented each other and so did those of the two roads. The Incas laid out a year-round circuit between two end-points outside Cuzco and with a use as precise in terms of time as of space. We recognized this last fact already by way of the dates chosen for its two components. The first (the pilgrimage) took into account the sun for the exact date of the June solstice and the second (the race) the first full lunar cycle after the December solstice; the second, moreover, could reach the date of the sun's passage through zenith. We discover a similar concern with precision in a third way, which it will be useful to describe too.

The pilgrimage followed a road almost exactly south-east from Cuzco. By itself, this fact was of no astronomical significance. However, the pilgrimage started outside its track at the point, called *Mutu*, marking sunrise on the day of the December solstice. Something similar happened with the procession from Huanacauri, over Cuzco to Quiancalla. Although Quiancalla marked the point of June solstice sunset, this event was observed from outside the road of procession. In addition, we remember that the race returned to Cuzco by way of the same Quiancalla. The three roads shared the same direction, although the procession used it in a way opposite the race and the pilgrimage. Let me call this common direction the "solstitial axis" in Cuzco cosmology. While the axis was not laid out for use in astronomical observation, the places that served the latter purpose were explicitly connected to the axis. They determined its calendrical uses.

A major question now rises, one that leads to the problem of how the Incas of Cuzco integrated Titicaca/Tiahuanaco and Pachacamac into their cosmology and possibly into their state-organized system of pilgrimages. Given the location of Quiancalla on the solstitial axis and its use for observing the June solstice sunset, why didn't the Incas orient the axis in such a way that by itself it could have served also the practical purpose of observing both solstices? The Incas may have taken into account the following practical considerations, ones that were not dependent only on Cuzco as capital of their state.

First, the local axis from Huanacauri over the temple of the Sun to Quiancalla was made part of the provincial axis between Villcanota and Ollantaytambo, places of wider, ecological concern in terms of the Villcanota River. In both last locations, at the borders of the Cuzco province, products were exchanged with other ecological zones.

Second, the pilgrimage and the race together expressed (in ritual as well as through comments about their meaning) a concern with seasonal changes: of rain, of the flow of water in the river and of the use of irrigation canals. The race was held in order to stop the rains and to send the ashes of sacrifices, by way of the river to the god Viracocha in the Ocean. Like the waters in the rivers, the runners had to go fast. Access to the irrigation canals was closed so that the canals would not be destroyed and that the crops could ripen. In June, the priests went slowly up to the source of the river in order to drink to the Sun and to warm him up with bonfires. Both actions were intended to attract rains and to let the river flow again. In the month after the pilgrimage, the irrigation canals were re-used for the first time.

Third, the solstitial axis was extended not only beyond the valley of Cuzco but also beyond its province. In both directions, myths support the intent. I will discuss first the south-eastern extension towards sunrise, which is to Villcanota and Titicaca and later come to the north-western extension towards sunset. At the beginning of time, the sun was said to be born in Villcanota as well as in Titicaca (Bertonio [1612], 1984: *villcanota*). Once, at the occasion of the birth of his son the crown prince, an Inca king had sent messengers passing by Villcanota to the top of the Titicaca rock obtaining sacred water there (Pachacuti Yamqui Salcamaygua 1993: 15, 18). The birth of a future king as "Son of the Sun" was connected to the place of birth of the Sun itself and apparently compared to this cosmic event.

Let me now turn to the myths that integrate Titicaca and Pachacamac into Cuzco cosmology and suggest an Inca pattern of pilgrimages to both places. I can then integrate the system of ritual movements of Cuzco into this larger pattern of pilgrimages. Questions about the history of Andean pilgrimages allow me to introduce the problem of how and to what extent, the concept of self-organizing systems could apply.

According to the Creation myth, as understood by the Spanish from their Inca informants, the god Viracocha first travelled from Titicaca to Cuzco, including the road along the Villcanota River and from Cuzco he continued to the sea. Different places on the coast, including Pachacamac, are mentioned from where he disappeared over the waters to the horizon. But the best-known place and the one most in agreement with imperial ideology is on the Ecuadorian coast, near the Equator, where the island now called "Isla de la Plata," "Island of Silver" can be found. Incaic occupation of this part of the empire was slight. Even so, important Inca offerings including golden and silver human figurines have been found on the otherwise unoccupied island; they suggest that important capac hucha sacrifices had been carried out there (McEwan & Van de Guchte 1992). The Isla de la Plata is located on the exact extension towards the north-west of the road from Titicaca to Cuzco. Apparently, people from Cuzco had been engaged in expeditions to the island that we can call pilgrimages.

This version of the myth of Viracocha probably had come about as a consequence of the idea of empire and we may ask how it could have grown out of an original version in the context of the ceremonial organization of the Cuzco province. The comparison with other myths of Viracocha or of deities with different names replacing him in other local contexts, allow us to detect one such original version from Cuzco.

Once, during a month of heavy rains, a supernatural man had floated down the river Villcanota toward Cuzco and had threatened to wash the town away. An Inca hero warded off the danger and then turned into stone and later was celebrated in the initiation rituals of the noble youths around the December solstice (Murúa 1946: 105-6). We are dealing with a local version of the myth of Viracocha coming from Titicacaca, now as a foundation myth of the ritual when the runners followed the ashes of sacrifices announcing the end of the rainy season.

The myth also implies the future conquest of empire.

Another myth with similar intent is told about the river that enters into the Ocean at Pachacamac (Taylor 1987: 53-73). At the headwaters of this river, the god *Cuniraya*, bearing the additional epithet of *Viracocha* had impregnated a woman who, after giving birth, fled down to Pachacamac. *Cuniraya Viracocha* pursued her along the river and on the way established various new conditions in the natural world. She escaped into the sea and became a coastal island. In the meantime, the wife of Pachacamac had filled the sea with fishes. Cuniraya Viracocha returned inland and his trickster acts caused other transformations.

Perhaps we do not want to call this story a foundation myth and it may not have gained the stature of an imperial myth. But its telling of Cuniraya's race gives the impression to reflect in a genuine pre-Hispanic way on the attraction of Pachacamac as a pilgrimage centre. Essential parts of the various myths of Viracocha or of similar deities seem to be that their field of action is laid out from the mountains down to the coast — never to the eastern lowlands — and that waters of a river are followed. In the various examples, the river may flow from north or south of *east* and go to south or north of *west*. Given the example from Cuzco, we may suspect that in the other cases the myths also took into account accurate astronomical observations for specific dates of the year. In all cases, the flow of water from sunrise to sunset may have symbolized a process of re-generation. The myth presented the process as one of Generation; Spanish chroniclers and theologians transformed this idea into one of Creation.

The situation in Cuzco gives cause to suspect that elsewhere the myths also referred to ritual movements. For instance, one other myth about Cuniraya Viracocha tells how he once travelled from Pachacamac to Titicaca — in fact had returned — to meet there the Inca king. After their meeting, the king rose to the sky and there adopted the role of his "Father" the Sun (Taylor 1987: 243-51). In Cuzco, the race of following the ashes and the myth of the man floating down on the waters of the Villcanota were both timed for the end of the rainy season. Assuming that Cuniraya went down the river for a corresponding seasonal reason, we might advance the hypothesis of still another similarity. The pilgrimage from Cuzco to the temple of Villcanota was intended to return to the Sun, his heat, his water and life-giving powers. The return of Cuniraya from Pachacamac to Titicaca and the rise of the Inca in Titicaca to the Sun may have implied similar motivations. The two movements of Cuniraya Viracocha, to and from Pachacamac, explain some of the reasons why Pachacamac was a pilgrimage centre. By the same token, we might conclude that the ritual movements of interest to Cuzco also contained qualities of pilgrimage.

When Spaniards talked about pilgrimages in pre-Hispanic Peru, they probably understood their information mostly in terms of pilgrimage events in Spain. We have no evidence that they themselves actually saw pilgrimages to places like Pachacamac and Titicaca. The three descriptions of ritual movements that I mentioned as executed by inhabitants of Cuzco, all go back to one early source, though supported by other information. They probably derive from eyewitness accounts. The journey to and from the temple of Villcanota is perhaps best comparable to pilgrimages as we think in other places of the world. However, as the motivation for this Cuzqueno pilgrimage is so similar to those of the procession and the race and so much integrated with these, I consider them all under the category of pilgrimage.

All ritual movements in Cuzco that we know of were precisely timed by the calendar. But were they all of equal strict concern to the state? At least two chroniclers mention that villages around Cuzco carried out races similar to the one following the ashes in the river (Fernández 1963: 86; Gutiérrez de Santa Clara 1963: 256). If there was a river nearby, the young men would follow it but if not, they would go through a field. Apparently, people were allowed some freedom in adapting to local circumstances but we don't know to what extent they exercised freedom in terms of the calendar.

Approaching the problem of self-organizing systems, let me briefly mention one other ritual movement in the valley of Cuzco. It concerns the horizon point where, as seen from Cuzco, the sun rose when passing through zenith. From this point, a hill called *Quispicancha* — in fact, it is the top of an old volcano — sunset toward Cuzco was observed on the two days (April 26, August 18) when the sun goes through nadir. It was the end point for the pilgrims returning in June from Villcanota. And from here, a new king entered the city for his crowning as if he were a conqueror. At the annual end of harvest in April — another kind of conquest — part of the route was used for a procession led by the king. Members of the high nobility and the mummies of their ancestors witnessed from the sides. Other people entered the harvest products along different routes into Cuzco and then were entertained, near the endpoint of the procession, with a bonfire and the distribution of huge quantities of llama meat (Zuidema 1996).

These were the known Incaic rituals along this second "axis". Our chroniclers do not write much about the horizon point of *Quispicancha*. Remarkable is, however, that this hill must have been of extraordinary ritual importance from long before Inca times. At its foot are found the remains of an Inca town and somewhat higher those of a large settlement of pre-Inca origin. The whole hill is enclosed by a high wall, not built by the Incas but by a city found in the next valley to the east, dating from much earlier *Huari* times. Cuzco defined the ritual importance of Quispicancha from its own astronomical and calendrical perspective. In fact, it redefined its use, as visits there must have served a quite different purpose for the Huari people. We don't need to ask which value these had placed on Quispicancha. Still, we must assume that after Huari times a fundamental shift in opinion had occurred.

Of course, it is also quite possible that places like Quispicancha — or Pachacamac or Titicaca for that matter — had different values for people when seen from different angles and directions or for people of different ranks and classes. The Inca state expressed its opinion, the one that descendants of its noble representatives communicated to us. But this need not have represented actual practice of all people.

In mentioning the procession for the harvest as joined by the king, I had also another issue in mind: that of the colonial development of the procession and its relationship to modern pilgrimage. The Inca harvest procession was witnessed by lords summoned from the whole empire and from all directions. In Cuzco, they were received by the king with presents and a state banquet. It was the most public feast in Cuzco. After the conquest, the Spaniards introduced into Cuzco their major public feast, the one of *Corpus Christi*. The most important component in celebrating Corpus was the procession in which people from all ranks and classes and again coming from all directions participated. As the two feasts of the Incas and the Spaniards fell at about the same time in the calendar, first they were combined, each feast keeping its own values. But soon, of course, the Spanish elements began to dominate in the city. However, one element remained: the road of the harvest procession, now being used by the images of two saints, *Saint Jerome* and *Saint Sebastian*, entering Cuzco from the same direction as the former procession.

Corpus Christi serves two purposes. For the church and especially for the Municipality of Cuzco it is an official feast. People visit the congregated saints from all parishes in the valley and Corpus now attracts many tourists as "new pilgrims". But at the same time, a place at the foot of glaciers in the mountains east of Cuzco — in about the direction from where originally the harvest procession had come but further away — attracts thousands, mostly indigenous, pilgrims from all over Southern Peru (Molinié 1996). According to a legend from the eighteenth century, here in *Coyllur Riti*, "Snow Star," Christ as a child had appeared to a herder boy. The modern feast grew spontaneously out of popular fervor and maintains many indigenous customs. Despite its founding legend, I suspect that it is of pre-Hispanic origin. Therefore, it would be of much interest to know whether, and how, the two celebrations, one as organized by the state and the other not, could have co-existed since Inca times.

Returning to the ritual movements as executed by people from Cuzco and to the pilgrimage centres of Titicaca and Pachacamac, our information on the first derives almost exclusively from an interest in their organization by the state. Still, I suggest that the particular form of this interest had grown out of and was based upon a much wider concern of all classes of people living in and around Cuzco. I keep constantly in mind that, next to the Sun as god of a head of government, Viracocha was a god associated with outside borders, primarily worshipped by people of lower classes. The ritual movements imitated not only the Sun's course through the sky but also Viracocha's mythical crossing through the country and along rivers. Let me present some arguments considering those wider concerns in ritual movements and pilgrimages; concerns that were not dependent, wholly or in part, on impositions by the state.

I mentioned already the information — rather isolated, it is true — that a ritual like the race following the ashes was also executed by any town or village on its own. People would choose the direction according to their own local situation, not necessarily the same as of the race in Cuzco. We know that the participants in Cuzco were non-noble or of very low nobility. The fact that they competed with each other may allude to an interest not organized by the state. We can equally question whether the Tarpuntay priests who participated in the procession and the pilgrimage were selected by the state. Their choice, by the Thunder, depended on natural criteria and as "planters" they served primarily the farming interests of people living outside town in the valley of Cuzco. The number of Tarpuntay in each event could have depended on the number of *ayllu* groups delegating them. And while the Incas came to design the road of Viracocha in its cosmic extension to the north-west, for which purpose they made and agreed the directions of their local river, the Villcanota River and the expansion of their empire, people living south of Lake Titicaca saw his road to the coast as going from here to the west of south. Titicaca/Copacabana as well as Pachacamac could be centres for attracting pilgrims from all directions. The Incaic road of Viracocha was only one of many, though it came to receive an almost exclusive institutional, propagandistic and paradigmatic representation.

The ritual movements that I considered here were tied to specific times of seasonal change that have remained of foremost concern to Andean agricultural calendars in general (Zuidema 1992). In this temporal sense, the Incaic rituals also would have been of interest to people of all classes.

Finally, a recognition of more general interest may have been reflected in the fact that the procession, the pilgrimage and the race were placed on an expanding scale of magnitude going from the king's observation of the June solstice sunset — all people of town joining him on his joyous return there — to the pilgrimage to Titicaca — where the sun first ascended to Heaven — and to Pachacamac — at the border of the Ocean as entrance to the Underworld. Such notions of self-similarity are still very much alive in southern Peru. We can study them from local ideas; one, for instance, concerns the cosmic return of water to the source of the Villcanota River as counterpart of the river itself (Urton 1981). There is no reason to assume that such ideas could not have existed without a form of state imposition. Various local or regional myths of travel from a higher to a lower source of water existed similar to Viracocha's, expressing their own ecological and seasonal concerns and with their own ritual reflections. Cuzco was not a central point where Viracocha ended his travel or even stopped but one that he passed by. Of major concern to pilgrims supplicating him were far-away Titicaca and Pachacamac and not Cuzco itself. Cuzco may have dominated pilgrimage travel but still participated in a wider and dynamic open system that covered the whole of the Central Andes.

Myths as recorded in seventeenth-century documents from Central Peru and even some modern myths reflect on the importance Titicaca and Pachacamac but only few mention travel of pilgrims. At least one document describes a pilgrimage to Cuzco as a sacred centre that was said to have actually happened (Zuidema 1977-78, 1989: ch. 4). The motivation for it was that the lord of a town had built a new irrigation system, obtaining help of neighbouring rulers. As a result, the Inca king allowed him to send on pilgrimage his daughter, qualified as *aclla*, "chosen one," with her retinue to Cuzco where she participated in the royal rituals of the December solstice. After her return she asked her father to be sacrificed, for which act he was honoured and elevated in rank. People came to visit her grave and worshipped there at times of planting and harvest. Later, a Catholic priest found her grave and that of her father and his descendants, learned about her story and wrote it up. While the Inca king had admitted her as *aclla* and while other documents allude to similar proceedings as condition for a lord to be elevated in rank, it had been local fervor that induced the succession of events. Myths from Central Peru even expressed opinions that in this way the Inca had been forced to seek political support from his subject lords, their peoples and their gods. He had to deal with extraneous factors that he could not always control.

Some 40 years after the Spanish conquest, a man of Copacabana made an image of the Virgin Mary and presented it to his town. After initial local resistance — having to do with variant ecological and seasonal concerns of factions in the population there — and having overcome objections of the church, the worship of the Virgin of Copacabana became popular. Justification for pilgrimage to Catholic Copacabana was totally different from that to pre-Hispanic Copacabana but the original dates of pilgrimage may have continued. Of most interest, here and in places like Coyllur Riti, is that their cults surged spontaneously, maybe as revivals of old habits.

Spanish information on pre-Hispanic pilgrimages does not readily allow us to analyse these as self-organized systems. But despite the fact that Incaic memories present pilgrimage as regulated by the state, details of the evidence make it likely that aspects of self-organization were not lacking. They may have been more important in pre-Inca times.

References

Bertonio, Ludovico, 1984, *Vocabulario dela lengua aymara*, Albo, Xavier and Felix Layme, ed. CERES, Cochabamba, LVIII, 399.

Betanzos, Juan de, 1987, Suma y Narración de los Incas, Martín Rubio, María del Cármen, ed. Atlas, Madrid, 317.

Calancha, Antonio de la, 1974, Crónica Moralizada, Transcription, critical study, bibliographic notes and indices by Ignacio Prado Pastor, ed. Prado Pastor, Ignacio, Lima, 6 volumes.

Cobo, Bernabé, 1956, Historia del Nuevo Mundo, Atlas, *Biblioteca de Autores Españoles*, vol. 92., Madrid.

Fernández, Diego, 1963, Primera y Segunda Parte de la Historia del Perú, in Crónicas del Peru, vols 1, 2. B.A.E. vols 164, 165, Juan Pérez de Tudela Bueso, ed. Atlas, Madrid.

Gade, Daniel W., 1975, "Plants, Man and the Land in the Vilcanota Valley of Peru," in *Biogeographica*, J.

Schmithusen, ed. Dr. W. Junk B.V., The Hague, 240.

Gutiérrez de Santa Clara, Pedro, 1963, Quinquenarios o Historia de las Guerras Civiles del Perú, in Crónicas del Perú, vols 2, 3. B.A.E. vols 165, 166, Juan Pérez de Tudela Bueso, ed. Atlas, Madrid.

Isbell, William H., and McEwan, Gordon F., editors, 1991, Huari administrative structure, Prehistoric monumental architecture and state government, Dumbarton Oaks Research Library and Collection, Washington, D.C., 321.

Jiménez Borja, 1985, Pachacamac, Boletín de Lima, 7 (38), 40-54.

Kolata, Alan L, 1993, *The Tiwanaku: Portrait of an Andean Civilization*, Blackwell, Cambridge MA.

Kolata, Alan L., 1996, *Valley of the Spirits. A Journey into the lost Realm of the Aymara*, John Wiley & Sons, Inc., New York.

MacCormack, Sabine, 1984, "From the Sun of the Incas to the Virgin of Copacabana," *Representations*, 8, 30-59.

McEwan, Colin, and Van de Guchte, Maarten, 1992, "Ancestral Time and Sacred Space in Inca State Ritual," in *The Ancient A mericas. Art from Sacred Landscapes*, Townsend, Richard F., ed. The Art Institute of Chicago, Chicago, 359-71.

Molina, Cristóbal, 1989, Fábulas y mitos de los Incas, Urbano, Henrique, ed. Historia 16, Madrid, 47-134.

Moliniè, Antoinette, 1996, D'un Village de la Mancha á un Glacier des Andes, Deux Célébrations "Sauvages" Du Corps de Dieu, in Le Corps de Dieu en Fêtes, Moliniè, Antoinette, ed. Les Éditions de CERF, Paris, 223-54.

Murúa, Martín de, 1946, Historia del Orígen y Genealogía Real de los Reyes Incas del Perú, C. Bayle, ed. CSIC, Instituto Santo Toribio de Mogrovejo, Madrid.

Murúa, Martín de, 1964, Historia General del Perú, Manuel Ballesteros Gaibrois, ed. Instituto Gonzalo Fernández de Oviedo, Madrid.

Pachacuti Yamqui Salcamaygua, Joan de Santa Cruz. 1993: Relación de Antigüedades deste Reyno del Pirú, Estudio Etnohistórico y Linguístico de Pierre Duviols y César Itier, ed. Institut Français d'Études Andines; Centro de Estudios Regionales Andinos "Bartolomé de Las Casas", Cusco, 276.

Pizarro, Hernando, 1938, A los Magníficos Señores, los Señores Oidores de la Audiencia Real de Su Magistad, que residen en la Ciudad de Santo Domingo, in Los Cronistas de la Conquista, Urteaga, Horacio H., ed. Desclée, de Brouwer, Paris, 253-64.

Ramos Gavilán, Alonso, 988, Historia del Santuario de Nuestra Señora de Copacabana, Transcription, note of the editor and indices by Ignacio Prado Pastor, ed. Prado P., Ignacio, Lima.

Rostworowski de Diez Canseco, María, 1992, Pachacamac y el señor de los milagros. Una trayectoria milenaria. Instituto de Estudios Peruanos, Lima.

Salles-Reese, Verónica, 1997, From Viracocha to the Virgin of Copacabana, Representation of the sacred at lake Titicaca, University of Texas Press, Austin.

Santillán, Hernando de, 1968, Relación del Orígen, Descendencia, Política y Gobierno de los Incas, in Crónicas Peruanas de Interés Indígena, Esteve Barba, Francisco, ed. Atlas, Madrid, 97-149.

Shimada, Izumi, 1991, Pachacamac Archaeology: Retrospect and Prospect, in Pachacamac. A Reprint of the 1903 edition by Max Uhle, Shimada, Izumi, ed. The University Museum of Archaeology and Anthropology. University of Pennsylvania, Philadelphia, XVI-LXVI.

Taylor, Gerald, 1987, Ritos y Tradiciones de Huarochiri. Manuscrito quechua de comienzos del siglo XVII. IEP, Instituto Francés de Estudios Andinos, Lima.

Urton, Gary, 1981, *At the Crossroads of the Earth and the Sky. An Andean Cosmology*, University of Texas Press, Austin.

Zuidema, R. Tom, 1973, Kinship and Ancestorcult in Three Peruvian Communities: Hernández Príncipe's Account of 1622. Bulletin de l'Institut Français des Etudes Andines, II (1), 16-33. Lima.

Zuidema, R. Tom, 1977-78, "Shafttombs and the Inca Empire," *Journal of the Steward Anthropological Society*, 9 (1/2), 133-78, Urbana.

Zuidema, R. Tom, 1981, "Comment on J. H. Rowe: Archaeoastronomy in Mesoamerica and Peru," *Latin American Research Review*, 16 (3), 167-70.

Zuidema, R. Tom, 1982, "Bureaucracy and Systematic Knowledge in Andean Civilization," in *The Inca and Aztec States*, 1400-1800, Collier, Rosaldo and Wirth, ed. Academic Press, New York, 419-58.

Zuidema, R. Tom, 1989, Reyes y Guerreros. Ensayos de Cultura Andina, Manuel Burga, ed. Fomciencias, Lima.

Zuidema, R. Tom., 1990a, "At the King's Table. Inca Concepts of Sacred Kingship in Cuzco," in *Kingship and the Kings*, Galey, Jean-Claude, ed. Harwood Academic Publishers, London, 253-78.

Zuidema, R. Tom, 1990b, *Inca Civilization in Cuzco*, University of Texas Press, Austin.

Zuidema, R. Tom, 1992, El Encuentro de los Calendarios Andino y Español, in Los Conquistados. 1492 y la Población Indígena de las Américas, Heraclio Bonilla, ed. Tercer Mundo editores, FLACSO, Quito, Ecuador, 287- 316.

Zuidema, R. Tom, 1996, Fête-Dieu et Fête de l'Inca. Châtiment et Sacrifice Humain comme Rites de Communion, in Le Corps de Dieu en Fête, Antoinette Molinié, ed. CERF, Paris, 175-222.

16

Conchero's Sanctuaries and Pilgrimages

Yolotl González Torres

PILGRIMAGES in Mexico are very common ritual practices, which generally take place in Catholic sanctuaries with a strong pre-Hispanic syncretism, as we shall explain later. According to written texts by the chroniclers, there were many places of pilgrimages in pre-hispanic times and several scholars think that many of the important pre-hispanic archaeological ceremonial centres were also pilgrimage centres (Martínez Marín 1972; Piña Chan 1998). Additionally, it is believed that some of them developed into urban centres like Teotihuacan (Heyden 1975). Besides, there is, for instance, the evidence of the Huicholes, an ethnic group very little affected by Spanish culture, for whom the pilgrimage to Wirikuta in search of the peyote plant plays a fundamental role in the religious life of the community; "they pass along the roads where the cosmos is built as they move to the sacred places. They serve the gods, doing what they established, repeating their actions and the world they created" (Rajsbaum 1999: 47). We must bear in mind also that one of the most important mytho-historical accounts of a journey of the Mexica people from Aztlan — their land of origin, somewhere in the north-west of Mexico — to the island in the lake in the Valley of Mexico where they founded their city, Tenochtitlan, was called a "pilgrimage." Even if it lasted about two hundred years, we may consider that they were actually in a pilgrimage, in a liminal state, as they had to perform throughout a series of common ritual activities to prove to the god who was guiding them that they were worthy of his protection. When they reached the promised place, marked by a sign: an eagle standing on a cactus and eating a snake, they came to the end of their pilgrimage, they returned to their usual and former activities and abandoned their wandering life.

The sanctuaries that attract pilgrims differ from common temples in that they go beyond the ordinary meeting places of the devotees. It is usually believed that in these places a saint or the image of one appeared miraculously or that the image behaves in a supernatural way, like crying or moving and that it grants favours and performs miracles, which become the main attraction for the pilgrims.

It is said that if mysticism is an interior pilgrimage, pilgrimage is exteriorized mysticism (Turner and Turner 1978: 7) and also that the pilgrim enters into a state of communitas or commonness of feeling shared with the rest of the people (Turner and Turner 1978: 13).

We shall talk on this occassion about the sanctuaries, which the concheros or dancers of tradition have as obligation to go on a pilgrimage to dance every year. The concheros are groups of people organized in brotherhoods or mayordomias, whose ritual activities include a diurnal and public one, which is dancing in honour of the saints and a nocturnal and private one which is a wake in honour of the souls of the departed spirits, mainly, of the chiefs or leaders of the brotherhood. Because of this activity they received formerly the name of "brotherhood of the holy count". The name concheros is derived from their musical instruments similar to *mandolines*, which have a box of resonance made of *conchas*, armadillo conchs or shells, which are considered their mystical arms full of power (*fig.* 16.1).

The concheros, according to González Anahuac (1997: 214), are grouped in "dance lineages" who are descendants of a common "dance forefather," who is made explicit in the standard. Each group is called a mesa — "table" — following a Spanish army's hierarchy pattern: captains, alferez, sergeants, soldiers plus a special post held by women called, Malinches. Malinche was the name of the woman who was given to Cortes as a gift by one of the Indian chiefs. She became a very important element in the conquest of Mexico, as she was Cortes official translator. The captain — who may be a man or a woman — is the leader of the mesa and his charge is usually hereditary. In his house there is an altar with the image of the patron saint of the mesa as well as the flag or standard, which has a sacred character and is considered a relic. The captain's house also serves as the location for "wakes" and, additionally, may have provided the meeting place for the dancers when they go to their ritual "obligations" like pilgrimages. The captain has to coordinate the organization of these pilgrimages as well as everything related to the ritual obligations. He must provide all the food needed for these pilgrimages. For instance, when they go to Chalma for one whole week, he has to carry food for all the members of his mesa as well as the utensils to cook it with. Sometimes he also has to pay for the bus fare and for the costumes of the dancers. He is the possessor of the knowledge of the tradition, of the music and of the dance steps and very often he is also a healer who knows the herbs and other elements for healing.

The sergeant is in charge of keeping order during the ritual activities and the malinches are in charge of the censers. The wafting of incense is a very important purifying activity, which is performed continually.

For their dances they wear fancy costumes, formerly a tunic, called the "naguilla," "little skirt" and a headdress made of ostrich feathers. Now only a few groups wear this type of costume and most wear costumes copied from the pre-hispanic codices with headdresses made of pheasant feathers and sometimes dresses that mimic the North American Indian costumes (*fig.* 16.2).

As mentioned before, one of the most important activities of the concheros is to dance ritually in the five sanctuaries (besides others which every mesa has as their own obligation), which are arranged in the form of a cross. The church of Santiago Tlatelolco is located at the centre of the cross and four sanctuaries or winds, radiate from this local: to the north, Our Lady of Guadalupe; to the west, Our Lady of Remedies; to the south, the Christ of Chalma; and to the east, the Christ of Sacromonte (*fig.* 16.3).

There is a devotional song or "praise" in which they mention the four winds linking them to the four evangelists, who are also linked to the four quadrants of the universe (after Zúñiga and Rodríguez 1996) (*fig.* 16.4).

This is the first wind
We have to conquer
It is St Lucas soul
Who in the Gospel is

This is the second wind
We have to conquer
It is St John's soul
Who in the Gospel is

This is the third wind
We have to conquer
it is St Marc's soul
who in the Gospel is

This is the fourth wind
We have to conquer
It is St Mathew's soul
Who in the Gospel is.

These sanctuaries are very popular not only with the concheros but also with other dancers and with all sorts of people. According to the range of their attraction, they fall in the categories of *international*, Guadalupe's, *national*, Chalma's, Los Remedios and *regional* Sacromonte (Turner and Turner 1978).

We shall now give a description and a brief historical view of each one of them, starting with the church of Santiago Tlatelolco, which is located in what was the ceremonial centre of the twin city of the Mexica. In this place, the archaeologists have found what they have called a "calendrical temple," with a mural of the god and goddess, Cipactonal and Oxomoco, who "created time." "It is possible that the calendar temple was a cosmographic monument where specialist who dealt with the worship through the abstraction of the flux of time...could know about man's destiny" (Guilliem Arroyo 1998: 53). In this place there was also a temple of Huitzilopochtl — their patron god of war and it was the last stronghold of the Mexica after the fall of their capital, Tenochtitlan. And at this same place, the Christian Friars built one of the first churches in honour of Santiago, the patron of the real and spiritual conquest not only of the Indians of America but also of the Muslims in Spain. This saint is also said to be the mythic patron saint of the concheros forefathers, after he appeared with a bright cross in the sky in July 1531, on a hill of Queretaro deciding a battle between Christianized and Pagan Indians, converting the latter who promised to celebrate this event by dancing to the cross.

fig. 16.4: Wind Sancturies (after Zuñiga and Rodriguez)

fig. 16.1: Concheros in Tlatelolco with musical instruments. (Photo: Rodríguez. Fototeca INAH)

fig. 16.2: Concheros with naguilla and feathers.

fig. 16.3: The Church of Tlatelolco. (Photo: Rodríguez. Fototeca INAH)

fig. 16.5: The new Basílica of Guadalupe. (Photo: Rodríguez. Fototeca INAH)

fig. 16.6: Our lady of Guadalupe with Juan Diego and the old Basîlica.

fig. 16.7: Chalma. (Photo: Carlos Jiménez)

fig. 16.8: Our lord of Chalma.

fig. 16.9: Rising the cross. (Photo: Jiménez)

fig. 16.10: The concheros in procession. (Photo: Jiménez)

fig. 16.11: The processional road. (Photo: Zúñiga. Fototeca INAH)

fig. 16.12: Amecameca. (Photo: Zúñiga. Fototeca INAH)

fig. 16.13: The entrance of Sacromonte. (Photo: Zúñiga. Fototeca INAH)

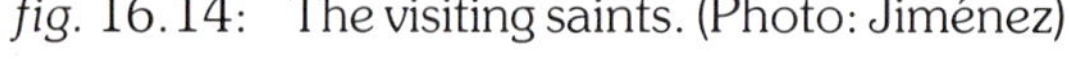

fig. 16.14: The visiting saints. (Photo: Jiménez)

Santiago is called the courier of the four winds and lord of dances. He is celebrated on July 25, a date that coincides with the last passage of the sun through the zenith of Mexico City. He is the axis of the "march" (pilgrimage) the concheros have the obligation to make around the year to the four winds' sanctuaries, which, as mentioned before, are located in the four quadrants of the cosmos and whose celebration also coincides with important solar moments.

Guadalupe

The Basilica of our lady of Guadalupe is possibly the most famous Marian sanctuary not only in Mexico but also in Latin America and perhaps in the world (*fig.* 16.5). Actually an average of about a million pilgrims come to the modern Basilica that was built in 1974 and is an

> architectural whole which was projected to receive 10,000 people under the huge roof which covers the nave, but besides, its semicircular form was designed to receive with ease the great masses of pilgrimages which constantly enter the precinct from the immensity of the atrium, which functions as a great enclosure which antecedes the interior, that is to say, it is an architecture of pilgrimage — Valero 1998: 71

The Basilica is located to the north of Mexico City and the place has since merged into the megalopolis. It is said that on the same site there was a temple dedicated to the goddess Tonantzin — "Our mother." The story explains that on December 12, 1531, the Virgin Mary appeared to a humble Indian peasant called Juan Diego in a hill called Tepeyac (*fig.* 16.6). She told him that she wanted a shrine to be built for her in that same place. Juan Diego went to the bishop to tell him about the apparition but the bishop wanted proof. When Juan Diego asked the lady for such a proof; she told him to gather some roses that had grown in the wilderness and to place them in his cloak and take them to the bishop. He did as commanded and when he opened the cloak, the roses fell and there appeared the very image of the Virgin Mary that is worshipped in the Basilica of Guadalupe. This image represents a young girl of brownish skin with a pink dress and a blue cloak with her hands held together as praying. She is standing on a crescent moon and surrounded by a solar halo. A cherub sustains the whole figure. It is said that in her mantle are painted the constellations and that in her pupils the figure of Juan Diego receiving the roses is reflected.

Plenty of literature exists pertaining to the Virgin of Guadalupe and about the origin of the image. There are two currents pertaining to the latter topic: the apparitionists, who believe that the image has a supernatural origin and the non-apparitionists who believe that it was painted by human hands. These two currents, which started in the sixteenth century, have had followers that include Catholic priests.

As far as we know, an Indian called Marcos painted the image and the Viceroy, Montufar, in 1555, ordered it to be placed in a hermitage that had been built by the conquerors on the place where the image of the goddess Toci had been. In 1570 a church was built which displaced the old hermitage.

In 1629 a great flood afflicted the city of Mexico and the Virgin of Guadalupe was offered many prayers to intercede and stop the rains. In 1648 the Catholic priest, Miguel Sánchez, published an essay entitled, "Image of the Virgin, Mother of God of Guadalupe" which was sustained by St. John's Apocalipse. In it, he argued that the image which had appeared to the apostle was the "prophetic original of the Virgin of Guadalupe," the prototype of the Mexican copy deposited in Juan Diego's cloak (Gruzinsky 1995: 128). He argued that Mexico had been conquered so that the image of Guadalupe appeared there as a symbol, "Mexico became then the providential receptacle in the theatre which was won after a great battle, so that the apparition could be reproduced in the country." All this gave a definitive impulse to her worship, from the Indian as well as from the Spanish side, which was later reinforced by several authors, turning among other things, the Virgin of Guadalupe into a national symbol.

In 1620, Pope Urbano VII consecrated the cult of the Virgin of Tepeyac and in 1666 an apostolic trial was conducted by the Church so that the traditional date of the miraculous appearance of the painting should be kept as a day of precept with a proper mass and Office.

In the following century the Virgin's cult acquired a diffusion with no limits and she became the official patroness of the City of Mexico in 1737. In 1810, Hidalgo, the priest who started the Independence movement of Mexico, took the standard from a church with the image of the Virgin and shouting, "Viva la Virgen de Guadalupe," went into battle. From then on Guadalupe became a symbol of the Insurgents.

It is curious that the very same president who secularized the State in 1857 and issued the Reform laws in Mexico, which curtailed the power of the church, was the one who made the twelfth of December a National Holiday. Juan Diego has been beatified few years back; in a way closing the argument, as far as the church is concerned, about his historicity.

Chalma

Chalmas' sanctuary, where the image of a crucified Christ is venerated, is about 20 miles south of Mexico City, at the mouth of a broad canyon (*fig.* 16.7). In older times the god Oztoteotl (god of the cave) was venerated there and, for some scholars, it was a form of Tlaloc, the god of water. It was an important pre-hispanic place of pilgrimage. His celebration is in Pentecost or "little Easter."

According to Augustinian records, on the day of Easter of the Holy Spirit of 1539, two Augustinian monks found the idol Oztoteotl in the larger cave of the canyon, who was worshipped by the inhabitants of the area. When they returned to the cave having made up their minds to preach there the word of Jesus Christ and to place a wooden cross inside, they found the idol shattered to pieces and the cave full of flowers of beautiful aroma and in the place where the idol was, they found an image of Christ crucified. This image of Christ remained in the cave for 143 years but in 1683 it was brought down to a specially consecrated church for his worship, which became the first sanctuary of Chalma (*fig.* 16.8).

In 1830 the sanctuary was renovated. The present building has neoclassic style and only one nave. Its main facade faces toward the south. From the middle of the sixteenth century, hostels were built in order to accommodate the pilgrims. These hostels lean against the wall of the canyon and have three superimposed bodies. A fire destroyed the original image of Chalma in the seventeenth century and the image venerated today was modelled with its remains.

Chalma's town is located at one side of the sanctuary and has grown out of its shadow. It is surrounded by cliffs crowned by crosses placed there to scare the evil spirits. Each cross belongs to a group of devotees. Every year they are brought down to the atrium, painted and ornamented and then taken up again. Some of the crosses are over seven meters high, which makes it a hard task to bring them up and down such a steep hill. However, the great numbers of people who participate in the job lessens the burden. When the cross is placed on the top of the hill, the dancers dance around it and spend the night guarding it, singing and lighting artificial lights (*fig.* 16.9).

The pilgrimages to Chalma take some time for preparation. One month before the journey, pilgrims meet at the house of the captain to discuss and arrange all the preparations. The night before the departure they may gather in the house of the captain or meet at a certain point and proceed together. Traditionally, the pilgrimage was done on foot and sometimes it is still done this way or walking is combined with cars and buses. On the way there are houses for pilgrims or private houses, where they are given lodging. On the way they sing and pray and the Malinches waft incense. Near Chalma there is an ancient tree, where they hang little bags with newborn baby's umbilical cords and sometimes women's hair. The women put their hands in a hole of the tree where water is coming out and anoint the water into their bodies in order to become fertile. Here, the pilgrims who come to Chalma for the first time choose a godfather or a godmother who puts a crown of flowers on their heads, and then, all dance. Once they reach the atrium of the church, the flowers are given to a mayordomo who places them in a stack.

A little farther down, there is a place called Chalmita, which is next to a cemetery and is marked by three crosses. This is the starting point of the trail of penitence, which leads to the sanctuary and is trodden on a particular day by the penitents. It is also the place where the different groups gather and go on a procession, carrying their standards, wafting incensing on the way, playing their musical instruments and singing their praises.

Many *quadrillas* of pilgrimages have carried the image of their patron saint, which has been covered by a blanket all the way from their village or barrio. Here it is uncovered and is received by a conchero captain who incenses it and sings some praises. After this they head to the church where they set their standards in the atrium.

Most members of the mesas of the dancers arrive on Saturday, if the groups have a long tradition of pilgrimage to Chalma. Then they may obtain a place in the hostel. Otherwise they will camp wherever they find a place. Some groups used to carry their *petates* (mats) and blankets — now they carry tents and sleeping bags. As mentioned before, the captain has to supply all the food for the members of his mesa. One captain has even bought some land for his people to camp.

Chalma is a very important meeting place for the concheros. Different groups get together to exchange opinions and decide all matters regarding their organizations and tradition. The captains get together in the night and very early next morning the concheros go along with people of the surrounding villages to bring down the crosses from the top of the hill. These crosses are decorated with a cloth called the *zendal*, which has hung from the arms of the cross for a year. The cloth is then taken down and cut into pieces which are kept as relics. The crosses are then placed in the atrium where they are cleaned, polished, painted and ornamented with a new zendal. Each day following, the dancers dance around their cross. Because the atrium is not very large, the groups of dancers are allotted a certain place and time during the day and the night, in such a manner that all day and almost all night there is the sound of the conchas or the drums accompanying the dancers, who most of the time are wearing their beautiful bright costumes, with feathered headdresses and anklets made of special seeds which sound along with the different steps (*fig.* 16.10).

Thursday, the day of penitence, the penitents gather in Chalmita where they chose a penitent godfather or godmother who places, on the road before them, the cloth for the penitent to walk or crawl on his/her knees to the sanctuary. The penitents may also go blindfolded or wear a crown of thorns. The concheros accompany them along the cobbled road singing praises (*fig.* 16.11). After this procession, they go to the sanctuary to thank the Lord for having received them, and, after this, they consider that their obligations as pilgrims have been fulfilled and that they are free to go back to their homes.

Amecameca

This site located to the east and here can be found the sanctuary of Sacromonte (sacred hill) at the base of the volcanoes, Popocatepetl and Iztacihuatl (*figs.* 16.12 and 16.13). There is also a cave where a supine, dead Christ, is worshipped. His celebration is on Ash Wednesday, according to the moveable calendar of Holy Week between February and the 10th of March.

Before the arrival of the Spanish, an image of Tlaloc, god of water, was worshipped in this cave. On the path to the cave there is also an old tree where the bags with the umbilical cords of newborn babies are hung.

Fray Martin de Valencia, one of the three first Franciscan friars who came to the New Spain to evangelize (and who was considered a saint), established himself in Tlalmanaco at the foot of the volcanoes. He used to go to pray, make penance, and to meditate in a cave on a hill nearby and later received the name of Sacromonte, "Sacred mountain." When he died the Indians kept as relics: his cassock, sackcloth and chasuble to give masses. Later, when a Dominican priest built an altar in the cave, he placed the relics next to the Christ image.

There are different versions about the mysterious finding of the image of Christ, whether it was found outside the cave or whether two mules carried it and later, mysteriously disappeared.

It is also said that some Indians tried to take Christ's image out of the cave in order to replace their idol but it became so heavy that they could not move it. Since then, they have asked the Christ's image for permission to move it every year during the Holy Week to the chapel below in the town of Amecameca and only then does he becomes light and allows the devotees to move him.

Los Remedios

It is said that the image of the Virgin of Remedies is the oldest brought by the Spanish conquerors and that an image of her was placed by Cortes in the first temple that he founded in Yucatan.

The Virgin of Remedies is celebrated on September 10. The sanctuary we are referring to is located in the hill of San Juan Totoltepec in Naucalpan in the State of Mexico, northwest of Mexico City, now also merged into the great city of Mexico. This place was also called the hill of Victory referring to the episode after the battle of the "sad night" when the Spanish were defeated by the Mexicas. The surviving soldiers gathered in that spot, out of gratitude to the Virgin of Remedies because she had saved them. Later some Spanish soldiers built a shrine in her honour.

It is believed that on that place, one of the soldiers lost a small wooden image of the Virgin that he was carrying, which was later found by an Otomí Indian chief called Juan Ce Cuautli (One Eagle) under a *maguey* (cactus) plant.

The story suggests that when Juan Ce Cuautli was going to the town of Tacuba, he saw a lady who came towards him and recognized her as the one who fought along the Spanish on the Sad Night. She asked him insistently to look for her the following day in the same place but he did not pay attention and just told the Franciscan friars about his encounter. Soon after that he fell from a pillar and was nearly dead when, again, he saw the lady coming towards him and she gave him a belt of St. Augustin. He then decided to pay attention to his protectoress and went to the place she asked. Under the maguey plant he found the lost image in which, he recognized the lady of the apparitions. Immediately he covered her with his cloak "so that they wouldn't see her or envy him" and took her to the altar in his house. Nevertheless, the Lady went back again and again under the maguey in spite of Juan's offerings, prayers and supplications. He came to the extreme of locking her up in a box with a key and putting her under his bed. But everything was useless; the image went back to her refuge in the wilderness. Juan ended giving up, and one day when he was very ill went to Tepeyac to beg to the Guadalupe and ask her for health. She started laughing and said, "Why do you come to my house, when having me in yours, you threw me out of it?" After that, the dark virgin gave him precise orders to build the hermitage dedicated to Mary of the Remedies, who, seeing her wishes properly fulfilled, came to set herself by her own will on the altar (Alberro 1997: 323).

The image of the Virgin of Remedies is small, about eleven inches high, as it was one of the so-called, saddle virgins the Spanish soldiers carried along with them in the saddles of their horses. She is made of painted wood and carries on one of her arms Jesus-child and in the other, a staff. She is standing on a crescent moon on a maguey plant. She is elegantly dressed and has a large wardrobe.

In 1550 a hermitage was built for her on the top of the hill, and in 1574 the town hall of the city of Mexico took charge of her sanctuary and promoted her, in such a way, that in the seventeenth century, her image was brought to the City of Mexico in procession many times more often that the one of the Virgin of Guadalupe. Around 1595, Alonso the Villasana painted the frescoes that decorate the hermitage of the Virgin telling her story.

The history of the Virgin of Remedies, somewhat parallels the one of the Virgin of Guadalupe. In spite of the words spoken to the chief Juan Ce Cuautli, the followers of each virgin started a fight between themselves in such a way that during the war of Independence the Virgin of Guadalupe became the patroness of the Insurgents and the Virgin of Remedies of the Spanish. Although for some time the latter was more respected, Guadalupe won by far in popularity.

Why did the concheros of the city of Mexico choose these particular sites as their main obligations? First of all we have to take into consideration that the concheros are quite heterogeneous; even if their general characteristic is that their main ritual activities are their dance obligations, their wakes in honour of the death, their organization in dance lineages and that they are urban dwellers. However, it seems that they are divided in geographic regions. It is commonly said that they originated in the area of Bajío (northwest of Mexico), which at the time of the Spanish conquest, was a border area between "civilized" and semi-nomadic Indians. Unfortunately, there are very few records about the dance fraternities during the following centuries.

We have our doubts about this origin of the concheros precisely because of the locations of the sanctuaries which we think are linked to a very old sacred geography of the people of the

Valley of Mexico. Also that the concheros of the city of Mexico — many of whom are masons by professions are the descendants of the Indian fraternities or brotherhoods which were created very early after the conquest by the Catholic priests who came to evangelize, in such a way that by 1585 there were more than 200 of these fraternities just in the city of Mexico (Gruzynsky 1995: 160).

We know from the people who have studied the archives that the friars promoted the Indian dances as a devotional expression (Alberro 1998: 120) and that they preserved their dances, some of their costumes and many forms of their organization on which the friars superimposed their own. There are descriptions of the early days of the Colony of Christian festivals in which the Indians displayed their costumes, including their feathered headgear and their arms: shields and native swords. Many of these objects had a ritual character like the shields and the musical instruments we have mentioned (Gruzynsky 1995: 66). Therefore, we think that the four winds, to which they say they have an obligation to go on pilgrimage and to dance, are linked to the sacred geography of the Valley of Mexico, and although the sanctuaries do not coincide exactly with cosmological points, ideologically they do: they mark the limits of their most sacred realm with Tlatelolco as the *axis mundi*, with Santiago, saint of conquest — god of war — sun god, surrounded by saints-gods who represent the time of the year and their sacred space which may extend without limits to the four quadrants of the universe (*fig.* 16.14). Santiago conquered the New Spain so that the cult of Christ and the Virgin Mary would spread on the four quadrants of the universe, symbolized by the four sanctuaries. But underneath them the old cosmo-vision of the Mesoamerican Indians permeates: we have mentioned that the four sanctuaries correspond to pre-hispanic sanctuaries and that all of them are located on hills that must have been important landmarks. It is not by sheer chance that the two Marian sanctuaries are located in the north and west and that their festivals, held during the "dark" side of the year, also coincide with pre-hispanic festivals to goddesses. Nor is it by chance that the two crucified Christs are located in the east and south, coinciding with the "bright" side of the year, the time of growth and fertility. In their sanctuaries we find caves and the trees of life with the babies' umbilical chords and as Rodríguez Carrasco (personal communication) points out, the festivities of these two places are on moveable dates of the Catholic Santoral related to the new and crescent moon, which is linked to fertility. On the other hand, we have male/female images in the north-south as well as in the east-west axis, which is also a Mesoamerican trait.

We may conclude that the four pilgrimage sites, the four winds of the concheros, cover space and time following the annual route of the sun: Santiago is at the centre in Tlatelolco where a calendrical temple was found and his feast day is on 25th July, the day of the second passage of the sun over the zenith in Mexico City. In this way the pilgrims, through their dance rituals on their pilgrimage sites, cover in space and time their whole sacred universe, which has strong roots in the pre-Hispanic cosmo-vision in spite of all the history of conquest and of modernity of the country.

References

Alberro, Solange, 1997, "Remedios y Guadalupe. De la unión a la discordia," in *Manifestaciones religiosas en el mundo colonial americano*, INAH Condumex, UIA. México.

———, 1998, "Bailes y mitotes coloniales como producto y factor sincrétic," in *La cultura plural. Homenaje a Italo Singorini*, UNA; y Universita di Studi di Roma, La Sapienza, México.

Barba de Piña Chan, Beatriz, 1998, "Peregrinaciones prehispánicas del Altiplano mesoamereicano," in *Caminos terrestres al cielo. Contriibución al estudio del fenómeno romero*, INAH. Col Científica, México.

Guilliem Arroyo, Salvador, 1998, "El tamplo calendárico de México-Tlatelolco" en *Arqueología Méxicana, Rito del México prehispánico*, INAH, México, pp. 46-53.

González, Anahuac, 1997, "Los concheros. La (re) conquista de México," *Las danzas de la conquista* F.C.E. México pp., 107-227.

Gruzynsky, Serge, 1995, *La guerra de las imágenes. De Cristóbal Colón a "Blade Runner*, FCE, México.

Heyden Doris, 1975, "An interpretation of the Cave Underneath the Pyramid of the Sun in Teotihuacan, Mexico," *American Antiquity*, vol 40, num 2, pp. 131-47.

Martínez Marín, Carlos, 1972, "Santuarios y peregrinaciones en el México prehispánico, religión en Mesoamérica," en *Religión en Mesoamérica XII Mesa Redonda*, SMA México, pp. 161-78.

Rajsbaum Godorezky, Ari, 1999, *Narratives and Pilgrimages*, D.K Printworld (P) Ltd. New Delhi. pp.139-56.

Shadow, Robert and María Rodríguez Shadow, 1944, "Símbolos que amarran, símbolos que dividen: hegemonía e impugnaciión en una peregrinación campesina a Chalma," *Las peregrinaciones religiosas:una aproximación*, UAM, México.

Turner, Edith, 1987, "Pilgrimage an overview," *Encyclopedia of Religion,* Mac Millan Publishing Co.,_New York, vol 11, pp. 328-30.

Turner, Victor and Edith Turner, 1978, *Image and Pilgrimage in Christian Culture*, Columbia University Press, New York, I.

Valero, Ana Rita, 1998, "Peregrinación al Tepeyac. Una observación analítica de las romerías guadalupanas," in *Caminos terrestres al cielo. Contriibución al estudio del fenómeno romero* INAH, México, pp. 17-39.

Zuniga Araceli and Rodríguez Carrasco Norberto, "Los concheros al fin del milenio," Homenaje al antropólogo Guillermo Bonfil Batalla. INAH Danzas de las conquista, vol.2 Los concheros al fin de milenio.

17

Transplanting Pilgrimage Traditions in the Americas

Carolyn V. Prorok

Introduction

TRANSPLANTING a pilgrimage tradition is a precarious endeavour. In theory the possibilities are endless, but in practice many difficulties must be overcome. Notions about how the sacred shows itself are carried easily enough from one land to another, but whether or not one will recognize the sacred there is an entirely different matter. The myths that tie specific supernatural entities to specific places at home may not be conducive to transplantation, and the collective conscious that produces a community of potential pilgrims might be so frayed by the migration experience that its original form cannot be recovered. Moreover, the new society may be unreceptive to, or outright intolerant of, one's traditions. Under these circumstances, diasporic communities with pilgrimage traditions have had varying degrees of success in recreating a sustained, organized, and functional pilgrim circulation system.

This paper is concerned with the prevailing strategies that underlie the transplantation and reinvention of an already established and deeply embedded pilgrimage tradition by migrant communities — primarily from Catholic Europe and Hindu South Asia to the Western hemisphere. This entails the struggle to make new sacred places. Making and remaking sacred place is essential to pilgrimage circulation systems. Three *meta-scenarios* for the potential emergence of a sacred place for transplanted peoples are presented in this essay. These scenarios, and their associated strategies, are not necessarily progressive or interdependent on each other, although more than one of them may have been deployed at any given site. It is also important to note that these scenarios are not based on specific ethnic, cultural, religious, political, social or economic predispositions and operant behavioral interactions. Countless empirical studies have already focused on some combination of such factors in the character and development of specific pilgrimage sites such that they are often presented as unique in time and space (e.g. Bhardwaj 1990; Bhardwaj & Rao, 1988; Jackson et al. 1990; Nolan & Nolan 1997; Prorok 1986, 1997: Rinschede 1990; Singh 1998; Stoddard 1997; Tyrakowski 1988; Zelinsky 1990). Earlier typologies tend to focus on the same types of surface features of sites instead of the processes that produced them (Bhardwaj & Rinschede 1988; Preston

1990; Stoddard 1997).

Here I seek to elaborate pan-human processes that underlie, drive, and ultimately (re)produce the surface features that appear as ethnic, religious, cultural, social, political and economic in their material forms — simply because these are the means of expression that specific groups of humans at certain times and places have at their disposal. Such underlying processes are linked to these very material forms so dear to a person's or people's heart. Reconciling, yet not assimilating, the material with the spiritual, the I with the We, and the past with the present is made possible when people redeploy their sacred travailing/travelling in new times and places. An end result is what can be called the "collective selfhood." Transplanting pilgrimage traditions is not the only way to create "collective selfhood" but it is a very successful means for doing so. Thus it remains a profoundly human endeavour that may diminish at times, but never wholly disappear. Although it is impossible to capture fully the multiplicity of actions and reactions of millions of people, of varying cultural heritage, on two continents, over several centuries of migration experience, I offer my typology as an initial means for creating dialogue on this topic.[1]

Sacred Place as the Basis of Pilgrimage Systems

In recent ruminations on traditions, or the lack thereof, V.S. Naipaul (1998, 50-51) shares with us his observation that his homeland, Trinidad, has no sacred places. He says,

> I began to feel when I was quite young that there was an incompleteness, an emptiness, about the place, and that the real world existed somewhere else. I used to feel that the climate had burnt away history and possibility. . . ., we who were Indian were an immigrant people whose past stopped quite abruptly with a father or grandfather. . . ., [This] agricultural colony, in effect a plantation, honoured neither land nor people. But it was much later, in India, in Bombay, in a crowded industrial area — which was yet full of unexpected holy spots, a rock, a tree — that I understood that, whatever the similarities of climate and vegetation and formal belief and poverty and crowd, the people who lived so intimately with the idea of the sacredness of their earth were different from us.

In this passage Naipaul eloquently captures an important and defining difference between peoples of the Old World homelands and the descendants of migrants to that other world across ocean. This divide also exists between the traditional and indigenous past, where the sacred infuses every nook and cranny of the lived world, and the modern, transplanted, and relatively desacralized present (Relph 1976:16). Naipaul recognizes for himself the absence of that critical element of all pilgrimage traditions, sacred place, and thus by implication he is also letting us know that Trinidadians, Hindu Trinidadians in particular, do not have a developed pilgrimage circulation system as it is known in the Indian homeland. His assessment of the lack of sacred connections in his homeland continues (1998, 52):

> Too late, then, I remembered with a pang a story I had heard about when I was a child, ... Every now and then, according to this story, groups of aboriginal Indians in canoes came across the gulf from the continent (where remnants of the tribes still existed), walked to certain places in the woods in the southern hills, performed certain rites or made offerings, and then, with certain fruit they had gathered, went back home across the gulf. This was all that I heard. I wasn't of an age to want to ask more or to find out more; and the unfinished, unexplained story now is like something in a dream, an elusive echo from another kind of consciousness. Perhaps it is this absence of the sense of sacredness — which is more than the idea of the "environment" — that is the curse of the New World . . .. And perhaps it is this sense of sacredness — rather than history and the past — that we of the New World travel to the Old to rediscover.

Naipaul is onto something here. Although I would disagree that the sense of the sacred is absent among the colonizing and colonized peoples of the Western hemisphere, it has certainly diminished. The depreciation of sacred consciousness of which he speaks did not occur overnight; it took centuries. Its roots are embedded in the rise of the modern era in western Europe, which brought with it the impersonality of industrialism and early capitalism — neither of which has need of sacred places in the traditional sense. The grand colonial projects of several Western societies, and the Protestant Reformation — with its focus on 'the word' over ritual (Richardson 1986, 1995) — also had their parts to play. In the face of such sweeping changes many sacred sites were destroyed or built over by the conquering party, especially in the Western hemisphere, and especially those of indigenous peoples whose lands were being absorbed or who were forcibly removed from favoured lands. Add to this the inundation by foreign migrants who arrived by the hundreds of thousands, and brought with them their own notions of what constituted a sacred place, even though transferring those ideas to their new circumstances would often prove to be difficult. Many communities wilfully abandoned practices; others simply lost them. For some communities, holding on to some aspect of their traditions became a foundation for their collective identity. Such projects are ongoing, and today, they are the basis for a resurgence of the search for the holy.

One could argue that the desire to travel — to briefly break away from the dreariness of the everyday — is a root cause of pilgrimage, and that journeying as existential quest is, in and of itself, a powerful motivation for many people to travel (Osterrieth 1997). Yet this desire alone is not enough reason to account for pilgrimage circulation in the traditional sense in that one needs a destination (Glazier 1983). Although there will always be those individuals who derive satisfaction from aimless wandering, such wandering is not the basis of traditional pilgrimage systems (Stoddard 1997). Rebecca Solnit (2000, 50) notes, "To travel without arriving would be as incomplete as to arrive without having travelled."

Before the advent of agriculture and its concomitant settled lifestyles our forebears were nomadic, and certainly they had their fill of journeying. During the course of their journeys certain places likely took on great significance and carried special meaning for them as "aggregation sites" where celestial confluences were conflated with special or unusual natural features that figured prominently in the travelling memories of countless bands of humans who gathered for companionship and friendly competition (Hitching 1977; Conkey 1980; Henry 1985; Nolan 1986; Malville et al. 1998; Shipman 2001). Quite possibly, pilgrimage by early agricultural peoples could have been an attempt to recover their nomadic heritage in an attenuated form, and it would have been directed towards specially remembered places of their nomadic pasts. J. McKim Malville, an astrophysicist, (1999) explains that Nabta Playa, an ancient site in the northern Sudan, was sacred to nomadic groups, and later to settled people, for millennia. He wrote to me:

> There was a ritual-like repetition of return, an act of synchronization between people and the cosmos, as they kept coming to that basin which would fill with water each summer solstice due to the monsoon rains. Not only were people in synchronism with the great cosmic cycle of rain and sun, but they were re-enacting the deeds of the past. . . . home was on the trail, and pilgrimage was at home; pilgrimage was not departure from home but a return to the center . . ..

We know, of course, that many sacred places are of more recent vintage and have been invented and reinvented many times. Without these sacred places religious journeys would not exist. Where the entire breadth of a people's lands are understood to be sacred, believers may distinguish between places with particular qualities or they may identify some places as more sacred than others (Bhardwaj 1973; Forbes-Boyte 1998). In either case, this relationship arises out of a traditional milieu whereupon a group of people have had a long, thorough, and intimate relationship with their local environments (Tuan 1974). Contemporary circumstances for ever-increasing numbers of people, especially in the lands of industrialization and colonial migration in the Western hemisphere, have shifted this relationship from one of intimacy with the living, breathing, earthiness of Earth to a search for such intimacy. The root of this shift largely derives from the rise of the modern era, and the cataclysmic ways in which millions of people were simultaneously uprooted, supplanted, and transplanted such that traditional systems have been "disembedded" from their specific time and place centered meanings (Giddens 1990, 20-25). More recently, individuals born into a (re)embedded postmodern sensibility are searching for a new intimacy with certain times and places, with the earthiness of Earth, by recovering them and reshaping them via slippery, and often fragmentary, processes deriving from the existential dilemma of creating a collective selfhood. Under such circumstances, Elvis Presley can sing,

"You Ain't Nothing But a Hound Dog," and still become a shining beacon of hope for life after death, and the desire to be close to an authentic voice (Richardson 1998, 7).

Pilgrimage Transplanting Scenarios

For Muslims, pilgrimage to a specific, extraordinarily sacred site is literally a commandment from the Almighty, and for over a millennium tens of millions of the faithful have turned their devoted gaze towards Mecca regardless of migratory experiences or the salience of local sacred sites. Hindus and Catholics have no such commandment that establishes the one and only sacred site for faithful observance, yet Hindu India and Catholic Europe have exceptionally well-developed pilgrimage circulation systems that incorporate thousands of sites of varying degrees of sacredness and importance (Bhardwaj 1973; Nolan & Nolan 1989).

Peoples of both faith systems have migrated to the Western hemisphere in large numbers, though Catholics more so than Hindus. Today Catholicism is the dominant faith in much of Latin America, with significant minorities in North America, while the Hindu presence tends to be concentrated in several of the former British and Dutch plantation colonies (e.g. Trinidad & Tobago, Guyana, Jamaica and Surinam), and is becoming more evident in contemporary North America (Clarke, et al. 1990; Helweg and Helweg 1990).

Indigenous peoples of the Americas felt the full brunt of an aggressive, colonizing Christianity in the first centuries of contact. Catholic migrants to an overwhelmingly Protestantized North America over the past two centuries generally met with intolerance through to the WW II era. During the late nineteenth and early twentieth centuries hundreds of thousands of South Asian Indians, primarily Hindus, were transported to already Christianized sugar colonies and met with intolerance for their faith traditions. Contemporary Hindu migrants to North America also face such difficulties despite civil laws that protect them (Johnson and Costa 1998). Even under the most conducive of migrant circumstances — such as moving to similar physical and social environments as the homeland, travelling voluntarily, migrating with the larger share of one's family and community, the ability to carry one's goods conveniently, being welcomed with open arms — it would be difficult to transfer a pilgrimage tradition because of its typically place-bound character. Yet, many migrants would have been fortunate to have even one of these facilitating factors prevail. Instead, alien environments, hardship, and intolerance were more often the order of the day, thus the transfer of pilgrimage customs was indeed a precarious one. Under these circumstances in the Western hemisphere several *meta-scenarios* emerge as primary strategies of recovery: co-opting indigenous sites, maintaining links with the homeland, and (re)creating sites for transplanting a pilgrimage tradition. Some sites perhaps have a history of multiple scenarios, either simultaneously or serially but none of these approaches are codependent on any other. The examples I use highlight only one of many possible strategies used by any given cohort of pilgrims.

Co-opting Indigenous Sacred Sites

Long before the Columbian voyage, indigenous people established sacred sites and created pilgrimage traditions in association with them (Turner & Turner 1978; Ingham 1986; P.O.V. 2001). Such sites still exist, many of which are still important to native communities. Contemporary worshipping communities visit them as native, syncretized, converted, and/or plural shrines where African traditions can also be incorporated into the ritual character of the site (Siemon-Netto 2000; Glazier 1983).

People, whether native themselves or not, visit native sites as native sites. The San Francisco Peaks and several other mountains in Arizona, for example, hold extraordinary meaning for the Navajo and Hopi peoples, but they are also open to the public at large (Dobbs 1997). For non-indigenous peoples, visits to these mountains and other such sites (as native sites) may take on a touristic quality or they can involve spiritual dimensions that include adopting some version of a native faith system or creating a new spiritual meaning for them within the context of their traditional meaning (Joseph 1992).[2]

Conquerors and the converted — however nominally — faithful imposed, adapted, and resisted conversion by syncretizing native sacred sites with Christian elements (Turner & Turner 1978; Waldman 1985, 58-59; Ingham 1986). While many indigenous religious sites and material culture were purposely destroyed or invalidated through elimination and renaming by Christian conquerors,[3] it was also common for Iberian conquerors to raze pyramids and other indigenous sites only to build cathedrals or churches on them. In addition, newly emerging native converts might have an extraordinary experience on or near an already established native site, thus making possible its rededication to a Catholic saint. The shrine of the Virgin of Guadeloupe in Mexico City (*fig.* 17.1), the patroness of all Mexicans, is one such example (Ingham 1986, 182-183; Torres 1999).

A plural shrine can be found in Trinidad (Trinidad & Tobago) where a Catholic shrine to Our Mother La Divina Pastora was established over two centuries ago on or near what is believed to have been a native sacred site in the town of Siparia. As more and more Indians from southern Asia (mainly Hindus) settled in the area, they too offered their devotions, so much so, that today she is also known as Sipari Mai and is honoured by them with a major festival and pilgrimage during the week before Easter when the statue of the Virgin Mary is moved to another room so that she can be adorned and worshipped in the Hindu manner. She is placed back on the main altar of the church on Good Friday for the Catholic services during Easter weekend (Temple-Thurston 1997; Vertovic 1992, 219-20). Thus, this place simultaneously has indigenous Caribbean roots and is Catholic and Hindu in its most crucial observances.

Finally, some sites are invested with a multiplicity of meaning by groups with varying beliefs and practices that conflict. Mount Shasta in California is one such contested site as the local native community struggles to maintain a traditional relationship with a place that now attracts thousands of New Age spiritual pilgrims as well as environmental pilgrims (Huntsinger and Fernandez-Gimenez 2000).

Maintaining Links with the Homeland

Contemporary Catholics and Hindus, particularly in North America, continue to go on pilgrimage by returning to the homeland. The return to the homeland can act as a pilgrimage in and of itself, in which case "Home" is distinguished as a nation-state and made sacred by its role in the diasporic imagination (Tuan 1977, 176-78). Still, some people return home so that they can visit remembered holy places and/or participate in the pilgrimage rituals of a knowable, traditional homeland with specific sacred sites to which they have access. Croatian-Americans visiting the Bosnian town of Medjugorje is such a place (Jurkovich & Gesler 1997; Prorok 1997).

In the Caribbean, Hindus have, by and large, lost their traditional pilgrimage circulation system although some have attempted to reconstruct a semblance of one over the years. While visiting communities in New Nickerie and Paramaraibo Suriname, I found no specifically Hindu sacred site. Some Surinami Hindus, who are generally third and fourth generation descendants of late nineteenth century migrants, indicated that going to India, or to a specific place in India (such as Varanasi), would constitute a pilgrimage for them but most could not afford the costs involved — thus, this is not a common practice. Surinami Hindu temples are important as ritual/social centres, but none of them play the role of pilgrimage place in a traditional sense. As with Surinami Hindus, Trinidadian Hindus have no Haridwar, Varanasi or a Kumbha Mela (Prorok 1988). Nor has the mythical nature of Indian holy sites been easily transferred by a group of people with knowledge of and experience with such places in India. Rama did not canvas this land searching for Sita, nor did dismembered parts of Sati — consort of Shiva — fall in Trinidad.[4] Yet Trinidadian Hindus did manage to (re)create local sacred sites.

Recreating/Reinventing Sacred Sites

If an immigrant group derives from a land with a significant pilgrimage circulation tradition, then its notion of what constitutes a sacred destination already has meaning and coherence. As such, any sacred destination in the new land is not simply created, but (re)created. This scenario entails at least five possible strategies: replication, (re)recognition, creating movable rituals, celebrating sites of sacred embodiment, and ritual historicizing.

REPLICATION

The first method involves the erection of a replica of the image, temple, or any other important sacred object from the homeland. Both Hindus and Catholics have deployed this strategy for establishing new sacred sites far away from the homeland. In the 1970s, Sri Venkateswara, an incarnation of Vishnu enshrined at Tirupati, in Andhra Pradesh, was replicated first in Pittsburgh, PA and later on at several other locations in North America with support from the homeland shrine. The Tirupati Temple supplied the artisans and priests necessary for the transferal projects, and the Pittsburgh temple depends upon support from a broad base of pilgrims across North America (Bhardwaj & Rao 1988; Bhardwaj 1990; Helweg & Helweg 1990, 117-19; Prorok 1994) to maintain its compound of religious structures. The Sri Venkateswara Temple in Pittsburgh hosts over 150,000 North American pilgrims annually (SV Fundraiser Brochure 1998).

Another example would be the National Shrine of Our Lady of Consolation in Carey, Ohio, about 50 miles south of the western end of Lake Erie. In the late nineteenth century a small Luxumbourgon community enshrined a replica of an image from their homeland that was subsequently associated with miraculous events. This shrine is now a centre of pilgrimage for Catholics in the Great Lakes region every year for the Feast of the Assumption (*fig.* 17.2) (Faiers and Prorok 1990).

(RE)RECOGNITION

The second process involves the (re)recognition of the sacred in one's midst with a direct relationship to traditional means for understanding hierophanic experience (when the sacred shows itself to us). This entails knowing the sacred when you see it, with the use of any of our other senses, or being able to recognize it again in a new context. This process has been especially significant for the descendants of immigrants who have strengthened demographically over the years.

The Hindu population in Trinidad became demographically stronger by the mid-twentieth century and was comprised of mainly Trinidad-born individuals when locally produced Hindu sacred sites began to emerge (Prorok 1988). Several temples in Trinidad have lingams, stones representing Lord Shiva, which Trinidadian Hindus believe have grown in size since discovered. Informants claim true faith and worship causes the lingams to grow. In each case a stone was found protruding from the ground, and a temple was erected. A sacred story is associated with the lingam of two separate temples, both similar in form. The most popular of the two is known as the Patiram Trace Shiva Temple located in southwestern Trinidad (*fig.* 17.3). According to informants, a man hired to clear out undesirable jungle growth sharpened his cutlass on a stone protruding from the earth. As a result the stone chipped and milk flowed (some say blood). This stone is said to have grown over a foot since the 1940s according to the informant Sanachariya (Prorok 1988). Now it appears that another stone is emerging out of its side. According to Sanachariya several people visit the temple every day to perform puja, the basic Hindu ritual of worship, as witnessed by numerous ceremonial symbols such as *jhandi* flags. She estimates over 5000 people pay their respects to the lingam on Shiva Ratri, a Hindu holy day (Prorok 1988).

In North America apparitions, weeping images, and other spontaneous miracle events have become more common over the last three decades (Root 1988; Milbank 1989; Chocoran 1994; Warner 1996; Wolf 1999).[5] In 1989, in Ambridge-Pennsylvania, devotees believe that a crucifix of Christ closed its eyes during the Good Friday Mass (Prorok 1997). No one actually saw the eyes of Christ's image close on that memorable day. The young men serving the mass simply thought the eyes of the crucifix were different. In an interview for the American television program Unsolved Mysteries, Mr. Leo (a local artist who had recently restored the image) reported that the eyes appeared fleshy and teary and, he added ". . . the left eye was closed and the right one was slightly open." Over the next year thousands of pilgrims flooded the church as more people learned of the miraculous event (Prorok 1997).

In both of these cases, as with countless others, the protagonists knew the sacred when they saw (or otherwise sensed) it and acted on that sensibility. Their respective communities validated the original encounter through continued, persistant visitation to the sites. If the stones in the Trinidad bush had been ignored or removed, and the changing demeanour of the Ambridge crucifix went unrecognized, then neither place would be so special to their communities today. Thus the ability to (re)recognize the sacred, as one's forbears recognized it in the homeland, would eventually disappear or it could reappear in a new form. A fascination with UFO's and ET's, and their association with sites like Roswell, New Mexico, is partly attributable to a reappearance of the ability to recognize the sacred. With the strategy of (re)recognition, a very ancient means of accessing the sacred can be maintained in new contexts and forms.

MOVABLE RITUALS

A third method for (re)creating the "sensibility" of traditional pilgrimage is to utilize movable rituals as temporary sacred destinations. Here, devotees take advantage of already institutionalized, and otherwise ordinary, ritual events in order to travel for a religious purpose. This method emerges most clearly in the absence of opportunities to visit especially sacralized sites (although an absence of such sites is not necessary for this process to occur) (Glazier 1983).

In Trinidad Hindus have created a ritual event known locally as the *jag* (Prorok 1988). This activity is centred around the classical ritual known as the *yagna*, although in Trinidad it has been altered in form. Traditionally the *yagna* is a Vedic sacrifice ritual but in Trinidad it has taken on new meaning and function. Travelling to *yagnas* sponsored by an extended family, a pundit, or a village temple is very popular. *Bhagwat Jag* usually lasts for seven days and *Ramayana Jag* for nine days. Handbills are prepared and distributed. Each night of the *jag* puja is performed, the *Ramayana* or *Bhagavad Gita* read, and *prasad,* sweets offered at the puja, distributed to the guests. On the final night a feast is served and most people attend at this time. The meetings accrue merit to those who prepare them, especially by feeding holy men and the poor who flock to the event (Koss 1959: 125-26). *Jags* can be held any time of the year and some people, especially elderly women, make their rounds to as many as possible. Families and pundits who sponsor such events do so only occasionally because they are so expensive. Temple committees usually sponsor a *jag* every year since donations given at this time are significant in supporting the temple's maintenance costs. Religious events like the *jag*, which have no special association with sacralized physical features or distance travelled, are more easily attended, at greater distances, and by a greater number of worshippers than many other religious events (Prorok 1988).

Similarly, some Catholics take advantage of the 'sunrise mass' offered by some churches at an open-air site on Easter Sunday to create a religious excursion, although this practice is not nearly as common or as important to the larger community as the Trinidadian one of attending *yagnas*. Yet, for some Catholics, seizing an opportunity to hear a mass conducted by the Pope is even more special, and it can draw thousands of people from great distances (Van Biema 1999). One such pilgrim announced to a reporter for NBC that she was spiritually fulfilled because she attended mass given by the Pope himself (NBC Evening News 2003).

SITES OF SACRED EMBODIMENT

An age-old practice from the homeland that transfers quite easily is the belief in an individual person embodying divine power. For Catholics, the public appearance of the Pope himself is reason enough to travel to "see" him, whether or not he performs mass. The same can be said of saints and those who are beatified, or blessed — or more commonly, the sites where they are buried or their relics are enshrined. Examples include the shrine for Santa Rosa de Lima (canonized in 1671 in Peru), the shrine of the Holy Relics maintained by the Sisters of the Precious Blood in west central Ohio, or the National shrine of the North American Martyrs in Auriesville, NY, west of Albany, for the eight Jesuit Martyrs of the seventeenth century who died Christianizing and colonizing north-eastern North America.[6]

Individual bodies may exhibit sacred characteristics such as stigmata or are believed to heal those who visit with full faith — such as an eighteen-year-old woman named Audrey Santo in Worcester, Massachusetts, who fell into a coma after an accident when she was three years old. Lying perfectly still, she receives many visitors seeking a divine experience. Some devotees call her a "victim soul" which is a traditional Catholic belief that some women suffer greatly to atone for the sins of the world, thus becoming a repository of divine power (Flecker

2003).

Hindus, similarly travel long distances to visit *swamis* (high-level spiritual authorities) or *gurus* (spiritual mentors) when they appear in public. Quite often, Hindus will travel to the *ashrams* (spiritual centres) of specific *swamis* or *gurus* to receive their blessings. Not surprisingly *swamis* regularly tour the Americas and some have established *ashrams* and/or temples in the Western hemisphere to serve its growing Hindu population as well as recent converts. The International Society for Krishna Consciousness (ISKCON) is probably the best known among a number of such groups to establish themselves, through the *swami* Bhaktivedanta Prabhupada, in the Americas and worldwide. Despite being a centre of controversy to non-believers, the temple commune of New Vrindaban in West Virginia continues to draw Hare Krishna pilgrims, and Hindus in general, from across North America partly because it was Swami Prabhupada's western home (Prorok 1986).

Conferring sacrality to the personhood of specific individuals is not confined to Hindus and Catholics. This practice is so ancient and so common that it (re)emerges even in populations that are theologically moving away from the material expression of the sacred to an emphasis on the 'word' as is the case for most Protestant Christians. In the latter half of his ministry, Billy Graham would fill stadiums and today Benny Hinn draws tens of thousands to any location where he appears in public. Moreover, Americans of many religious and nonreligious persuasions invest a similar sense of the sacred in specific individuals not usually thought of as religious. The greatest such example of this is the reification of Elvis Presley through his voice, his body and his public persona. Pick up any newspaper or magazine, or watch any news broadcast from August of 2002, to see that the twenty-fifth anniversary of his death was more than a media event; it was memorialized by millions. Graceland, his home and burial site near Memphis, Tennessee, receives several thousand people daily while tens of thousands visit on his birth and death anniversaries (Davidson et al. 1989; Gregory & Gregory 1997; Polman 2002; Siegel 2002)

RITUAL HISTORICIZING

The fifth method whereby people (re)create sacred destinations is an especially complex one that entails the reification of particular historic moments as epitomized in the structures, people, and/or locational features associated with those moments, or period of time in some cases (Foote 1997). This is quite different from the often desacralizing act of simply explaining an important event. Indeed, these structures and sites represent more than ordinary sacralized place. A church or temple encompasses ordinary sacred space where prescribed rituals are an ongoing part of their raison d'etre. All churches and temples are not automatically pilgrimage destinations by virtue of their ritualized character, nor are they necessarily historically important — although all of them have a history. Instead, epitomized sites and structures are ritually invested with the emotional, political and social moment that captures a people's recognition of their own history; their own identity. It answers the question, "Who are we?" with "We are Mormons," "We are Vietnam veterans and Americans," "We are Trinidadian Hindus," "We are Cuban Exiles," and so on.

Contributing to what Zelinsky (2001, 565) calls, "the uniqueness of the American religious landscape," are Mormon sacred sites. These sites are embedded in the formative history of Mormonism and include such important places as Kirtland, Ohio, site of the first temple; Nauvoo, Illinois, where the martyred Joseph Smith is buried and the temple was burned by anti-Mormon mobs; and Salt Lake City, Utah, with its grand temple and Brigham Young's home. Ritually historicized sacred sites conflate moments in time with points on Earth's surface to the degree that the group believes that it owns such places to the exclusion of other groups of people because of what was experienced — and such a sense of ownership is crucial to group identity (Jackson et al., 1990; Van Biema 2000). Recently, Mormon pilgrims retraced Brigham Young's great trek to Utah, thus revalidating that journey as the epitome of their own historical sense of selfhood (Underwood 1997; Attache 1998).

A site that reflects the investment of a deeply felt spiritual sensibility into what is otherwise a secular or civil site is the Vietnam War Memorial on the Washington Mall as it captures a particular period in the American collective conscious (*fig*. 17.4). It is a memorial that reminds us that death is *real* and not merely absurd or noble (Menand 2002, 62).

Miles Richardson (1994, 161) explains:

> . . . on the Mall, we follow a path leading among the trees to a grassy knoll. Presently, we can discern a V of black marble extending into the knoll. At first the wall of the V is at our feet, but it rises as we go down toward the apex. At the apex, the wall rises over our heads. We are in the middle of a black mirror of names: Melvin G. Cormier, Walter L. Burroughs, Hector S. Acevedo, Michael L. Poletti, Grady E. McElroy, Mary T. Klinder. Your hand, with a will of its own, reaches out to trace the curve of letters; mine follows. In the black mirror of dark marble we see our hands touching the words, and we see the self and the other, the living and the dead, meet. As a monument, the Vietnam Veterans Memorial achieves its power through the manner in which it, a controversy itself, encapsulates the greater controversy. . . . The memorial's unique reinsertion of the past into the present permits us now, at long last, to place the past into a perspective that ameliorates our nightmares and eases the burden of our guilt.

Unlike many of the other monuments on the Mall, which play their own role in American civil religion, the Vietnam Veterans Memorial is the centre of much ritualizing on the part of its visitors, from leaving mementos at its base to taking home a rubbing of its surface. It is a traditional pilgrim's destination.[7] Every day is a day to visit the site, but Memorial Day has taken on special significance known as *Rolling Thunder*, when over 250,000 motorcyclists descend on the site in remembrance of POW's and MIA's (Today Show 1999).

In Trinidad a temple is perched on a platform in the sea.[8] This is no ordinary Trinidadian Hindu temple. Its history captures the history of its people in an extraordinary way. In this case, a people's civil history intersects symbolically with their religious history, and is exceptionally epitomized by the Temple in the Sea. Just after WW II a gentleman known simply as 'Sadhu' to the local people, erected a small temple on the beach near the village of Waterloo. All beaches in Trinidad & Tobago are government property, and unlike Christian Churches, Hindu temples were not tolerated on public property until recently. Caroni Limited, the government sugar company, destroyed the temple. Sadhu built it again. The government fined and jailed Sadhu, and they destroyed the temple again. Sadhu rebuilt the temple in the sea itself — on a platform he made of rocks. He built a rocky pathway out to the temple, such that the temple was only accessible at low tide. The temple was now safe from colonial interference, but not from the elements or neglect after Sadhu died in 1970 (*fig.* 17.5). Yet this place was special. Before WW II people had illegally cremated their dead nearby, and after the war, when cremation was made legal, they continued to do so and spread the ashes in the sea. This site has always been popular for the performance of *puja* by the sea in celebration of the full moon of the Hindu month of Kartik (ca. October) when the tide waters enter the temple. Indeed, until 1994, people continued to perform *puja* on the temple platform long after the structure began to deteriorate and emptied of its ritual paraphernalia. The past ten years have seen a resurgence of pride in Hindu identity in Trinidad, and 1995 saw the election of Trinidad's first Hindu prime minister. Since then a memorial statue of Sadhu and a visitor's centre now awaits the pilgrim and tourist alike (*fig.* 17.6). A new, contemporary, Trinidadian style, temple has been built on a platform behind the original one, and it has become the focus of the annual "Indian Arrival Day" ceremonies which commemorate the first landing of South Asian Indians in 1845. Already, thousands of Trinidad's Hindus have come to this site to simultaneously honour their gods and celebrate their own survival of colonial history.

Cuban exiles in Miami have created an extraordinary shrine on Biscayne Bay just south of the downtown centre of business (Tweed 1997). Here the patron saint of Cubans, the Virgin Mary as Senora de la Caridad del Cobre or Our Lady of Charity from Cobre, is honoured simultaneously in her Catholic role of charitable mother, as Oshun — the Yoruba goddess of fertility, beauty, love and generosity, as well as a symbol of national pride and longing. Periodically *romerias*, or pilgrimage picnics, are held at the shrine for people from specific provinces in Cuba and La Caridad's feast day, 8 September, is celebrated with thousands of worshippers gathered in one of Miami's stadiums or parks as the priest calls for Cuban liberation during the mass (Tweed 1997, 123-27). Tweed (1997, 61) also noted that Cubans in Miami recognize two key changes in their religious practices here as compared to Cuba. All exiles are more religious in Miami than they are in Cuba, and a significantly higher number of men worship at the Miami shrine than in the original shrine in Cuba. While fighting for independence from Spain Cuban soldiers wore La Caridad's image during battle, and today Cuban exiles are drawn to her in even greater numbers as a unifying and liberating force. The Shrine of Our Lady of Charity in Miami is ritually historicized repeatedly as its role of symbolizing collective selfhood achieves greater depth and significance for increasing numbers of *Exilio Cubanos*.

Unlike the holy wells of Ireland, where historicization has led to the atrophying of localized spiritual power (Brenneman & Brenneman 1995, 96-109), the temples and memorials of the post-Columbian Americas have been raised up and ritually epitomized into thick, sturdy and sublime places that shoulder the weight of a people's burdened past while simultaneously mirroring a collective consciousness of selfhood.

Conclusion

What this is all about is a collective selfhood within which individuals are straining to define themselves through (re)sacralization, replicated over and over in the places we make sacred so that we can visit them and remind ourselves of ourselves. As we move from the edge of one millennium that ushered in the full-throttled transformations of modernity, of impersonality, of desacrality and slide into another, re-linking the fragments of our remembered pasts becomes a reification of an imagined heritage for posterity. At the cusp of that modernity giving way to postmodernity, we search for meaning, for relevance, for that which elevates us, by rooting around in our indigenous and migratory pasts, where co-opting native spiritual sites, maintaining ties with the homeland — or losing them for that matter — and (re)creating the sacred in our midst has taken on heightened significance.

This heightening of the significance of sacred places in our lives is created over and against the pervasive desacralized, rationalized world around us. Just like the exaggerated peaks resulting from the slope profile exercises we do in our map reading classes, we make sacred places stand out more than ever in an exaggerated way. And their numbers are growing — not diminishing — as we become more technologically advanced and more "connected" with the world around us, a connection that is simultaneously to ill-defined somewheres and nowheres which produces an existential dilemma that is, in part, solved by anchoring one's relationship to the divine through knowledge and experience of places with 'real' meaning.

For Sartre (1956, 319), the world around us was like a fine printed table cloth with his gloves upon it. To see the gloves, or in our case the sacred places, is to not see the cloth's design which has faded into the background of our view. To focus on the print design, or for us our modern desacralized milieu, is to lose sight of the gloves or sacred places which then lose their acuity and significance. Thus contemporary (re)creation of sacred place — and an active engagement with it — requires highlighting the sacred places in the geographical space that surrounds them. This perceptual process is easier than ever with new technologies; what a paradox, when we consider the role of new technologies in desacralization and spiritual disconnection through its focus on an "explained" geographical space that hides the sacred places that abound within it. We must search for them, and if we are fortunate they present themselves to us. An openness to a mystical interpretation of earthly phenomena (Chamberlain 2001) may be a requirement for some, but is not necessary for all.

Over the past century a number of great minds foresaw the conundrum we are currently facing in the search for a relevant selfhood. According to Mugerauer (1994, 55), Jacques Derrida and Michel Foucault would have us continue to "undo tradition and create whatever temporary meanings and values we can for ourselves . . .." In light of this perspective, the search for the sacred in visitations from outer space, alongside images of the biggest baby in the world, and the chimp who shoots people at the zoo,[9] seemingly becomes fanatical for some people as our ability to hold on to relevance slip-slides away in a world where meaning is increasingly plasticized and fragmentary. In the marketplace of globalized choices and localized experiences, the search for the sacred is becoming increasingly decentralized — the Catholic hierarchy rarely validates reports of miracles any more (Prorok 1997) despite the powerful role of a central authority in creating a media-oriented diocese without official parishoners (Starrs 1997). The plethora of new sacred places being identified in our nightly news are as fleeting as the words used to describe them (God Decentralized 1997; Designer God 1998). Thus old, peeling paint on an Ohioan barn became the Madonna holding her child in 1990, and in 1995, Surnami Ganeshas drank milk from teaspoons in empathy with those in India. Did the paint stop peeling? Are Ganesha idols in Suriname still drinking milk? Is the spirit of Elvis really a healer? (Rosenbaum 1995; Nickell 1996; Stern & Stern 1998). Postmodern skeptics would see devotees swimming in a soup of credulity.

Mircea Eliade (1959), and according to Mugerauer, Martin Heidegger too, would have none of this (Mugerauer 1994, 55-56). Unlike Foucault and Derrida, Eliade believed that historicism (not ritual historicizing) as an explanatory model had not yet taken the upper hand, and that it is still possible to rejuvenate our experience of the sacred for our time and place. I believe that Eliade would see in Elvis the healer and Ganesha the milk-drinker an attempt to recover substantive meaning by those who participate in their making. Moreover, Eliade thought it possible to retrieve the sacred from cultures to which we never did, or no longer, belong (Mugerauer 1994, 56).

Both perspectives have something to contribute to our understanding of how we make sacred places in new times and new lands. While the salience of particular traditional meanings may be (re)cast, (re)presented, and even temporary, they are still drawn from that deep well of historically particular, collective consciousness; a consciousness of collective selfhood constantly (re)negotiated and constantly relevant.

The phrase "collective selfhood" would seem to be an oxymoron, but it is not. Instead, it reconciles without assimilating, thus obliterating, one or the other state of being, collectivity or individuality, the We with the I. (Re)making sacred places, and visiting them, is an intensely personal, material, experience for so many individuals. Pilgrims see the sites on their own terms. They smell the smells and walk the walk on their own, all the while capturing the past and the spiritual and making it relevant to a present sensibility. When visiting a sacred site, the pilgrim can really feel that sense of belonging to a group that requires no explanation or validation of one's publically expressed, personal experience. This is not simply the communitas described by Victor and Edith Turner (1978, 250-55), though communitas may be experienced by the pilgrim (for example; liminality, anti-structural belonging, rite of passage or undifferentiation). Collective selfhood does not require the obliteration of the I, nor does the sense of belonging thus created end with the pilgrimage event. It expands and solidifies through the pilgrimage experience into the everyday world existence to which the pilgrim returns. What a wonderful way to stave off the ever-threatening — sitting right there on the edge of the horizon — existential darkness of being alone in the world. Giving up one's individual sense of self is one solution — a solution that is not uncommon (Smith 1978, 93). But why give up so much when you can have your cake and eat it too! The post-modern lifeworld of so many in the Americas seems to require an increasing frequency and intensification of experiences that produce collective selfhood that does not simultaneously threaten individuality in order to innoculate oneself against the ever present threat of aloneness. To this end, one can recount an endless number of attempts to resacralize space, even temporarily, in the name of collective affirmation as a stop-gap measure against personal annihilation.

American Indians temporarily produce movable sacred places in a series of sacred commons in the form of powwows where their collective selfhood becomes both a destination and a journey (*fig.* 17.7). Sri Ganapathi Sachchidananda, a guru from Mysore-India, finds Shiva-Vishnu-Brahma on a rock 100 kilometres north of Pittsburgh–Pennsylvania (*fig.* 17.8). He tells us (Bhakti Mala-USA 1992, 2),

> This is a powerful rock. . . . Now it is a powerful soul. There is a good vibration here, come and touch it! It is not for testing with machines. If you touch with that kind of intention, nothing happens. If you feel there is something, if your heart, mind and soul's power make a connection with the rock's power, then the healing power is coming. This rock is the same shape as the Kedarnath lingam . . .. So I call this as the American Kedarnath.

When Swami Sachchidananda visits this site his devotees — both Indian and Anglo Hindus — converge to honour him, God, this place, and themselves. What then of the pilgrims celebrating

fig. 17.1: Many Mexican pilgrims still climb the hill to worship in this original shrine dedicated to the Virgin of Guadeloupe, the patron saint of Mexico. A new, massive basilica is at the base of the hill. (photograph by author, 1984)

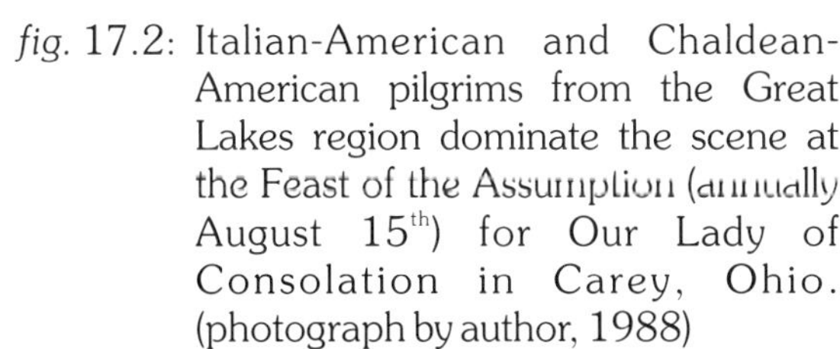

fig. 17.2: Italian-American and Chaldean-American pilgrims from the Great Lakes region dominate the scene at the Feast of the Assumption (annually August 15th) for Our Lady of Consolation in Carey, Ohio. (photograph by author, 1988)

fig. 17.3: A Hindu woman honors Shiva as she pours water to cool the lingam at Patiram Trace Shiva Mandir in Penal, Trinidad. (photograph by author, 2003)

fig. 17.4: Our reflections speak to us in the inscribed granite of the Vietnam War Memorial in Washington, D.C. (photograph by author, 1996)

fig. 17.5: This faded photograph captures the poignant deterioration of the Temple in the Sea at Waterloo, Trinidad. (photograph by author, 1985).

fig. 17.6: Sewdass Sadhu is prominently memorialized as the original builder of the Temple in the Sea at Waterloo, Trinidad. Note the contemporary form of the rebuilt temple in the background. (photograph by author, 2003)

fig. 17.7: Dancer pilgrims from over 30 different native nations performed at the Three Rivers Pow Wow just north of Pittsburgh, Pennsylvania. (photography by author, 1998)

fig. 17.8: A sacred rock that expresses the power of the great Hindu gods, particularly Shiva, is enshrined by the Dattatreya Yoga Center in West Sunbury, Pennsylvania. (photograph by author, 1999)

the Feast of the Assumption with Our Lady of Consolation in Carey, Ohio? Or Trinidadian pilgrims honouring Shiva's growing lingam on his most holy day? And those who adamantly attest to the closing of Christ's eyes on his crucifix in their local church? What about those who were healed by Sipari Mai in Trinidad, the Virgin of Guadeloupe in Mexico, the Black Christ of Esquipoulas in Guatemala, or even the spirit of Elvis himself? Then there are those who persist in building temples in the sea, and those who leave a piece of themselves at the base of a black wall. What they are doing is making sacred places — sacred destinations that will capture this moment in their life's journey and give it collective meaning, at least for now. Some of these endeavours grow in significance and solidify a sense of "collective selfhood" through repetition; many others wither and disappear, only to be reborn in another time and place.

Notes

1. The vast differences in social, political and economic experiences between, say, Spanish conquistadors of the 16th century and Slavic peasants of the early 20th century, not to mention the differences between north Indian Sudras of the 19th century and highly educated, south Indian Brahmins of the late 20th century would certainly influence the political and social basis for producing specific sacred places. These differences would likely reveal themselves in terms of an emphasis on one particular scenario over another, but I believe that they can all be accommodated by the processes I analyze in this paper. Identifying which scenario is likely to be used by which particular group of people could be the subject of another project.
2. In this last case, some New Age religionists are attempting a postmodern co-opting of indigenous sites which is often contested by native peoples through restricted access to reserved lands (P.O.V. 2001). Still, some sites are on public lands or held privately and open to a multiplicity of uses (such as Mt. Shasta or Devil's Tower). In 1993, 70,000 people visited the *Indian Wheel*, a sacred site located in the Bighorn Mountains of Wyoming. As recently as 1990, fewer than 6,000 people visited this site. Pilgrims circumambulating the wheel have worn a trench around its perimeter (Attache 1998).
3. The Turners (1978, 51) refer to this as a "baptizing of local customs" and point to the writings of Gregory the Great in 601 as an early recognition of the efficacy of the practice — in this case, the absorption of European Pagan traditions.
4. Many sacred places on the Indian subcontinent are linked directly to the sacred stories of the deities. In the great epic story of Lord Rama, called *Ramayana*, the God-King Rama searches for his wife Sita who had been kidnapped by the demon Ravana. He canvasses the subcontinent. As a result, countless sites are associated with his (remembered) presence. Additionally, the great God Shiva and his primordial consort Sati are associated with many sites. A complex story results in her body being dismembered in flight across the subcontinent. Pieces of it fall and are memorialized in many locations (e.g. an eye, a hand).
5. Countless such events are reported every year in the United States alone. From Conyers, Georgia and Lubbock, Texas where the Virgin Mary is believed to have appeared, to Lake Arthur New Mexico where the image of Jesus was seen in a tortilla (the miracle tortilla) or in rural Ohio where the image of Jesus has been seen in the peeling paint of a barn as well as in the oil stain on a soybean silo (see websites noted in bibliography).

6. The Jesuit Martyrs include: Saint Rene' Goupil, Saint Isaac Jogues, Saint John de Lalande, Saint Anthony Daniel, Saint John de Brebeuf, Saint Gabriel Lalemant, Saint Charles Garnier, Saint Noel Chabanel — this location is also the birthplace of the Blessed Kateri Tekakwitha, the Lily of the Mohawks, born at Ossernenon in 1656 and has since become a centre of Marian devotion.
7. A movable replica of the Vietnam War Memorial travels across the country on a month to month basis so that Americans who cannot make the journey to Washington D.C. can still honor those who lost their lives in Vietnam. One can google the term "movable vietnam war memorial" to find upcoming venues.
8. I have been visiting this site and interviewing local people about it for twenty years. The background on the site is derived from this fieldwork.
9. Many supermarket tabloids regularly "report" on traditional types of hierophanies along with outlandish, exaggerated events as if they are of the same category of experience. The front cover of an issue of the *Sun* (1992) shows this with headlines that include a story on the famous shrine at Chimayo, New Mexico with the birth of the world's largest baby (35 lbs), a caged chimpanzee shooting a tourist at a zoo, or a man charged with bigamy for marrying conjoined twins.

References

Attache, 1998, *Pilgrimage Issue*, (July): 66-69.

BHAKTI MALA-USA, 1992, *Newsletter of the Datta Yoga Center*, 147 Moniteau Road, West Sunbury, PA., December.

Bhardwaj, S.M., 1973, *Hindu Places of Pilgrimage in India: A Study in Cultural Geography*, Berkeley: University of California Press.

———, 1990, Hindu Deities and Pilgrimage in the United States, *Geographia Religionum* 5: 211-28.

Bhardwaj, S.M., and M. Rao, 1988, Emerging Hindu Pilgrimage in the United States: A Case Study, *Geographia Religionum* 4: 159-88.

Bhardwaj, S.M., and G. Rinschede, 1988, Pilgrimage — A World Wide Phenomenon, *Geographia Religionum*, 4: 11-19.

Brenneman, W. and M. Brenneman, 1995, *Crossing the Circle at the Holy Wells of Ireland*, Charlotte: University of Virginia Press.

Chamberlain, P.G., 2001, Topomystica: An Investigation into the Concept of Mystic Place, *Journal of Cultural Geography* 19 (1): 97-123.

Chocoran, T. 1994, Mary Visions: A Virgin in the Sky With Diamonds, *OMNI* 17 (1): 54-60.

Clarke, C. et al., eds, 1990, *South Asians Overseas: Migration and Ethnicity*, Cambridge: Cambridge University Press.

Conkey, M.W., 1980, The Identification of Prehistoric Hunter Gatherer Aggregation Sites: The Case of Altamira, *Current Anthropology* 21 (5): 609-30.

Davidson, J.W., A. Hecht, and H.A. Whitney, 1990, The Pilgrimage to Graceland, *Geographia Religionum* 5: 229-52.

Dobbs, G.R., 1997, Interpreting the Navajo Sacred Geography as a Landscape of Healing, *Pennsylvania Geographer* 35 (2): 136-50.

Eliade, M., 1959, *The Sacred and the Profane: The Nature of Religion*, trans. by W. R. Trask, NY: Harcourt, Brace & Co.

Faiers, G.E., and C.V. Prorok, 1990, Pilgrimage to a "National" American Shrine: "Our Lady of Consolation" in Carey, Ohio, *Geographia Religionum* 5: 137-48.

Flecker, S., 2003, On the Trail of Miracles, *PITT Magazine* 17 (4): 31-35.

Foote, K.E., 1997, *Shadowed Ground: America's Landscapes of Violence and Tragedy*, Austin: University of Texas Press.

Forbes-Boyte, K. 1998, It is All Sacred: Foothill Konkow Perceptions of Sacred Places, *Pennsylvania Geographer* 36 (1): 5-29.

Giddens, A., 1990, *The Consequences of Modernity*, Stanford: Stanford University Press.

Glazier, S.D., 1983, Caribbean Pilgrimages: A Typology, *Journal for the Scientific Study of Religion* 22 (4) 316-25.

Gregory, N., and J. Gregory, 1997, When Elvis Died: Enshrining a Legend, In, *In Search of Elvis*, ed. V. Chadwick, 225-42, Boulder, Colorado: Westview Press.

Helweg, A.W. and U.M. Helweg, 1990, *An Immigrant Success Story*, Philadelphia: University of Pennsylvania Press.

Henry, D., 1985, Preagricultural Sedentism: The Natufian Example, In, *Prehistoric Hunter-Gatherers: The Emergence of Cultural Complexity*, eds. T.D. Price and J. Brown, 365-84, Orlando: Academic Press.

Hitching, F., 1977, *Earth Magic*, NY: William Morrow & Co.

Huntsinger, L., and M. Fernandez-Gimenz, 2000, Spiritual Pilgrims at Mount Shasta, California, *Geographical Review* 90 (4): 536-84.

Ingham, J.M., 1986, *Mary, Michael, and Lucifer: Folk Catholicism in Central Mexico*, Austin: University of Texas Press.

Jackson, R.H. et al., 1990, Pilgrimage in the Mormon Church, *Geographia Religionum* 5: 27-62.

Johnson, J. and Frank J. Costa, 1998, Hindu Temple Development in the United States: Planning and Zoning Issues, *Journal of Cultural Geography* 17 (2): 115-24.

Joseph, F., ed., 1992. *Sacred Sites: A Guidebook to Sacred Centers & Mysterious Places in the United States*, St. Paul, MN: Llewellyn Publications.

Jurkovich, J.M. and W.M Gesler, 1997. Medjugorje: Finding Peace at the Heart of Conflict, *Geographical Review*, 87 (4): 447-67.

Koss, J.D, 1959, *Hindus in Trinidad: A Survey of Culture Change and Cultural Continuity*, Master's thesis, University of Pennsylvania.

Malville, M., 1999, Note to author, 24 February.

Malville, J.M. et al., 1998, Megaliths and Neolithic Astronomy in Southern Egypt, *Nature* 392: 488-91.

Menand, L., 2002, The Reluctant Memorialist, *The New Yorker* 78 (18): 54-65.

Milbank, D., 1989, Miracles: They Seem to Come in Waves, *Pittsburgh Post-Gazette* July 6: 4.

Mugerauer, R., 1994, *Interpretations on Behalf of Place* Albany: SUNY Press.

Naipaul, V.S., 1998, *Beyond Belief: Islamic Excursions Among the Converted People*, NY: Random House.

NBC (National Broadcasting Corporation), 2003, Interview with a Catholic pilgrim, *NBC Evening News*, October 12.

New York Times Magazine, 1997, *GOD Decentralized*, (A Special Issue) December.

Nickell, J., 1996, Milk drinking idols, *Skeptical Inquirer* 20 (2): 7.

Nolan, M.L., 1986, Pilgrimage Traditions and the Nature Mystique in Western European Culture, *Journal of Cultural Geography*, 7 (1): 5-20.

Nolan, M.L., and S. Nolan, 1989, *Christian Pilgrimage in Modern Western Europe*, Chapel Hill, NC: The University of North Carolina Press.

———, 1997, Regional Variations in Europe's Roman Catholic Pilgrimage Traditions, In, *Sacred Places, Sacred Spaces: The Geography of Pilgrimage*, eds. R.H. Stoddard and A. Morinis, 61-94. Baton Rouge: Geoscience Publications.

Osterrieth, A., 1997, Pilgrimage, Travel & Existential Quest, In, *Sacred Places, Sacred Spaces: The Geography of Pilgrimages*, eds. R.H. Stoddard and A. Morinis, 25-39, Baton Rouge, LA: Geoscience Publications.

Polman, D., 2002, "Elvis' truest fans at Graceland resent the kitsch, revere the King", *The Philadelphia Inquirer,* August 16: A1,14.

P(oint).O(f).V(iew). 2001, *In the Light of Reverence*, Public Broadcasting Service Documentary, August 14.

Preston, J., 1990, The Rediscovery of America: Pilgrimage in the Promised Land, *Geographia Religionum* 5: 15-26.

Prorok, C.V., 1986, The Hare Krishna's Transformation of Space in West Virginia, *Journal of Cultural Geography* 7 (1): 129-40.

———, 1988, Patterns of Pilgrimage Behavior Among Hindus of Trinidad, *Geographia Religionum* 4: 189-99.

———, 1994, Hindu Temples in the Western World: A Study in Social Space and Ethnic Identity, *Geographia Religionum* 8: 95-108.

———, 1997, Becoming a Place of Pilgrimage: An Eliadean Interpretation of the Miracle at Ambridge, Pennsylvania, In, *Sacred Spaces, Sacred Places: A Geography of Pilgrimage*, eds. R.H. Stoddard and A. Morinis, 117-40. Baton Rouge, LA: Geoscience Publications.

Relph, E., 1976, *Place and Placelessness*, London: Pion Ltd.

Richardson, M. 1986, Place and Culture: Two Disciplines, Two Images of Christ, and a Single Goal, In, *The Power of Place: Bringing Together Geographical and Sociological Imaginations*, eds. J. Agnew and J. Duncan, 140-56. Boston: Unwin Hyman.

———, 1994, Looking at a World That Speaks, In, *ReReading Cultural Geography*, edited by K. Foote, et al., 156-63, Austin: University of Texas Press.

———, 1995, Speaking and Hearing (in Contrast to Touching and Seeing) the Sacred, In, *Religion in the Contemporary South: Diversity, Community, and Identity*, eds. O. White, Jr. and D. White, 13-22, Athens: University of Georgia Press.

———, 1998, The Gift of Presence: The Act of Leaving Artifacts at Shrines, Memorials, and Other Tragedies, Paper read at the 94th Annual Meeting of the Association of American Geographers, March, at Boston.

Rinschede, G., 1990, Catholic Pilgrimage Places in the United States, *Geographia Religionum* 5: 63-136.

Root, D., 1988, Revelations: From Weeping Icons to the Face on the Freezer, *The Pittsburgh Press Sunday Magazine* October 2: 12-15.

Rosenbaum, R., 1995, Among the Believers, *New York Times Magazine* September: 50-57, 62ff.

Sartre, J.P., 1956, *Being and Nothingness*, trans., by H.E. Barnes, New York: Gramercy Books.

Shipman, P., 2001, On the Nature of Violence, *American Scientist* 89 (6): 488-89.

Siegel, L., 2002, Long Live the King, *Time,* August 12, 160 (7): 70.

Siemon-Netto, U., 2000, Bewitched by Bolivar, *Civilization* April/May: 78-85.

Singh, R.P.B., 1998, Sacred Journey and Faithscape: An Experience of the Panchakroshi Pilgrimage, Varanasi, *Pennsylvania Geographer* 36 (2): 55-91.

Smith, J., 1978, *Map is Not Territory*, Chicago: University of Chicago Press.

Solnit, R., 2000, *Wanderlust: A History of Walking*, NY: Viking Press.

Sri Venkateswara Temple 1998, *Prakaram Project Features* (Fundraising Brochure), December.

Starrs, P.F., 1997, The Sacred, The Regional and The Digital, *Geographical Review* 87 (2): 193-218.

Stern, J., and M. Stern, 1998, Amazing Graceland, *Attache* July: 82-85.

Stoddard, R.H., 1997, Defining and Classifying Pilgrimages, In, *Sacred Places, Sacred Spaces: A Geography of Pilgrimages*, eds. R.H. Stoddard and A. Morinis, 41-60, Baton Rouge: Geoscience Publications.

SUN, 1992, *Front Cover*, December 1, 10 (48): ff.

Temple-Thurston, B., 1997, All o'We is One, (http://www.plu.edu/~prism/thurston.html), accessed 1/25/2003.

Today Show, 1999, May 31, NY: NBC Studios.

Torres, Y.G., 1999, Conchero's Sanctuaries and Pilgrimages, Paper read at the International Conference on Pilgrimage & Complexity, Indira Gandhi National Centre for the Arts, January, at New Delhi.

Tuan, Y., 1974, *Topophilia: A Study of Environmental Perception, Attitudes, and Values*. NY: Columbia University Press.

_____, 1977, *Space and Place: The Perspective of Experience*, Minneapolis: University of Minnesota Press.

Turner, V. and E. Turner, 1978, *Image and Pilgrimage in Christian Culture: Anthropological Perspectives*, NY: Columbia University Press.

Tweed, T. 1997, *Our Lady of the Exile: Diasporic Religion at a Cuban Catholic Shrine in Miami*, New York: Oxford University Press.

Tyrakowski, K., 1988, Pilgrims to the Mexican Highlands, *Geographia Religionum* 4: 193-246.

Underwood, A., 1997, Onward, Mormon Pilgrims: A Second Great Western Trek, 150 Years Later, *Newsweek* 129 (17): 65.

UTNE Reader, 1998, *Designer GOD: In a Mix-and-Match World, Why Not Create Your Own Religion?* (A Special Issue), July/August.

Van Biema, D., 1999, A View From the Flock: One Woman's Pilgrimage to the Heart of Her Faith & the Place of the Pontiff in Catholic America, *Time,* 153 (5): 46-48.

———, 2000, The Invasion of the Latter-day Saints, *Time,* 156 (2): 64-65.

Vertovec, S., 1992, *Hindu Trinidad: Religion, Ethnicity and Socio-Economic Change*, London: MacMillan.

Waldman, C., 1985, *Atlas of the North American Indian*, NY: Facts on File.

Warner, M., 1996, Blood and Tears, *New Yorker* 8: 63-69.

Wolf, N., 1999, There's Something About the Virgin Mary, *George* January: 42-43.

Zelinsky, W., 1990, Nationalistic Pilgrimages in the United States, *Geographia Religionum* 5: 253-67.

———, 2002, The Uniqueness of the American Religious Landscape, *Geographical Review* 91 (3): 565-85.

http://www.roadsideamerica.com/attract/NMLAKtortilla.html accessed february 10, 2004.

http://wovoca.com/prophecy-venezuela-maria-esperanza.htm accessed february 10, 2004.

http://www.mcn.org/1/Miracles/Visions.html accessed february 10, 2004.

http://www.visionsofjesuschrist.com/weeping273.htm accessed february 10, 2004.

List of Figures

fig. 17.1: Many Mexican pilgrims still climb the hill to worship in this original shrine dedicated to the Virgin of Guadeloupe, the patron saint of Mexico. A new, massive basilica is at the base of the hill. (photograph by author, 1984)

fig. 17.2: Italian-American and Chaldean-American pilgrims from the Great Lakes region dominate the scene at the Feast of the Assumption (annually August 15th) for Our Lady of Consolation in Carey, Ohio. (photograph by author, 1988)

fig. 17.3: A Hindu woman honors Shiva as she pours water to cool the lingam at Patiram Trace Shiva Mandir in Penal, Trinidad. (photograph by author, 2003)

fig. 17.4: Our reflections speak to us in the inscribed granite of the Vietnam War Memorial in Washington, D.C. (photograph by author, 1996)

fig. 17.5: This faded photograph captures the poignant deterioration of the Temple in the Sea at Waterloo, Trinidad. (photograph by author, 1985).

fig. 17.6: Sewdass Sadhu is prominently memorialized as the original builder of the Temple in the Sea at Waterloo, Trinidad. Note the contemporary form of the rebuilt temple in the background. (photograph by author, 2003)

fig. 17.7: Dancer pilgrims from over 30 different native nations performed at the Three Rivers Pow Wow just north of Pittsburgh, Pennsylvania. (photography by author, 1998)

fig. 17.8: A sacred rock that expresses the power of the great Hindu gods, particularly Shiva, is enshrined by the Dattatreya Yoga Center in West Sunbury, Pennsylvania. (photograph by author, 1999)

18

Washington, D.C. and Power of Pilgrimage

Jeffrey F. Meyer

THE first question that must be answered is whether or not it is legitimate to consider Washington, D.C. as a pilgrimage site. Wilbur Zelinski, who has written about the religious foundations of nationalism, claims that "one's first pilgrimage to Washington can be a blinding religious experience, a rite of communion." (Zelinski 1988: 180). While perhaps an exaggeration, Zelinski's statement points to a long history of using religious terms to refer to the U.S. capital. Its buildings have been called "shrines" and "temples," its precincts "hallowed," its founding documents, the Declaration of Independence and the Constitution, "sacred texts."

In the nineteenth century Representative Rufus Choate said, "We have built no national temples but the capitol. We consult no common oracle but the constitution" (U.S. Capitol Historical Society 1991: 5). Senator Charles Sumner made explicit the connection of the capitol with the Temple to Jupiter Optimus Maximus, classical Rome's most important shrines. Architecturally modelled on the Pantheon, Jefferson had earlier called the Capitol the "first temple dedicated to the sovereignty of the people" (Brown 1971: 76-77). Its first dedication and subsequent additions were solemnized by elaborate Masonic rituals.

Washington the city has often been described as a centre of pilgrimage. Richard Oulahan, a nineteenth-century poet, writes in 1879: "When our patriot pilgrims of freedom/To our National Mecca repair. . ." (Bergheim 1992: 75). More recently Edward Linenthal has described how Americans have created sacred spaces, the most obvious example being Washington, D.C., "which was consciously designed as the ceremonial centre of the nation" (Linenthal 1991:1-2). In a 1995 editorial in the Chronicle of Higher Education, Michael Nelson, a political scientist, wrote as follows: "When Americans travel to Washington with their families or high-school classes (as most of my students have done), they see themselves as making a pilgrimage of a sort. Their attitude is serious, even reverential." (Nelson 1995: A44) At the same time, the leading functionaries of this city called the "new Jerusalem on the Potomac" have been described in religious terms. Martin Marty calls the presidents "the priests of public religion," (Marty 1987: 61) and Robert McCloskey, leading historian of the Supreme Court, has described the Justices as "a kind of secular papacy" and says that Americans' devotion to the Constitution has allowed the court to "assume the priestly mantle" (McCloskey 1994: x, 8-9).

This paper takes the position that such language is not simply hyperbole, mere analogy, but it points to a deeper possibility in the experience of visitors to the city. In so doing I am following more recent anthropologists and historians of religion, cited by Juan Eduardo Campo, who adopt a broad definition of pilgrimage viewing it as "a set of ritual actions involving specific human communities, institutions and organized travel to and from sacred places." Such a broad definition of pilgrimage allows Campo to posit three types of pilgrimage found in the American context: "pilgrimages of organized religion, civil religion and cultural religion" (Campo 1998: 40-41).

The present article examines the United States Capital as a centre of pilgrimage in civil religion. Since it is not a site made sacred by its central role within one of the traditional religions but rather as an expression of civic or public religion I will conclude with some thoughts on the issue of why it is both legitimate and hermeneutically useful to analyse the U.S. capital as a centre of pilgrimage.

The creation of Washington, D.C. is closely tied to the creation of the United States as an entirely new political entity, a revolutionary polity in which the people, rather than hereditary monarchs, should exercise sovereignty. After the Founding Fathers had published the Declaration of Independence and proclaimed themselves separate from Great Britain they immediately underlined the finality of the act by seeking to assume all the rights, duties and symbolic accouterments of a fully independent nation. One of their first acts was to create a Great Seal for the United States. Because the seal would be a concise expression of the core ideals of the new republican form of government, Congress appointed its leading thinkers, Franklin, Jefferson and Adams to design it. Three committees and six years later Congress was still not satisfied with the results. Yet though many symbolic details changed over that time period, one idea persisted throughout the entire process. When Congress finally gave the responsibility for the seal to Charles Thompson, the secretary for the committees, he kept this persistant idea, depicting it on the reverse side of the seal, the Masonic pyramid with the all-seeing eye of the Deity. He explained the symbolism as follows:

> The pyramid signifies Strength and Duration: The Eye over it & the Motto allude to the many signal interpositions of providence in favour of the American cause. The date underneath is that of the Declaration of Independence and the words under it signify the beginning of the New American Aera, which commences from that date.
>
> — Patterson and Dougall 1976, 84-85

The words he refers to indicate the new Latin mottoes he had chosen in place of the phrase *deo favente* (with God's favour). The two new mottoes on the Seal would be *annuit coeptis* (He [God] approved their undertakings), and *novus ordo seclorum* (a new world order, a new age). The word *seculum* (in its contracted genitive form *seclorum*) refers to both a "world" and an "age" in space and time, although the temporal dimension is primary. Applying this concept to the plan of Washington, the city, with the Capitol at its centre, was designed to be placed at the centre of the world and to signal a crucial turning point in human history. According to Perry Miller, American colonists believed that

> God governed the universe not only in space but also in time and as there was intelligent purpose in each enactment, so all events were connected in a long-range program which men call history. — Mead 1963: 77

It can be shown that all the Founding Fathers shared the belief that the American experiment was unprecedented, the Providential ushering in of a new and glorious age for all humanity. They saw previous history as a slow and painful progress towards this great moment and future history would see its development and eventual triumph.

Symbols of spatial centrality also abound in Washington. The District of Columbia was planned as a perfect square of ten miles on a side, its corners oriented to the four cardinal directions. L'Enfant's original plan shows that the Capitol was clearly to be the centre of the city, with the numbered and lettered streets radiating out from the building to create the four quadrants which still define the city today. The plan shows clearly that the Capitol, not the President's House would be the "pivot of the four quarters." Major boulevards, named after the 15 States of the Union which existed in 1790, are ranged around the Capitol like a kind of microcosm of the nation, with the New England States to the north, the mid-Atlantic States in the central area and the southern States to the south. One supporter of the Potomac location of the capital (also a local landholder), George Walker, had asserted that Providence had chosen the site, even the precise location between Alexandria and Georgetown, because it was the central point between the St. Croix and St. Mary's rivers which then marked the northern and southern boundaries of the existing states.

In 1809 William Lambert submitted a proposal to the House of representatives to establish a prime meridian "through the dome of the Capitol in Washington," to replace that of Greenwich, "since the calculation of longitude from the meridian of a foreign nation . . . implied a "degrading dependence" and was "a shackle of colonial dependence"' (Edney 1994: 384). The meridian issue had been important to Andrew Ellicott, the original surveyor of Washington, who wrote to Jefferson: "I have taken the liberty of sending you an almanac for the year 1793, which I calculated. . . . The Astronomical part is adapted to the meridian and latitude of the City of Washington." (Padover 1945: 160) Lambert's proposal was of course rejected but it received the support of some in congress, some cartographers and from James Monroe, who would become President seven years later. Monroe said that the establishment of a meridian had become "an appendage, if not an attribute of sovereignty."

Using new and more scientific concepts current in the late eighteenth century, the creators of Washington accomplished what ancient planners had done in the designing of sacred cities, temples, palaces and monasteries — they placed their capital at the centre of space and time. By the time of the Civil War the Capitol had assumed the form it has today, the central rotunda above all a symbol of unity and spatial centrality as the place where Senate and House came together and where the people could come to meet their representatives. Despite the pressures of the Civil War, Lincoln demanded that the work on the building continue. "If the people see this Capitol going on, they will know that we intend the Union shall go on." (Maroon 1993: 43) It also reflected the traditional three-storied universe, the central rotunda representing this world, the dome with its fresco showing Washington worshipped in heaven like a god, and the basement crypt, where early plans had called for the mausoleum of the first President, symbolizing the underworld. Thus the city took shape during the period of over a century, its organization reflecting old cosmological ideas in a new garb. Its buildings and major Memorials — the Capitol, White House, Washington Monument, Lincoln and Jefferson Memorials — became sites on a kind of pilgrimage route recalling the Founders and sacred events in national history.

Rituals of Order and Chaos: Self-organizing Systems

The major rituals of Washington are familiar to most Americans. Beginning with the death of William Henry Harrison in 1841, the city has been the site for funeral and mourning rites for deceased Presidents and other heroes of the republic. It has also been the place for the celebration of national triumph: victory parades of Union troops celebrating the end of the Civil War, Admiral Dewey's victory parade after the war with Spain, General Pershing's after First World War and the triumph of Charles Lindberg after his flight over the Atlantic.

Without doubt, however, the most important periodic ritual is the inauguration of the President. Beginning as a minimal ritual with Jefferson in 1801, it has subsequently grown in importance and grandeur to meet a felt need, to define and affirm the nature of the national community. The culmination comes at the Capitol when the President takes the oath of office. The entire government is present at this ritual event as well as the whole nation, which is in effect represented by their Congressional members and Senators but also by tens of thousands of ordinary visitors who have come on pilgrimage.

At the same time, another type of pilgrimage ritual has developed, not affirming the *status quo*, but quite the reverse. It calls for attention to new causes, challenges the establishment and attempts to redefine the nature of the national community. Its existence and the tensions it creates mirror the perennial suspicions held by orthodox religious authorities concerning religious pilgrimage. In Turners' words:

The apparent capriciousness with which people make up their minds to visit a shrine,

> the rich symbolism and communitas quality of pilgrimage systems, the peripheral character of pilgrimage *vis-à-vis* the ritual or liturgical systems as a whole, all make it suspect. Pilgrimage is too democratic, not sufficiently hierarchical.
>
> — Turner and Turner 1978: 31

Some examples of this more spontaneous type of pilgrimage would be Jacob Coxey's army in 1894, women suffragists in 1913 and the Bonus Army in 1932; all marched down Pennsylvania Avenue to show support of their various causes.

After Second World War, these protest pilgrimages changed their venue to the Mall and their numbers increased exponentially. Since the 1963 march for racial equality led by Dr. Martin Luther King there have been a total of 853 demonstrations, rallies, sit-ins and marches through 1985. The various causes have included civil rights, racial equality, anti-Vietnam protests, pro-abortion, anti-abortion, the environment, women's rights, Indian rights and gay rights.

Over the course of time, these mass journeys, which are highly spontaneous compared to the established pilgrimage rites in traditional cultures, have evolved ritual patterns of their own, including speeches, prayers, singing, processions and sit-ins. They may be considered pilgrimages in that they come to Washington as the centre of power (and the birthplace of that power), believing that by making connections with the symbols of the capital, their messages may be more efficacious. They can be viewed as contestations for the sacred space at the centre of the nation, claiming rights and seeking to form a new communal identity for the American nation. Again the Turners note that "there is something inveterately populist, anarchical, even anticlerical about pilgrimages", and they have at times been linked with "popular nationalism" (Turner and Turner 1978: 32).

Daniel Boorstin has written of Washington protest pilgrimages in the following terms: "The messages change (and seldom are heard where it counts) but the messengers keep coming, reminding us that in this city *everybody* can say his piece, even if nobody listens." (Boorstein 1994: 100) Rather than adopting this cynical view, one could argue the opposite. American views towards the issues of these protest pilgrimages, e.g., racial and gender equality, immigration and imperialism, have changed profoundly since the early twentieth century. Although these protest-movements and ritualized demonstrations have not achieved their goals immediately nor have been the sole cause of the changes, overall, they have played their part in the process of transforming popular attitudes as well as governmental policies. They have been effective because they utilized the symbols and monuments of public religion, occupying at least temporarily the *templum*, the sacred arena at the centre of things.

At the same time there have been pilgrimages to Washington meant to reaffirm more traditionally religious values, such as the National Washington Pilgrimages of the 1950s, which were well financed and widely supported by both political and religious leaders. They cannot be described as self-organizing and spontaneous events. Howard Pyle, assistant to President Eisenhower, wrote to commend the pilgrimage leaders for stimulating a "quickening and deepening of the spirit that characterizes this annual recognition of the basic sources of our nation's religious heritage" (Washington Pilgrimage brochure 1957).

Symbolic and Social Complexities

Washington provides an abundance of political/religious symbols, some well defined and relatively stable, others open to progressive change. The Lincoln Memorial is an example of a national symbol whose meaning has evolved, almost in spite of the intention of its creators. It is an icon, like the Capitol and the White House, which every citizen can see on the Lincoln penny and the five dollar bill. It is precisely the pilgrims to Washington, not the political leaders, who have transformed the building's meaning from an emblem of the reunion of the States to an emblem of emancipation and racial equality. Their pilgrimages were self-organizing events not only because they developed their own rituals but because these actions fundamentally changed the intended meaning of the Lincoln Memorial. There is abundant evidence, for example, that the builders of the memorial wanted to downplay if not completely ignore Lincoln's work as an emancipator, focusing on the reunion of the white brothers, blue and grey, who had both fought nobly for the cause in which they believed. Although Robert Moton, the President of the Tuskeegee Institute, was given the honour of delivering the major speech at the dedication of the memorial in 1922, the seating at the event was segregated. The three events that were most significant in changing the meaning of the memorial as a symbol were the Marian Anderson concert there in 1939, the March on Washington of August 1963, organized by Martin Luther King, and the demonstrations in the spring of 1964 while the civil rights bill was being debated in Congress. They and many subsequent pilgrimage marches on Washington have woven a new fabric of meaning, rendering the Lincoln Memorial as a symbol of black freedom and more generally of racial equality and of resistance to all forms of social oppression. Through these largely spontaneous demonstrations, the various pilgrims have shaped a new and more inclusive communal identity for themselves and for the American people. In the words of the conveners of this conference, these new systems of meaning and social cohesion have *self-emerged* from the "collective behaviour of free individuals, each in search of a spiritual ideal."

Power of Pilgrimage

I believe that using pilgrimage as an interpretative category to understand the U.S. capital reveals the power it exerts over the imaginations and feelings of Americans and its consequent potential to effect social transformation. Without paying attention to this latent religious element, it is impossible to understand the power of the place. I do not claim that this analysis would apply to other important capitals, like London or Paris, but I am certain that it does apply to

Washington because of the particular religious sensibilities of the American people. As Chesterton observed many decades ago, the United States is a nation with the soul of a church. The words of the founding Fathers and subsequent leaders have contained the same message. Washington had stated that the great experiment in democracy was under the protection of Providence and that the United States had a mission to bring this new form of government to the rest of the world. Lincoln, during the darkest days of the crisis of the war between the States, had claimed that the United States was "last best hope of the earth." This is the mythology that pilgrims contact and have reinforced when they visit the capital.

Adopting a contrary argument, one could object that the sort of pilgrimage I am describing contains no "transcendent," —element, seeks no ultimate salvation, and that most of those who come to visit the city are merely tourists. While transcendence is a fundamental characteristic of pilgrimage in the case of historical religions, the goals of many pilgrims were far less transcendent; they sought this worldly blessings, — like health, wealth and offspring. Pilgrimage in many tribal cultures was never soteriological but focused on the "attainment of a new socio-cultural status and state" in this world. Washington pilgrimage may therefore be closer to the world of tribalism than that of the historic religions.

Even if most of those who visit Washington come as tourists, that is still a situation common to all pilgrimage traditions in the historical religions. From Chaucer's Canterbury pilgrims to today's visitors to popular tourist destinations, tourism and pilgrimage have been regular bedfellows. "A tourist is half a pilgrims, if a pilgrim is half a tourist." (Turner and Turner 1978: 20) What may have begun as a simple tour, may be transformed by a powerful inner experience into an authentic pilgrimage. Recent studies have generally tended to blur the distinction between tourism and pilgrimage, with the final judgment depending more on the inner response of the tourist-pilgrim than upon any absolute definition of the two activities (Naquin and Yu 1992; Higgens 1985; Sears 1989; Albanese 1990; Chidester and Linenthal 1995).

The ultimate test of a political system lies in its ability, without using coercive means, to enlist the loyalty and cooperation of its citizens. At times when the American political system was under challenge, such as during the Civil War and the Vietnam era, spontaneous pilgrimages to Washington have taken place, giving an excluded group the opportunity to occupy the sacred space at the center of the American universe and to demand their inclusion in the national community.

> The power of a shrine, therefore, derives in large part from its character almost as a religious void, a ritual space capable of accommodating diverse meanings and practices — though of course the shrine staff might attempt, with varying degress of success, to impose a single official discourse. — Eade and Sallnow 1991: 15

In these religious or quasi-religious acts of pilgrimage, the visitors to Washington have laid claim to a new self-identity and effected a transformation of national symbols. If they came as aimless tourists or members of a rag-tag group of protestors, many of the pilgrims have left the capital with a new sense of identity and a conviction of new empowerment.

References

Albanese, C., 1990, *Nature Religion in America: From the Algonkian Indians to the New Age*. Chicago: University of Chicago.

Bergheim, L., 1992, *The Washington Historical Atlas,* Rockville, MD: Woodbine House.

Boorstin, D., 1994, *Cleopatra's Nose: Essays on the Unexpected*, New York: Random House.

Bowling, K., 1991, *The Creation of Washington D. C. : The Idea and the Location of the American Capital,* Fairfax, VA: George Mason.

Brown, G., 1971, *History of the United States Capitol,* 2 vols., New York: Da Capo.

Campo, J., 1998, "American Pilgrimage Landscapes," *Annals of the American Academy of Political and Social Sciences,* 558 (July).

Chidester, D., and Linenthal, E., 1995, *American Sacred Space,* Bloomington: Indiana University.

Concklin, E., 1927, *The Lincoln Memorial in Washington,* Washington, D.C.: U.S. Government Printing Office.

Eade, J. and M. Shallnow, 1991, *Contesting the Sacred: The Anthropology of Christian Pilgrimage.* London: Routledge.

Edney, J., 1994, "Cartographic Culture and Nationalism in the Early United States: Benjamin Vaughn and the Choice for a Prime Meridian, 1811," *Journal of Historical Geography,* 20, no. 4.

Linenthal, E., 1991, *Sacred Grounds: Americans and their Battlefields,* Urbana: University of Illinois.

Maroon, F., 1993, *The United States Capitol*, New York: Tabori and Chang.

Marty, J., 1987, *Religion and Republic: the American Circumstance*, Boston: Beacon.

McCloskey, R., 1994, *The American Supreme Court*, Chicago: University of Chicago.

Mead, S., 1963, *The Lively Experiment: The Shaping of Christianity in America*, New York: Harper and Row.

Naquin, S. and C. Yu., 1992, *Pilgrims and Sacred Sites in China*, Berkeley: University of California.

Nelson, Michael., 1995, Editorial, *Chronicle of Higher Education*, August 18, 1995.

Padover, S. (ed.), 1946, *Thomas Jefferson and the National Capital*, Washington, D.C.: U.S. Government Printing Office.

Patterson, Richard S. and Douglas Richardson, The Eagle and the Shield: A History of the Great Seal of the United States. Washington, D.C.: Department of State, 1976.

Turner, V. and E. Turner, 1978, *Image and Pilgrimage and Christian Culture: Anthropological Perspectives,* New York: Columbia University.

United States Capitol Historical Society, 1991, *We the People, The Story of the United States Capitol: Its Past and Its Promise*, Washington, D.C. : U.S. Government Printing Office.

Zellinski, Wilbur, 1988, *Nation into State: The Shifting Symbolic Foundations of American Nationalism.*

PART IV

SACRED LANDSCAPES AND PERSONAL TRANSFORMATION

19

Pilgrimage as Spatial Representation of Complexity

Pradeep A. Dhillon

CONTEMPLATING an intricately woven Kashmiri shawl might well help solve the problem of meaning. However, it is unlikely that such a solution would come from decoding encrypted messages or hidden pictures. The idea rather is to move perceptually between all the individual details within the seamless overall design. In this essay I will take up the difficulties presented for thinking about meaning in relation to spatial environments. In regarding the seamlessness of space, philosophers often make theoretical distinctions between absolute and egocentric space in thinking about spatial regions. These are problematic distinctions for physics no doubt, however, they are discursively useful when thinking about pilgrimage. Such distinctions provide different ways of representing the same spatial region as opposed to different regions. Spatial design in its entirety is difficult to think about because it requires that the theorist removes him or herself from a particular environment while remaining a subject within that very world. Egocentric representations of spatial regions rely on narratives, which can become so particular as to suggest entirely different, particular, spatial regions.

The study of pilgrimage as a representation of complexity is useful, I will argue, to find a way to negotiate the problem of the particularity and incompleteness of representations and the complexity as well as vastness of space. That different cultures developed the practice of pilgrimage suggests a persistence in the awareness of the significance of spatial complexity in the making of meaning for the self in a not-always benign world which is theoretically knowable but given to us partially. In other words, the practice of pilgrimage receives its religious and ethical functions from twofold awareness of the significance of the spatial environments we inhabit and the frailty of our attempts to negotiate its complexity. A discussion of the problem of the representation of spatial regions should go some way towards explaining the linkage between aesthetics and ethics in narrative meaning. Finally, such a discussion should take us some way towards solving the problem of objectivity while avoiding the Scylla and Chryabadis of relativism on the one hand, and a dogmatic universalism on the other.

In thinking about pilgrimage as a representation of spatial complexity and the making of meaning I have two main thoughts: The first runs roughly along lines which consider ways in which pilgrimages are enactments of our awareness of complexity and our attempts, through ritualistic movement, either to ward off feelings of complete helplessness, or reflect an acceptance of our fragility. The second considers the complex patterns of pilgrimage as they carve out the matrices along which meaningful travel, including the whole of life as pilgrimage, is described. Both rely on thinking of pilgrimage as experience that links the particular and the whole; the individual bootis, the plant motifs, of the Jamawar shawl to its overall, garden design.

In thinking about these matters I have been greatly helped by focusing on a particular text namely that of Heinrich Harrer's description of his seven years in Tibet, but also John Bunyan's *The Pilgrim's Progress* and Chandrakriti's treatise on Buddhist philosophy. These texts together traverse several oppositions: Western/non-Western, secular/religious, outer/inner, oral/literate, high/popular culture. In reading Harrer's text doubly as pilgrimage, a journey that caused a conversion in his way of orientating himself towards the world and our acts of reading as pilgrimage, I, too became a pilgrim. As regards complexity, before I got interested in pilgrimage, I was drawn to Kant and Wittgenstein as thinkers of limits. Broadly, the two philosophers speak of the partial nature of our ability to know and represent the worlds we inhabit. The pathos of the human condition comes from our having to act in this world, to be judged and judge others, under conditions of partial and incomplete knowledge. It is this tension between our awareness of the partiality of what we can know and the necessity to judge and the resulting terror, that Imannuel Kant describes in the dialectic of the sublime in his *Critique of Judgement*. It is not surprising that Ludwig Wittgenstein concludes his discussion of the possibilities of representation in his *Tractatus Logico-Philosophicus* with the reminder that "Whereof one cannot speak, thereof one must be silent."

The concept and practice of pilgrimage can be taken up as spatial representations of our awareness of complexity as well as the epistemological limits within which we live out our lives. In other words, they reflect our awareness of that which we can never neither fully know nor adequately represent. In the sixteenth-century *Japji* hymn of the Sikhs, we find a reflection of just such awareness.

Layer upon layer in landscape,
Hundreds of thousands of skies,
Finally, the Vedas grow tired
repeating this reality,
As also all the other sacred texts.
The infinite cannot be represented
All representations destroy this reality.
Nanak says, that which we call on as the ultimate
is self-referential. — Japji, *Adi Granth*, (author's translation).

Pilgrimages, then, are attempts to occupy that liminal space which enables a coupling, unstable and fleeting though such a coupling might be between the cosmos and the individual. Furthermore, the individual, through such a journey grows aware of the vastness of the interior landscape the self is capable of occupying. Kant provides nice imagery, at the end of *The Critique of Reason*, when he talks of "the starry skies above and the moral law within." The ethics of humility as well as recognition of our dependence on and responsibility towards others is often the outcome of such a turning towards the world. Not surprisingly, the term "pilgrimage" carries religious weight regardless of the manner of its practice. Its opposing term would be "tourism."

I now turn to my reading of Harrer's text. At the conference on Pilgrimage and Complexity, at the end of my presentation, Alfred Wuerful, who divides his life between New Delhi and Stuttgart, came up to me and told me that he had been imprisoned with Heinrich Harrer and Peter Aufschneiter in the prisoner of war camp at Dehradun. Despite having made New Delhi his home, after the war he visited Heinrich Harrer and Austria every year. The circle was complete for me for a while — complete, but not closed. This brief reflection on the practice of thinking about pilgrimage suggests not only the complexity of interlinking representations, circles within circles, but also its spatiality and spirituality. We catch a glimpse of the vastness and the design of an open-ended yet metastable system.

Seven Years in Tibet (Harrer 1996) is a textual representation of Harrer and Aufschneiter's journey — physical, intellectual, and psychic movement — across spaces which link Tibet to Europe, India to Tibet, and the outer regions of Tibet to Lhasa. It also links ideologies and religions, and self-directed to other-directed action. After a long and arduous journey from the prisoner of war camp in Dehradun, Harrer and Aufschneiter arrived sick, tired and without papers in Lhasa, expecting to be turned back to the Indian border. Instead, to their surprise, they found a warm welcome. The Tibetans, with their own traditions of pilgrimage, extended traditional hospitality to the Europeans out of respect for the life-changing nature of the ordeal experienced by Harrer and Aufschneiter as they travelled through the Himalayan passes and the Tibetan landscape. In other words, the Tibetan system was open to others since the arduous journey undertaken by the Europeans could sustain the ascription of meaning related to the reorientation of the self towards the environment.

It is important to note, however, that Harrer and Aufschneiter, but particularly Harrer, did not ascribe the same meaning to their journey. Growing up in the Alps, Harrer had developed acquired fame as a downhill skier and a mountaineer. His success, however, bored him and victory over human rivals and public recognition no longer satisfied him; "I began to feel that the only worthwhile ambition was to measure my strength against the mountains." But, his travels across the plateau of Tibet changed him from someone who saw himself as over against others as well as nature to one who can no longer tell the difference between himself and others. It seems fair to say that he developed a sense of self that encompassed east and west, Europe and Asia. "Wherever I live," we find him writing from Berlin, "I shall feel homesick for Tibet. I often think I can still hear the wild cries of geese and cranes and the beating of their wings as they fly over Lhasa in the clear cold moonlight" (Harrer, 1996: xviii).

This is the universal story of pilgrimage. It is a story of travel, struggle, learning and teaching in search of wisdom — a reorientation towards the world — that enables us to live richer lives. Pilgrimage entails the recognition that the learning self inhabits an educational world that is not only temporal but also spatial. It raises the significance of the body in linking the physical to the spiritual world. It involves not only learning, but also teaching, since pilgrims carry a pedagogical charge to perform ethical acts of representation and interpretation. At the very least, the presence of a pilgrim within a community serves as a reminder of the metaphysics shaping daily moral action. Full accounts like texts, poems, paintings and even the cadences of songs, representations of space, and the possibilities of movement through it, are guides that lead others on the quest. These are some of the dimensions of thinking about pilgrimage as education and of thinking about the significance of space in learning.

There has been considerable study in the formation and formalization of Christian pilgrimage (Ousterhout 1990). In the main these studies focus on the formation and meaning of sacred places in early to medieval Christianity. Pilgrimages, as Sabine McCormack tells us, were exercises in holy learning, attempts to gain closer proximity to the divine and a search for places where, through the suspension of spatial distance and temporal duration, "the tomb of the martyr could (thus) be the distant gate of heaven" (McCormack 1990: 29). There is a sense, however, in which any journey, even if not taken for an explicitly sacred purpose can become a pilgrimage as the traveller becomes aware of complexity and interdependence that characterize our inhabited world. Furthermore, there are ways by which such journeys can be undertaken without the pilgrim ever leaving a particular place. Such journeys link the aesthetic to thoughtful reflection and spiritual growth. Something similar is present in thinking about the sacred power of places in traditional pilgrimage. The difference between these two types of pilgrimage — the one without travel and the other an actual journey — lies in the fact that the one relies on a sacred sense of space, the other on the designation of particular places as sacred. It is the former sense of pilgrimage as instruction in developing a sacred sense of space, which provides the focus of this essay.

There is an important difference in thinking about these matters that arises from taking space to mean not only place. The restricted sense of space places all the emphasis on the goal. A more extended understanding of space makes attending to the educational journey not only as important as the goal, but rather is the goal itself. Regardless, all pilgrimages bring together particularity and universality, in a highly unstable and fleeting moment, through the pilgrim's physical presence in a sacred location. More importantly, they do so through the pursuit of a goal whereby egoism dissolves into universal awareness. In other words, space, far from being neutral or even specifically sacred, *loca sancta*, on this reading is the very ground of the ethical self.

McCormack reminds us that early Christian pilgrimage grew out of and was continuous with, pagan institutions of sacred places and objects. These objects, "blessings," brought home from the pilgrimage, took on the same power as the places and shrines of which they were tokens. Meaning was transferred from the holy place or the saint to the object. In turn, the blessing served as a durable way of connecting the divine with the earthly particularity of a pilgrim. Blessings, therefore, reconfigured the pilgrim's home environment in a very concrete way. Protestantism, however, through its grounding of faith in reason in the practice of Christian piety developed a strong case against pilgrimage. Thomas Hobbes, in *The Leviathan*, published in 1651, lays out a clear case against pilgrimage, aspects of which already exist in Luther and Calvin. According to Hobbes, "to inanimating or inhabiting . . . an image or place, that is to say an infinite substance in a finite place is idolatry" (Cited in McCormack 1990: 9). Space here is equated with place. This as we have seen is only one sense of sacred space. There are others, the most significant of which being that of space as the ground against which the self maintains and orients itself. Interestingly, Hobbes's second objection to pilgrimage, however, is easily folded into this view. For Hobbes, no particular place could be holy. "Holy . . . implies no new quality in that place . . . but only a new relation by appropriation to God. Holy ground not by inherent sanctity but by separation to God's use." (Cited in McCormack 1990: 9) This is entirely consonant with Protestantism. All actions, guided by such a metaphysics, become instances of worship. Pilgrimage, then, is no longer based only in the sense that the relationship of the self to the divine is better performed in one place than another. Rather it is the journey of discipline and knowledge, which leads to a new relation towards the ground of space which enfolds the places we inhabit and pass through.

But pilgrimage is not only a search for establishing a link between the self and the divine. It could well reflect the establishment of a relationship with our immediate and extended environment. These relationships would include, but not be limited to, other humans. According to Buddhist philosopher Chandrakirti this is the sixth ground of wisdom (see Klein 1994). Dissolution of ego does not imply the denial of subjectivity; rather it suggests a spaciousness of the interior self such that it renders the distinction between self and other irrelevant. In the Buddhist view, a pilgrimage of ethical learning does not depend on a transcendental view of the universal; rather, it seeks to link the particular to the universal in a very real and concrete sense. In other words, the spiritual journey teaches the pilgrim the increasingly complex connection between his or her historical, specific self to the environment at large.

On the Buddhist view, then, it is this understanding of the self in relation to an expanding, ultimately, universal context — an awareness of the relation between part and whole — which gives rise to reasoned compassion. Such compassion resists pity as an equivalent just as it holds off nihilistic passivity. In Harrer's case, the fact that he recognized his connection with others, that such a recognition served to arouse compassion for their suffering and that such suffering had enough become his own to motivate him to strive to alleviate it, makes his journey spiritual. For Harrer, home and abroad, Asia and Europe, self, mountains and wild geese had all become one. His assistance with matters related to Tibet was not the "intervention" of a European in non-European matters as Jacques Anaud's film implies. Rather, he was seeking to alleviate his own suffering. The divine, on this view, can be invoked but only as a metaphor for the dissolution of self-other distinctions in interpersonal relations and for universal community.

Martin Scorsese presents a masterful image of this linkage in his film *Kundun* through a representation of the compassionate Dalai Lama standing among an infinitely growing number of corpses of monks. As the camera recedes from a focus on the particular figure of the Dalai Lama to encompass thousands of bodies, the Dalai Lama loses his particularity and the viewer is drawn into the frame. The objectivity achieved through this inclusive movement arouses profound compassion.

It is important to note, however, that this move towards the other and the universal recognition of our interdependence as well as the contingency of all things — is not unique to Buddhist, non-Western thought. John Donne in his famous seventeenth meditation calls for just such an awareness when he reminds us that "no man is an island" and so we are not to ask "for whom the bell tolls," for it tolls for us all. St. Francis of Assisi goes further and includes all sentient beings as deserving of our care and attention. The Buddhist view takes this relationship a step further by justifying respect for all sentient beings through the concept of reincarnation. Nor is a re-orientation towards a particular place — without undertaking physical travel — to be seen as pilgrimage unique to Buddhist, non-Western, aesthetics and ethics.

Emily Dickinson, for example, alerts us to the spiritual significance of such an attentive turning towards the environment in most of her poems. But nowhere near as clearly as in her description of the bird that came down her walk,

Like one in danger; cautious,
I offered him a crumb,
And he unrolled his feathers,
And rowed him softer home.
Than oars divide the ocean,
Too silver for a seam,
Or butterflies, off banks at noon,
Leap, splashless, as they swim.

— Dickinson 1959: 104

Such close attention to those who share our environment opens ways of knowing which are in the spirit of seeing and saying the real gained by a focus brought to our engagement with the other through a loss of ego. This turning towards the environment or the acknowledgement of a universal community quite explicitly holds off the privileging of one position over another. Dickinson has made her ego so small that she never claims the role of teacher for herself. Rather, she calls out for a spiritual traveller — a teacher — who will lead her out of her dark night;

> O some scholar! O, some sailor!
> O some wise man from the skies!
> Please tell the little pilgrim
> Where the place called morning lies.
> — Dickinson 1959: 55

If Dickinson exemplifies the development of a sacred sense of space through care and attention towards those with whom we share our immediate environments, Walt Whitman seeks wider connections. Where Dickinson as pilgrim teaches by erasing herself, Whitman positions himself as a teacher of pilgrims. In his poem "Passage to India," Whitman gives us a narration of America which not only has Asia, Africa and Europe in the past which shapes its present but also has them in its future. On his view nationalism is internationalism. In contemporary terms, perhaps not with contemporary meanings, the world is global, a "vast Rondure," in descriptive and normative terms.

> Passage to India!
> Lo, soul, seest thou not God's purpose from the first?
> The earth to be spann'd connected by network,
> The races, neighbours, to marry, to be given in marriage,
> The oceans to be cross'd, the distant brought near,
> The lands to be welded together.
> — Whitman 1892

Whitman is aware, however, of the risk of repeating patterns of imperialism when national space is narrated in an international context. Furthermore, as we can see in Virgil's Aeneid among others, he is aware of the significance of the stories a nation tells of itself in a bid to find its place within a congress of nations. This is a new world, this America, and so everything must be done anew. Therefore:

> A worship new I sing,
> You captains, voyagers, explorers, yours,

You engineers, you architects, machinists, yours,
You, not for trade or transportation only,
But in God's name, for thy sake O soul.
— Whitman 1892

Assuming a sacred, complex, sense of space, he exhorts all those thinking and working to do so in ways which link the immediate to the universal, the national to the international. He could be said to exhort those working with educational technology and distance learning over the worldwide web, in cyberspace or deep space, to do so with a commitment to a higher purpose. Such work is ritual; it is work undertaken in service of the divine and for the sake of the spiritual self. The notion of indeterminacy which such a reading of work as ritual implies is captured by the advice offered by Krishna in the *Bhagavad Gita* that we do our duty as well we can while remaining disinterested in the outcome. How could we have any interest, much less seek control over the outcome, once we are cognitively aroused to the idea that we inhabit a vast unspeakably complex spatial system? Walt Whitman as teacher of pilgrims does not give us a representation of a journey undertaken. He wants us to undertake all journeys, metaphorical or real, in the spirit of pilgrimage. We must all take on the attitude of pilgrims as we turn towards our various tasks great or small, far or near.

Clearly, questions of spatial representation, of maps, play an important role in thinking about pilgrimage in traditional or new ways, in real or metaphorical terms. Allegory has been one of the central tropes in thinking about representations of pilgrimages. McCormack draws our attention to the significance of allegory for the "late antique Christian exegetes" for whom the "convergence of history and allegory, spirit and letter, provided the means of universalizing the content of Scripture" as the focal point of doctrine and help explain "difficult or controversial passages" (McCormack 1990: 23). This turn to allegory helped make sense of pilgrimages and holy places to the extent that the entire universe "had become one great allegory spelling out diverse sacred meanings" (McCormack 1990: 28). By the sixteenth and seventeenth centuries, however, such allegorical transference of geographical meaning was increasingly curtailed with the rise of scientific map-making. Early modern theological scholarship focused on literal not transferred textual meaning. Influenced by secular scholarship theologians were more interested in literal exegeses of texts than in the ambiguity, complexity and multiplicity of meaning of allegory used by late antique Christians in reflecting on the spatial presence of the holy.

As a result, Reformation debates separated and polarized the different meanings an ancient or late antique holy place could convey to the visitor, and allegory was for the most part discounted. Catholics found defensible one set of meanings and Protestants another. — McCormack 1990: 29.

Nevertheless, allegory remains central to a discussion of pilgrimage as a way of reorienting the self. We take the allegorical turn even in the quite commonplace idea of human life as journey — as pilgrimage. Through a turn to allegory, journeys of sacred instruction or sacred journeys of instruction can be undertaken both literally and figuratively. They can, for instance, be undertaken in actual physical space, as in the case of Harrer, or through acts of reading which convert representations of travel through historical and geographical space into the space of a spiritual allegory. Sacred journeys can also be undertaken in the space of spiritual allegory made identical with historical and geographical space. Such journeys can be undertaken by following an instruction manual, a map. This is quite explicit in the case of certain spiritual texts — as in *Madhyamika* Buddhism, Kensur Yeshey Tupden's *Path to the Middle* (Klein 1994) for example — where the reader as pilgrim is led step by step through the journey to a non-dualist freedom. The motivation to guide, to teach, is easily apparent in most spatial representations of spiritual journeys or journeys become spiritual. Most of these allegorical representations, however, rely on either a sense of sacred space or a sacred sense of space. The second sense, which seeks to relate the self to the real, would wish to eschew allegory. No matter how concrete the relations between the self and the world at large, however, all tellings must rely on allegory for the complexity that is to be represented always exceeds the narrator. In other words, any telling of the sublime, no matter how it is conceived, has to be allegorical.

As maps, representations of these spiritual journeys mark the territory in ways that are specific to the spiritual-religious commitments of the cartographers. John Bunyan, writing during the Reformation period in England, provides us with an allegory in which we traverse historical and geographical space. The goal of pilgrimage in Bunyan's sense is to make oneself worthy of entering the City of God. The journey, the development of the self, links the particular and the universal. In Harrer's text the physical geography of the vast plateau of Tibet becomes an allegory for space in a universal sense. Harrer's journey to Tibet and back to Europe links the allegorical sense of sacred space to real space — to a sacred sense of space. Tupden's journey to the middle ground allegorizes an interior space where the distinction between subject and object disappears making spatial relations sacred.

Bunyan explicitly positions his book not only as a map to guide others to the City of God — universal space — but also as a motivation for those who have not yet resolved to undertake such a journey. In Bunyan's words:

> This book will make a traveller of thee,
> If by its counsel thou wilt ruled be;
> It will direct thee to the Holy Land,
> If thou will its directions understand.
> Yea, it will make the slothful active be,
> The blind also delightful things to see. — Bunyan 1954

Motivation to embark on such a journey depends on a glimpse of sacred space. Such a journey demands a conception of absolute space, which is characteristically rejected by philosophers with a pragmatist bent. For these pragmatists all spatial understanding connects with the embodied subject through perception and action. Henri Poincare, for example, asserts: "absolute space is nonsense, and it is necessary for us to begin by referring space to a system of axes invariably bound to our body" (Poincare 1913: 257). To embark on a pilgrimage, which leads to the dissolution of subject and object, one requires a mental image — a glimpse — of the space that motivates pilgrimage. It directs our actions even as the journey of becoming relates us to temporality leading us from a state of confusion and despair to clarity and peace. John Bunyan has a glimpse of absolute space in his dream. In the opening paragraph of his Pilgrim's Progress, Bunyan describes his desperate condition in the City of Destruction and in his desire to write of the "race of saints" he falls suddenly into an allegory. "As I walked through the wilderness of this world," he says, "I lighted on a certain place where was a den and I laid me down in that place to sleep, and as I slept I dreamed a dream." In that dream an Evangelist, a teacher, appears to Christian. Desperately seeking to escape the wrath that is to come: "Whither must I fly?" asks Christian. Evangelist replies: "Do you see yonder shining light? Keep that light in your eye and go up directly thereto; so shalt thou see the gate, at which when thou knockest, it shall be told thee what thou shalt do" (Bunyan 1954: 19). Similarly, Tsong Kha Pa's text tells us that a bodhisattva's journey begins with his or her first glimpse of emptiness.

The initial glimpse is one over which the student-traveller has no control. It is given as a result of grace on the Protestant-Christian view. Of course, following Bunyan, the glimpse could possibly come from a text even as it could "out of the blue" as it did for Augustine. Within the Buddhist tradition this first glimpse is the result of such journeys undertaken in previous lives. Tsong-kha-pa, a fifteenth-century Buddhist master, lists in order and explains the ten bodhisattva perfections on the path to wisdom within the Mahayana tradition. On this view, the purpose of all lives, including the present, is to complete this journey of self-knowledge. This glimpse of the goal of self-development occurs during the very first stage and sets the pilgrim on the Mahayana path of seeing and will not be fully realized till the traveller has reached the "sixth ground of wisdom."

> The sixth is called the Approaching
> Because they (pilgrims) are approaching the good qualities
> of the Buddha.
> Through familiarity with calm abiding and special insight
> They attain cessation and hence are advanced [in wisdom].
>
> — Nagarjuna: 197

Following the initial glimpse, the pilgrim follows the path of seeing, through discipline and knowledge, reaching the sixth where the mind grows subtle and all difference, which rests on dualism, dissolves. The pilgrim is now prepared to embark on the last stages of his journey, which lead to the tenth ground of perfection. In Nagarjuna's words:

> The tenth is the Cloud of Doctrine
> Because the rain of holy doctrine falls,
> The Bodhisattva is bestowed empowerment
> With light rays by the Buddhas.
> Through the maturation of those [good qualities]
> They become master of the gods of Pure Abode.
> They are supreme great lords,
> Master of the sphere of infinite wisdom.
>
> — Nagarjuna: 159

Harrer's desire to conquer the Himalayas was shaped during visits to the university library in Berlin between climbing and skiing expeditions in the Alps. His specific desire to visit Tibet was shaped in childhood when he "read only geography books and my great role model was the Swedish explorer Sven Hedin, who had written fascinating books on his adventures in Tibet" (Harrer 1996: 327). Here the first glimpse of the destination of pilgrimage is caught in a representation of a journey already undertaken.

The memory of absolute space regardless of how it is conceived helps orient the traveller at every point in his or her journey. It is the glimpse of the tenth ground, which motivates the Buddhist pilgrim, on the Madhyamika view, to struggle through the ethical disciplines leading to the sixth ground. Once this ground has been achieved the pilgrim is no longer in danger of slipping back and losing the way. Also, this place of calm abiding is sufficiently free from strife to make the journey onward to the tenth ground a matter of choice again. Christian, the pilgrim in Bunyan's allegory, set out on his journey following the first glimpse of the celestial city offered by the Evangelist. During this journey he falls in with Mr. Worldly Wise. Taken in by the counsel offered by Mr. Worldly Wise, he is turned away from the path shown by the Evangelist. On realizing that his new friend's advice has not liberated him from pain and confusion but rather has increased it, he is distraught. The Evangelist approaches him again and after having reproached him for his lack of faith, as also reason, sets him on the true path again. As Christian travels on his journey he is offered timely reminders of the dangers of straying from the path just as he encounters and overcomes all the distractions of the world. Having fallen in with a flatterer, he is taken in hand by Hope:

> Come hither, you that walk along the way;
> See how the pilgrims fare that go astray!

They catched are in an entangling net,
Cause they good counsel lightly did forget,
'Tis true, they rescued were, but yet you see
They're scourged to boot. Let this your caution be.
— Bunyan 1954: 123

When Harrer and Aufschneiter, being Austrian, are taken prisoner by the British army in India during the Second World War and held in camp in the foothills of the Himalayas, Harrer's "ambition to escape naturally focused on the direction north to Tibet" (Harrer 1996: 327). Caught twice in his attempts to escape, Harrer is placed in solitary confinement. On the third attempt, he successfully crosses into Tibet but is caught by the Tibetans and turned back towards the Indian border. Through ruse, Harrer and Aufschneiter avoid going back into India, where they would have found themselves prisoners again and struggle on to Lhasa, where they are honoured as pilgrims.

There are two additional genres relevant to the understanding of the development of the self in relation to space. The first of these is philosophical writings on personal identity that take space into consideration. The second adheres to writing on the significance of pilgrimages in religious education. These genres, however, treat the self in space in a static rather than dynamic manner, which has consequences for our discussion. In *Individuals* (Strawson 1959), Peter Strawson holds that reidentification of places depends on the reidentification of things. We identify places in relation to the things we see. In this manner things, including stable illusions like shadows, enable our knowledge of the spaces we inhabit, locate and identify. From this insight Strawson drew the conclusion that we inhabit a unified spatio-temporal field. While this thesis may be too strong, its weaker version is hard to deny. Things are densely interwoven in our identification and re-identification of places. An initial orientation allows us to locate ourselves and all other objects into a relational spatial field. This view, however, is limited. Such a rendering of ourselves in space would be fine if we never moved and neither did the things about us. On Strawson's account this should not prove significant to his argument because we can and often do orient ourselves based on a single particular in a spatial field. But, it is not trivial to observe that we do move as do things around us. Moreover, we do not always move in familiar environments. Travel through unfamiliar places should have epistemological and educational significance. What is missing in accounts, such as Strawson's, of space and personal identity is the effect movement in space would have on the shaping of such an identity. This is the point at which these issues of personal identity in relation to space intersect with those raised within the discourse of pilgrimages. The question of identification, however, is not the only thesis in question here. There is the further, deeper and still relatively unexplored question of how our knowledge of ourselves relies on this relation with objects in our environment. For Richard Ousterhout the institution of pilgrimage raises the following question: How does the physical world address the spiritual world? Medieval pilgrimage assumed that the two worlds came together in certain places, *loca sancta*, where the power of heaven were more easily tapped either for earthly benefit or for aid in salvation (Ousterhout 1991: 1). Thus the pilgrim could share in a profound spiritual experience and bring home a token, called a blessing. This object is now one of Strawson's spatial particulars.

Three issues arise from the discussion so far. The focus on the *loca sancta* and the blessing speak only to a particular moment of being in the sacred place. The place also is particular. This is the place where, mystically, the distinction between subject and object is erased. This moment of non-dualist experience in a particular place is certainly significant. It provides, on Bunyan and Tsong Kha Pa's account, that first glimpse of the celestial city or the "sixth ground of wisdom". Such an account of pilgrimage, one linked to a particular place and time, however, is only the initial moment that motivates the actual pilgrimage. This is the journey to developing a sense of the spatial dimension of the self such that particularity extends outward towards universality. Thus, reason moves across the ground of faith and ethics is not a calculation but a felt commitment.

Perhaps there is no finer example of such an educational journey in the Western tradition than St. Augustine's *Confessions*. Augustine, an Italo-Maghreb, traveled from the peripheral regions of the Mediterranean to the metropolitan centre of Rome in search of wisdom; a wisdom he did not find. He returned home, with a new orientation towards his immediate environment and those he shared it with, and with the realization that that which he was seeking lay there in "*remota intcriore loco, non loco*," an interior space which is not space (Augustine 1979; bk. 10, chapt. 17). Reading was the practice by which this interior space is to be negotiated and the educational journey, the pilgrimage of the self, was to be negotiated.

References

Augustine, 1979, *Confessions*, bk. 10, chap. 17, Cambridge: Harvard University Press.

Bunyan, John, 1954, *Pilgrim's Progress*, New York: Everyman's Library, Dutton.

Dickinson, Emily, 1959, *Selected Poems and Letters*, ed. Robert N. Linscott, New York: Anchor Books.

Harrer, Heinrich, 1996, *Seven Years in Tibet*, New York: Putnam.

Klein, Anne (tr.), 1994, *Path to the Middle: The Spoken Scholarship of Jensur Yesshey Tupden*, Albany: State University of New York Press.

McCormack, Sabine, 1990, "The Organization of Sacred Topography," in Richard Ousterhout, *The Blessings of Pilgrimage*, Urbana: University of Illinois.

Nagarjuna, *Precious Garland* [2nd. century], tr. Jeffrey Hopkins, Ithaca: Snow Lion Publications.

Ousterhout, Richard, 1990, *The Blessings of Pilgrimage*, Urbana: University of Illinois.

Poincare, Henri, 1913, *The Foundations of Science*, New York: The Science Press.\

Strawson, P.F., 1963, *Individuals*, Garden City: Doubleday.

Whitman, Walt, 1892, "Passage to India", in *Leaves of Grass*, New York: Bantam Classics.

List of Contributors

Thomas Barrie
Associate Professor
College of Architecture & Design
Lawrence Technical University
2100 West Ten Mile Road
Southfield, MI 48075-1058 (USA)

Kurt Behrendt
Assistant Curator
Department of Asian Art
The Metropolitan Museum of Art
1000 Fifth Avenue
New York, NY 10028-0198 (USA)

Surinder M. Bhardwaj
Department of Geography
436 McGilvrey Hall
Kent State University
Kent OH 44242-0001 (USA)

R.K. Bhattacharya
Head, Janpada Sampada Division
Indira Gandhi National Centre for the Arts
Central Vista
New Delhi 110 001

R.K. Bhattacharya
Deer Park
Santiniketan 731235
Distt. Birbhum (West Bengal)

Pradeep A. Dhillon
College of Education
University of Illinois
Urbana-Champaign, 86182 Illinois, (USA)

Niels Gutschow
Ortsstr. 26, (Odenwald)
D-69518 Absteinach (Germany)

Marianna Kropf
Department of Contemporary History, Science of Religion, and Social Anthropology
University of Fribourg
Avenue de l'Europe 20
CH-1700 Fribourg (Switzerland)

Alexandra Mack
Workplace Anthropologist
Pitney Bowes
Advanced Concepts and Technology
MSC 26-31
35 Waterview Dr.
Shelton, CT 06484 (USA)

John McKim Malville
Department of Astrophysical and Planetary Sciences
University of Colorado
Campus Box 391
Boulder CO 80309 (USA)

Anne L. Marshall
Department of Architecture
University of Idaho
Moscow, 83844-2451 ID (USA)

Jeffrey F. Meyer
Department of Religious Studies
HWY 49 North Str.
University of North Carolina
Charlotte NC 28223 (USA)

Kaj Noschis
Department of Architecture
Swiss Federal Institute of Technology
Case 555, Ave.de l'Eglise-A'nglaise
CH-1001 Lausanne (Switzerland)

Carolyn V. Prorok
Department of Geography, Geology and the Environment
Slippery Rock University
Spotts World Culture Building,
Box 111
Slippery Rock PA 16057-1326 (USA)

Baidyanath Saraswati
N.K. Bose Memorial Foundation
B-8/9, Bara Gambhir Singh
Varanasi - 221 005, (UP)

Hiroshi Tanaka Shimazaki
Faculty of Management
4401 University Drive
University of Lethbridge
Lethbridge, Alberta T1K 3M4 (Canada)

Rana P.B. Singh
Department of Geography
Banaras Hindu University
No. B29/12A (II Floor)
Lanka; P.O. B.H.U., Station Road
Varanasi - 221 005 (UP)

Amita Sinha
Deptt.of Landscape Architecture
101 Temple Hoyne Bruell Hall
611 East Lorado Taft
University of Illinois at Urbana Champaign
Champaign IL 861820 (USA)

Robert L. Stoddard
Department of Geography
313 Avery Hall
University of Nebraska - Lincoln
Lincoln NE 68588 - 0135 (USA)

Yolotol Gonzales Torres
A.V. Revolucion 4y6
Col San Angel Mexico
Mexico D.F. 0100 (Mexico)

R. Tom Zuidema
Center for Advanced Studies
University of Illinois
Urbana - Champaigne, 86182 Illinois (USA)

Index